THE CAMBRIDGE COMPANION TO
VIRTUE ETHICS

Virtue ethics has emerged from a rich history to become one of the fastest-growing fields in contemporary ethics. In this volume of newly commissioned essays, leading moral philosophers offer a comprehensive overview of virtue ethics. They examine the theoretical structure of virtue ethics and its place in contemporary moral theory, as well as the history of virtue-based approaches to ethics, what makes these approaches distinctive, what they can say about specific practical issues, and where we can expect them to go in the future. This *Companion* will be useful to students of virtue ethics and the history of ethics, and to others who want to understand how virtue ethics is changing the face of contemporary moral philosophy.

DANIEL C. RUSSELL is Professor of Philosophy at the Center for the Philosophy of Freedom and the Department of Philosophy, University of Arizona, and the Percy Seymour Reader in Ancient History and Philosophy at Ormond College, University of Melbourne. He is the author of *Plato on Pleasure and the Good Life* (2005), *Practical Intelligence and the Virtues* (2009), and *Happiness for Humans* (2012).

T0381711

OTHER VOLUMES IN THE SERIES OF CAMBRIDGE COMPANIONS

ABELARD *Edited by* JEFFREY E. BROWER *and*
    KEVIN GUILFOY
ADORNO *Edited by* THOMAS HUHN
ANCIENT SCEPTICISM *Edited by* RICHARD BETT
ANSELM *Edited by* BRIAN DAVIES *and* BRIAN LEFTOW
AQUINAS *Edited by* NORMAN KRETZMANN *and*
    ELEONORE STUMP
ARABIC PHILOSOPHY *Edited by* PETER ADAMSON *and*
    RICHARD C. TAYLOR
HANNAH ARENDT *Edited by* DANA VILLA
ARISTOTLE *Edited by* JONATHAN BARNES
ATHEISM *Edited by* MICHAEL MARTIN
AUGUSTINE *Edited by* ELEONORE STUMP *and*
    NORMAN KRETZMANN
BACON *Edited by* MARKKU PELTONEN
BERKELEY *Edited by* KENNETH P. WINKLER
BOETHIUS *Edited by* JOHN MARENBON
BRENTANO *Edited by* DALE JACQUETTE
CARNAP *Edited by* MICHAEL FRIEDMAN
CONSTANT *Edited by* HELENA ROSENBLATT
CRITICAL THEORY *Edited by* FRED RUSH
DARWIN 2nd edition *Edited by* JONATHAN HODGE *and*
    GREGORY RADICK
SIMONE DE BEAUVOIR *Edited by* CLAUDIA CARD
DELEUZE *Edited by* DANIEL SMITH *and*
    HENRY SOMERS-HALL
DESCARTES *Edited by* JOHN COTTINGHAM
DEWEY *Edited by* MOLLY COCHRAN
DUNS SCOTUS *Edited by* THOMAS WILLIAMS
EARLY GREEK PHILOSOPHY *Edited by* A. A. LONG
EARLY MODERN PHILOSOPHY *Edited by*
    DONALD RUTHERFORD
EPICUREANISM *Edited by* JAMES WARREN
EXISTENTIALISM *Edited by* STEVEN CROWELL
FEMINISM IN PHILOSOPHY *Edited by*
    MIRANDA FRICKER *and* JENNIFER HORNSBY
FOUCAULT 2nd edition *Edited by* GARY GUTTING

Continued at the back of the book

The Cambridge Companion to

VIRTUE ETHICS

Edited by Daniel C. Russell
University of Arizona

CAMBRIDGE
UNIVERSITY PRESS

CAMBRIDGE
UNIVERSITY PRESS

University Printing House, Cambridge CB2 8BS, United Kingdom

Cambridge University Press is part of the University of Cambridge.

It furthers the University's mission by disseminating knowledge in the pursuit of education, learning and research at the highest international levels of excellence.

www.cambridge.org
Information on this title: www.cambridge.org/9780521171748

First published 2013
3rd printing 2014

A catalogue record for this publication is available from the British Library

Library of Congress Cataloguing in Publication data
The Cambridge companion to virtue ethics / edited by Daniel C. Russell.
     p.   cm.
Includes bibliographical references (p. 339) and index.
ISBN 978-1-107-00116-9 (hardback)
1. Ethics.   2. Virtue.   I. Russell, Daniel C.
BJ1521.C17   2013
179'.9 – dc23   2012024122

ISBN 978-1-107-00116-9 Hardback
ISBN 978-0-521-17174-8 Paperback

CONTENTS

List of contributors   *page* ix

Acknowledgments   xiii

List of figures   xiv

   Introduction: virtue ethics in modern moral
   philosophy   I
   DANIEL C. RUSSELL

1 Virtue ethics, happiness, and the good life   7
   DANIEL C. RUSSELL

2 Ancient virtue ethics: an overview with an
   emphasis on practical wisdom   29
   RACHANA KAMTEKAR

3 Virtue ethics and the Chinese Confucian
   tradition   49
   PHILIP J. IVANHOE

4 Virtue ethics in the medieval period   70
   JEAN PORTER

5 Hume's anatomy of virtue   92
   PAUL RUSSELL

6 The historic decline of virtue ethics   124
   DOROTHEA FREDE

7 Virtue ethics in the twentieth century   149
   TIMOTHY CHAPPELL

8   Virtue ethics and right action   172
    LIEZL VAN ZYL

9   Virtue ethics and bioethics   197
    JUSTIN OAKLEY

10 Environmental virtue ethics: what it is and what
    it needs to be   221
    MATT ZWOLINSKI AND DAVID SCHMIDTZ

11 The virtue approach to business ethics   240
    EDWIN HARTMAN

12 Virtue and politics   265
    MARK LEBAR

13 The situationist critique of virtue ethics   290
    GOPAL SREENIVASAN

14 The definition of virtue ethics   315
    CHRISTINE SWANTON

Bibliography   339
Index   363

CONTRIBUTORS

TIMOTHY CHAPPELL is Professor of Philosophy and Director of the Ethics Centre at the Open University. He has published extensively on both ancient and contemporary ethics, and his books include *Aristotle and Augustine on Freedom* (1995), *The Plato Reader* (1996), *Understanding Human Goods* (1998), *Reading Plato's Theaetetus* (2004), *The Inescapable Self* (2005), and *Ethics and Experience* (2009). He has also edited *Philosophy of the Environment* (1997), *Human Values* (with David Oderberg, 2004), *Values and Virtues* (2006), and *The Moral Problem of Demandingness* (2009).

DOROTHEA FREDE is Professor Emerita at the University of Hamburg, and Honorary Professor at Humboldt University, Berlin. Her publications include *Plato's Philebus* (1993), *Plato's Phaedo* (1999), *Traditions of Theology* (with Andre Laks, 2002), *Language and Learning* (with Brad Inwood, 2005), and *Body and Soul in Ancient Philosophy* (with Burkhard Reis, 2007), as well as numerous articles on the ethics of Plato, Aristotle, and Hellenistic philosophers.

EDWIN HARTMAN taught in the Business School and the Philosophy Department at Rutgers University for many years before finishing his career at the Stern School of Business at New York University. He is the author of *Aristotle on Soul and Body* (1969), *Substance, Body, and Soul: Aristotelian Investigations* (1977), *Conceptual Foundations of Organization Theory* (1988), and *Organizational Ethics and the Good Life* (1996), as well as numerous articles on ancient philosophy and business ethics. His new book on an Aristotelian approach to business ethics will be published in 2013 by Cambridge University Press.

PHILIP J. IVANHOE is Professor of Philosophy at the City University of Hong Kong. He is the author, translator, and editor of numerous books in Chinese moral philosophy and virtue ethics, including *Confucian Moral Self Cultivation* (2000), *Ethics in the Confucian Tradition* (2002), *The Daodejing Laozi* (2003), *The Essays and Letters of Zhang Xuecheng* (2009), *Readings from the Lu-Wang School* (2009), and *Master Sun's Art of War* (2011). His numerous edited works include *Virtue, Nature, and Moral Agency in the Xunzi* (with T. C. Kline, 2000), *Working Virtue: Virtue Ethics and Contemporary Moral Problems* (with Rebecca Walker, 2007), *Taking Confucian Ethics Seriously* (with Kam-Por Yu and Julia Tao, 2010), and *Mortality in Traditional Chinese Thought* (with Amy Olberding, 2011).

RACHANA KAMTEKAR is Associate Professor of Philosophy at the University of Arizona. She is the author of numerous articles on ancient as well as contemporary virtue ethics and moral psychology, and has edited *Plato's Euthyphro, Crito, and Apology: Critical Essays* (2004), *A Companion to Socrates* (with Sara Ahbel-Rappe, 2006), and *Virtue and Happiness: Essays in Honour of Julia Annas* (2012). She is currently working on a manuscript entitled *The Powers of Plato's Psychology*.

MARK LEBAR is Associate Professor of Philosophy at Ohio University. He is the author of numerous articles on ancient and contemporary ethics, practical reasoning, and well-being, and his book *The Value of Living Well* is forthcoming.

JUSTIN OAKLEY is Associate Professor and Deputy Director of the Centre for Human Bioethics at Monash University. He has published extensively on applications of virtue ethics to a wide range of issues in bioethics and the health-care professions. He is the author of *Morality and the Emotions* (1993) and *Virtue Ethics and Professional Roles* (with Dean Cocking, 2001), and is editor of *Informed Consent and Clinician Accountability* (with Steve Clarke, 2007), and *Bioethics* (2009).

JEAN PORTER is Rev. John A. O'Brien Professor of Theological Ethics and member of the Medieval Institute at the University of Notre Dame. She has published extensively on moral theology and the history of Christian moral thought, and her books include *The Recovery of Virtue* (1990), *Natural and Divine Law* (1999), *Nature as Reason* (2005) and most recently *Ministers of the Law* (2010).

DANIEL C. RUSSELL is Professor of Philosophy in the Center for the Philosophy of Freedom at the University of Arizona, and the Percy Seymour Reader in Ancient History and Philosophy at Ormond College, University of Melbourne. He has published numerous articles on ancient and contemporary ethics and moral psychology, and is the author of *Plato on Pleasure and the Good Life* (2005), *Practical Intelligence and the Virtues* (2009), and *Happiness for Humans* (2012).

PAUL RUSSELL is Professor of Philosophy at the University of British Columbia. He is the author of numerous articles on the history of early modern philosophy and moral psychology. His books include *Freedom and Moral Sentiment* (1995) and *The Riddle of Hume's Treatise* (2008), as well an edited collection *Free Will and Reactive Attitudes* (with Michael McKenna, 2008). At the present time he is preparing two edited collections, *The Oxford Handbook of David Hume* and *The Philosophy of Free Will* (with Oisin Deery), and is at work on another book, *The Limits of Free Will*.

DAVID SCHMIDTZ is Kendrick Professor of Philosophy, Joint Professor of Economics, and founding director of the Center for the Philosophy of Freedom at the University of Arizona. He has published extensively on political philosophy, ethics, and practical reasoning and is the author of *The Limits of Government* (1991), *Rational Choice and Moral Agency* (1995), *Social Welfare and Individual Responsibility* (with Robert Goodin, 1998), *The Elements of Justice* (2006), *Person, Polis, Planet* (2008), and *A Brief History of Liberty* (with Jason Brennan, 2010). He has also edited *Environmental Ethics: What Really Matters, What Really Works* (with Elizabeth Willott, 2001), *Robert Nozick* (2002), and *Creating Wealth: Ethical and Economic Perspectives* (2011).

GOPAL SREENIVASAN is Crown Professor of Ethics and Professor of Philosophy at Duke University. He is the author of numerous articles on ethics, political philosophy, and philosophical psychology, and his books include *The Limits of Lockean Rights in Property* (1995) and *Emotion and Virtue* (forthcoming).

CHRISTINE SWANTON is a professor in Philosophy at the University of Auckland. She is the author of numerous articles on virtue ethics, the history of philosophy, and political philosophy, and her books include *Freedom: A Coherence Theory* (1992) and *Virtue Ethics: A Pluralistic View* (2003).

LIEZL VAN ZYL is Senior Lecturer in Philosophy and Ethics at the University of Waikato. She is the author of *Death and Compassion* (2000), as well as numerous articles on virtue ethics, with a particular focus on applied ethics and theories of right action.

MATT ZWOLINSKI is Associate Professor of Philosophy and Codirector of the Institute for Law and Philosophy at the University of San Diego. He has published numerous articles on issues at the intersection of ethics, politics, business, and economics, often focusing on liberty or exploitation. He is the author of *A Brief History of Libertarianism* (with John Tomasi, forthcoming), and has edited *Arguing About Political Philosophy* (2009).

ACKNOWLEDGMENTS

I would like to thank all of the authors who have contributed to this volume, for lending not only their expertise but also their enthusiasm to its creation. I also thank the Social Philosophy and Policy Center at Bowling Green State University for generous financial support during the editing of the majority of the chapters included here. Very special thanks are due to Hilary Gaskin and Anna Lowe of Cambridge University Press, for their unflagging support and excellent guidance throughout the preparation of this volume. Thanks also to Julia Annas for assistance in selecting a cover image suitable for a volume on such a heterogeneous field as virtue ethics. Lastly, my greatest thanks go to my wife, Gina Russell, and our daughters Jocelyn, Grace, and Julia, for their support while I put this volume together, all while shifting between Wichita, Bowling Green, Tucson, and Melbourne.

FIGURES

10.1 Population size and average quality of life.   *page* 226

10.2 Quality of life and increasing population size.   227

xiv

Introduction
Virtue ethics in modern moral philosophy

Virtue ethics has a very long history – longer than any other tradition in moral philosophy – stretching back to the ancient Greek philosophers and, a world away, ancient Chinese philosophers as well. Its central concepts are the excellences of character, such as fairness, courage, and self-control, and it focuses on how such excellences help us live good lives, treat ourselves and others well, and share thriving communities.

What makes virtue ethics different from other approaches in moral philosophy? One way to answer that question would be to point out the distinctive way that it treats the notion of rightness: right action, in virtue ethics, can be understood only with the aid of an account of the virtues, which in turn can be understood independently of right action (see Watson 1990; Hursthouse 1999, chap. 1; D. Russell 2009, chap. 2). The trouble with this answer, though, is that it is so very broad, and there is enormous diversity among virtue ethicists as to how the relation between rightness and virtue might be made more precise (see van Zyl, this volume). More than that, virtue ethicists disagree over how important the notion of "right action" is in the first place (see the chapters by Chappell and Swanton in this volume).

However, even setting all that aside, to think of virtue ethics as giving a different answer to the same questions about rightness addressed by other approaches – utilitarianism and deontology, most notably – would be to understate what is really distinctive about virtue ethics and the radically different alternative it offers. As Matt Zwolinski and David Schmidtz observe in their chapter in this volume, virtue ethics is so different it might be best to see it, not as an alternative answer to the same question, but as responding to a different question altogether. Often associated with Aristotle, but with roots in various traditions as discussed in this volume, virtue ethics tells us that what is right is to be a certain kind of person, a person of virtue: courageous, modest, honest, evenhanded, industrious, wise. A virtuous person will, of course, express his or her virtue through action. But, for virtue ethics, the specification of rules of right action is largely a secondary matter – one that in many ways presupposes the kind of practical wisdom possessed by the person of virtue. (p. 221)

What sets virtue ethics apart is that it treats ethics as concerned with one's whole life – and not just those occasions when something with a distinctly "moral" quality is at stake. For virtue ethics, the focus is not so much on what to do in morally difficult cases as on how to approach all of one's choices with such personal quali- ties as kindness, courage, wisdom, and integrity. That difference in focus is an important one. People who may feel confident in the rightness of their actions can sometimes be brought up short when asked whether they are also being generous, or considerate, or hon- est. Rightness is about what we're doing; virtue is also about how we're living. It resists compartmentalization.

Writers of textbooks in ethics are becoming increasingly appre- ciative of this feature of virtue ethics. For instance, one textbook in engineering ethics considers an imaginary case of a dangerous and expensive spill at a chemical plant (Harris *et al.* 2008, chap. 4). The spill occurs in an outdated part of the plant that has raised the eyebrows of several engineers and technicians, although all of them accepted the situation as "just how things are." Now, in one way it's obvious what the plant workers should do: clean up the spill, fix the outdated fittings, perhaps implement new maintenance and reporting procedures, and so on. But the textbook's authors don't stop there, and for good reason. This is a textbook for future engi- neers, and they already know that spills need to be cleaned. What they need to learn is how to avoid getting into these kinds of jams in the first place. As the authors point out, the real problem was not that anyone perpetrated any heinous act; it was that several people might have taken responsibility for addressing the problem, but none of them did. The point is a crucial one: really what engineers need are virtues, because it's a virtue to take responsibility. The imagi- nary engineers who did nothing needed virtues like that because we must also imagine that neither their professional nor their personal lives end here, with the clean-up of this spill. And the real engineers who learn from them need, not a decision procedure from a textbook, but the practical wisdom to understand for themselves how to be people who take responsibility and why taking responsibility matters.

AN OVERVIEW OF THIS BOOK

As I said above, virtue ethics is extremely rich in its history, and it is no less so in the diversity of forms it can take. As a result, it is impossible to give a brief characterization of virtue ethics that is both specific enough to be informative and general enough to be suitably inclusive. (Brief, specific, inclusive: pick any two.) So it would surely be wiser for me to quit while I am ahead and turn instead to giving an overview of the fourteen chapters that follow. They have all been specially commissioned so that, taken together, they might introduce readers to virtue ethics with all of its historical background, variety of interpretations, and diversity of applications. Several of the chapters deal with some basic concepts in virtue ethics, others with some major points in its development at different times and places, and the rest with some of its main contributions to moral philosophy today.

Virtue ethics: central concepts

The volume begins and ends with discussions of the virtues and how they come to bear on ethical thought. The first chapter (Daniel C. Russell) examines one approach – shared by all ancient virtue ethicists and still prevalent today – on which the virtues are those character traits that are essential to living a fulfilling human life, a life in which one both cares about the right things and has the wisdom and skill to act intelligently about those things. Christine Swanton closes the volume with a subtle discussion of the many different varieties that virtue ethics can take and has taken, arguing for a characterization of virtue ethics that is broad enough to include not only such obvious figures as Aristotle, but potentially some less obvious candidates as well, such as Hume and Nietzsche. This approach suggests new avenues for exploring innovative directions both within virtue ethics itself and in the study of its history.

Virtue ethics: its history and development

The wealth of the history of virtue ethics is the subject of no fewer than six chapters in this volume. Rachana Kamtekar discusses the development of virtue ethics among the major ancient Greek philosophers – Plato, Aristotle, the Stoics, and the Epicureans – paying particular attention to their various treatments of wisdom or practical intelligence, which they all agreed in treating as the master virtue. Philip J. Ivanhoe explores two main lines of development within ancient Confucian virtue ethics: the view, represented by Mengzi, that the virtues are excellences of human fulfillment, and the view of Wang Yangming that the virtues are dispositions contributing to harmonious social interaction. Each of these chapters not only offers an instructive way to understand different ancient traditions in virtue ethics, but also illustrates where those traditions resonate with their modern counterparts.

Like other parts of ancient Greek thought, virtue ethics had a complex and often turbulent relationship with early Christian philosophers and, subsequently, with the philosophers of the early modern period. In her chapter, Jean Porter discusses the different ways in which ancient virtue ethics was received in the Middle Ages: among scholars, as a complement to the "theological" virtues of faith, hope, and charity, and among the pastorate as a central strand of a moral and disciplinary tradition. By contrast, as Paul Russell explains, David Hume explored the virtues as part of a larger and purely secular investigation of human nature, one that would both cast light on an array of social practices and explore the bases of human happiness.

While the virtues never disappeared from moral theory entirely, virtue ethics itself was eventually eclipsed in the West (but not, it is worth noting, in the East) by the major traditions of the early modern period, namely the utilitarianism of Jeremy Bentham and the deontology of Immanuel Kant. Although the decline of virtue ethics during this period is a familiar datum among philosophers, its explanation has been controversial. Some have argued that virtue ethics was cast aside because of a general shaking off of Aristotelian philosophy, or because it was simply found to have a theoretical center that could not hold. By contrast, Dorothea Frede argues in her chapter that the political catastrophes of the early modern period led to a decline in confidence in aspirational ideals of virtue and social unity, and in consequence to a search for new bases for moral philosophy. Lastly, Timothy Chappell argues that the revival of interest in virtue ethics in the mid-twentieth century was in fact a consequence of precisely that kind of search: philosophers like Elizabeth Anscombe and Philippa Foot, so far from pointing out an obvious but overlooked alternative in modern moral philosophy, advocated a turn to virtue ethics as the logical conclusion of the contemporary quest to clarify and ground the central concepts of ethics.

Virtue ethics in contemporary moral philosophy

The remaining six chapters examine the contributions of virtue ethics to moral philosophy today, both in theory and in application. Liezl van Zyl surveys the major alternatives within virtue ethics for characterizing right action: the view of Rosalind Hursthouse that an action is right if and only if it is what a virtuous person would do; Michael Slote's definition of right action in terms of the virtuousness of one's motive; and Christine Swanton's account of right action as hitting the "targets" associated with the various virtues. Just as important, van Zyl also looks critically at the very idea of a criterion of right action, clarifying what we should (and should not) expect such a criterion to tell us by way of action guidance.

Several of the chapters in this part of the volume survey the contributions of virtue ethics to various areas of contemporary applied ethics: human bioethics (Justin Oakley), environmental ethics (Matt Zwolinski and David Schmidtz), and business ethics (Edwin Hartman). As these authors point out, the advances made by virtue ethicists in these fields are especially important for our assessment of virtue ethics: there is no better reply to the early doubts as to whether the then newly revived field of virtue ethics could be "action guiding," after all, than for virtue ethicists to actually provide useful guidance to action.

In recent years, virtue ethics has also begun to make increasing inroads into political philosophy. Mark LeBar critically assesses several virtue ethical accounts of political justification that have been particularly influential: that acts of the state are justified when they are virtuously motivated, or when they enable persons to cultivate human capabilities (including capability for the virtues), or when they provide the background conditions for self-direction (including self-directed pursuit of the virtues). LeBar argues that while proponents of these views have focused on their theoretical merits, they must also ask whether it can be virtuous to unilaterally require others to live according to one's own preferred theory, whatever its merits.

Of course, if an ethical theory is to be able to guide action, even in principle, its guidance must be applicable to creatures like us, with the kind of psychology that we have. Gopal Sreenivasan assesses recent claims that thinking of action in terms of virtues is antiquated, on the grounds that modern social psychology has revealed that even minor features of a person's situation have more to do with his behaviors than any alleged dispositions or character traits do. Sreenivasan argues that these critics have failed to make their case: their crucial objection is that behavior is inconsistent across different situations, but this objection has rested on assessing inconsistency from the researcher's point of view rather than the experimental subject's.

Aims of this volume

Our hope in producing this collection of new work on virtue ethics is threefold. One, we hope to give readers a sense of how virtue ethics has evolved to its current state, by tracing its development through the main periods of its history. Two, we also hope to clarify the theoretical structure of virtue ethics and its place in contemporary ethical theory. And three, we hope to explore the contemporary relevance of virtue ethics, some of the main challenges it now faces, and new avenues of exploration and development within virtue ethics. In all of these ways, our overarching aim is that the volume should be a very useful resource for a wide array of readers: hopefully for readers all the way up to full-time philosophers, but certainly for students of philosophy eager to understand this simultaneously very old and very new approach to ethics.

1   Virtue ethics, happiness, and the good life

In its earliest versions, virtue ethics began not with the question "What is the right thing to do?" but with the question "What is the best way to live?" The first is a question for ethical reasoning specifically, while the second is for practical reasoning about one's life more broadly: it concerns what to do with one's life and how to make it a happy one. Answering these questions involves, among other things, reflecting on what sort of person to be and what sort of character to develop. And it is here that practical reasoning leads to thought about the virtues, excellences of character that consist in both caring about the right sorts of things and having the wisdom and practical skills to judge and act successfully with respect to those things. It seems appropriate, then, to open this volume on virtue ethics with an overview of this traditional approach to the virtues.

This approach is called "eudaimonism," from the Greek word 'eudaimonia,' the ancient Greek philosophers' term for a good human life, or more succinctly, happiness. By "happiness" here we do not mean a mood or a feeling but a life that is rich and fulfilling for the one living it. Specifically, 'eudaimonism' can refer to theories about practical reasoning, or about the nature of happiness, or about the virtues – or, more usually, to a theory of the relation between these three. Eudaimonism of this latter sort is the focus of this chapter: eudaimonism is the idea that we grasp which character traits are

This chapter was written during my appointment as a Visiting Scholar at the Social Philosophy and Policy Center at Bowling Green State University in summer 2011. I thank Hilary Gaskin of Cambridge University Press for the invitation to contribute this chapter, as well as Tim Chappell and Mark LeBar for their comments on earlier drafts.

the virtues by understanding what traits practical reasoning recommends as essential to living a fulfilling human life.

Eudaimonism dates to ancient Greece, where all of the major camps in moral philosophy (Platonists, Aristotelians, Epicureans, Stoics) were eudaimonists, and their influence in virtue ethics is still strong today. This is due to the work of philosophers like G. E. M. Anscombe, Philippa Foot, John McDowell, Rosalind Hursthouse, Julia Annas, Martha Nussbaum, and others who have seen in the ancient focus on human nature and flourishing a source of new vitality for contemporary philosophy.[1]

The most influential exposition of eudaimonism is still Aristotle's, so in the first three sections I outline eudaimonism along broadly similar lines. Then in the final two sections, I consider some challenges for eudaimonism as a contemporary approach in ethics.

EUDAIMONISM ABOUT PRACTICAL REASONING

Eudaimonism makes two main claims about practical reasoning. First, practical reasoning requires a "final end": an end we pursue for its own sake and for the sake of nothing else, and for the sake of which we pursue all other ends. Second, the final end is eudaimonia.

Take the first idea first, beginning with the notion of doing something for a reason. We don't do everything for a reason: someone might tap his foot while listening to music, but not for any *reason*. But think about someone making something: perhaps he begins with a long, flat piece of wood, cuts it into a certain shape, rounds one end of it into a handle, gives the other end of it a curved, flat face, and so on. We understand his reason for doing all of these things when we understand what his end is – in this case, making a cricket bat. Furthermore, we can ask about his reason for having that end; perhaps it is his job. We can keep going: someone employs him in order to sell cricket bats; people buy cricket bats to play cricket; and so on. In each case, we explain what people do in terms of their ends, and these ends fit together into a hierarchy, each end explained by the next end in this "chain" of ends.

What do we mean by doing something "for the sake of" an end? The bat-making example gives one answer: we make a bat for the sake of selling it – making the bat is a *means* to that end. But that is only one answer; obviously, there are many things we do for their own sake, such as playing cricket. It is also possible to do something both for its own sake and for the sake of another end: for instance, a person might make bats both as a hobby and as a means of making some extra money. Or consider someone who plays a game of cricket for the sake of enjoying a sunny day. Obviously, playing cricket is not a means to the end of enjoying the day: the bat-maker thinks how to make the bat so that someone will want to buy it, but the player does not think how to play the next ball so that he can enjoy his day. Rather, playing cricket is for the sake of enjoying the day in the sense that it is a *way* of enjoying the day; and in order to enjoy a day of cricket, one must play cricket on its own terms, for its own sake.[2] And so on. The point is that we should interpret the "for the sake of" relation in these chains as broadly as the variety of our reasons demands.

Now, each "chain" has to end somewhere. If it were infinitely long or looped back on itself, then we could never say what the whole chain was for the sake of, and practical reasoning couldn't halt anywhere; the thought that the whole enterprise might have a point couldn't withstand scrutiny.[3] This is why practical reasoning requires a *final* end that all of the other ends in the chain are for the sake of, but which is not for the sake of anything else.

This is how Aristotle introduces the notion of a final end.[4] However, Aristotle immediately says a couple of surprising things about it: there is exactly *one* final end per person, and what's more, it is the *same* final end for each of us.[5] Strangely, Aristotle doesn't argue for these claims,[6] but they actually make a lot of sense: multiple final ends could conflict, and practical reasoning couldn't settle that conflict.[7] Besides, practical reasoning doesn't just work out how to reach our ends, if we have any; it also tells us to have ends, and more than that, to have ends *we can live for*, ends that give us a reason to go on in the first place, ends that our lives can be about. In other words, we have one very central end – the end of giving ourselves a good life. If that is so, then there really *is* just one end that makes sense of every other end, and it is the *same* one for all. That doesn't mean that everyone should live the same life, only that everyone needs to find a good life.

The idea that there is just one final end has led some to suppose that there must be some single theme or purpose, some "grand end" to one's life, and that one must deliberate about everything one does as fitting into a sort of blueprint of a life organized around that grand end. The notion of such a blueprint also suggests a kind of fixity, laying out a master plan for the rest of one's days. However, that should strike us as an odd way of thinking about doing things for the sake of a good life; at the very least, it would be odd to suppose that that is generally how practical reasoning works. People find all sorts of things to live for – a loving relationship, raising a child, pursuing a career, enjoying pastimes – but usually not as part of a master plan, and not for the sake of some single grand end. One does not deliberate about how to pursue a career or raise a child so that doing so will lead to a grand end. One deliberates about them on their own terms. That is, one lives one's life.[8]

In what sense, then, do we do all of these things for the sake of a good life? Since the things we live for are in fact our ends, the question more precisely is how we might adopt these various ends for the sake of the single end of having a good life. The answer, I think, is that there are some ends we seek only by coming to have other ends, and that having a good life is the ultimate end of that sort. Consider an end like having a satisfying career: that just is the end of finding another end that one can pursue for its own sake.[9] (Consider how common such ends are among university students, for instance.) Ultimately, one's end in life is to give one's life meaning and to make it about something. When that process succeeds, one has several ends to pursue for their own sake and the life one lives in living for these ends is a good life. Of course, it would go too far to suggest that this is Aristotle's view; we are, after all, discussing a *gap* in his argument.[10] But I find it plausible in its own right, and at the very least it illustrates the kind of flexibility that the eudaimonist notion of a final end can have.

This brings us to the second main idea in eudaimonism about practical reasoning: the final end is a good human life, eudaimonia. For Aristotle says that when we talk about the final end, we are looking for the greatest good in life – and that is exactly what we are looking for when we talk about eudaimonia.[11] In both conversations, the central idea is that of the sort of good that could bring focus and direction to a person's life. Of course, people disagree about what exactly eudaimonia is: maybe pleasure, or fame or riches, maybe indulgence or, by contrast, being a good person, maybe it is just having good luck, etc. Aristotle rejects these views, but they reveal that to talk about eudaimonia is to try to say what the best thing is that anyone could hope for in life. In fact, that is why Aristotle rejects indulgence, say: it might be the best that cows could hope for, but we're not like that. These views also seem to be attempts to say what sort of life is good, fulfilling, and desirable for the one living it. In sum, eudaimonia seems to be a good life that involves both *human* fulfillment and *individual* fulfillment. And that does sound like what we all want out of life, even though we don't all want the same things.

EUDAIMONISM ABOUT HAPPINESS

Whatever eudaimonia *is*, we know what it is *like*: the kind of good that can be the final end for practical reasoning. But is *happiness* like that? When we talk about "happiness," often we mean a positive emotion, feeling, or mood, but surely we don't want everything else just for the sake of *that*. So how could eudaimonia give us a way of thinking about happiness?

Sometimes we mean something else by "happiness." For instance, people often say to new parents that they wish their child "every happiness." They don't mean, "I wish your child a future of mostly good moods, whether it actually has a good life or not."[12] This wish is not for a kind of *feeling* but for a kind of *future*: one that can count as a *good life*.

When we think about *that* kind of happiness, it is more plausible that it could have a lot to do with our major ends in life, as eudaimonia does. For example, consider the popular film *Spiderman*, in which a young man (Peter Parker) on the verge of graduating from high school unexpectedly develops spectacular superhuman powers. The focus of Peter's story is his suddenly being forced to figure out what to do with his life, all at once: either devoting himself to helping others as an anonymous hero, or going about the normal life and relationships he had always dreamed of. An amount of "growing up" that is usually spread out over many years, even decades of a person's life, is thrust upon Peter literally overnight. I don't know exactly what a friend would advise Peter to do, but it seems clear that a friend would think about Peter's *happiness* – that is, about the kind of future that will amount to a good life for Peter.

So, when we wish someone a good life, one thing we clearly wish for them is that their lives be rich and fulfilling for the unique individuals they are.[13] There is an analogy here to giving someone a gift: a good gift-giver tries to give a friend a gift that the friend will like, not a gift that the *giver* likes or thinks the friend *ought* to like. Likewise, we can think of happiness as the good life that one gives oneself, and it should be one that "fits" one as an individual, and is experienced and felt as meaningful. At the same time, that is certainly not *all* that we wish for: for instance, someone might find his life rewarding as a result of manipulation or even brainwashing, and that is obviously not a future anyone would wish for a friend, or for himself.[14] Likewise, we saw above that to wish someone "every happiness" is to wish him a good life – the real thing, not merely contentment with whatever life he might end up with. For instance, we wish for children to grow up to be emotionally fulfilled, but we mean the emotional fulfillment of a normal *grown-up*, not of a mentally childish adult (like Chauncey Gardiner in the film *Being There*). So in addition to individual fulfillment, a good life also involves *human* fulfillment. In fact, notice that individual fulfillment is itself one *kind* of human fulfillment: fulfillment as the sorts of creatures we are requires individuality and self-expression of a sort that dogs, say, simply do not require.[15]

So when we think about happiness in the sense of a good future and good life, happiness is remarkably like eudaimonia. Happiness, like eudaimonia, is an end that we pursue for its own sake and nothing further. Happiness is also the kind of end for the sake of which we can pursue all of our other ends: to pursue happiness, after all, is to pursue a number of other ends that one finds fulfilling, and pursue them in a way that adds up to a whole life that is a good life. And happiness, like eudaimonia, is life that is fulfilling for one as an individual and as a human.

Perhaps it is not so surprising that happiness and eudaimonia should turn out to be rather alike after all. For instance, the English word 'happy' originally derived from the word 'hap,' meaning "chance" or "fortune," as in 'perhaps'; similarly, the Greek word '*eudaimonia*' originally conveyed having a favorable (*eu-*) guardian spirit (*daimōn*), that is, having good fortune. In fact, Aristotle says that in his own time a lot of people still thought that eudaimonia and good luck were the same thing.[16] And as we saw above, many thought that eudaimonia was pleasure or being famous or rich,[17] and all of these sound a lot like things that people in our culture might say happiness is. Yet "happiness" is a malleable enough notion that we can think of it in more sophisticated ways too, just as ancient philosophers thought about eudaimonia.

Thinking further about human nature can help us say more about what the "human fulfillment" in happiness is. As Martha Nussbaum has put it, here we reflect on what goods are so crucial in our lives that we cannot imagine a *human* life without them: our sociality, for instance, or our ability to trust each other.[18] Not surprisingly, different philosophers have gone in different directions at this point, even in the ancient world. For instance, Epicurus argued that the fundamental feature of humans and human motivation is their basic urge to avoid all forms of physical and mental pain. This had two major implications for Epicurus' account of happiness: one, human happiness is above all a *passive* life of tranquility and freedom from pain, and so, two, the use of reasoning is not part of our happiness, even though it is useful for it.

However, by far most eudaimonists, ancient and modern alike, have believed that we are defined instead by our capacity for practical reasoning, both in thinking intelligently about what to do and in acting with emotions that can be intelligently trained. Aristotle understands living by practical reasoning to be our distinctive mode of life, or what he calls our "function," and argues that only a life lived wisely could genuinely count as a fully human life.[19] This is not to deny the significance of our basic physical and other psychological needs. Rather, the idea is that our capacity for practical reasoning shapes and "interpenetrates" every other aspect of our nature, and makes our whole nature distinctively human.[20] This is true of even our most basic drives, such as the drive to eat: humans can reflect intelligently on how, whether, when, and what to eat, and this makes human *dining* completely unlike animal *feeding*. Whatever human happiness is, then, it must be the happiness of a creature whose characteristic mode of life is to live by directing itself through practical reasoning.

This idea has also been an important theme in the work of Rosalind Hursthouse. Although the flourishing of animals and humans alike can be understood in terms of their characteristic ways of life, including their characteristic enjoyments, the possession of practical reason totally transforms human flourishing: our characteristic way of going on is a "rational way," Hursthouse says, and this is to live in "any way that we can rightly see as good, as something we have reason to do."[21] Even our "characteristic enjoyments" are anything that we can enjoy and find compatible with practical reasoning.

However, eudaimonists have differed, not only regarding what they think human nature is, but also regarding what kind of reflection is involved in saying what human nature is. Some have regarded facts about our nature as lying outside the realm of normative thought, serving as a basis or foundation for normative thought. For instance, Anscombe argued that it is good to keep one's promises because, as a purely natural fact, we must cooperate in order to attain our goals and a convention of promising is the most effective way to cooperate.[22] However, this approach has often drawn the reply that normative ("ought") statements cannot be inferred from nonnormative factual ("is") statements – the "naturalistic fallacy" – although this objection is contested.[23]

By contrast, other eudaimonists think of human nature as itself a normative notion, and understand the process of thinking of happiness in terms of human nature as calling on a body of normative notions that are mutually supporting and enlightening.[24] Moreover, while such thought might involve natural facts, reasons are not "discovered" in those facts; those facts can have only the normative weight we give them. For example, John McDowell has argued that the very ability to engage in practical reasoning requires the ability to contemplate alternative courses of action, choosing as there is most reason to choose. Of course, this will apply also to actions that are presented as purely "natural"; for instance, if we are told that our teeth and digestive system make it "natural" for us to eat meat, we must still choose to eat meat from among our alternatives in order to do so for a reason. In that case, it is never the bare "naturalness" of a fact that gives it any practical or normative weight for us.[25]

EUDAIMONISM ABOUT THE VIRTUES

In eudaimonism, happiness is two things at once: it is the final end for practical reasoning, and it is a good human life for the one living it. The next step is to say what things make a human life good in this sense, and here we have to think about what it would take for a good life to be *both* of the things that happiness is. For instance, even though money may well be important for happiness, just making money cannot be the final end, because we want money for the sake of what we can do with it. If we could continue in this way, we could rule out a number of candidate goods that cannot be the same as happiness, and hopefully we could also begin to home in on the sorts of goods we are looking for.

This is exactly what Aristotle does, and he identifies what we can call several "formal constraints" on the kind of good that happiness is:

(1) Happiness must be an *active* life: we live by choosing and acting, so happiness must be a good life of that sort.[26]
(2) Happiness must lie in one's *own* activity: happiness depends on what a person does in and with his own life, not on what someone else is doing in his life; other people cannot just give or take away happiness.[27]
(3) Happiness must be *stable*: although luck can shift a lot, happiness depends on how one acts and is therefore more stable than luck.[28]
(4) Happiness must be good *in its own right*: happiness is not the sort of thing that is good only because of something else that is good (as e.g. money is).[29]
(5) Happiness must be *final* or *comprehensive*: happiness is good for its own sake; it is never for the sake of anything else; and everything else is for the sake of happiness.[30]
(6) Happiness must be *self-sufficient*: because happiness is final, it is therefore the greatest thing one could want in life.[31] "Self-sufficiency" here doesn't mean being very rich or powerful[32] or having no need of others, but having all one needs for the sake of the life one is living.[33]
(7) Happiness must be distinctly *human*: a good life for a human includes fulfillment of a distinctly human sort.[34]

These constraints rule out a lot of candidates for happiness, like moneymaking; but it also cannot be prestige or honor (which is good only as recognition for something even better); it cannot be indulgence or consumption (that's fine for cattle but not for us); it cannot be the same as good luck (that is too unstable, and has too little to do with one's own actions); it cannot lie in just *being* a certain way (that is compatible with chronic inactivity); and so on.[35] However, notice a further defect of each of these candidates: it is difficult to see how any of them could be something we want *everything else* for the sake of, and it would be at least as difficult to see how *all of us alike* could want that same thing. Furthermore, it seems inevitable that *every* good thing we might propose would have the very same problem. Have we reached a dead end?

Fortunately, there is one way to meet these constraints and move ahead: make happiness not one kind of activity but a *way* of doing other kinds of activities. A person can find individual and human fulfillment by choosing fulfilling ends and then acting for those ends with good practical reasoning and sound emotions. That kind of reasoning and emotion is what makes us fully human, since our characteristic human way of living is a *rational* way, rational in both wisdom and emotion.[36] In Greek, one would say that such a thing is part of being fully human by saying it is a human *aretē*, which is often translated "excellence" or, more frequently, "virtue." Acting with wisdom and sound emotion is what Aristotle means by "virtuous activity."

So Aristotle concludes that virtuous activity, so understood, is the most important thing for happiness, and it is at this point that we reflect on human nature in order to tell what counts as success in practical reasoning and emotion, and thus what is an excellence or virtue in a person.[37] For instance, this reflection will probably lead us to conclude that a good human life is social, a life in the company of others for whom we have genuine concern and with whom we share interests. In order to find real fulfillment in such a life, it will be important to treat one another fairly and honestly, to share generously, to be civil in our reactions to each other, to be friendly, even to be witty. Another part of a fulfilling human life might be having realistic attitudes about oneself, both one's successes and one's shortcomings. Likewise, one must be able to stand by one's ends despite fear and temptation. And of course one needs intelligence about all of these things: when a certain sort of sociality is appropriate, how to deal with successes and shortcomings realistically, what fears and desires are worth resisting, what counts as generous.

Fulfillment in these areas is something one has reason to want for the sake of one's happiness, whatever else one may happen to want, and here we can identify certain personal attributes – "excellences" – that make a life a good human life. Judging from the fulfillments just mentioned, these traits will include fairness, honesty, generosity, even-temperedness, friendliness, and wit; proper pride and, when appropriate, even a sense of shame; courage and temperance; and in every case, practical wisdom. These attributes or excellences are of course the *virtues*, both the virtues of character and (in the case of practical wisdom) the virtue of practical intellect. In fact, the virtues I have listed here are just the ones that Aristotle himself identifies.[38] Furthermore, practical wisdom is especially significant, because it is the virtue of deliberating well, which we can now see involves deliberating about how all of one's ends might fit together into a whole life that is a happy one.

So eudaimonism identifies the virtues as those attributes of character and practical intellect that are important for happiness. In what way are they "important" for happiness, more precisely? Are they necessary for happiness? Are they sufficient for it? Both? Ancient eudaimonists all agreed that the virtues are necessary for happiness, and most of them argued that it was sufficient as well (the Aristotelians were the exception).[39] Today, philosophers generally side with Aristotle that virtue is not sufficient for happiness: in addition to virtue, as Aristotle said, happiness also needs bodily as well as external goods.[40] Furthermore, many believe that it is not strictly necessary for happiness, either, since by all appearances rotten people sometimes seem to live very well anyway. Even so, this is consistent with saying that the best bet we have for a happy life is to develop the virtues; in this way, as contemporary eudaimonists say, the virtues "benefit their possessor."[41]

Understanding the virtues in this way has several important implications for virtue ethics. For one thing, it yields a distinctive picture of the virtues: the virtues are human excellences, and this means they are both "deep" and "broad." They are deep insofar as they are steady, reliable, and intelligent dispositions, rather than mere habits, say; they involve caring strongly about certain things and reasoning wisely about them. And they are broad in that they have a broad reach across one's psyche, involving emotional reactions, attitudes, desires, values, and so on.[42] Furthermore, these excellences of character are inseparable from the excellence of practical wisdom. As Aristotle puts it, the virtues of character give us the right sorts of ends, such as helping a friend in the case of generosity, and practical wisdom (*phronēsis*) enables us to deliberate intelligently about those ends, such as what would really count as helping as opposed to merely having one's heart in the right place.[43]

Eudaimonism also makes for a distinctive sort of virtue ethics in its understanding of ethical reasoning. On this approach, there is not a distinction between "moral" and "nonmoral" forms of practical reasons. Eudaimonism takes its start by thinking about the nature of practical reasoning, understood in a perfectly ordinary way as deliberating about what to do. Consequently, eudaimonistic virtue ethics treats ethical reasoning as a case of ordinary practical reasoning as we employ it everywhere in our lives. This is not to say that practical reasoning is "prudential" rather than "moral" but to question that very distinction. Likewise, eudaimonistic virtue ethics treats virtues not as counterbalancing more "selfish" interests in one's happiness, but as sources of wise action, and wise action is continuous with one's own happiness.

Lastly, eudaimonistic virtue ethics takes a distinctive approach to ethical evaluation. Modern moral theory often focuses on acts, and policies for evaluating acts: whether that act was right, and whether this act ought to be done, are the central sorts of questions, and generally the aim is to formulate some policy or rule for sorting acts into one evaluative category or the other. These evaluations usually seem compartmentalized and disconnected from the rest of one's life (i.e. from its "nonmoral" elements), and that engenders a sense that morality is not so much a part of one's life as a set of rules that keep it within certain boundaries. Because of its heritage in eudaimonism, however, virtue ethics tends to be different in both of these ways. Eudaimonistic virtue ethics does of course concern itself with what is right and what one ought to do, but here the focus is on how to deliberate well about such questions, for which rules are generally insufficient. This focus also tends to be diachronic rather than episodic: at least as important as saying what act would be right, here and now, is what an act says about the person who does it, and that tends to shift attention onto the long process of developing into the kind of person who is skilled at such deliberations. Virtue ethics offers us action guidance less by giving us rules to follow than by telling us how to become people who can do what rules never can.

CAN THE FINAL END BE HAPPINESS?

In the last two sections I want to clarify a number of important details about eudaimonism by thinking about some main concerns that philosophers sometimes have about it. It will be useful to divide these concerns into a couple of groups: first, concerns about the idea that something that is the final end, as eudaimonia is supposed to be, could really be what happiness is; and second, concerns about whether the sort of good that happiness is supposed to be could really be the final end.

I

The final end is an "objective" good, we might say, in the sense that pursuing that good is important for one's happiness whether one thinks so or not; and in that case, a person is not the final authority on what his or her happiness requires.[44] Now, recall my argument above that happiness (as a good life) is objective in this way too, since (e.g.) we don't think that brainwashed people have happy lives just because they think they do. Perhaps that argument was too quick: according to L. W. Sumner, this point is consistent with thinking that each person really is the final authority on his or her happiness. More than that, Sumner argues that the very idea of objectivity is incompatible with our whole notion of happiness.

On Sumner's view, a person has a genuinely good, happy life just in case (a) he feels and thinks that his life is happy, (b) his judgment is genuine in the sense that it is not based on ignorance of anything that would change his judgment if he knew it, and (c) the judgment is not the result of manipulation, that is, the judgment is "autonomous." Now, even though one's judgments about his happiness must be genuine, Sumner argues, this does not mean that happiness is objective: his happiness still depends solely on his own judgments, and all that requirements (b) and (c) do is to ensure that his judgments really *are* his.[45]

However, even if such a theory of happiness is *consistent* with the idea that happiness must be autonomous, still it cannot explain *why* that idea should have mattered in the first place. After all, Sumner doesn't think that autonomy is important for the welfare of dogs, say, only of humans.[46] But in that case, autonomy isn't part of welfare just as such, but only part of *human* welfare, or happiness; *for a human*, then, autonomy must be *objectively* important for happiness, important whether one thinks it is or not.[47]

2

It is because eudaimonism thinks of happiness as crucially involving *human* fulfillment that it can identify virtues as those character attributes that are important for happiness. But is that really the right way to think about happiness? Recall the point about giving gifts to friends: the right gifts are ones that the *recipient* will like, not ones that someone *else* likes. Happiness is like that, too; even eudaimonism says that happiness involves individual fulfillment, since what will be a good life for someone depends on what he is like and what sorts of things he finds fulfilling. But in that case, why should anything *else* matter for his happiness, since it is just *his* happiness we are talking about?[48]

A proponent of this line of thought could even make sense of the idea that happiness requires autonomy: to be fulfilled as an individual is to live a life that reflects and expresses who one really is, and autonomy just is the latitude to live that way. Now, this means that autonomy is important for a person's happiness whether he thinks so or not; this view of happiness is still objective. However, on this view autonomy is still important for happiness just for the sake of one's fulfillment as an individual.

Notice, though, that the individuality a being needs must still depend on what kind of creature that being is. Human individuality involves exercising practical reasoning, making choices, and living with what follows from those choices. By "autonomy," we mean the sort of latitude that is indispensable to living that kind of life. To be sure, a dog needs some latitude too: a dog's life would be pathetic if it were made to live in a way that it found miserable, boring, or frustrating. But the latitude a dog needs is not autonomy – it is not the latitude that *we* need. In that case, the need for autonomy depends not just on being an individual but on being an individual *of a certain kind* or *species*. That is why eudaimonism holds that even our need for individual fulfillment ultimately stems from our need for human fulfillment, which includes directing our own lives by our choices.

3

Lastly, how far is this emphasis on human fulfillment to go? If we keep pushing this thought, we might end up characterizing happiness as "being a good specimen of humanity," for instance; but that sounds more like our *goodness* than like our *good*. The life of a good human specimen is obviously some sort of "good life," but recall that happiness is a good life *for the one living it*, and being a good specimen is not *that* sort of good. Furthermore, by the time eudaimonism tells us that the virtues are important for happiness, we might suspect that it has made exactly this misstep.[49]

Mistaking our goodness for our good would be a serious misstep indeed, but eudaimonism as I have characterized it here doesn't do that – on the contrary, it reveals precisely why that misstep would be so serious. Because happiness is the final end, it has to be the sort of good life that *we want for its own sake*, and for the sake of which we could want whatever else we want. As Aristotle puts the point, the whole idea behind a final end in the first place is to give desire a focus, so that it doesn't turn out to be pointless. But happiness understood as "being a good specimen" (say) couldn't give desire the focus that it needs, and could not bring deliberation to a halt. In other words, happiness must be a good life for the one living it, not in *spite* of being the final end but precisely *because* it is.

That is why happiness must be a kind of individual fulfillment. However, we have seen that the only kind of individual fulfillment that could really count as happiness in the first place, is fulfillment as the distinctly *human* individual that each of us is. These two ideas come together in the thesis that virtue is important for happiness. As we have seen, virtuous activity is not some special kind of pursuit.[50] It is instead activity for the sake of one's ends, insofar as one adopts and acts for them in a wise and emotionally healthy way.

CAN HAPPINESS BE THE FINAL END?

This brings us to the other set of issues: can a good like happiness – a good life for the one living it – make sense of practical reasoning, which the final end is supposed to do? There are four issues about practical reasoning that we should consider here: reasons to act for the benefit of others; reasons to sacrifice for others; reasons that we are obligated to act for; and the very idea that there are reasons to seek one's own happiness in the first place.

I

First, if the final end for the sake of which I do everything else is my own happiness, does that mean that all I really have reason to do is to look out for my own interests? Here we should think about the different sorts of ends that people might adopt as a way of giving themselves a good life. Should we suppose that all of those ends would be self-serving? It is hard to see why. On the contrary, we can easily recognize that people usually live happy lives in taking the good of others as an end of their own. Such ends are ones that happy people usually choose to love in their lives: helping the poor or the homeless can be such an end, but more commonly people take devotion to a partner as an end, or raising their children.[51] In other words, eudaimonism is a view about *how* we adopt our ends – for the sake of a good life – but it does not say that *which* ends we adopt should be self-serving. On the contrary, we would likely agree that living a purely self-serving life would be a particularly *poor* strategy for happiness.

Even so, we might ask, if the ends need not be self-serving, then why not just adopt those ends *directly*, and leave one's happiness out of it? What is gained by thinking of those ends as being for the sake of one's happiness in the first place? Rather a lot, I think. For one thing, it is important to keep the proper perspective on a relationship: each person in the relationship needs to be sure that the relationship occupies a place in his life that he can live with. When that doesn't happen, devotion can become "selfless" in the pejorative sense of self-abnegating, losing perspective on one's life as a whole.[52] When a very close relationship thrives, the difference between acting for one's own sake or one's partner's sake begins to break down: acting for each other's sake just is part of the happiness each has chosen for himself or herself by joining lives with the other person. However, that intimacy is destroyed when one partner becomes too demanding; so each partner must be ready to assert his or her interests, so that the difference between their interests can once again be happily effaced and the relationship can thrive.

For another thing, committing to an end means committing *one-self* to it, in a couple of ways. First, one must judge whether the end in question is worth making part of one's life, devoting the necessary resources to live up to that end. Indeed, every choice to do one thing is also a choice not to do all of the other things one might have done instead – that is, a choice to bear certain "opportunity costs." Part of choosing an end for a reason is to assess its merits *taken with* its opportunity costs, so it is unclear what it would be to choose an end on its merits without first looking at that end from the broader perspective of one's life. And second, one must also judge whether one's life is worth investing in by making that end a part of it. In both cases, one begins from the perspective of committing to make a good life.

2

Another question concerns rational self-sacrifice: if my final end is my happiness, then how could any act of mine be *both* self-sacrificing *and* rational? Consider the following dilemma from *The Return of Tarzan*: Tarzan is the rightful Lord Greystoke, but in order to take his title and its benefits he would have to expose the man now pretending to be Greystoke; however, Jane is betrothed to that man, and so by taking his title Tarzan would hurt the woman he loves. In the novel, Tarzan makes a sacrifice and protects Jane. Surely we should describe this as an act of rational self-sacrifice, but if eudaimonism is true, we might worry, then sacrificing some good of one's own could not be rational – unless the loss is balanced by a compensating gain, but then it no longer counts as a sacrifice.[53]

Notice that the question sets up a conflict between a pair of ends: an end that calls for sacrifice (protecting Jane), and the end that is one's happiness (having the title). But I think we should instead see this conflict as one between sacrificing some good for the sake of an end – foregoing the title for the love of Jane – and sacrificing another good for the sake of another end: hurting Jane for the sake of the title. Or think of it this way. If loving Jane is part of the good life Tarzan is giving himself, then there is sacrifice either way: either giving up his title by acting for the sake of the end of loving Jane, or giving up on the end of loving Jane by not acting for the sake of that end.

In short, the question assumes that one's happiness is something independent of how one makes the choice about sacrificing. By contrast, happiness is the kind of good that is sometimes best when one's ends give one something to lose. For instance, loving someone is an end one can adopt for the sake of happiness even though it exposes him or her to loss – in fact, precisely *because* it does. Even when our ends can cost us something, it can make sense to adopt those ends for the sake of happiness. Those costs are real, and they are real sacrifices. But the point is that the costs grow out of the ends that make one's life a happy life in the first place.

3

Even if a person whose final end is eudaimonia *might* act for the good of others and *might* even make sacrifices for others, could that final end really make sense of an *obligation* to act in those kinds of ways?[54]

I think that it could. If one's final end is eudaimonia, then doing well by others is much more than something he just *might* do; it is something he would *have* to do.[55] Recall that eudaimonia is *human* happiness and involves fulfillment as a human being. A crucial part of our humanity is our sociality, which involves a certain kind of reciprocity: treating each other as having the authority to give each other reasons to act.[56] For instance, if I step on your foot and you tell me to stop, you are both announcing your authority to address that reason to me and, in addressing it to me, recognizing my ability to understand that reason and its force; you thereby recognize that I too have the sort of authority that you have. Now, if treating each other with this kind of reciprocity is crucial to human fulfillment, then none of us can rationally have any option but to stand in this reciprocal relation with other people. And to stand in that relation with each other just is to give each other the authority to be sources of binding obligations.

It is important to see that once I occupy that reciprocal relation with you, the reason that I treat you decently – by getting off your foot, say – is for *your* sake, recognizing that you obligate me to do so. Of course, my reason for occupying that reciprocal relation in the first place is that it is indispensable to my happiness. Does that mean my reasons are less than "moral" reasons? That is our next and final question.

4

Does the fact that I stand in that reciprocal relation with others for the sake of my happiness undercut the idea of being obligated to do so? Immanuel Kant argued that there is no obligation to seek one's own happiness, and this has led to a widespread sense that we cannot make sense of obligation by starting from the perspective of an agent's happiness. In very broad outline, Kant's position comes down to two main ideas. One is the idea that obligations are directives from practical rationality as such (e.g. to respect beings with practical rationality, to avoid any action that would contradict reasoning, etc.).[57] The other idea is that practical rationality does not direct us in that way to seek our own happiness.

I see no reason to reject Kant's first idea (though eudaimonists do not usually speak in those terms). Rather, I think Kant's second idea is the suspicious one. Now, Kant doesn't say that practical reason is indifferent about *happiness*: we are (imperfectly) obligated to promote the happiness of others.[58] Nor is practical reason indifferent to *self-benefit*: we are (imperfectly) obligated to develop our talents.[59] Why, then, is there no obligation to seek *one's own happiness*? One plausible answer is that Kant thinks of happiness as the satisfaction of desire, so that we all seek our own happiness anyway, without having to be directed to do so by practical reason.[60]

But in that case, where philosophers like me disagree with Kant is less over the nature of *obligation* than over the nature of *happiness*. Happiness, or eudaimonia, is entirely different from desire satisfaction; in fact, it is a normative notion, in a couple of ways. First of all, it is the very nature of practical reasoning that shapes our understanding of happiness, since happiness is the final end (recall the "formal constraints" on happiness). And second, the conception of human nature employed in our account of happiness is, I would argue, part of a broader ethical outlook (recall McDowell's point, above, p. 14). Now, I argued early in this chapter that it is part of our practical rationality to need, not just to have ends, but to have ends to live for – and to live for them wisely. Furthermore, it is obvious that people regularly fail to seek that end (even if they think they are seeking happiness). Consequently, if *that* is the sort of end that happiness is, then practical reason obligates us to seek happiness – even on *Kant's* view of what an obligation is. Where I would part ways with Kant, therefore, is not so much over obligation as over happiness.

NOTES

1 See also the chapters in this volume on ancient virtue ethics (Rachana Kamtekar), Anscombe and Foot (Timothy Chappell), and eudaimonism about politics (Mark LeBar).
2 See Ackrill 1999.
3 Mark LeBar discusses this point in "Challenges to the Structure," unpublished at the time of this writing.
4 *Nicomachean Ethics* (cited as *NE*) 1.1–2. In Greek, an end is called a *telos*.
5 *NE* 1.2.
6 See Broadie 1991, pp. 8–17.
7 See Annas 1993, pp. 32–3; S. White 1992, pp. 13–15. See also N. White 2006, pp. 19–20, for discussion of a similar point in Plato's *Rep*.
8 For critique of the "grand end" view, and for discussion of eudaimonist deliberation in general, see Broadie 1991; see also D. Russell 2009, chap. 1.
9 For discussion of such ends see Schmidtz 1994, who calls them "maieutic" ends. The term is from the Greek word for midwife, since these ends "give birth" to other ends.
10 Some might even suggest that this cannot be Aristotle's view, since he says that we deliberate not about ends but about things for the sake of ends (*NE* III.3, 1112b10-ish). However, many scholars take Aristotle to mean that to deliberate *now*, one must take some end as given, even though one might deliberate about that end at some *other* time. See D. Russell 2009, pp. 6ff. and references.
11 *NE* 1.4–5.
12 See Kraut 1979.
13 Fulfillment of this sort is the topic of Haybron 2008.
14 See Sen 1987.
15 See Hampton 1993, pp. 149–50.
16 *Eudemian Ethics* (cited as *EE*) 1.1, 1214a21–5.
17 *NE* 1.4–5; cf. *EE* 1.3, 1214b34–1215a3; 1.4.
18 Nussbaum 1995. See also 1988, pp. 175, 177; 1990a, pp. 217–19, 224; 1992, p. 208.
19 *NE* 1.7, 1098a3–18. See Korsgaard 1986.

20 See Nussbaum 1990a, pp. 219–26; see also 1988, 1992, and 1993.
21 Hursthouse 1999, p. 222.
22 Anscombe 1981, chap. 2. Foot 2001 develops a version of this type of naturalism as well.
23 This is only one version of the naturalistic fallacy; other versions can be semantic, epistemological, motivational, etc. I thank Doug Rasmussen for this point.
24 See esp. McDowell 1995a, 1995b, and 1996.
25 See McDowell 1995b, pp. 151–3. See also Hursthouse 1999, chap. 8 and Nussbaum 1995. McDowell (1995a; 1995b, pp. 149–51) argues persuasively that Aristotle thinks of human nature in this second way as well; see also 1988; Broadie 1991, p. 35; Nussbaum 1995; 1986, chap. 8. By contrast, Williams 1985 assumes that eudaimonism, in Aristotle and elsewhere, is based on a purely metaphysical thesis about human nature.
26 *NE* I.5, 1095b31–1096a2, x.6, 1176a33–1176b2; *Politics* VII.3, 1325a32–4, 1325b12–16; cf. *EE* I.3, 1215a7–19. See McDowell 1995a, pp. 210–11; Broadie 1991, p. 36.
27 *NE* I.5, 1095b22–6.
28 *NE* I.10, 1100a32–b30.
29 *NE* I.5, 1095b26–31, 1096a5–10; *EE* I.7, 1217a29–40.
30 *NE* I.7, 1097a15–1097b6.
31 *NE* I.7, 1097b6–21, x.6, 1176a35–1176b9; cf. *Magna Moralia* I.2, 1184a7–14. There is a lot of controversy, however, over whether a "self-sufficient" good is greater than every other good, compared one by one, or whether it is a whole set of goods that cannot be improved upon. But we don't need to review that controversy here.
32 *NE* x.8, 1179a3–9.
33 *NE* I.7, 1097b8–11.
34 *NE* I.7, 1098a3–18.
35 See esp. *NE* I.4–5.
36 *NE* I.7, I.13; cf. *EE* I.5, 1215a30–1216a10. See Annas 1988, pp. 157–8; Broadie 1991, p. 35; McDowell 1980, p. 360; 1995a; Hursthouse 1999, pp. 214–16, 227–8.
37 *NE* I.7, 1097b22–1098a18; I.10. However, Aristotle says elsewhere (x.6–8) that happiness lies most of all in "contemplation" (*theōria*), and there he focuses on *intellectual* virtues. The relation between this view and his account of happiness in *NE* I is one of the most controversial issues in Aristotelian scholarship, but I shall leave it aside here since the *NE* x account has never had a major impact on either ancient or modern eudaimonism.
38 On the character virtues, *NE* III.6–v; on friendship, VIII–IX; on practical intelligence, VI.

39 As Cicero makes clear in *On Goals* (see esp. Book v), a central debate in ancient ethics was over the sufficiency of virtue for happiness. For discussion, see Annas 1993; S. White 2002; D. Russell 2010 and 2012.

40 *NE* 1.8–10.

41 See Hursthouse 1999, chap. 8; see also Foot 2001, pp. 96–7; Swanton 2003, p. 60.

42 See Hursthouse 2007b, sec. 2.

43 *NE* vi.12. See also D. Russell 2009; Annas 2011.

44 See Foot 2001, pp. 85–6; LeBar 2004.

45 Sumner 1996, pp. 160–71. What we are calling "happiness" Sumner calls "well-being"; by "happiness," Sumner understands a certain kind of satisfaction with one's life, in both judgment and feeling.

46 Sumner 1996, p. 179.

47 So argues LeBar 2004; cf. Haybron 2008, pp. 189–92.

48 See Haybron 2008, chap. 9.

49 See Haybron 2008, chap. 8; Sumner 1996. Haybron and Sumner call the view they target "perfectionism," although different philosophers mean different things by that term.

50 As Hursthouse (1987, p. 222) observes, happiness as the "good life" is not to be thought of as the "good moral life," i.e. a life full of saintly deeds, say.

51 See Hampton 1993, p. 157.

52 Here and elsewhere in this section I have benefited greatly from Hampton 1993.

53 For this worry, as well as the example, see esp. Darwall 2002, pp. 22–7.

54 For these general sorts of worries, see Korsgaard 1993; Scheffler 1988, 1992.

55 For this argument, see LeBar 2009.

56 See also Darwall 2006, who calls such reasons "second-personal reasons."

57 This is what it means to say that those directives – or "imperatives" – bind us "categorically." See Kant, *Groundwork* 4: 414ff.

58 *Metaphysics of Morals* 6: 387–8, 393–4.

59 *Metaphysics of Morals* 6: 386–7, 391–3.

60 On happiness as desire satisfaction, see *Groundwork* 4: 399 (although elsewhere he characterizes happiness as a mental state of contentment, *Critique of Practical Reason* 5: 22). On the inevitability of seeking one's happiness: *Groundwork* 4: 414–15; *Metaphysics of Morals* 6: 386. Kant does say that there is an "indirect" duty to preserve one's happiness, but only because dejection can lead to temptation (*Groundwork* 4: 399).

2 Ancient virtue ethics

An overview with an emphasis on practical wisdom

WHY WISDOM?

Writing *On Ends* in the first century BCE, Cicero can say that all philosophical schools see a close connection between virtue – comprising wisdom, courage, justice, and moderation – and the final end, happiness. Their disagreement is not about whether, but *how*, virtue secures happiness, and about what, if anything, apart from virtue is needed in a happy life. In the fifth-century-BCE world represented in Plato's dialogues, however, where philosophical thinking about the virtues begins, the situation is subtly but importantly different. While Plato's *Laches*, *Charmides*, *Protagoras*, and *Meno* all assume that the various virtues, or virtue as a whole, conduce to happiness (*eudaimonia*) or living well (*eu zēn*), and try to determine *what virtue must be* if it is to be so related to happiness, Plato's *Gorgias* and *Republic* argue, against a sophisticated opposition, *that* justice conduces to happiness. Arthur Adkins' classic (1960) *Merit and Responsibility* explains that in the Homeric scheme of values, which persists into Plato's day, a good (*agathos*) man who possesses virtue (*aretē*) is a man of worldly success; such a man does not undermine his claim to virtue by taking what another has reasonably laid claim to (e.g. Agamemnon by taking Briseis from Achilles), but he does if he suffers a defeat in battle. Building on such observations, Adkins shows that in the Homeric scheme of values, the warrior's courage and cunning are predominant virtues, but justice is not. In fifth-century Athens, however, justice, more obviously vital to the

I would like to thank Dan Russell and an anonymous reader of Cambridge University Press for their comments on an earlier version of this chapter.

life of the city than it was to the battlefield, begins to claim the title of virtue, although the claim does not go unopposed.

A modern reader thinking about ancient virtue is naturally drawn to justice, the ancient virtue that best corresponds to modern moral thought's focus on our relationship to others. However, the fifth-century controversy about justice's claim to be a virtue makes it nonrepresentative of the virtues in general. Consequently, this survey of ancient virtue ethics takes wisdom as the representative virtue. Among the ancients, wisdom is uncontroversially a virtue and contributor to happiness: despite their many differences about the nature of happiness, the nature of the virtues, and the manner of the virtues' contribution to happiness (cf. Frede, this volume, pp. 126–9), ancient philosophers from Socrates to the Roman Stoics and Epicureans agree that wisdom is the master virtue, necessary for the other virtues as well as for happiness. The *Iliad*'s Nestor shows that Homeric society values good counsel as much as the fifth century. From the fifth century on, sophists and philosophers, assuming in common that wisdom is a virtue and so contributes to happiness, disagree about wisdom's content: what is its subject matter and what is its relationship to this subject matter? Gorgias advances rhetoric and Protagoras, the art of politics; Hippias is a polymath; it remains for Socrates to subject these competing claims to an investigation.

In addition to wisdom's universal acceptance as a virtue, recent developments in contemporary virtue ethics give us another reason to be interested in ancient conceptions of wisdom. In the last few years, prominent virtue theorists such as Julia Annas (*Intelligent Virtue*, 2011) and Daniel C. Russell (*Practical Intelligence and the Virtues*, 2009) have defended the Aristotelian claim that real virtue must be animated by practical wisdom, but many contemporary philosophers suspect that the Aristotelian conception of practical wisdom is too intellectualist, too demanding, or too elitist. More pressing still for today's Aristotelians is the need to elaborate the (sketchy) Aristotelian tag for practical wisdom, namely "good deliberation and sensitivity to salient factors." Some Aristotelians have turned to the disciplines of cognitive and social psychology to learn more about the strengths and weaknesses of the human mind in its practical mode, with the thought that practical wisdom would be built on the strengths and would correct for the weaknesses. Revisiting alternative ancient conceptions of the wisdom that (allegedly) makes us virtuous and happy should inform the neo-Aristotelian project of elaborating practical wisdom, for considering anew which alternatives Aristotle rejects, and for what reasons, provides a useful comparison and contrast with our contemporary alternatives. Perhaps, depending on what similarities and differences we find, neo-Aristotelians will be able to adopt parts of the conceptions of the wisdom advanced by other ancients, or to clarify the desiderata for a better-elaborated conception of practical wisdom. In what follows, we will be investigating such questions as: What do different ancient philosophers say is the content of wisdom such that it is so vital to virtue and happiness? What is wisdom's precise relationship to the rest of virtue – is it sufficient for virtue or does virtue require nonintellectual dispositions as well? Does wisdom itself have nonintellectual prerequisites? Does (and if so how does) wisdom improve nonintellectual traits? Does (and if so how does) wisdom relate to right action?

In what follows, we will trace the evolution of the notion of wisdom and its relationship to the rest of virtue and to happiness through Socrates and Plato, Aristotle, the Epicureans, and the Stoics.

PLATO: FROM THE ART OF MEASUREMENT TO THE TRANSFORMATIVE OBJECT OF CONTEMPLATION

Wisdom and success

In the dialogues conventionally regarded as belonging to Plato's "early" period, Socrates presents wisdom as making the difference between a life lived well and a life lived poorly. The dialogues explore this idea in a number of ways. Sometimes, Socrates scrutinizes a sophist's claims to possess a knowledge that makes its possessor successful (e.g. *Protagoras*, *Gorgias*). On other occasions, Socrates himself tries to define virtues like courage or temperance on the assumption that, since they always benefit their possessor, the virtues must be some kind of knowledge (e.g. *Laches*, *Charmides*). A supporting argument for this assumption is provided in the *Meno*: without knowledge, courage would be recklessness, a quality of the soul that brings harm rather than benefit (88b). On still other occasions, Socrates elaborates the difficulties in specifying the content of wisdom, given that it must always be beneficial (*Euthydemus*

288d–292e, *Charmides* 165c–176a). In the *Protagoras* and *Euthydemus*, Socrates argues directly that wisdom uniquely enables us to live well, or to be happy. In the *Protagoras*, on the assumption that we live well by having what is good, and what is good is pleasure, Socrates introduces a conception of wisdom as an art of measurement that would guide our choices in life so that rather than being taken in by appearances of pleasantness, which might be distorted due to their proximity or distance from us, we could always calculate how great or small any given pleasure is. Here wisdom's value is instrumental, but Socrates also calls it "our salvation in life" (356c–357a). Socrates proposes a different account of wisdom in the *Euthydemus*, arguing that the wisdom that makes us happy must be a superordinate knowledge of, not only how to procure good things, but also how to use them correctly once procured. On this view, wisdom is the only thing good by itself, and other things in one's possession become beneficial when accompanied by wisdom (whereas accompanied by ignorance, they are harmful).

It is important to Socrates to distinguish between success and failure due to good or bad fortune, on the one hand, and success and failure due to virtue or vice, or wisdom and ignorance, on the other. But can't success be enjoyed by someone who has, instead of wisdom, the good fortune of an adviser to supply her with true opinions as to where the greater pleasure is to be found, or as to how best to use whatever she has (cf. *Meno* 97a–98c)? And can't bad fortune make a person's life wretched despite his possession of wisdom, if wisdom is coupled with poor circumstances in which there is no pleasure to be had, or no other goods to be procured?

Plato responds to such difficulties in a couple of ways, considering what in addition to wisdom is required for happiness (e.g. in his late dialogue, *Philebus*), and examining what, besides guidance in action, wisdom contributes to a good life. This second response takes us into his "middle"-period dialogues.

Wisdom as knowledge of the forms

In the *Phaedo* and *Republic*, Socrates characterizes wisdom in terms of its theoretical objects, Forms. Knowledge of Forms on the one hand perfects our souls (*Republic* 518c; cf. *Phaedo* 79d–80a) and so makes us virtuous and happy in the sense of realizing our best capacities; and on the other hand, motivates and guides our actions:

the attractive power of Forms both outshines that of any bodily goods, thereby doing away with any motivation to unjust action, and positively motivates the knower to imitate the Forms in action (*Republic* 485d–486b, 500b–c). (Mackie calls the Forms "queer" because they, uniquely, both direct and motivate immediately upon comprehension [Mackie 1977, p. 40].) Further, because knowledge of Forms is the most accurate knowledge possible, it can guide correct action by enabling correct judgments in the ordinary world of messy facts. The idea that a life is made good by its contact with something supremely good can be found in certain contemporary religious outlooks: for example, it is believed by some that God's goodness is so great that apprehending it transforms us morally. This account goes some distance towards showing how wisdom is preferable to the good fortune of an adviser directing one's actions, and why the bad fortune of poverty in external goods cannot harm one's possession of what is most valuable in life. Plato never considers the point that poverty or ill-health could prevent intellectual development, and so prevent the acquisition of this most valuable good. Perhaps it is too obvious to be mentioned, or perhaps his focus on what makes a life good, as opposed to what are the necessary preconditions for having that good in a life, makes it seem beside the point.

The properties of Forms that make it good simply to know them and that make knowledge of them capable of transforming our motivations are their purity and eternity. However, these are formal properties of *all* the Forms; they do not yet give us the content of the knowledge that makes us live well by enabling correct judgment about mundane matters. The formal properties may first inspire and then guide our search for that content, but to live well we must possess definitions of the virtues, for which it is necessary to practice dialectic.

Plato's *Republic* suggests that the study of dialectic is a lengthy and difficult one, which only very few are capable of, and which requires extensive prior training in mathematics; Plato's *Statesman* displays dialectic aimed at defining political knowledge, which, despite the accomplishments of its exponent in the dialogue, succeeds only in identifying the sphere with which this knowledge is concerned. Plato's consistent message is that wisdom, the knowledge that makes for virtue, is rare and difficult. This naturally raises the question, is there no virtue for nonphilosophers? Plato briefly discusses virtue without wisdom in a few contexts. In the

Phaedo, although he calls "so-called" courage and temperance without knowledge "illusory" (68d–69c), he also ranks people who have practiced "popular and social virtue, which they call moderation and justice and which was developed by habit and practice, without philosophy and understanding" as happiest among the nonphilosophers (81e–82b). In the *Republic*, he describes a "political courage," which consists of stable true beliefs about what is to be feared and what is not to be feared, and is produced by education and law; this, he says, is superior to mere behavioral compliance motivated by fear of punishment (429b–430c). In the *Statesman*, political knowledge, which is at once theoretical and directive, is to unite "naturally courageous and temperate" citizens with a bond of true opinion (309b–c). Up until his last and unfinished work, the *Laws*, Plato remains more interested in the nature of the knowledge that makes for perfect virtue than in the psychological states of the imperfectly virtuous; however, because he sees wisdom as qualifying its possessor for political rule, the aim of which is the improvement of citizens, he also sketches the kind of virtue which philosophers bring about in their fellow citizens (on this topic see further Kamtekar 1998).

In addition to the question of whether there can be any kind of virtue without wisdom there is one about whether virtue requires any traits of character in addition to wisdom, either as accompaniments to or prerequisites of wisdom. While Plato's early dialogues do not take up this issue, the description of the just soul in the *Republic* indicates that virtue includes, in addition to wisdom, that our nonrational capacities be disposed to follow our rational determinations. Such a disposition seems to be in part a prerequisite for wisdom, for without a prerational commitment to virtue, exposure to dialectic turns one against it and makes one mistrustful of reason (537d–540a), and in part a result of wisdom's contact with the Forms, the desire for which weakens one's desire for lesser things (485a–486b). Plato's student Aristotle develops the idea that virtue involves both wisdom and a disposition of our nonrational capacities that is obedient to reason.

VIRTUE AND PRACTICAL WISDOM IN ARISTOTLE

Aristotle defines virtue as "a state concerned with choice, lying in a mean relative to us, this being determined by reason and in the way in which the person of practical wisdom [the *phronimos*, who possesses *phronēsis*] would determine it" (*Nicomachean Ethics* [cited as *NE*] II.6, 1106b35–1107a2). Aristotle thinks that virtuous activity, which is the exercise of the state of virtue, constitutes happiness (1.7), and he emphasizes the difference between this view and the view (found in some Platonic dialogues) that happiness is virtue (1.8). A consequence of Aristotle's position is that happiness requires enough nonmoral goods (e.g. health, moderate wealth, freedom from pain) to enable virtuous activity. A virtuous person who spent his life asleep or was for some other reason unable to act on his virtue would not have a happy life, on Aristotle's view. Whether virtue is sufficient for happiness or happiness also requires other nonmoral goods becomes a central issue in, for example, Cicero's presentation of ethical views in *On Ends*. However, Aristotle's most distinctive and, in the long run, influential, contributions to thinking about the virtues can be seen in the views about wisdom he develops in response to Plato.

Virtue, reason, and passion

Aristotle's definition of virtue refers to both the intellectual and nonintellectual dispositions in which virtue consists. First, virtue is "concerned with choice," which means that it is a disposition with respect to our desires on the one hand and reasoning on the other, for our choices are deliberated desires, desires made determinate by reasoning about how to realize some end (*NE* III.3, 1113a2–12; cf. VI.2, 1139a21–3). So according to Aristotle virtue is a disposition not only of the rational or intellectual faculty but also of the emotional and desiderative one. The inclusion in virtue of emotional and desiderative dispositions allows Aristotle to draw a distinction between virtue (a condition of harmony among the various faculties in one's soul) and mere continence (a condition in which one's reason may direct one correctly, but one's desires rebel against reason's directives).

Second, the "mean" in which virtue lies consists of feelings that are neither excessive nor deficient – e.g. courage is a mean in feelings of fear and confidence between rashness or excessive confidence, and cowardice or excessive fearfulness – but the mean itself is determined by practical wisdom. Aside from expressing a rejection of asceticism – virtue is not just the curbing of natural human passions, but may involve encouraging their expression – Aristotle's famous "mean" contributes little to his account of virtue, for the mean varies from one circumstance to another, and is sometimes nearer one extreme and sometimes nearer the other. Even the general definitions of virtues in terms of a mean misses important cases: as Rosalind Hursthouse (1980–81) points out, the one-time adulterer is intemperate not because he enjoys sexual pleasure too much or too little, for his sex drive may be entirely unremarkable; it is rather that he enjoys a dishonorable sexual pleasure. Practical wisdom is a more promising standard to refer virtue to than the mean.

Third, Aristotle's account of habituation, the process by which performing acts of a certain kind produces in us dispositions of the corresponding kind (*NE* II.4, 1103a30–b25), involves intellectual and nonintellectual mechanisms. On the one hand, it seems that in the course of performing just or courageous actions we come to see their value and so to perform them for themselves (for a developed account of this sort see Burnyeat 1980). On the other hand, repetition makes us used to performing certain actions and feeling the emotions that accompany those actions, so that we perform them without resistance (cf. *Politics* VII.17, 1336a11–21, VIII.5, 1340a24–9). Upon habituation to virtue, the virtuous person performs virtuous actions in a virtuous manner: with knowledge, choosing them for themselves (*di' auta*, which may mean either noninstrumentally or under the right description), and from a stable disposition to do so (1105a31–2).

Practical wisdom and deliberation

What is practical wisdom (*phronēsis*)? Aristotle tells us in *Nicomachean Ethics* VI, a book which distinguishes the various intellectual virtues, that the practically wise person deliberates well about what is good and expedient for himself, not in some particular respect but in respect of the good life in general (1140a25–9). Here and in his earlier discussion of deliberation (III.3), Aristotle delineates the sphere of that about which we deliberate: things that can be otherwise than they are, things that we can bring about by our own actions, and things for which there is no art to prescribe what we are to do. This distinguishes practical wisdom from scientific knowledge (for that concerns unchanging things), from the study of natural things (for although they can be otherwise than they are, it is nature that brings them about, not we by our actions), and from art (for there are precise rules by which to write our letters or make shoes).

Deliberation is concerned with "the things towards the ends" (*ta pros ta telē*), i.e. with determining the means by which to bring about certain ends. Although what else is included under deliberation is controversial, many scholars add specifying the constituents of one's ends and handling competing considerations (*NE* VI.5, 1140a24–8, VI.7, 1141b8–18, VI.9, 1142b31–3; for further discussion, see Wiggins 1980 and Broadie 1991). Another important component of practical wisdom seems to be what David Wiggins calls "situational appreciation": perceptiveness of which, of the innumerable features of a situation, are relevant to the right response and which may be ignored (*NE* VI.8, 1142a23–30, VI.11, 1143a25–b5). In addition, Aristotle credits the practically wise person with goodness of judgment about others' opinions about practical wisdom's subject matter (VI.10, 1143a13–16). For an account that weaves these different ingredients together and shows of how life experience develops practical wisdom, see Hursthouse 2006a.

Deliberative skill in turn needs to be informed by good desires and emotions if it is to make us happier than would mere cleverness in determining means relative to any ends whatsoever (*NE* VI.12, 1144a20–36; cf. VI.9, 1142b18–35). Because the moral virtues and practical wisdom develop hand in hand, Aristotle says he agrees with Socrates that all the virtues require wisdom, but disagrees with his claim that they are the same as wisdom (on the grounds that they also involve nonrational elements). Aristotle develops Plato's account in the *Meno* (see above) of how virtue requires wisdom: without wisdom, traits (Aristotle dubs these traits "natural virtue") are like a body that moves about without sight, and so is prone to stumble (*NE* VI.13, 1144b10–15). A blind body simply moves in the direction it is disposed to move in; a sighted body can alter its movements to respond to information it receives about what is in the path it was initially disposed to take.

Aristotle's differences with Plato

Aristotelian practical wisdom is nowadays contrasted with consequentialist calculation (e.g. determining which action maximizes utility) or with assessment by conformity to certain higher-order principles (e.g. determining whether your maxim for action could be universalized without contradiction), but the views in opposition to which Aristotle defines practical wisdom are those found in Plato. Although Aristotle emphasizes his differences with Plato, shining a bright light on what they have in common helps us better understand Aristotle's distinctive position on the relationship between wisdom, virtue, and happiness. Plato thinks that the contemplation of Forms (i) is itself good, (ii) motivates rational agents to imitate the Forms, and (iii) guides action correctly. Aristotle thinks that contemplation (not of Forms but of the first principles, especially God), (i) is itself good and (ii) motivates rational activity throughout the world. But Aristotle disagrees with Plato about (iii), because determining what to do is not a matter of imitating perfectly rational activity in some other sphere, but requires attention to the particulars of the situations in which we find ourselves.

Plato's mistake, according to Aristotle, is to treat ethical matters as if the same degree of precision could be obtained in ethical knowledge as in scientific knowledge (cf. *NE* 1.3 1095a12–27 for Aristotle on the inevitable imprecision in ethical discussions). But scientific knowledge can be so precise because its objects are as they are by necessity. By contrast, the connections between actions and a good outcome vary with all kinds of situational factors. Further, while Plato thinks that all good things are good by participation in the Form of the Good, in fact, "good is said in many ways," namely, what it is for a human being to be good (given by the human function) is so different from what it is for a substance to be good (God) or for a time to be good (the right moment, *kairos*) that there can be no account of what they have in common (*NE* 1.6). For guiding action, we neither need nor can have a science with the distinctive subject matter "the good"; what we need and can develop through experience and reflection are deliberative skills concerning what is good or bad for us, and perceptiveness with respect to which particulars instantiate the universals which direct our actions (vi.8, 1141b8–16, 1142a23–30).

It is worth noting that Plato agrees with Aristotle's claim that correct action requires attention to particulars (in the *Republic* he requires fifteen years of practical experience for his philosopher-rulers, and in the *Statesman* he insists on the difference between wisdom, which is flexible and responsive to particulars, and law, which is not), and that Aristotle does not deny that ethical general-izations offer useful action guidance (see further Irwin 2000). Their differences over (iii) are rather that, first, Aristotle thinks that the ability to perceive particulars is partly constitutive of practical wis-dom itself, and not just something that comes in when one has to apply wisdom to particular situations to make a correct judgment. Second, and more importantly, although Aristotle counts theoret-ical activity as supremely good, he thinks this is by its being an ingredient of the happiest life, but not by its organizing that life and telling us what to do – as practical wisdom does (VI.13, 1145a6–11). A slightly more familiar parallel: the activity of playing music makes a musician's life good, but not because music instructs her when to pay the bills or how to raise her children.

Modern readers see Aristotle as making a significant advance over Plato in distinguishing between the content of theoretical and that of practical wisdom, and explaining their different values or con-tributions to happiness. Practical wisdom is that excellent state of soul that enables us to choose well with respect to human goods and evils, in particular situations and for the course of our lives; theoret-ical wisdom is that excellent state of soul that enables us to engage in the most intrinsically good, happiness-constituting activity, con-templation. One consequence of Aristotle's distinction between the-oretical and practical wisdom is that nonphilosophers may have full virtue and lead happy lives so long as they possess practical wisdom, which neither is the same as, nor presupposes, philosophic wisdom, and which at least seems to be more widely available.

Is Aristotle relevant today?

However, we need to think hard about whether or not the arguments Aristotle levels against Plato's views about how theoretical wisdom could make life go well rather than badly have contemporary appli-cation. For example, if we are pluralists about value, we may agree with Aristotle that "good is said in many ways," but Aristotle's point doesn't obviously rule out either consequentialist or deonto-logical forms of deliberation. It is true that if determining what to do requires that one bear in mind the moderate in quantity, the oppor-tune in time, the useful in relation, and so on (NE 1.6 1096a20–8), it is not clear how maximizing would yield a solution, and it is true that considering the different senses of good would require more than one principle against which to assess an intended action. Still, Aristotle seems less concerned than we are that a plurality of values to be considered in deliberation produce conflicts.

Another question about contemporary applicability is raised by new developments in social sciences such as economics and psychology. If these produce rules for bringing about an outcome where previously we would have had to rely on good judgment, should we conclude that the subject they cover is no longer in the purview of practical wisdom, or should we remove from our characterization of practical wisdom that it excludes any subject for which there is an art that specifies what its practitioner should do? For example, if cognitive and social psychology discover that our decision-making is subject to such biases as the framing effect (e.g. whether the outcome of an action is described as a loss to be sustained or a gain not achieved) or the bystander effect (i.e. that we tend not to register situations as calling for our action when no one else viewing the situation is intervening) or such fallacies as ignoring the base rate (the background frequency with which some event occurs), fairly precise recommendations suggest themselves as fixes: reframe the information; factor the bystander effect explicitly into your deliberations; redescribe the statistical information using sampling terminology (n out of 1,000 events) instead of in percentages (see further Gigerenzer 2000; D. Russell 2009). Should we see these fixes as part of practical wisdom and see the social sciences as included in the reflection and experience by which Aristotle says we would develop practical wisdom? Or should we say that some of what used to be determined by deliberation is now determined by rules that come from new disciplines? For the new disciplines are theoretical and their rules are more precisely formulable than our judgment; further, it is unclear whether we can internalize their prescriptions as second nature or must always use them consciously to override the heuristics which we use more or less by nature.

EPICUREAN VIRTUE AND THE KNOWLEDGE OF NATURE

For the Epicureans physics, the knowledge of nature, has life-changing practical import. In the *Letter to Menoeceus*, Epicurus says that practical wisdom is the source of all the other virtues,

teaching that it is impossible to live pleasantly without living virtuously and impossible to live virtuously without living pleasantly
(132; cf. *Principal Doctrines* 5). The outline of this wisdom is given
in the famous "fourfold medicine" (*tetrapharmakon*): (i) the gods
are blessed beings, not such as to intervene in our lives; (ii) at death
we cease to experience and so to be subjects of good or evil; (iii)
the limit of what is good is easy to get; and (iv) the limit of what
is bad is short-lived. As their name for it suggests, the Epicureans regard wisdom as a cure; the disease is anxiety caused by false
beliefs.

Epicureans posit in each of us an inborn desire for the goal of
life, namely pleasure and freedom from pain; however, during our
upbringing we develop the false beliefs that the gods intervene in
our lives, that our souls survive death and suffer, and that the pleasures we need to live a happy life are not securely ours. As a consequence we become anxious, ascetic, acquisitive. To dispel our false
beliefs, we need physics, a true account of nature, which shows
us that the gods do not intervene in the world, that the soul dis-
solves at death and so experiences nothing, and that the good, i.e.
the pleasant, life requires only the satisfaction of necessary and natural desires, for which nature affords us abundant supplies. Once we
understand these things, we will have attained our goal of a pleasant
life, for our knowledge will have removed anxiety and the consequent flurry of activity to address that anxiety. Although Epicurean
physics is atomistic, Epicurus countenances multiple explanations
of natural phenomena (*Letter to Herodotus* 80, *Letter to Pythocles*).
If the point of physics is to alleviate anxiety, it makes sense that
he should not be concerned about which of the multiple possible
theoretical explanations is true. The noninvolvement of the gods in
our world is equally established by any naturalistic explanation of
lightning or earthquakes. Further, knowing which desires are necessary and natural and which are neither, but are based instead on
groundless opinion, positively guides our choices, not only of which
objects of desire to pursue in order to avoid pain and enjoy pleasure,
but also of which desires to eliminate so that we can be in the blessed
condition of having no unfulfilled desires.

How is Epicurean wisdom related to the other virtues, to justice,
courage, piety, and so on? Knowing the truth about the nature of the
gods, that they are blessed and uninvolved, presumably engenders in

one the right attitude towards the gods – of admiration and emula-
tion, not of fear or deal-making. Knowing that there is nothing to fear
in death, and that what is painful is either not very painful or else
is short-lived presumably also contributes to courage. Knowing that
the limit of pleasure is the absence of pain and that the absence of
pain can be achieved by fulfilling one's necessary and natural desires
by what is at hand presumably removes incentives to intemperance
and at least greed-driven injustice. Epicurus also says that injustice
(the violation of a contract establishing justice) is bad only insofar as
it produces fear of detection in the wrongdoer (*Principal Doctrines*
34), thereby suggesting that such a calculation – injustice brings on
too much anxiety – will be the reason the wise and virtuous person avoids injustice – rather than out of a commitment to justice
for its own sake. And this is consistent with Epicurus' frequent
reminder that every choice should be referred to our natural goal
of living pleasantly (*Principal Doctrines* 25). (It is noteworthy that
Epicurus is not revisionist about what justice is: although he does
have a distinctive account of justice's origin, he lets the convention,
originating in the supposed contract, say what is its content.)

Epicurus makes a relatively modest claim about the merits of
wisdom as compared to fortune for bringing about a happy life: the
wise person "thinks it better to be unlucky in a rational way than
lucky in a senseless way; for it is better for a good decision not to
turn out right in action than for a bad decision to turn out right
because of chance" (*Menoeceus* 134–5).

STOIC WISDOM

The Stoics hold that only virtue (and what participates in virtue) is
good and contributes to happiness, and that only vice (and what participates in vice) is bad and contributes to unhappiness. Everything
else is indifferent, so that having more or less of health, wealth,
fame, beauty, and so on can make no difference to one's happiness
whatsoever. Whereas in Plato the claim of a trait to be a virtue had to
be shown by way of its connection to happiness, in Chrysippus (279–
206 BCE), the leading exponent of Stoicism, it is the virtues that are
canonized and happiness that has to be increasingly moralized to fit
the claim that only virtue is good. The Stoics reject Aristotle's *Nicomachean Ethics* idea that the external goods like health and wealth

contribute to happiness insofar as they enable the exercise of the virtues in activity. And their position on Plato's *Euthydemus* idea that external goods only become good in the possession of a wise person would seem to be that these external goods are in their nature indifferent (see further Long [1988] 1996). On the Stoics' view, for something to be good it must be such as to cause benefit, and since only virtue is always beneficial, only virtue is good by nature.

For the Stoics, the value of anything other than virtue is also defined in terms of its relation to virtue: "appropriate actions" (*kathēkonta*), defined as those for which a reasonable defense can be given (i.e. by the virtuous person), are those which a virtuous person would do in the circumstances; "correct actions" (*katorthōmata*) are those done from virtue (Arius Didymus, *Outline of Stoic Ethics* in Stobaeus, *Anthology* II.8). Similarly, the passions, which are based on false beliefs about value, are in the virtuous person replaced by good emotions (*eupatheia*) so that, for example, instead of feeling fear, the virtuous person feels caution, a watchfulness that avoids bad things (Diogenes Laertius, *Lives* VII.116).

Virtue and knowledge

The Stoics identify all the virtues with knowledge of some kind or another: virtue as a whole is expertise in living (Arius, *Outline* II.5b10); practical wisdom (*phronēsis*) is knowledge of what is to be done, what is not to be done, and what is neither; temperance is knowledge of what is to be chosen, what is not to be chosen, and what is neither; justice is knowledge of the distribution of proper value to each person; courage is knowledge of what is terrible, not terrible, and neither (II.5b1).

It may seem that if virtue is the only good and vice the only evil, then the knowledge in terms of which all the virtues are defined is very simple: it is the knowledge that one should do virtuous actions, choose virtue, recognize that the only terrible thing is vice, and aim for everyone to have virtue. This is the position taken by the renegade Stoic Aristo. The problem with this conclusion, however, is that it leaves the content of virtue utterly obscure. The content problem is familiar to us from Plato; here, we see it if we ask, what concrete choices does one need to make (in a given situation) to count as virtuous? This is not a question about earning the title to virtue, but about *what is virtuous* in a particular situation. By hypothesis the content of virtue, even for a particular situation, cannot be given by common sense or convention, for it is supposed to be some sort of specialized knowledge Stoicism imparts.

Reporting on the various Stoic formulations of the end (*telos*) or "living virtuously," Diogenes Laertius tells us that according to Zeno's successor Cleanthes, the end "is living in agreement with nature"; according to his successor Chrysippus, it is "living according to the experience of events which occur by nature" (*Lives* VII.87). This suggests the following answer to the content-of-virtue problem: the virtuous person knows what is to be done, because she knows what is according to nature in the circumstances. So practical wisdom (defined above as knowledge of what is to be done) would seem to be knowledge of nature.

What is it about nature that could be relevant to living virtuously? One relatively uncontroversial (i.e. widely held in antiquity) idea is that the study of a species reveals what members of that species naturally do and also what they ought to do, so the study of human beings would reveal what is natural and right for us. However, this cannot be just read off human behavior, since according to the Stoics, most of us, after the age of reason, live badly. Perhaps what studying human specimens provides is the realization that our ability to reason is central to human nature, and that even though most specimens of humanity use their reason poorly because of their social upbringing, there must be such a thing as reasoning well and that for us, following nature involves reasoning well. But what is it to reason well?

The Stoics do not restrict the nature we should follow to human nature; they think that we live virtuously and well by knowing the whole of nature, "common nature." Chrysippus says, "there is no other, and certainly no more appropriate, way to approach the discussion of good and bad things or the virtues or happiness, <except> on the basis of common nature and the administration of the cosmos," and, "for the discussion of good and bad things must be linked to them, since there is no better starting point or reference point and since the study of physics is not to be taken up for any other reason than to distinguish good from bad" (Plutarch, *On Stoic Self-Contradictions* 1035C–D, trans. Inwood and Gerson 1988). The claims Plutarch attributes to Chrysippus are not merely those about what else, in addition to human nature, the virtuous person must know. For the reason at the core of human nature is identical to Zeus's reason, which is the nature of the cosmos. Zeno defines nature as "a craftsmanlike fire which proceeds methodically to the task of creation" and says that "the nature of the cosmos has all the voluntary motions, endeavours and impulses... and carries out the actions consequent on them, just as we ourselves do who are set in motion by our minds and senses... [T]he mind of the cosmos is like this and can for this reason be properly called prudence or providence..." (Cicero, *On the Nature of the Gods* II.57–8, trans. Inwood and Gerson 1988). It belongs to human nature to take on the perspective of cosmic nature.

This is not to say that Chrysippus thinks we should try to derive ethical terms or precepts from physical ones, for the Stoics think of their philosophy as a tightly interconnected whole which may be approached from different perspectives in different contexts (see further Annas 2007). However, that is consistent with physics having a special and essential role to play in Stoic ethics (see further Menn 1997). Indeed, the various metaphors the Stoics use for the relationship between the parts of philosophy and philosophy as a whole suggest this: philosophy is like an animal, with logic the bones and sinews, ethics the flesh, and physics the soul; philosophy is like an egg, with logic the shell, ethics the white, and physics the yolk; philosophy is like a field, with logic the surrounding wall, ethics the fruit, and physics the land and trees (Diogenes Laertius, *Lives* VII.40). The metaphors of animal, egg, and field tell us that physics is what animates the body, what grows into the animal, what bears the fruit. These metaphors fit the idea that physics is the content-giver for ethics' otherwise formal statements about what is good, virtuous, appropriate or correct, and so on.

Virtue and indifference

Cicero raises the content problem to motivate the admission of 'according to nature' and 'contrary to nature' as terms of value in Stoicism, writing, "that very prudence [*prudentia* is Cicero's Latin for *phronēsis*] which we are seeking and praising would be utterly destroyed if there were no grounds for choosing between those [*sc.* indifferent things] which are contrary to nature and those which are according to nature" (On Ends III.31; cf. 50). Although the Stoics restrict "good" to virtue and what is related to it, they must appeal to nature to accord another, independent, kind of value to some of the indifferents; they call this secondary value, "selective value" and the indifferents that possess it, "preferred." While indifferents like health, wealth, and so on have no potential to contribute to happiness directly, there is such a thing as correctly selecting health (or sometimes sickness), wealth (or sometimes poverty), and so on, on the grounds that these selections are in accordance with nature. To live in conformity with the nature of a species would be to select what is healthy for that kind of being. To live in conformity with cosmic nature is to select what is to be selected, all things considered. But this is not really foreign to human nature, because human nature is rational – it points beyond any particular human being to the perspective of the cosmos. Now wisdom is exercised in the selection, among indifferents, of those that are "according to nature." If there were no difference in value among any of these indifferents, then there would be nothing for wisdom to be wise about.

Our texts illustrate "according to nature" and "preferred," on the one hand, and "contrary to nature" and "dispreferred," on the other, with types of events: health is in accordance with nature, sickness is contrary to it; bodily integrity is in accordance with nature, bodily injury or dismemberment is contrary to it. But it seems that we should speak of these as only prima facie according to nature because cosmic nature, or Zeus's plan for the whole, may involve one's being sick and dismembered rather than healthy and with all one's limbs intact. "Preferred" and "according to nature" function as a guide for those who do not yet have Zeus's perspective and so do not know which token events are fated. Epictetus reports Chrysippus as saying, "As long as what comes next is nonevident to me, I always cling to what is better suited to getting what is in accordance with nature. For god himself made me such as to select those things. But if I knew for sure that it was fated for me now to be ill, I would even seek illness. For my foot, if it had brains, would seek to be muddied" (Epictetus, Discourses 2.6.9–10; cf. 2.10.5–6).

Now one implication of this is that one should be accepting of one's fate, but Chrysippus seems to be talking about one's attitude, not only towards what happens, but also towards what one must do. If one does not know what is fated, one should choose the sorts of things one is already disposed by nature to seek: one's own health, wealth, and so on. If one does know what comes next, whether because one has perfected oneself in physics and understands Zeus's plan for the cosmos, or because one has made enough progress to understand which considerations might override the general considerations in favor of health and wealth, then right reasoning might lead us to select sickness, poverty, and so on, in the circumstances. For progress in physics would be knowing more and more, not only of what will happen, but also what should happen because it is ordained by wisdom and providence. Seneca adds another dimension to the attitude we should have towards our selections if we lack knowledge of nature: we should make our plans "with reservation," that is, with the recognition that what we have planned may conflict with what will and ought to happen, and a consequent nonattachment to the projected outcomes of our actions, so that we are not overly emotional when things do not turn out as we planned (Seneca, *On Peace of Mind* 13.2–14.2).

Are the Stoics relevant today?

If we do not share the Stoics' view that what happens is what ought to happen, with the result that living according to nature at the highest level would be sharing Zeus's perspective (and acting in harmony with it), can the Stoic account of practical wisdom have anything to teach us? It seems to me that without committing to the Stoic's particular conception of nature, we can adopt the thought that practical wisdom involves an enlarging of perspective (because of the kind of being humans are, rational and social) to include concerns other than the states of one's own body. We can reject the goal of taking on Zeus's perspective (or deny that there is such a perspective), but still take on a perspective of the communities of which we are part that includes seeing ourselves in terms of the role(s) we play in those communities; such a perspective should lead us to behave in ways that better serve our communities than if we thought of ourselves in isolation.

Further, and this is a thought common to Aristotle, the Stoics, and the Epicureans, practical wisdom involves a knowledge of the kind of natural creature one is – what are one's abilities and inabilities, especially the abilities likely to fulfill one most, and what conduces to the fulfillment of a creature with such abilities. The Epicureans add that we are not only agents with abilities and disabilities but also patients or experiencers, and that our lives can go pleasantly or painfully for us in this capacity as well, but that even in this capacity, we can make our lives go more or less pleasantly if we understand our own nature and that of the world.

CONCLUSION

Contemporary moral philosophers sometimes complain that ancient conceptions of virtue are overly intellectualist in requiring wisdom of some kind, even if it is only practical wisdom, for virtue. This survey has tried to show that wisdom cannot be optional for virtue if virtue is supposed to be the way we ourselves can bring it about that we live well rather than badly; the real question is, what is the content of that wisdom?

3   Virtue ethics and the Chinese Confucian tradition

My primary aims are to introduce representative examples of thinkers from different periods within the Chinese Confucian tradition who advocated forms of virtue ethics, Mengzi 孟子 ("Mencius," 391–308 BCE) and Wang Yangming 王陽明 (1472–1529), and to use their views to suggest a way to distinguish distinct types of virtue ethical theory.[1] Mengzi and Wang are among the most famous and influential Confucian philosophers in the Chinese tradition; their philosophies are complex, rich, and powerful and represent different and important aspects of virtue ethical theory. In many ways, Mengzi seems to advocate the kind of theory one finds in thinkers like Aristotle, whose conception of virtue is connected to a theory about human nature and a related view of human flourishing described in terms of an ideal agent.[2] I will refer to this type of theory as virtue ethics of *flourishing* (VEF). On the other hand, parts of Mengzi's view, particularly his emphasis on the role of the emotions and empathy, reveal significant similarities with thinkers like Hume and other sentimentalists, who describe the virtues primarily in terms of certain broadly construed emotions. I will refer to this type of theory as virtue ethics of *sentiments* (VES). Wang Yangming appears to be even closer to Hume and other sentimentalists; nevertheless, Wang's form of virtue ethics is more like Aristotle's in relying upon a theory about human nature and a conception of human flourishing described in terms of an ideal agent. These similarities

Thanks to Erin M. Cline, Eirik L. Harris, Eric L. Hutton, Pauline C. Lee, Daniel C. Russell, Michael R. Slater, Michael Slote, David W. Tien, and Justin Tiwald for comments on earlier drafts of this chapter.

and differences explain why contemporary philosophers have disagreed about the true nature of Mengzi's and Wang's forms of virtue
ethics. I hope to describe distinct types of virtue ethical theory that
will allow us to settle such disagreements.

A GENUS AND NOT A SPECIES

Christine Swanton (2003, p. 1) makes the important point that as a
type of ethical theory, virtue ethics is a genus and not a species. In
other words, virtue ethics is a class of ethical theories that share a
common emphasis on virtues as central features of their account of
morality. Different species of virtue ethics disagree not only about
what the proper list of virtues is but also about the nature of the
virtues, how they relate to one another, and how they do or do not
fit or hang together to define a good life. In order to prepare the way
for our discussion of Chinese forms of virtue ethics, it will help to
have a general description of two of the main types of virtue ethics
found in the Western tradition.[3]

Virtue ethics and flourishing

The most familiar and widely analyzed form of virtue ethics in the
Western tradition finds its source and model in the writings of Aristotle; Aristotle describes a distinctive version of VEF. For our purposes, two related features of his theory are most significant: (1) it
is grounded in a comprehensive and detailed conception of human
nature that seeks to describe the content, structure, and overall shape
of that nature; (2) it describes the virtues in terms of a teleological
view about the flourishing of human nature expressed in an ideal or
paradigmatic model of what it is to be human. Both these features
are familiar and widely studied aspects of Aristotle's philosophy and
are prominent features of most Chinese Confucian forms of virtue
ethics. However, we discover significant differences between Aristotle and Confucians when we move from the general down to the
particular level of description. For example, Confucians hold very
different beliefs about the content, structure, and shape of human
nature. Aristotle's view is intimately connected with his claims
that the most characteristic function or *ergon* of human beings is
rational activity and that the good life for human beings will have

such activity not only at its core but as its acme: the most valuable type of activity human beings can engage in is contemplation.[4] The Chinese Confucians, whose thought we will explore, share a belief in the critical contribution reflection and attentiveness make to the process of self-cultivation, but they do not share Aristotle's views on the nature, role, and value of reason. The second feature of Aristotle's view also is an important feature of Chinese Confucian forms of virtue ethics. In this case too, there are critically important differences, which do not lie in the general features of their respective ethical philosophies but in the particular ideals and paradigms they recommend.

Virtue ethics and sentiments

VES describes a second very influential form of virtue ethics in the Western tradition. Sentimentalist virtue ethics finds its most distinguished representatives in thinkers such as Shaftesbury, Hutcheson, Hume, and Smith. Contemporary proponents of an ethics of care, such as Noddings (1986) and Held (2006), offer views that share important features of such an approach. The most sophisticated and comprehensive attempt to defend a modern version of VES is found in the work of Michael Slote (2007, 2010), who emphasizes the critical role of empathy or more precisely empathic caring as the basis of moral value. As in our discussion of VEF, we will focus on two features of VES as most significant: (1) it is grounded in a general conception of human nature that focuses on aspects of human psychology; (2) it describes the virtues in terms of dispositions conducive to smooth, agreeable, and beneficial interactions between individuals within and between different societies.

In regard to the first feature, VES resembles VEF, but while VEF seeks to provide a comprehensive and detailed account of human nature that describes its content, structure, and shape, VES focuses more exclusively upon general emotional resources, tendencies, and capacities. As for the second feature, unlike VEF, the set of virtues VES describes does not fit together to yield a single ideal of human flourishing expressed in a related paradigmatic model. Instead the virtues hang together only loosely to form a conception of what kind of life is most agreeable and beneficial under certain circumstances. In contrast to those who promote versions of VEF, advocates of VES are more concerned with ideal traits and their benefits than ideal persons and their character. One consequence of this difference is that for VES the virtues are more expressions of features of human psychology within the confines of particular social conditions than they are direct manifestations of human nature in its authentic, full, or proper form.[5] For example, instead of describing and holding up the man of practical wisdom as the ideal standard for the good and the aim of every human life, Hume describes what people must be like in order to form and maintain a humane and cooperative society and interact with other societies around the world in an agreeable and beneficial manner. He distinguishes what people in *his age* need for successful and harmonious living from what was needed in past ages, when life was simpler and people lived in more intimate arrangements. In other words, for Hume, the virtues are practical expressions of what is needed to live well in particular social conditions; human nature serves as a resource for crafting the best kind of life, but the virtuous life is not in any direct way the expression of human nature's flourishing. VES has a firm but general psychological foundation, not a specific trajectory or goal. Modern advocates of VES regularly appeal to the findings of contemporary psychology in order to support their views, and contemporary psychologists tend to focus on psychological capacities, tendencies, and mechanisms and eschew the kind of comprehensive, normative accounts of human nature characteristic of VEF. Overall, the approach is more empirical than what one finds in VEF and more oriented toward discovering what is agreeable and beneficial than in revealing the most authentic form of human flourishing.

MENGZI

Mengzi's ethical philosophy exhibits both of the characteristic features of VEF discussed above. He relies explicitly and directly on a comprehensive and detailed theory of human nature that seeks to describe its content, structure, and shape; and he presents a program of moral self-cultivation that leads to a distinctive conception of human flourishing, which he describes in terms of the paradigmatic models of the "gentleman" (君子 *junzi*) and "sage" (聖人 *sheng ren*). Let us explore the particular form these features take in the *Mengzi* and how together they describe his distinctive expression of VEF.

Human nature

Mengzi is famous for his theory that human nature is good, by which he means not that people are innately perfectly good but that they are born with moral sensibilities, which incline them toward becoming virtuous. Specifically, Mengzi argues that human beings possess four "sprouts" (端 *duan*) of virtue.[6] Mengzi's use of the agricultural metaphor of "sprouts" to describe our nascent moral sensibilities or tendencies is not an isolated or unimportant feature of his view. Such metaphors are found throughout his descriptions of the content, structure, and proper course of human development.[7] For example, he likens the growth or failure of the moral sprouts to the natural but still contingent development of barley plants (*Mengzi* 6A7). Through such analogies, Mengzi seeks to show that all humans have an equal capacity for moral development; that such development, while natural, requires human attention and effort; and that barring differences in environment, influence, attention, and effort people all will tend toward a common moral end. Self-cultivation is very much like agriculture: it consists of reflective endeavor aimed at realizing a natural end, and that end is an ideal of flourishing thought to apply to all human beings. Mengzi offers one of the clearest examples of an ethic of human flourishing as his agricultural metaphors consistently invoke or imply the notion that moral self-cultivation seeks to facilitate the blossoming or "flourishing" (Latin *florere*) of human nature.

Mengzi's use of agricultural metaphors is not just a literary embellishment; his repertoire of agrarian images not only expresses his fundamental claims about moral self-cultivation but also informs and conveys subtle and distinctive features of his ethical view. For example, in the parable of the "Farmer of Song" (*Mengzi* 2A2), he uses another agricultural metaphor to warn against trying to force the process of moral cultivation. The central point of this parable is that one can try too hard to be moral and such effort not only will not improve one's character but will in fact harm and perhaps even doom one to failure. Self-cultivation is like farming, and we must learn to be dedicated but patient farmers.

Flourishing and ideals

There remains but one final feature of Mengzi's ethical philosophy left to complete the case that he was an advocate of VEF: we need to show that his account of the virtues and the flourishing of human nature is expressed in an ideal or paradigmatic model of what it is to be human. The evidence is easy to find and unambiguous. Mengzi relies directly and explicitly upon numerous examples of actual sages and worthies in order to craft his account of the moral ideal. In this regard, it is important to recognize that he used "the Way of Yao and Shun"[8] (*Yao Shun zhi dao* 堯舜之道) as a more complete expression of the Confucian Way. This exemplifies an important feature of most versions of virtue ethics: they rely upon thick descriptions of the virtues and this often leads virtue ethicists to invoke the lives of actual historical individuals as part of their explanation of what the virtues are. This practice is characteristic of Confucian thinkers. Many scholars have noted that Chinese thinkers tend to see a very close relationship between history and ethics; when we understand these thinkers as advocates of VEF, we understand the reason for this close association.[9]

The appeal to sages and other worthies plays numerous roles in Mengzi's ethical philosophy. One point he was careful to emphasize and repeat is that these paragons of morality are not different in kind from the rest of humanity; they represent the best in all of us and offer a goal which we should take as both a standard and inspiration, "Yao and Shun were the same as any other human being" (*Mengzi* 4B32, 6B2). Mengzi also notes that sages from different places and widely diverse backgrounds all develop toward the same moral ideal (*Mengzi* 4B1). He makes clear that these moral paragons are models of a shared conception of flourishing that is within the reach of all normally endowed human beings. This is made even more explicit in passages such as *Mengzi* 6A7, which claims proper standards of taste in cuisine, music, and aesthetics – as well as morality – display an informed and cultivated consensus that reflects the refined expression of human nature. The sages are simply the first to discover what all human beings will approve and delight in, when given proper knowledge, experience, and time to reflect.

Mengzi's use of the sage or gentleman as moral exemplar is not limited to actual historical figures. He deploys a general concept of such exemplars throughout his work. For example, Mengzi quotes with approval a disciple who extols Kongzi ("Confucius") as the greatest sage ever to have lived, but lest we be led to think the standard he sets is somehow beyond us, in the same passage, the disciple reminds us, "The sages are the same in kind as other human beings" (*Mengzi* 2A2, 6A7). Mengzi also invokes the idea of future sages and insists that they will share the same moral sense and reach the same moral judgments as cultivated people in his own place and time: "Were a sage to arise once more, surely he would agree with what I have said" (*Mengzi* 2A2, 3B9). From all that has been shown above, it is clear that Mengzi made extensive use of an ideal or paradigmatic model of what it is to be human to express his conception of human flourishing. These paragons of humanity offer examples of how the virtues function and hang together to constitute a good life.

Mengzi has a carefully worked out account of human flourishing. His panoply of agricultural metaphors rely upon a teleological view of human nature that offers an analogy between the growth of plants – from nascent sprouts to fully flowering, mature specimens – and the development of the moral sense, from "sprouts" to virtues. His ethical philosophy expresses the successful completion of the process of moral self-cultivation in terms of actual and hypothetical ideal agents. Such paragons of virtue are presented as the healthy specimens of the species and offer a normative standard for measuring a person's moral progress and level of achievement. Mengzi uses agricultural metaphors to describe not only human nature and moral self-cultivation but also his account of moral failure. This makes him one of the clearest exponents of VEF one ever could hope to find.

A number of contemporary philosophers (Yearley 1990; Van Norden 2007) have argued that Mengzi is productively and even best thought of as an exponent of VEF. Others (Liu 2002, 2003) have noted similarities between his views and those of David Hume, and on this basis have argued that Mengzi should be understood as a proponent of VES. Opinions on this matter will turn for the most part on the particular conceptions of VEF and VES that one embraces, and so it is essential to begin with clear and workable definitions of these types. Those who hold Mengzi is an advocate of VEF tend to point to his discussion of virtues and claim that he described an ideal of flourishing; those who hold Mengzi is an advocate of VES focus on his discussions of the four sprouts and highlight how each of these describes an emotional response that enables us to empathize with others. There is truth in all these claims, but in addition to making clear what one means by VEF and VES, one also needs to offer a careful account of things like: (1) what one means by flourishing and how the virtues relate to this ideal, and (2) the nature of empathic caring and what role it plays not only in understanding but also in justifying moral claims. I have provided two ideal types, VEF and VES, and used these to argue that Mengzi is an advocate of VEF. In the concluding section of this chapter I shall explore some additional and distinctive features of Mengzi's form of VEF.[10]

WANG YANGMING

One of the most dramatic and distinctive features of Wang Yangming's ethical philosophy is the emphasis he places on achieving and living in light of a sense of oneness between self and world; this ideal is captured in his teaching about heaven, earth, and the myriad creatures as one body (*tian di wan wu wei yi ti* 天地萬物為一體). Along with other aspects of Wang's philosophy, this ideal of *feeling one with* all the people, creatures, and things of the world gives the very strong impression that empathic care is an important part of Wang's ethics, and such an impression is not incorrect. As will become clear from the following discussion, Wang's conception of empathic care and the role it plays in moral life are critical features of his ethical philosophy; we will devote considerable attention to these issues in our analysis of Wang's teachings and return to them in drawing our conclusions. Nevertheless, as in the case of Mengzi, the importance of empathy per se is not our central concern. The question we are seeking to answer is whether Wang is a virtue ethicist and if so what kind of virtue ethicist he is.

Until recently, modern scholars who wrote about Wang tended to focus on the more religious aspects of his philosophy and not simply his ethical theory (Tu 1976; Ching 1976; Tien 2004). This is because they recognized the degree to which all of Wang's views depend upon an underlying comprehensive metaphysical scheme that is more characteristic of religion than contemporary analytic ethics. While there surely is no impediment to analyzing Wang's metaphysical views as an integral part of his ethics, modern philosophers interested in ethics, as a whole, have tended to avoid philosophers whose ethical systems depend upon strong metaphysical commitments. In this respect, Wang's ethical philosophy is more like many forms of Buddhism or the ethical philosophy of Thomas Aquinas, which are more often discussed in departments of religious studies than philosophy. I have argued (Ivanhoe 2000, 2002) that Wang's views cannot be understood accurately or adequately without appreciating the degree to which they were influenced by Buddhism and to a lesser but not insignificant extent, Daoism, and I will build upon this work in arguing that Wang is best thought of as an advocate of VEF.

Human nature

The core of my case for understanding Wang as a proponent of VEF is that his ethical philosophy exhibits both the characteristic features of VEF we described earlier and found in Mengzi's philosophy. Wang relies explicitly and directly on a comprehensive and detailed theory of human nature that purports to describe its content, structure, and shape. His theory of human nature shares certain similarities with Mengzi's, but the influence of Buddhism and Daoism alters the fundamental basis of his conception of human nature. Instead of grounding his account of human nature in a philosophical anthropology, as Mengzi does, he relies on a comprehensive metaphysical theory. As we shall see, this shift transforms not only the nature but also the range of his ethical sensibilities. Wang presents a program of moral self-cultivation that leads to a distinctive conception of human flourishing, which he describes in terms of an ethical and spiritual ideal of the "sage" (聖人 sheng ren).[11] Here too we see continuities with the philosophy of Mengzi but also quite profound differences as well. For example, under the influence of Buddhism and especially Chan (Japanese: Zen), Wang and his contemporaries were preoccupied with a Confucian form of "enlightenment" (悟 wu) resulting in the attainment of sagehood. This emphasis and the possibility of this occurring "suddenly" were not part of Mengzi's way of thinking.[12] Let us explore more of the similarities and differences between Mengzi and Wang as we describe Wang's ethical philosophy and present the case for understanding him as an advocate of VEF.

Wang embraced a constellation of related beliefs that were common among neo-Confucian thinkers, many of which would be viewed as highly untenable today. I have referred to such beliefs as the "heroic metaphysical" aspects of Wang's view and here seek only to describe and not defend them. In drawing conclusions, I shall discuss some of the ways versions of Wang's views remain important resources for contemporary virtue ethics. Wang accepted the view that all human beings are endowed at birth with a pure and perfect moral heart–mind (xin 心).[13] In its original and unadulterated state, this heart–mind consists of the set of "principles" (li 理) that determine the underlying, normative patterns and processes of the world. The pure form of the human mind is the active and knowing mode of the principles of the universe. This happy correspondence offered Wang a way to account for a wide range of phenomena and resolve several vexing philosophical problems. For example, it offered him a way to explain how it is that we can come to understand the world around us. Since our mind is principle, we understand the world whenever the principles of our mind properly match up with the principles of things and events.

Connectedness with others

This correspondence played a critical role in another of Wang's signature teachings: the idea that we and the world "form a single body" (yiti 一體). The basic metaphysical belief behind this teaching is that we and the world share the same principles or, as expressed in other ways Wang often invokes, we share a common "original heart–mind" (ben xin 本心) or "nature" (ben xing 本性). The practical effect of this shared principle, heart–mind, or nature is that we *feel* connected to every single thing in the world, in a way analogous to the way we feel connected to every part of our physical bodies.[14] The only thing that prevents us from realizing – both in the sense of understanding and feeling the full force of – this fact is that our minds are embodied in physical forms that separate us from, and tend to generate misleading impressions of, the true state of affairs. Our embodied physical form subjects our pure heart–minds to the influence of a kind of ether (qi 氣), which obscures our true nature and underlying relationship with the rest of the world.[15] This separation leads to the mistaken view that we exist as unconnected and independent creatures and leads us to an excessive concern with satisfying our individual needs and desires. This is why most people tend to be self-centered and fail to see the world for what it is: a unified and interconnected whole.[16] Such a perspective only works to deepen our alienation, frustration, and delusion, generating ever more numerous and intense "self-centered desires" (*si yu* 私欲) which, in turn, further muddies our *qi* and distorts our perception of both ourselves and the world around us.

Following earlier neo-Confucian thinkers, Wang described a lack of feeling for the welfare of people, creatures, and things as being "numb" (*buren* 不仁) to the world. This expression fits well into his overall picture, within which we and the world are "one body," for in the language of Wang's day, the term *buren* not only meant to be "unfeeling" toward suffering or distress; it was a medical term describing paralysis in some part of the body. Neo-Confucians were quick to point out that someone who is unfeeling (i.e. lacking in benevolence) toward the world is like someone with a paralyzed limb. He might deny connection with his arm and even pay no attention when it is injured, but still he is "one body" with both the world and his afflicted limb.[17] As this picture suggests, Wang insists that no matter how deluded people become, at some deep level they still possess a pure and perfect moral heart–mind; even though one's moral heart–mind may be blocked and has disappeared behind "clouds" of self-centered desires, above these clouds, the sun still shines (Ivanhoe 2002). The only way out of this sad state of affairs is an active program of self-cultivation focused on the removal of self-centered desires and the consequent refinement of one's *qi*.

Wang used a special term of art, "pure knowing" (*liang zhi* 良知), which he picked up from Mengzi, to describe the original heart–mind's response to moral situations.[18] For Wang, pure knowing is a faculty of moral sapience; if unobstructed by self-centered desires or obscuring *qi*, it spontaneously responds to any moral situation in a seamless process of perceiving, understanding, judging, willing, and action (Ivanhoe 2002, pp. 99–100). Wang likened the responsiveness of pure knowing to the reflective quality of a mirror or the ways in which we are spontaneously drawn to beauty or repelled by a bad odor. These and other metaphors describe pure knowing as an innate, fully formed, complex, and spontaneously functioning faculty. Wang was adamant and eminently clear about how such *moral vision* functioned in a properly ordered life and how it alone was sufficient to ensure complete and unerring moral understanding and action. The real risk was not any inherent *lack* on the part of the pure knowing of our heart–mind but a lack of confidence or faith in its power and ability. We must trust in pure knowing thoroughly and completely, not interfere with its spontaneous operation, and not make even the slightest effort to help it along. Any attempt to improve upon our pure knowing adds something alien to the heart–mind, some less-than-pure element, which can only "stick to" and interfere with our naturally clear moral vision (Chan 1963, pp. 256–7).

Self-cultivation and discovery

As a result of Wang's very different views about human nature, our moral faculty, and the source of moral failure, he presented a different account of self-cultivation. While Mengzi described an agriculturally inspired *development model* of self-cultivation, Wang advocated an individually focused, therapeutic, *discovery model* (Ivanhoe 2002, pp. 88–108). Mengzi counseled a gradual, steady course of care, nurture, and attention; Wang sought to inspire his students to maintain an intense attentiveness, a Confucian form of Buddhist mindfulness, to the movements and responses of their own heart–minds. The goal was to be ever alert and vigilant, to search out and eradicate any taint of self-centeredness in order to purify one's *qi* and allow the myriad principles of the original heart–mind to shine forth and illuminate the Way (Ivanhoe 2002, p. 102).

Wang's ultimate aim was to engage and bring into complete play the power of pure knowing. Once we begin to cultivate the required awareness and attentiveness, our pure knowing will start to inform and guide us. Pure knowing has the power to melt away and loosen the grip of selfish desires and light our path along the Way. As we succeed in freeing pure knowing from the grip of self-centeredness and interfering *qi*, we feel a more extensive and profound sense of oneness with all things.[19] For Wang, empathic concern is not simply a feature of human psychology; it is the practical result of appreciating the true nature of the self and its relationship to the world. Wang's conception of empathic concern was not the source of or justification for regard for other people, creatures, and things or an expression of altruism; both the causal and justificatory relationship were very much the other way around: it is *because* and as a function of our sense of oneness that we experience empathic concern and act in the interests of other people, creatures, and things. Wang was not exploring the possibility of altruism; he was describing the implications of oneness.

Flourishing and ideals

Like Mengzi, Wang offers a comprehensive and detailed conception of human nature that seeks to describe the content, structure, and overall shape of human nature. All that remains to complete the case that Wang is an advocate of VEF is to show that his teachings about moral self-cultivation are developed in terms of a view about the flourishing of human nature expressed in an ideal or paradigmatic model of what it is to be human. This is easy to demonstrate; like Mengzi, Wang made extensive and critical use of the concepts of the "gentleman" (君子 *junzi*) and "sage" (聖人 *sheng ren*) in describing his moral ideal. While there is complete agreement between Mengzi and Wang in regard to employing both historical figures and general conceptions of such ideal individuals, Wang focused much more upon the ideal of sagehood.[20] Moreover, unlike Mengzi, Wang was regarded by his followers and thought of himself as a living example of his ideal.[21] This claim may seem less startling in light of the fact that Wang repeatedly insisted that "the streets are full of sages" (Chan 1963, p. 240). This, in turn, is something we could infer from the parts of his philosophy we already have introduced. Since everyone is endowed with a pure and perfect original heart–mind and thereby possesses all the principles of the world, each and every person is a hidden sage; all one needs to do is to discover or uncover what lies within.

DRAWING CONCLUSIONS

Mengzi: flourishing and sociality

If we look to Mengzi as a source for contemporary ethical philosophy, two aspects of his thought are of particular interest and importance. The first is a feature not only of Mengzi's ethics but arguably of all Confucian thought: his notion of flourishing is explicitly linked to the good of larger social units and not just to the good of individuals.[22] Mengzi's discussion of historical sages and his more general account of the virtues make clear that what makes a Confucian life good is inextricably connected with what makes families thrive and society orderly and humane. While Mengzi believes that a morally good life is good for the person who lives it and that such a life constitutes that person's proper state of flourishing, such flourishing has at its core the good of families and society at large. Families and society in general are not simply the context or enabling conditions for human flourishing; they set constraints upon our behavior and offer core elements of what makes life good. These features of Confucian virtue ethics explain a number of qualities that distinguish it from most of its Western cousins. Confucianism is well known for its emphasis on the family and virtues such as filial piety;[23] many scholars have noted Confucianism espouses a more communal conception of the good and that the Confucian notion of the self is more relational than individualistic.[24] While Mengzi does link his account of the virtues to a fairly clear and detailed conception of human flourishing, which he illustrates with a corresponding notion of sagehood, we must keep in mind that his notion of what makes a life good is intimately linked in complex ways to a wide range of people beyond the individual in question. This is one reason why it is correct to see his view as sharing important similarities with certain versions of VES and especially with contemporary feminist advocates of VES who emphasize the centrality of relationships both to a good life and to the individuation of the self (Li 2000).

Mengzi: human nature

The second aspect of Mengzi's ethical philosophy I would like to explore concerns the specificity and detail of his notions of human nature and flourishing; in important respects these are too specific and narrow to serve informed and reflective modern people and require reinterpretation and modification. This weakness is not avoided and is made even more severe by the fact, noted above, that he links his views on human nature and flourishing to normative accounts of larger social units. No one should want to defend Mengzi's historical views on these issues since they present too restricted and implausible an account of what human beings are, can become, and enjoy and the kinds of societies they can fashion and be proud of.[25] It is not clear, though, that one cannot argue for a looser and more plausible version of Mengzi's vision; one that leaves open the question of how human needs, desires, and capacities can be developed and brought into harmony within larger familial and social orders. This would require a pluralistic form of Confucianism and might even allow for a version of what I call ethical promiscuity.[26]

Wang: oneness with others

If we bracket parts of Wang's teachings, we can retain valuable insights about the nature of certain moral problems and the practical business of overcoming them. For example, if we set aside his views about an innate moral faculty and simply assume we are talking about the sensibilities possessed by mature moral agents, Wang's way of describing the interference of self-centered desires often makes a good deal of sense and captures important features of moral epistemology and the phenomenology of moral perception. In at least a wide range of situations, when we fail to act morally our problem is not a lack of knowledge but an excessive concern with our own, self-centered desires (Tien 2010). Desires often operate in a quite subtle and convoluted manner that leads us to "see" things in ways that make improper action look pretty good and make it difficult to perceive or pay attention to ethically preferable alternatives. Self-centered desires can enlist reason in the service of excessive self-concern and lend further force to its cause, reinforcing such a view of the world. This often is roughly what we mean when we talk about "rationalizing" self-serving actions, decisions, or beliefs.[27] Breaking free of the grip of such errant perceptions requires us to become aware of and focus attention upon our excessive self-centeredness and turn to concentrate on more other-directed desires, already present within us.[28] It often requires us to recognize that other people, creatures, and things, while clearly not part of our physical bodies, are parts of our lives and our conception of who we are. In Wang's terms, we must come to recognize and appreciate that we are "one" with at least many parts of the world. On such a view, moral perception is more about one's fundamental conception of the self and one's related view about personal welfare than it is about the proper use of reason.[29] Altering or shifting from one self-conception to another can greatly affect one's perception of events; one can experience a kind of gestalt shift that results in seeing the same thing in a dramatically different way.

Wang: self-cultivation

Wang's views about moral self-cultivation have many other things to offer. Among these is the idea that moral learning occurs most often and effectively when it is grounded in and engages the actual events of one's own life.[30] Wang roundly criticized many of his contemporaries for detaching moral learning from the actual actions and affairs of daily life and instead casting it excessively or even exclusively in terms of the study of overly abstract speculative theories, staid historical accounts, or hollow displays of ritual (Ivanhoe 2002, p. 130). In contrast, he insisted that we learn to be better, if at all, when we work on engaging pure knowing as it operates in the actual actions and affairs of our own lives. Wang would urge us to concentrate on cultivating a heightened awareness and attentiveness to how we think, feel, and behave as we live out our lives rather than to dedicate ourselves to the *study of morality* in its various forms. We should reflect on whether we have been living up to the standard we already possess within, our pure knowing, and whether we are being the kind of father, mother, husband, wife, child, sister, brother, teacher, truck driver, judge, cashier, etc., we know we should be, or are allowing excessively self-centered desires to block and misdirect us.

Wang: the relevance of oneness

Wang's claims about the role a sense of oneness between the self and the rest of the world plays in our moral lives are also remarkably revealing and important (Tien 2012). We need not think of ourselves as linked to the rest of the world directly, through the sharing of "principles" or some other metaphysically obscure entity, but can still defend a robust sense of being inextricably connected with the world in ways that reveal aspects of it we fail to see and that can and should guide our understanding and move us to action. In fact, several contemporary psychologists have argued that a sense of oneness and *not* empathic concern is what motivates people to help others (Cialdini *et al.* 1997). Such research relies upon the idea that most often people feel *and act* in a benevolent manner not because they experience more *empathic concern* for another, but "because they feel more *at one* with the other – that is because they perceive more of themselves in the other" (Cialdini *et al*. 1997, p. 483).[31] On such a view, our concern for others is not purely selfless or altruistic, because it is grounded in an expanded view of the self. In addition to a growing number of experimental results, this view is supported by notions like "inclusive fitness" in evolutionary theory. Here, the sense of oneness is more palpable and related to shared genetic inheritance. A sense of oneness, though, is not limited to or even primarily related to genes; we can feel one with others in many different ways; for example, we can identify with ideas, beliefs, images, symbols, and practices transmitted and inherited across generations just as strongly.

Wang's way of looking at the phenomenon of oneness takes us considerably beyond the work of contemporary psychologists, who tend to focus exclusively on the possibility of genuine concern for other *human beings*. There is every reason to think that we in fact can and to some extent already do feel a sense of oneness with other animals, plants, and even inanimate objects and that such a sense is essential for getting us to act on behalf of these other creatures and things. In fact, a *denial* of – or in Wang's terms being "numb" to – our intimate connection to the natural world, properly understood, and our linked common future is clearly contrary to our best scientific understanding, irrational, and a dire threat to human welfare as well as that of many other forms of life on earth. Wang's view suggests that one of the most powerful bases of our concern for other people, creatures, plants, and things is an enlarged sense of self; at least in a number of cases, for example in the cases of inclusive fitness and our general, evolutionary interrelationship with Nature, this is more than just a stance on the world, it reflects important facts about how we are related to things in the world that we hold dear.

One challenge to this kind of view is that it seems to deny the possibility of altruism, for it appears to say that when we act in the interest of other people, creatures, plants, and things we really are simply helping ourselves.[32] Altruism requires that our acts be *selfless* but to some extent oneness includes the other within the self. This is a complex and subtle issue, which I will not attempt to settle here. I do, though, want to suggest that some have sought to settle it too quickly. For example, Cialdini *et al*. claim that "When

the distinction between self and other is undermined, the traditional dichotomy between selfishness and selflessness loses meaning" (Cialdini *et al.* 1997, p. 491). I am not so sure about this. If
we could not *in any way* distinguish between self and other, the
notions of excessive self-centeredness and selflessness would indeed
lose meaning. That, though, is not what modern psychologists, like
Cialdini, or neo-Confucians, like Wang Yangming, have argued for.
They have described an expanded sense of self and identified vary-
ing types and degrees of "interpersonal unity" (Cialdini *et al.* 1997,
p. 490). For example, while Wang insists that underneath it all there
are shared principles, he does not dissolve the self into the world;
qi preserves the world of physical things and a hierarchy of concern
even for the sage. What the proposed, modern conception of oneness brings with it is a need to *rethink* the meaning of notions like
selfishness and selflessness.

NOTES

1   While Mengzi and Wang agree, for the most part, about what virtues are
    important, their respective theories entail different conceptions of what
    the virtues fundamentally are. This issue, while important and inter-
    esting, will not be explored in this chapter. Thanks to Daniel Russell
    for raising this issue.
2   The relationship between the virtues and the related conception of the
    ideal life, like that between the virtues and the good person, is a matter
    of debate, but this issue does not affect the general point I am making
    here.
3   These two types by no means exhaust the full range of theories that fall
    within the family of virtue ethics.
4   This reading depends on how one understands the relationship of
    Book x of the *Nicomachean Ethics* (cited as *NE*) to the rest of the work.
    Some insist that the parts which support this reading, for example *NE*
    x.6–8, do not represent Aristotle's mature view and should be removed
    from the text.
5   Maria Merritt (2000) makes this point in a very clear and forceful way
    and argues that for this reason VES is better equipped than Aristotelian
    versions of VEF to rebut situationism. Thanks to Eric Hutton for bring-
    ing Merritt's work to my attention.
6   For more detailed accounts of Mengzi's view of human nature and self-
    cultivation see Ivanhoe 2007b, pp. 15–28, 2002, and Van Norden, 2007.

7 I have argued for the central role of such agricultural metaphors, as distinct from vegetative or craft metaphors, in Mengzi's philosophy in numerous publications but most thoroughly in the two books noted above. This is what makes his view a "development model" of self-cultivation. His later rival, Xunzi, employs a set of craft metaphors that present self-cultivation as a process of reshaping and orienting a recalcitrant original nature, which is prone to error. He offers a "reformation model." Within the development versus reformation scheme, Aristotle is much closer to Xunzi than Mengzi. For an insightful essay comparing Aristotle and Xunzi on the related issue of moral reasoning, see Hutton 2002a.

8 I illustrate my point by focusing on the sage kings Yao and Shun, but the point can be supported with numerous other examples.

9 Chinese thinkers also anticipate current debates about the role of literary figures in ethics. Though fiction came in for criticism by some later neo-Confucians, it has also been an immensely important resource for ethics in the Chinese tradition. For a discussion of this relationship, see Ivanhoe 2007a.

10 One of the reasons Mengzi is important for contemporary virtue ethicists is that he fits the core features of VEF and yet presents a form of VEF not found in the Western tradition. Studying his philosophy offers us a way to enrich our understanding of VEF and our ethical lives more generally.

11 For a study which explores the ethical implications of neo-Confucian ideals of sagehood, see Angle 2009.

12 Mengzi had neither the term nor any concept resembling "sudden enlightenment." For more on this difference, see Ivanhoe 2000, pp. 60 etc. and 2002, pp. 106 etc.

13 I translate the Chinese word *xin* as "heart–mind" to indicate that it was thought to contain faculties of cognition and emotion as well as intention or volition.

14 Wang made use of the fact that we feel more or less connected and concerned with different parts of our bodies to support the traditional Confucian view of graded forms of love and care. I say "analogous" because, as will be clear, on Wang's view, the relationship is not part to whole. Wang believed each thing in the world contained within it *all* the *li*, somewhat like the way in which every cell contains within it all of a creature's DNA.

15 Neo-Confucians believed that a number of factors contribute to the presence of what is morally bad. Most scholars focus on the turbidity or impurity of one's *qi* which surely is one important source of what is bad, but the mere fact of being physically embodied contributes to

our tendency to misconstrue our true nature and connection with the rest of the world and hence contributes to bad thoughts, feelings, and actions.

16 One finds a similar view in early Hinduism, which describes the central religious task as realizing that *atman* is *Brahman*. Because the *atman* misidentifies itself with the ego, humans tend to see themselves as separate individuals instead of as fundamentally connected to all other things. Thanks to Erin Cline for suggesting this comparison.

17 This description already makes clear the need to be careful in equating Wang's version of empathic concern with the views of people like Hume or modern advocates of sentimentalism such as Slote who make it clear that caring for another does not involve a loss of self or the merging of individuals. As we shall see when we discuss oneness below, this issue is very much in play among psychologists as well as philosophers.

18 This is important for those who want to explore further the respects in which Wang is a proponent of VES. For his claims about pure knowing make clear that he believes in a distinct *faculty* of moral perception. This makes him more like Western sentimentalists such as Butler and Hutcheson and unlike Hume. For a study that offers a comparative exploration of Wang's views about moral perception, see Ivanhoe 2011. For Mengzi's original use of *liang zhi*, see *Mengzi* 7A15.

19 Wang makes clear that pure knowing is not just a *response to* things in the world but the morally consciousness aspect or mode of the principles shared by things and the heart–mind. See Ivanhoe 2009a, pp. 114–15.

20 In Wang's most representative philosophical work, the *A Record for Practice*, he uses the term *junzi* a total of 24 times and *sheng ren* 196 times. In addition to this comparative frequency of use, the importance of attaining sagehood was central to Wang's philosophy while not an explicit goal of moral practice for Mengzi. Mengzi did believe every person was *capable* of becoming a sage (see e.g. *Mengzi* 6B2), but he did not expect even morally committed people to attain this goal. In fact, he thought sages were extremely rare historical phenomena. Thanks to Eric Hutton for discussion on this and other topics.

21 Wang was more of a *guru* figure or Chan master to his immediate disciples. See Ivanhoe 2002, pp. 103, 121–34.

22 This first point is also a feature of Wang's philosophy, but as is true of so many similarities between Mengzi and Wang, it takes a distinctive shape in the latter.

23 For a defense of a modern conception of filial piety as a virtue, see Ivanhoe 2007b.

24 This general feature of Confucian philosophy will be discussed in greater detail below in my remarks on Wang's conception of oneness.

25 I have in mind Mengzi's strong claims about the degree of consensus we can expect to find among informed and reflective people on matters of values and tastes. See for example, *Mengzi* 6A7.

26 Van Norden explores a number of issues concerning how one might fashion a more pluralistic form of Confucianism (which he refers to as Ruism) in Van Norden 2007, pp. 315–59. For "ethical promiscuity," see Ivanhoe 2009b.

27 Human beings show a regular and pervasive tendency to favor themselves in numerous ways, for example by claiming personal successes as evidence of excellence while attributing failure to situational factors or by interpreting ambiguous evidence in ways that are self-serving (Epley and Dunning 2000, and Pronin *et al.* 2002).

28 Wang does not discuss the feminist idea that some of us need to become more self-assertive and seek our own good when others are trying to make us feel guilty for doing so. This is not a common theme among neo-Confucians, though Dai Zhen offers a prominent exception and presents a careful analysis of these very concerns. For Dai's views on this issue, see Tiwald, 2011. Thanks to Michael Slote for raising this issue in comments on an earlier draft of this chapter. For his splendid discussion of this set of problems, see chapter 4 of Slote 2007.

29 For a study comparing Eastern and Western conceptions of self and their implications for issues related to moral perception, response, and action, see Markus and Kitayama 1991.

30 As a general claim, such a view finds support in important contemporary psychology. For example, see Hoffman 2007 for "empathy-based interventions." Angle 2009 relates Hoffman's views to neo-Confucian philosophers like Wang Yangming.

31 The current literature often describes other-regarding feelings as either empathy or oneness, but I see no reason to draw a sharp line here or to regard these as mutually exclusive.

32 Ensuring that human beings do at times act selflessly or altruistically is a central concern of the so-called "empathy-altruism hypothesis" championed by people like C. Daniel Batson. For example, see Batson 1987.

4   Virtue ethics in the medieval period

Ideals and theories of the virtues play a central role in the moral discourse of medieval Western Europe. This should perhaps surprise us more than it does. In contrast to categories of law and sin, "virtue" is not a scriptural motif, nor does this concept have obvious theological connotations. Yet by the third century, if not earlier, conceptions of virtue play a central role in Christian speculative thought, apologetics, and pastoral literature. The virtues were too deeply entrenched in the moral discourses of late antiquity to be ignored by educated Christians, who were just as much the products of late classical culture as anyone else. What is more, classical reflections on the virtues turned out to offer much of value to theological speculation, including illuminating perspectives on key doctrines, and practically accessible approaches to spiritual formation and pastoral care.

Siegfried Wenzel remarks that in the Middle Ages, any reasonably well-informed Christian, asked to identify the central virtues, would have replied that that depends on one's point of view.[1] The virtues commended by St. Paul, now identified as the theological virtues of faith, hope, and charity, taken together with the classical cardinal virtues of prudence, justice, fortitude, and temperance, provided the basic framework for most doctrinal and theological speculation on the virtues. However, monastic and ascetic traditions, focused on personal formation and the care of souls, would identify another set of key virtues as effective remedies for the deadly vices and sins that threaten one's salvation. While this list would overlap with the first to some extent, they would be organized differently, and different virtues would be given prominence; for example, humility, which plays a secondary role in a doctrinal analysis of the virtues, is regarded as a leading virtue within monastic and pastoral traditions, given its importance as a remedy for the capital vice of pride. The doctrinal approach is most familiar to us today, because it was taken up by the scholastics and embedded in later Catholic thought through the influence of Thomas Aquinas. However, the monastic/ ascetic approach continued to play a central role in the preaching, pastoral care, and increasingly the literature of the medieval period. It is prominently reflected in the works of Chaucer and Dante, and in less obvious forms, it continues to shape pastoral thought and its secular counterparts to this day.

My aim in this chapter is to trace the development of medieval virtue ethics, focusing on the two central strands identified above. After a brief review of the classical and early Christian sources, I will examine the main lines of scholastic and monastic/pastoral reflection on the virtues during the twelfth and thirteenth centuries. Finally, I will comment briefly on later medieval transformations of the earlier approaches to the virtues.

SOURCES AND EARLY CHRISTIAN ANTECEDENTS

Classical traditions and theories of the virtues have been covered elsewhere in this volume (chapters by Rachana Kamtekar and Philip J. Ivanhoe). At this point, I want simply to identify those aspects of classical virtue ethics which were especially influential in the medieval period.

Beginning in Athenian society in about the fifth century BCE, the virtues which developed in the warlike society of archaic Greece were gradually transformed into virtues more appropriate to a settled, urban existence. This process led to the first attempts to provide systematic accounts of the nature of virtue, and these accounts, in turn, helped to crystalize the idea of a distinctively human form of excellence which is proper to the human being as such, without reference to particular circumstances or roles.[2] From this point onward, reflection on the virtues was intimately bound up with more fundamental questions about the purpose of human life, as philosophers and other reflective thinkers attempted to determine the place of virtue in a well-lived life and to correct their initial intuitions about the virtues in light of wider theories of human flourishing and excellence. Indeed, the main lines of Greek and Hellenistic theories of ethics can be identified in terms of competing theories about the nature of virtue and its relation to human flourishing. As Julia Annas argues, these debates presupposed that the virtues are fundamentally dispositions towards characteristic kinds of perceptions, judgments, and actions, which combine both rational and affective elements in a relatively stable way.[3]

Plato (c.428–348 BCE) offered the first extended philosophical dis-cussion of the virtues that has survived intact, through a series of dialogues supposedly representing the views of his teacher Socrates (469–399 BCE).[4] These dialogues are notoriously difficult to inter-pret, and any broad summary of their overall position should be treated with the greatest caution. Yet it does seem safe to say that on the Socratic/Platonic view, the virtues should be analyzed as forms of knowledge or insight into what is truly good. Hence, the diverse virtues are essentially one and the same quality, a view which came to be known as the doctrine of the unity of virtue (see, for example, *Laches* 198a–199c). Plato appears to have interpreted this basic account in terms of his doctrine of the Forms, arguing that the knowledge proper to virtue can only be attained through an immediate perception of the Forms of Beauty, Goodness, Justice, and the other Forms. This perception enables the individual to bring the different components of his soul into right relation with one another, and this inner harmony, in turn, enables the individual to act appropriately in dealings with others, while his vision of the Forms motivates him to do so. (For an example of a passage bringing these themes together, see the *Republic* 514a–520e.) This brief sum-mary is almost certainly an oversimplification, but it gives a fair idea of what Plato and Socrates were thought to be saying by generations of followers and commentators.

At any rate, Plato's student Aristotle (384–322 BCE) offers what is in many respects a strikingly different approach to the virtues.[5] Like Socrates as Plato depicts him, Aristotle begins with commonly held moral opinions regarding ideals of character, excellence, and obliga-tion. However, in contrast to Plato's emphasis on general transcen-dental ideals, Aristotle takes the properly human forms of goodness, proper functioning, knowledge, and desire as the touchstones for his analysis. On this basis, he attempts to offer systematic accounts of the true nature and the proper interrelationships of diverse kinds of human excellence, in the process distinguishing between true excellences or virtues and their similitudes. In this way, Aristotle distinguishes the virtues both from the faculties of the soul and its passions. Rather, a virtue is a stable state of character which is expressed through a range of characteristic actions pertaining to some broadly defined field of human life. More specifically, true virtue is expressed through the attainment of a mean; this does not refer to an intermediate state between extremes of passion, but rather, an appropriate balancing of responses as determined by practical wisdom or prudence (*Nicomachean Ethics* [cited as *NE*] II.6, 1106b35–1107a25). In this way all the virtues are connected because they are all grounded in practical wisdom, yet they are distinct qualities (*NE* VI.13, 1144b30–1145a6); however, Aristotle rejects Plato's view that the virtues are diverse expressions of one and the same fundamental quality.

Stoicism, which emerged as a philosophical school shortly after Aristotle's death and continued well into the Christian era, offers a third distinctive approach to the virtues.[6] It is more difficult to give a summary of the Stoics' views, both because of the complexities introduced by the development of their thought, and because our sources are fragmentary. However, it seems safe to say that on their view, the virtues are closely linked to the agent's intention to act in accordance with right reason in every aspect of life. Furthermore, like Plato but unlike Aristotle, they defended the unity of virtue. The role of the passions in the life of the virtuous person was another point of debate between them and the Aristotelians, and they have often been criticized, in their own time and in ours, for promoting detachment and a lack of feeling as ideals of virtue. However, closer examination suggests that they did not consider emotion as such, but excessive or inappropriate passions, as contrary to reason and therefore to virtue. Understood in this way, the passions were regarded as delusional or morbid distortions of rationality, distressing because they undermine serenity, and even more because they keep the individual from perceiving reality as it is, and acting accordingly. This view led naturally to disciplines of virtuous living, informed by philosophical reflection, as a remedy for the sickness of distorted passions; thus understood, Stoic views of the passions, reasonableness, and the virtues were to have a profound impact on the monastic and pastoral traditions of Christian virtue ethics.

Stoic reflection on the virtues was mediated to Christian authors through a number of sources, including preeminently the Roman philosophers Seneca (4 BCE–65 CE) and Cicero (106–43 BCE).[7] Seneca's account of the rational character of the virtues, and his insistence that the ideals of virtue are the same for all persons, were to have considerable influence on later Christian thinkers. Cicero's influence on Christian ethics can scarcely be overstated. His own eclectic theory of virtue included both Stoic and Aristotelian elements (the latter mediated predominantly through the Peripatetics), and he played a key role in mediating both approaches to later Christian reflection. Subsequently, the Neoplatonist Macrobius (circa fourth century CE), in his commentary on Cicero's account of the dream of Scipio – which is recounted near the end of the latter's *De Republica* (6: 9–29) – set forth yet another analytic division of the virtues: political virtues, which are expressed within civil society; purgative virtues, which purify the soul and prepare it for contemplation; the virtues of the purified soul, which has overcome the passions; and the exemplary virtues, that is to say, the divine exemplars of the virtues as they exist in God. This analysis too was popular among medieval authors.

Although they differed greatly with respect to particulars, ancient theories of the virtues set the agenda and framework for scholastic virtue ethics. On this view, the virtues are first of all to be understood as stable qualities of the individual's soul or character which are expressed through characteristic kinds of actions. These qualities involve both affective and intellectual components; that is to say, the virtuous person is characterized both by the kinds of desires or feelings which he has, and by the intellectual judgments concerning action which he forms. At the same time, the virtues are active dispositions, oriented towards acting in such a way as to attain the mean, that is to say, the ideal and appropriate balance of responses and judgments, in diverse areas of life. The virtues were generally regarded as interrelated in some way, whether as expressions of one fundamental quality or as diverse capacities held together through the architectonic virtue of prudence. Debates over virtue were cast in terms of controversies over the meaning and interrelationships of these components.

As they attempted to come to terms with rapidly changing circumstances, and to address the practical concerns of expanding Christian communities, Christian intellectuals, ascetics, and pastors drew freely on classical traditions of virtue ethics. These reflections gave rise to the distinctively theoretical and practical approaches noted above. On the one hand, Christian intellectuals entered into philosophical debates over the virtues and the good life, entering freely into wider debates over the proper analysis of the virtues, seen in relation to the overall shape and purpose of human life. Their aim in doing so was, in part, apologetic – they appropriated and transformed classical ideals in such a way as to display the integrity and praiseworthiness of the Christian way of life. At the same time, classical traditions of the virtues offered a framework within which to think through key theological concepts such as sin, grace, and conversion, in ways which went beyond the narrowly apologetic discourses.

The most prominent of these early Christian intellectuals (at least in the West), both for the power of his analysis and his long-term influence, was Augustine of Hippo (354–430), who combined Stoic and Neoplatonic elements with Christian traditions of reflection on the theological virtues.[8] Like Plato and the Stoics, Augustine claims that the virtues are all fundamentally expressions of one quality, but in his view, that quality is Christian love (*De moribus Ecclesiae catholicae* I 15). As such, true virtue can only be bestowed by God. What characterizes the man or woman of charity is the ability to place all human affections in their right order, loving God above all, and loving creatures as expressions of God's goodness and, in the case of rational creatures, potential companions in the enjoyment of divine goodness. Thus, even though the seeming virtues of non-Christians are genuinely praiseworthy and beneficial to the human community, they cannot be true virtues, because they are directed towards the wrong ends (*De civitatis Dei* 5.12, 14).

On the other hand, the ascetic movements which came to prominence in the early third century gave salience to an alternative way of thinking about the virtues, in terms of remedies for the vices of the soul.[9] As the collected sayings of the desert monastics illustrate, the men and women who withdrew from society in pursuit of salvation were persuaded that the passions of the soul, understood in broadly Stoic terms as distorted or morbid desires and aversions, could only be countered through the cultivation of humility, obedience, chastity, and self-restraint. Seen from this perspective, the virtues are not so much qualities of character necessary to living a good life, which lend themselves to systematic analysis in terms of a unified conception of the human good, as they are correctives to vices which could potentially lead to deadly sin and damnation. Thus understood, the cultivation of the virtues was an urgent task for all Christians, lay men and women as well as ascetics; and those responsible for pastoral care were focused above all on facilitating this process. The urgency and practicality of this kind of virtue ethic is well represented in the influential accounts of the deadly vices and their corrective virtues which were developed by John Cassian (c.360–c.435) and Gregory the Great (c.540–604). Cassian wrote primarily for monks and ascetics, whereas Gregory was more concerned with the struggles of lay Christians. But for both of them, the most urgent challenge of the Christian life is to identify and root out the vices which lead to sin. To aid the Christian in this task, the abbot or pastor needs some practical knowledge of the kinds of qualities which correct the vices, and that is what both Cassian and Gregory attempt to provide. Their efforts were widely influential and much imitated throughout the medieval period. As a result, patristic thought bequeathed two ways of analyzing the virtues: one schema combined the classical cardinal virtues and the Christian theological virtues, whereas another organized them in terms of the seven deadly vices which they served to correct.

THE MEDIEVAL PERIOD

So far, we have focused on the distinctiveness of the two broad approaches to the virtues, the one systematic and (broadly speaking) academic, the other more immediately practical and pastoral. These two approaches persisted throughout the medieval period, when the virtues were a favorite theme for literary works, preaching, and practical pastoral advice. These treatments of the virtues tended to employ the older schema of the virtues as correctives to the vices, yet in the writings of Chaucer and Dante (for example), this old schema took on unprecedented beauty and power.

At the same time, we should not lose sight of the fact that from the beginning, and even more in the early Christian period, these two approaches developed together, each shaping the other in creative ways. Early medieval pastoral writings and homilies generated a rich literature on the virtues, the vices, and related topics such as the gifts of the Holy Spirit and the Beatitudes, all of which shaped scholastic as well as pastoral accounts of the virtues. The high-water mark of monastic speculation on the virtues, as on many other topics, occurred in the late eleventh and twelfth centuries, leading to noteworthy advances in the analysis of the virtues.[10] These advances reflected both a general trend towards intellectual and spiritual renewal which began to emerge in the late eleventh century, but also, more specifically, the need to rethink the normative implications of ideals of the virtues in the light of rapidly changing institutional and social contexts. At the same time, monastic and proto-scholastic authors began to reexamine traditional conceptions of sin, vice, and culpability, generating a rich and psychologically acute body of literature on the underlying dynamics of human action. These discussions highlight the extent to which reflection on the virtues, the vices, and sin brings together practical concerns and theoretical sophistication, whether it is situated in monastic or more strictly scholastic contexts.

Abelard and Lombard

That being said, systematic reflection on the virtues in the classical mode, i.e. analyzing them in relation to some overall account of human well-being, only got underway with the emergence of scholasticism in the early twelfth century.[11] Two of the earliest and most influential scholastics, Peter Abelard (1074–c.1142) and Peter Lombard (c.1100–1160), offered contrasting approaches to the virtues which were to set the agenda for much subsequent discussion.[12] In his *Dialogus inter philosophum, judaeum et christianum*, Abelard offered an Aristotelian analysis of virtue as a habit through which persons are able to act in a truly moral way, and to merit supreme beatitude (*Patrologia Latina* 178, 1651C–1652A). In contrast, in his *Sentences* Peter Lombard sets forth a pointedly theological analysis of virtue. In his view, virtue is closely linked with grace and the gifts of the Holy Spirit (II 27.1). More specifically, he defines virtue in terms taken from Augustine's writings as a good quality of the mind, which God brings about in us without our activity (II 27.5). Strictly speaking, God brings about virtue in the soul, and we bring about acts of virtue through the exercise of free will in cooperation with God's grace. Hence, "grace is not inappropriately called virtue" (II 27.9), and by implication, there can be no virtue without grace. This would seem to imply that Christian analysis has no place for a distinctively philosophical analysis of the virtues, but even if this was Lombard's own view, it represents a misleading oversimplification. Lombard's Augustinian analysis of the virtues is clearly, if indirectly indebted to a Platonic analysis of the virtues as modalities of knowledge or right love. This approach might be better characterized in terms of the broadly Platonic philosophical theology so prevalent in early twelfth century thought – in contrast to a broadly Aristotelian approach, which can also be construed in theological terms.

William of Auxerre

At any rate, early scholastic theology could accommodate positive appraisals of so-called natural virtues, attainable by all without the need of grace – at least, up to a point. One influential approach offered by the secular theologian William of Auxerre (c.1150–1231) in his *Summa aurea* (cited as *SA*), was to distinguish between the theological virtues, which are dependent on grace, and the political virtues, which are appropriate to human life in society and can be acquired through human effort. According to William, the political virtues are grounded in fundamental principles of the natural law, which are in turn known to all through a vision of God as supreme good innate in all human persons (*SA* III 18 intro, 18.4). The political virtues are both the preparation for the theological virtues, and the medium through which they are expressed in external acts once grace is received. As such, they are good in themselves, although not salvific without grace (*SA* III 19 intro). In this way, Macrobius' categories were appropriated as a starting point for a theological interpretation of the cardinal virtues.

William expressly (and almost certainly wrongly) attributes his view that the fundamental principles of virtue are known through direct divine illumination to Augustine (*SA* III 18.4). We find another very different development of Augustine's thought in the account of virtue offered by the Franciscan theologian Bonaventure (1217–1274) in his last work, the *Collations on the Hexameron*, which is a disquisition on the limitations of human knowledge cast in the form of a commentary on the six days of creation set forth in Genesis.[13]

Bonaventure

Bonaventure sets forth his understanding of the virtues in the seventh collation, which takes its starting point from Genesis 1:4, "God saw the light, that it was good, and He divided the light from the darkness..." He takes his starting point from Macrobius' analysis, remarking that according to the "most noble Plotinus" and Cicero, the virtues come into the human soul through illumination by God, the exemplary cause of all virtues (VII 3; Macrobius is not named). Nor does this view seem altogether wrong to him, although he insists that we receive the cardinal virtues through faith rather than philosophical illumination. Nonetheless, he adds, the pagans could not arrive at a right understanding of virtue, because without revelation, they could not understand the true point and the proper functioning of the virtues (VII 4).

As he goes on to explain, the virtues work in the human soul by means of a threefold operation, namely, directing the soul to its end, rectifying its dispositions, and healing its sickness, and none of these operations can be understood rightly apart from revelation (VII 5). More specifically, the philosophers could not understand how the virtues direct the soul to its end, because they did not know that our ultimate destiny is resurrection and eternal life (VII 6); they did not realize that the passions of the soul can only be rectified through grace (VII 7); and finally, they could not understand how the virtues can be healing, because they did not realize that the sicknesses of the soul are the results of sin (VII 8). Christian charity, which presupposes faith and hope, is the only possible remedy for the sicknesses of the soul, and the form of all the virtues (VII 14). This suggests that the pagan philosophers were incapable, not only of understanding the virtues, but of attaining them, and in fact we go on to read that the virtues of the pagans were unformed or vestigial versions of their Christian counterparts (VII 15).

Clearly, Bonaventure believed that full virtue is impossible without grace, but it is not clear how far his rejection of the virtue traditions of classical antiquity would go. Some scholars have suggested
that his account of the virtues reflects a thoroughgoing suspicion
of classical philosophy. However, it is not clear, even in the *Hexae-
meron*, that he rejects classical moral philosophy completely, and he
elsewhere makes use of elements of Aristotelian virtue theory with
evident approval.[14]

Aquinas

At any rate, it is certainly the case that scholastics in the twelfth
and thirteenth centuries generally draw freely on Aristotelian terminology and themes in developing their theories of the virtues,
thus continuing along the broad lines set out by Abelard. It may
seem surprising to find Aristotelian motifs before Aristotle's works
were reintroduced to the West by Muslim translators and commentators in the thirteenth century, but as Cary Nederman points out,
the main lines of Aristotle's moral thought were accessible through
multiple sources, including Aristotle's own works on logic and their
commentaries, as well as the writings of later Peripatetic and (so-
called) Neoplatonic philosophers.[15]

This is the context within which to place the extended theory of
the virtues developed by Thomas Aquinas (c.1225–1274). Aquinas is
often credited (or blamed) for his seemingly innovative synthesis of
Christian theology and Aristotelian philosophy, but with respect to
moral theory at least, that project was already well underway. At the
same time, Aquinas does depart from the views of his interlocutors
in some striking ways, and unless we take account of this fact, we
are likely to come away with a misleading sense of the overall shape
of medieval thought on this topic.

Aquinas frames his analysis of the concept of virtue in terms
taken from Lombard's definition: "Virtue is a good quality of the
mind, by which we live righteously, of which no one can make bad
use, which God brings about in us, without us" (*Summa theologiae*
[cited as *ST*] I-II 55.4, quoting II *Sentences* 27.5). He immediately
goes on to qualify this definition in one critical respect, adding that
the last clause of Lombard's definition applies only to the infused
virtues, which God bestows on us without action on our part, in

contrast to the acquired virtues, which as the name suggests can be attained through human effort without grace. Aquinas goes on to interpret this definition in decidedly Aristotelian terms, grounded in an analysis of virtue as a *habitus*, that is to say, a stable disposition of the intellect, will, or passions inclining the person to act in one kind of way rather than another (*ST* I-II 55.1). Such dispositions are necessary if we are to be capable of action at all; for example, the child's innate capacities for speech must be developed through the *habitus* of a particular language before the child can actually talk (*ST* I-II 49.4). Those virtues which shape the passions and the will, and the intellect insofar as it is oriented to action, are necessarily morally significant, because they incline towards actions of a kind which are good without qualification (*ST* I-II 58.1).

The distinctiveness of his theory lies in the way in which he synthesizes these approaches by means of a systematic development of the claim that the virtues are perfections – singly, perfections of the faculties of the soul that comprise the subject of the particular virtues, and taken together, a perfection of the human agent (on virtues as perfections of faculties, see for example *ST* I-II 55.3, 56.1; on virtue as a perfection of the agent, see *ST* I-II 4.7, in tandem with I-II 3.2).[16] In this way, he integrates his analysis of virtue, and by implication his overall account of human agency and the acts expressing it, into his overarching metaphysical and theological system, integrating it with his overall analysis of intelligibility, goodness, and causality.[17] While this line of analysis is broadly Aristotelian, it seems to owe more to the Peripatetics than to Aristotle himself. More generally, Aquinas' systematic analysis of the virtues in terms of a metaphysics of perfection is the most striking aspect of his distinctive theory of the virtues. Nearly every scholastic theologian up to Aquinas' time would have agreed that the virtues are perfections of the agent, but Aquinas stands out for the systematic way in which he interprets and integrates this claim in the light of his overall metaphysics.

Correlatively, Aquinas interprets the kinds of actions traditionally associated with particular virtues in such a way as to display these as perfections of specific faculties, as well as exemplifications of general ideals of praiseworthy behavior. The passions, which are naturally oriented towards what is perceived as desirable and away from what is perceived as noxious through the senses, are shaped through reason in such a way as to aim towards the overall good of the person through virtues of temperance and fortitude (*ST* I-II 58.2). Shaped, but not suppressed – otherwise, the virtues of the sensitive part of the soul would render their subject otiose, rather than perfecting it (I-II 59.5). Thus, the kinds of actions characterizing temperance and fortitude are irreducibly identified with the passions and the external behaviors typically expressing these – for example, the characteristic exterior acts of chastity always take the form of some kind of sexual behavior or abstinence, reflecting a rational and appropriate disposition of the faculty for sexual desire itself. Similarly, the will, which is intrinsically oriented towards self-love, is shaped by the virtues of justice and ultimately charity to move beyond natural self-love to wider loves, towards the community, one's neighbors, and ultimately towards God himself (*ST* I-II 56.6, 60.2; II-II 24.1, 58.4). And yet, the proper disposition of the will towards a wider range of loves does not do away with, much less destroy, a properly informed self-love – otherwise, as Aquinas remarks, charity would represent the corruption, rather than the perfection of human (or angelic) nature (*ST* I 60. 5; cf. I-II 109.3).

Aquinas acknowledges that we can legitimately regard the traditional cardinal virtues as general qualities of every praiseworthy action, but he prefers a second construal, according to which these are distinct virtues, informing the distinctive faculties of the soul (*ST* I-II 61.4). Thus understood, the virtues are perfections – which is to say, the full and appropriate development of the faculties that they inform, actualized in distinctive kinds of good actions. Because the faculties of the intellect, the will, and the desiring and irascible passions are all distinct, each has its proper virtue, identified with one of the four traditional cardinal virtues: prudence or practical wisdom, strictly speaking an intellectual virtue, enables the agent to choose in accordance with rightly ordered desires for one's final end, as these are expressed in particular actions; justice orients the will towards the good of others or the common good, as discerned by reason; and temperance and fortitude shape the passions in such a way that the agent desires what is truly in accordance with reason, and is prepared to resist obstacles to attaining it (*ST* I-II 59.2, 60.3–5; cf. *Quaestiones disputatae de virtutibus in communi* [cited as *QDVC*] a.12, which sets forth the relation of the virtues to the different faculties of the soul in more detail).

Because the particular virtues represent dispositions of distinctive faculties, Aquinas does not endorse the classical and Augustinian thesis that diverse virtues, properly understood, are all expressions of some one virtue or ideal of goodness, rationality, or charity (*ST* I-II 60.1). Rather, particular virtues represent perfections of the distinct faculties of the soul, as these are informed by rational reflection and judgment and (in the case of the infused virtues) the deliverance of faith. Yet the acts of the virtues will always be good without qualification, and for that reason, they must be coordinated – through the rational judgments of prudence, (perhaps) directed by charity – towards action in accordance with the agent's overall good and with right relations with others and God (*ST* I-II 65.1). Thus, Aquinas affirms the connection, rather than the sameness of the virtues – the thesis that the operations of the virtues are necessarily interconnected in such a way that it is necessary to possess all the central virtues in order genuinely to have any particular virtue (*ST* I-II 65.1). It should be noted, however, that this does not imply that the virtues are only possible through charity. While only the infused virtues can be described as such without qualification, the acquired virtues, fully formed through rational reflection and connected through prudence, are also genuine virtues seen in relation to the connatural end of the human person (*ST* I-II 65.2)

This brings us to a further point. Not only do the virtues consist in perfections of the constitutive faculties of the human soul, they operate in tandem to direct the individual towards his or her overall perfection as a rational creature, that is to say, towards beatitude or happiness. At the same time, happiness can be understood in a twofold way. There is a kind of happiness proportioned to our natural capacities, to which the virtues that we acquire by our own efforts are oriented. Indeed, Aquinas frequently identifies this kind of happiness with the practice of the cardinal virtues themselves, regarded as jointly constituting the full development of the principles of action characteristic of the rational creature (*ST* I-II 4.7, 5.5; cf. *QDVC* a.10). But in addition, we have been called to a higher form of happiness, namely direct personal union with God in the beatific vision. This form of fulfillment completely exceeds the natural capabilities, not only of the human soul, but of any creature; thus, it must receive new principles of action in order to attain such an end (*ST* I-II 62.1, 110.3). Correlatively, these new principles of action are only brought about through God's immediate action on the soul (ST I-II 62.1). This transformation is brought about by grace, and the operative dispositions through which grace is rendered active are the infused virtues, including infused versions of the cardinal virtues as well as the theological virtues of faith, hope, and charity, and the gifts of the Holy Spirit (ST I-II 110.3; with reference to the gifts in particular, I-II 68.1,2).

We need to consider one further distinction between the infused and acquired virtues. That is, the infused cardinal virtues are specifically different from their acquired counterparts because they are directed towards a different end, and therefore observe a different mean (ST I-II 63.3, 4). Acquired temperance takes its standards from the overall well-being and health of the body, and leads to an appropriate moderation in food and drink. Infused temperance, in contrast, takes its ultimate criterion from the person's desire for salvation, and incorporates forms of restraint and discipline, fasting for example, which will promote the individual's spiritual, as well as her physical health. Note, however, that ascetical exercises which damage one's bodily well-being are vicious, rather than virtuous (ST II-II 147.1 ad 2). The end of the acquired virtues, namely the overall well-being of the organism and the community, is thus transformed by the infused virtue, rather than being obviated or undermined by it (ST II-II 104.6, 141.6 ad 1); again, grace perfects, rather than destroying nature, as we are frequently reminded (for example, see ST I 60.5).

At this point, we come to one of the most interesting and original aspects of Aquinas' analysis of the virtues. Most of Aquinas' predecessors and interlocutors organized their accounts of the virtues in accordance with a dichotomy between the theological virtues, which are necessary to salvation and depend on God's grace, and political or (later) acquired virtues, which are appropriately directed towards human flourishing in this life and can be attained through human effort. The latter can be said to serve as a preparation for the theological virtues, and they provide a medium through which the theological virtues are expressed in external acts. Nonetheless, scholastics up to this point typically hold that the theological and the political or acquired virtues remain in an external relation, with the former directing the latter – there is no need, within this schema, to postulate infused political or cardinal virtues. Aquinas is clearly familiar with this approach (QDVC a.9, ST I-II 61.5), but in the

Summa theologiae he replaces it with a more complex set of distinctions between the theological and the cardinal virtues, on the one hand, and between infused and acquired virtues on the other, with specifically distinct forms of the cardinal virtues falling on either side of this line. At first glance, this would seem to introduce unnecessary complications. Why should he have done so?

At least part of the answer to this question lies in the specifics of Aquinas' concept of grace, as developed in terms of his overall analysis of the virtues as perfections of the agent. Recall that for Aquinas, the infused virtues are the operative principles through which grace can be expressed through one's acts (*ST* I-II 110.3). Correlatively, in order for an action to be meritorious, it must stem from grace in some way (*ST* I-II 114.2). What this implies is that the earlier view, according to which the theological virtues direct the political or cardinal virtues, is inadequate. In order for grace to be fully operative and efficacious in every dimension of human life, it must transform all the faculties of the human soul involved in the processes of deliberation and action (*ST* I-II 63.3, especially *ad* 2, 65.3). Thus, it is not enough that the theological virtues should command the acts of the other virtues; rather, grace must be expressed directly through virtues appropriate to every faculty of the soul, which is to say, through infused versions of all the cardinal virtues.

This still does not explain why Aquinas prefers to speak of the cardinal, rather than the (infused) political virtues. We can better appreciate why Aquinas frames his discussion in these terms when we turn to the detailed moral analyses of the *secunda secundae*. We find that the division between virtues oriented towards beatitude, and those oriented towards social life, is too simple for Aquinas' purposes. Only one of the cardinal virtues, justice, has a direct and defining relation to the good of the community as a whole; indeed, strictly speaking this is the case only for legal justice (*ST* II-II 58.7, 8). Both fortitude and temperance are primarily oriented towards maintaining the individual's equilibrium between passions and reasoned judgments about the overall good, and in that sense they both have the good of the individual as their primary focus (*ibid.*). Similarly, particular justice, which is further divided into commutative and distributive justice, is concerned with right relations towards individuals (*ST* II-II 61.1). Prudence ranges over both sets of considerations and integrates them, and for that very reason Aquinas distinguishes between individual and political prudence (ST II-II 47.11).

Aquinas analyzes the specific ideals of cardinal virtue in terms of the Aristotelian doctrine of the mean, according to which the virtues are expressed through passions and actions in accordance with a mean as determined by reason (ST I-II 64.1). The rational criterion, that is to say, the mean of the virtues of the passions is determined by the overall good of the organism, which places sensual goods in their correct relation to that overall good; hence, these virtues are said to observe a rational mean only (ST I-II 64.2). The mean of justice, in contrast, is set by the good of the neighbor or the community as a whole (depending on which form of justice is in question), in such a way as to reflect objective criteria of equity and fairness. For this reason, the mean of justice is said to be a real, as well as a rational, mean (ibid.; also see I-II 56.6, II-II 58.10). As already noted, the infused cardinal virtues observe a different mean than do the acquired virtues, and the theological virtues are not defined by reference to a mean at all because there can be no question of moderation with respect to believing, hoping in, and loving God (ST I-II 64.4).

LATE MEDIEVAL DEVELOPMENTS

Already in the late thirteenth century, and continuing throughout the fourteenth and fifteenth centuries, scholastic analysis of the virtues was shaped, and eventually transformed, by controversies over free will and the relationships among the will, the intellect, and the passions. These controversies are notoriously complex and the exact meaning and implications of the diverse positions remain contested to this day. However, it is safe to say that these controversies were driven by two approaches to human agency.[18] On the one hand, we find (mostly) Dominican masters defending intellectualism, according to which rational judgment determines the choice of the will; on the other, the (mostly) Franciscan masters defended versions of voluntarism, which gives more or less absolute priority to the will. Whatever the merits of these two approaches might be, neither leaves much space for an Aristotelian approach to the virtues, such as we find dominating thirteenth-century discussions.

Aristotelian theories of the virtues characteristically take their starting points from some account of human agency as a complex phenomenon, dependent on the coordinated exertions of diverse faculties. The agenda for such a theory is thus set by two related problems:
to explain how this coordination can take place in such a way as to
lead effectively and easily to desirable or praiseworthy actions; and
to do so in such a way as to show that the virtuous agent is well
disposed to act in accordance with the ideals of the virtuous life. In
scholastic terms, this implies that virtue renders both an action and
the agent herself good.

It will be apparent by now that neither of the approaches to human
agency dominating late scholasticism leaves much space for a distinctively Aristotelian problematic arising out of the complexity of
human agency. (That may, indeed, have been part of their attraction.)
Whatever their differences, these approaches share the tendency to
analyze human agency in terms of one dominant faculty, whether
intellect or will, which operates in such a way as to lead more or less
directly to determinate choice and action. On such a view, there is
no need to account for the coordination of diverse faculties, because
these faculties, even though they are present and operative, do not
have the independence needed to generate real internal conflicts
or distorted judgments. By the same token, the agent's character
is tied much more closely to some assessment of the kinds of things
he actually does. There is little point in asking whether someone's
actions stem from a stable disposition, reflecting the successful coordination of diverse faculties – if one's actions are determined, more
or less, by right judgments or a good will, then presumably so is one's
character as an agent.

Scotus

The Franciscan theologian Duns Scotus (c.1265–1308) offers what
are probably the most influential accounts of will, moral law, and
moral goodness to emerge in this period, and for that reason, his
remarks on the virtues merit attention, even though they have
received less notice than other aspects of his moral views, at least
in modern times.[19] Scotus' traditional sobriquet was "the subtle
Doctor," and philosophers continue to debate the interpretation of
his views. However, we can safely say that the Franciscan master

Duns the Scot defended a voluntarist theory of human agency, although his voluntarism is carefully qualified (in his later writings) by the acknowledgment that the will is informed (although not determined) by the intellect. Even so, his subtle and nuanced voluntarism leads him to an account of virtue that is strikingly different from Aristotelian views.[20]

On Scotus' view, the will operates in independence from the judgments of the intellect, in such a way as to yield actions apart from, or even contrary to intellectual judgments concerning the good. Only in this way can the will be said to be truly free – and by the same token, the will likewise operates in independence of passions or sensual desire. What is more, he appropriates a distinction from the monastic theologian Anselm of Canterbury (c.1033–1109) to identify a more profound sense of human freedom. That is, following Anselm he identifies two wills in each individual, a will to seek one's own well-being or perfection, and a will towards justice or the good in general. These two wills open up the possibility of truly disinterested choice and action, in this way freeing the human agent to choose in a real and meaningful sense between her own well-being and justice or the good, understood in nonagential terms. It is important to note that Duns Scotus does not regard the will towards one's own perfection as in itself iniquitous – properly exercised, it plays a natural and proper part in human action. Nonetheless, if the agent is to act in accordance with God's law, the latter will has to exercise, as it were, the controlling voice.

This line of analysis opens up a space for virtue. On Scotus' account, virtue is essentially a disposition to act in accordance with the will towards justice, operating as the controlling will to which self-interest is subordinate. However, it is worth noting that on this account, virtue in the most unqualified sense would seem to be identified with the agent's disposition to choose just, or at any rate morally acceptable acts. Scotus thus does not need the kind of complex analysis of virtue that we find in the scholastic Aristotelian – he simply needs to show how the architectonic virtues (above all, charity) work in such a way as to dispose the individual to subordinate self-love to the love of God in the appropriate way. This may explain why Scotus denies that virtue adds anything to the moral value of either particular actions or the character of the agent, although he adds that virtue does facilitate good action through disciplining and constraining our sensuality. By the same token, Scotus rejects any distinction between infused and acquired moral virtues, and indeed he denies that meritorious action depends on infused virtues at all. We are naturally capable of carrying out the characteristic acts of charity, including self-sacrifice and the love of God above all, and while God's grace may render these kinds of actions easier, it is in no way a necessary condition for their performance or their salvific value.

These views represent radical departures from earlier scholastic views on the distinctiveness and necessity of grace, and yet they follow readily from his overall views of human agency and the virtues. Wolter observes that Duns Scotus, in contrast to Aquinas, does not believe that the soul is really (as opposed to formally) distinct from its faculties. This means that he need not, and indeed cannot postulate a distinct principle of action, directed to a new end, which is infused into the soul without altering its fundamental nature – which is simply to say, he cannot, and need not, postulate grace understood in Aquinas' terms as a new operative principle, distinct from natural inclinations. For Scotus, whatever elevates the faculties of the soul necessarily elevates the whole soul, since these are not two distinct realities. I would suggest a further reason for Scotus' distinctive views on nature and grace. For earlier scholastics, including Aquinas, infused virtues are necessary because they enable men and women to act for a new set of aims, apprehended and loved in a way that goes beyond natural capacities – thus, they qualify the mode of action, as well as its ultimate determinants. On Scotus' view, however, there is no space and no need for principles that might qualify or direct the righteous will – all that matters is that this be the will that is in fact engaged.

Scotus is often blamed, or credited, with the collapse of scholastic virtue ethics. Certainly, he influenced Luther's wholesale rejection of the idea of Christian virtue, together with Aristotle and all his pomps. Nonetheless, it would be too quick to say that Scotus and his followers did away with virtue ethics in its entirety. While he departs radically from his Aristotelian predecessors, and offers a view strikingly at odds with earlier Christian thinkers on the proper character of grace, his view can arguably be traced, in part, to alternative conceptions of the virtues. In particular, while Augustine would certainly have rejected his overall views, Scotus might still claim to offer a defensible construal of Augustine's view that the virtues are all modalities of love, with *righteous will* substituted for *love*. At any rate, it is by no means clear that the earlier Aristotelian virtue ethic did collapse. It underwent an eclipse, but is currently enjoying a revival in both philosophical and theological circles. Virtue ethics is always located within a wider context of intellectual debates and practical concerns, and so long as key issues remain in play, we can expect to see diverse approaches to the virtues appearing, receding, and returning again.

NOTES

1   Wenzel 1984, p. 7; more generally, see pp. 2–12 for a more extended discussion of the complexities of literary, pastoral, and theological discussions of virtues and vices in this period.
2   For this point, see MacIntyre 1984, pp. 121–45; more generally, throughout this section I rely especially on Annas 1993, 3–134.
3   Annas 1993, pp. 120–2.
4   In my account of Plato's theory of virtue, I rely on Irwin 1989, pp. 68–84, and Vlastos 1995, pp. 69–146.
5   For an illuminating comparison of Aristotelian and Stoic accounts of the virtues, see Annas 1993, pp. 47–134.
6   In addition to Annas, see Colish 1990, pp. 61–79 and 85–9, for further discussion of Stoic theories of the virtues.
7   For the views and later impact of Seneca, see Colish 1990, ·pp. 13–19; with respect to Cicero, see Colish 1990, pp. 61–158, and Watson 1971.
8   For an especially illuminating account of Augustine's theory of virtue seen in relation to its classical antecedents, see Rist 1994, pp. 148–202.
9   See Wenzel 1986 for more particulars.
10 In addition to Wenzel 1986, see Blomme 1958 for an extended treatment of late monastic and early scholastic analyses of the psychological and theological dimensions of vice and sin.
11 The best account of the development of medieval theories of virtue remains the essays collected by Lottin 1942–60, vol. III; for a more recent and most illuminating account focused on later medieval thought, see Kent 1995.
12 On Abelard and Peter Lombard, see Lottin 1942–60, vol. II, pt. I, pp. 100–4; for an extended discussion of Abelard's remarks on virtue, see Marenbon 1997, pp. 282–7.
13 For my account of Bonaventure's views, I rely on Emery, 1983; for a somewhat different interpretation, see Kent 1995, pp. 46–58.

14 Emery 1983 takes this view; for the contrary (and in my view, more persuasive) interpretation, see Kent 1995, pp. 46–8.

15 See Nederman 1991 for particulars.

16 I argue for this interpretation in more detail in Porter 2005, pp. 163–203.

17 For further details, including further textual references, see Pasnau 2002, pp. 143–51; in addition, see Porter 2005, pp. 158–63.

18 I rely here on Kent 1995, pp. 94–149.

19 See Kent 2003, p. 352. More generally, in my account of Scotus' understanding of the virtues, I rely on Wolter 1997, pp. 31–123, and more specifically pp. 75–89, and Kent 2003, pp. 352–76.

20 In contrast to most of the authors previously discussed, Scotus does not lay out a systematic theory of the virtues in any one text (Kent 2003, 352). His most important remarks on the virtues can be found in the *Ordinatio* III suppl., dist. 33–6. In what follows, I rely on Wolter's translation of these texts, Wolter 1997, pp. 223–74.

5 Hume's anatomy of virtue

> I never balance between the virtuous and vicious course of
> life; but I am sensible, that, to a well-disposed mind, every
> advantage is on the side of the former.
>
> – David Hume, *Enquiry concerning Human*
> *Understanding* (11.20/140)[1]

In his *Treatise of Human Nature* Hume makes clear that it is his aim
to make moral philosophy more scientific and properly grounded
on experience and observation.[2] The "experimental" approach to
philosophy, Hume warns his readers, is "abstruse," "abstract" and
"speculative" in nature. It depends on careful and exact reasoning
that foregoes the path of an "easy" philosophy, which relies on a
more direct appeal to our passions and sentiments.[3] Hume justifies
this approach by way of an analogy concerning the relevance of
anatomy to painting. "The anatomist," he says, "ought never to
emulate the painter." At the same time, the painter cannot afford to
ignore the anatomist:

An anatomist ... is admirably fitted to give advice to a painter ... We must
have an exact knowledge of the parts, their situation and connexion, before
we can design with any elegance or correctness. And thus the most abstruse
speculations concerning human nature, however cold and uninteresting,
become subservient to *practical morality*; and may render this latter science
more correct in its precepts, and more persuasive in its exhortations.[4]

I am grateful to Dan Russell for helpful and insightful comments and suggestions
relating to this chapter.

As these remarks suggest, Hume's anatomy of virtue is not without its own practical aims and objectives. It is advanced with a view to identifying and carefully delineating the true foundations of morality in human nature and correcting our practices in light of this. With this improvement in our understanding of the nature and basis of virtue, we can better appreciate the way in which virtue secures happiness for ourselves and others and may also avoid the distortions and corruptions of morality by religious superstition.

PASSION, CHARACTER, AND THE MECHANICS OF VIRTUE

Hume introduces his account of the nature of virtue and vice in the context of his discussion "Of the Passions" in Book II of the *Treatise*. According to Hume, the way in which virtue and vice are related to moral evaluation must be understood with reference to the causal mechanism that generates the indirect passions of love and hate, and pride and humility. The passions themselves, he claims, are pleasant or painful feelings, love and pride being pleasant and hate and humility being painful. The *object* of these passions is always a person or thinking being.[5] In the case of love and hate it is some other person, and in the case of pride and humility it is oneself. The *causes* of these passions, although they vary greatly, must be "either parts of ourselves, or something nearly related to us."[6] For the cause to produce the relevant indirect passion it must (a) be related to the person in the appropriate way, and (b) have an *independent* pleasant or painful tendency, one that is relevantly similar to the pleasant or painful quality of the indirect passion that it gives rise to (e.g. for a house to give pride it must itself be found pleasant and belong to me or my family). Hume describes the principles involved in the production of these passions with particular reference to the role of sympathy and the association of impressions and ideas.[7] He then proceeds to categorize the various qualities and features of things that may serve as causes of our indirect passions.

There are, according to Hume, four main categories of objects or features of human beings that serve to generate the indirect passions: our wealth, external goods, or property; our immediate relatives or people who are closely related to us; our bodily qualities or attributes (i.e. beauty and deformity); and, most important of all, our qualities of mind or character traits.[8] Those character traits or mental qualities which produce an independent pleasure in ourselves and others also generate love or pride (i.e. depending on whom these qualities or traits belong to). Character traits or mental qualities of this nature are virtues. Similarly, those mental qualities or character traits which are found painful will produce hate or humility and, as such, are deemed vices. Well into Book III Hume summarizes his account:

We have already observ'd that, moral distinctions depend entirely on certain peculiar sentiments of pain and pleasure, and that whatever mental quality in ourselves or others gives us satisfaction, by survey or reflection, is of course virtuous, as every thing of this nature, that gives uneasiness, is vicious. Now since every quality in ourselves or others, which gives pleasure, always creates pride or love; as every one, that produces uneasiness, excites humility and hatred: It follows, that these two particulars are to be consider'd as equivalent, with regard to our mental qualities, *virtue* and the power of producing love or pride, *vice* and the power of producing humility and hatred. In every case, therefore, we may judge of the one by the other and may pronounce any quality of the mind virtuous, which causes love or pride; and any one vicious, which causes hatred or humility.[9]

It is Hume's view, therefore, that virtues and vices are pleasurable or painful qualities of mind. By means of the general mechanism that produces the indirect passions, these qualities of mind give rise to that "faint and imperceptible" form of love and hatred which constitutes the moral sentiments.[10] It is by means of this "regular mechanism"[11] which generates the moral sentiments, understood as modes of the indirect passions, that human beings are able to distinguish between virtue and vice.

While it is clear that Hume holds that our character traits are capable of generating moral sentiments, whereby we distinguish them as virtuous or vicious, this still leaves us with the question of what character itself consists in.[12] Hume speaks of "character" in two quite different senses. The narrower sense refers to a specific character trait (e.g. honesty, courage, etc.). The wider sense, by contrast, means a person's complete set of moral traits and qualities – that is, her whole set of character traits. It is clear enough that when Hume is speaking of virtues and vices he is referring to specific traits of character, which he takes to be "durable principles of the mind."[13] What, then, do character traits consist in? In certain contexts Hume explicitly identifies virtues and vices with specific passions.[14] On this interpretation it is perceptions that constitute the ontological basis of qualities of character – because passions are one kind of perception. A passion, Hume maintains, may become "a settled principle of action" and, as such, may be "the predominant inclination of the soul."[15] So considered, a passion may serve as an enduring or persisting cause of actions, such that the agent's will and choices are governed by it.[16] This observation explains the very important and evident connection between character and action.

According to this interpretation, a person's character may be understood in terms of the structure or pattern of various passions that animate that person and direct her conduct. There are, however, at least two aspects of this account that require some further refinement or qualification. First, Hume does not construe character entirely in terms of its relation to a person's will and actions. A person's gestures, mannerisms, and countenance may also betray a passion, even though no intentional action is involved. Not every passion engages the will and leads to intentional action, but it may, nevertheless, be expressed or manifest and, as such, betray qualities of mind that can be found pleasant or painful. Second, Hume maintains that our natural abilities and talents (e.g. intelligence, imagination etc.) constitute important qualities of mind and that they are also liable to arouse our moral sentiments of approval and disapproval. So considered, these qualities of mind must be included among a person's virtues and vices and as aspects of her moral character. (Hume's views concerning the natural abilities are discussed further below, pp. 105–8.) Clearly, then, Hume's account of character cannot be interpreted entirely in terms of the relation between passions and intentional action.

Although action is not the only evidence that we have concerning a person's character, it is, nevertheless, the principal sign of character that we have available to us. The immediate relevance of action is that it reveals the nature of the agent's motives and qualities of mind, and thereby arouses moral sentiments which are the basis of moral evaluation.[17] In several passages Hume emphasizes the (distinct and further) point that people are responsible for their actions and the motives that produced them only insofar as they reveal *enduring* qualities of mind or character traits. In the following passage in Book III of the *Treatise* he pursues this point:

If any *action* be either virtuous or vicious, 'tis only as a sign of some quality or character. It must depend upon durable principles of the mind, which extend over the whole conduct, and enter into the personal character. Actions themselves, not proceeding from any constant principle, have no influence on love or hatred, pride or humility; and consequently are never consider'd in morality.[18]

He continues:

This reflection is self-evident, and deserves to be attended to, as being of the utmost importance in the present subject. We are never to consider any single action in our enquiries concerning the origin of morals; but only the quality or character from which the action proceeded. These alone are *durable* enough to affect our sentiments concerning the person.[19]

According to Hume it is a matter of "the utmost importance" for moral philosophy that our action be indicative of *durable* qualities of mind if a person is to be held accountable for it.[20] Although this claim is crucial to his moral philosophy – and fundamental to his commitment to virtue ethics – it is a claim that has puzzled and perplexed many of Hume's commentators, while others have simply ignored or dismissed it. What, then, is the basis of this puzzling and controversial claim? In order to understand Hume's position we need to return to his account of the indirect passions. Hume claims that for an indirect passion to be aroused in us, the cause of the passion (i.e. some item or feature which we find independently pleasurable or painful) must stand in some relevant or appropriate relations to the object of the passion (i.e. oneself or someone else). In general, the relationship between the cause and the object of the passion must be close.[21] The quality or feature must be "part of ourselves, or something nearly related to us" if it is to produce these passions.[22] Related to this point, Hume also notes that the relationship between the quality or feature which gives rise to the passion and the person who is the object of the passion must not be "casual or inconsistent."[23]

Hume describes what happens when the relationship between the cause and the object of the passions is brief and temporary in the following passage (where he is specifically concerned with pride):

What is casual and inconsistent gives but little joy, and less pride. We are not so much satisfy'd with the thing itself; and are still less apt to feel any new degrees of self-satisfaction upon its account. We foresee and anticipate its change by the imagination; which makes us little satisfy'd with the thing: We compare it to ourselves, whose existence is more durable; by which means its inconsistency appears still greater. It seems ridiculous to infer an excellency in ourselves from an object, which is of so much shorter duration, and attends us during so small a part of our existence.[24]

The language here is closely in accord with the language Hume employs when he is arguing that moral evaluation, interpreted in terms of the generation of moral sentiment, is grounded on character and not action as such.[25] The reason for this is that the latter claim, relating to the importance of character for the production of our moral sentiments, is simply a particular application of the more general claim he makes in respect of the importance of the required close and enduring relationship between the causes and objects of our indirect passions. Any object or quality which bears only a casual or inconstant relation to the person or agent will be unable to arouse an indirect passion. Actions by their very nature are "temporary and perishing." Moral sentiments can be generated only when they proceed from something that stands in the required *close and lasting* relation to the agent or person concerned. Only constant and enduring principles of mind satisfy this demand, whereas actions do not. This observation explains the basis of Hume's commitment to virtue ethics as opposed to an action-based theory, and shows that this commitment must itself be understood in terms of Hume's analysis of the mechanism of the indirect passions. It is not possible to separate his virtue theory from his account of the psychology of the passions, as governed by the general principles and operations of sympathy and association.

THE VARIETIES AND VAGARIES OF VIRTUE

Hume's anatomy of virtue suggests two different ways of classifying the virtues and vices. In Book III of the *Treatise* he introduces a fundamental distinction between two kinds of virtue, natural and artificial.[26] Some virtues are artificial, as opposed to natural, in the sense that they depend on a contrivance or convention of some kind.[27] The conventions concerned, which relate primarily to property and promises, establish the basic rules and obligations of justice.

The just person is one who scrupulously adheres to these rules and fulfills her obligations in this regard. Hume explains this basic distinction in the following terms:

> The only difference betwixt the natural virtues and justice lies in this, that the good, which results from the former, arises from every single act, and is the object of some natural passion. Whereas a single act of justice, consider'd in itself, may often be contrary to the public good; and 'tis only the concurrence of mankind, in a general scheme or system of action, which is advantageous.[28]

While the particular conventions and laws invented by humans to secure peace and social cooperation vary, the basic need or requirement for some such scheme is universal and all schemes of this kind must be judged with reference to the advantages that they secure for the individuals and society concerned. By way of analogy, Hume points out that people in different times and places build their houses in different ways but all structures of this kind are universally required and can be evaluated with reference to the basic needs that they are designed to satisfy.[29] In the second *Enquiry* he contrasts the (natural) virtue of benevolence with the (artificial) virtue of justice by means of another analogy, contrasting a wall and a vault. The happiness secured by benevolence is like a wall "which still rises by each stone heaped upon it, and receives increase proportional to the diligence and care of each workman."[30] In contrast with this, happiness secured by justice is better compared with a vault, where each stone must be supported by all the others in the structure and would otherwise "fall to the ground." In general, Hume's aim is to point out that there exists a crucial divide between two kinds of virtue, those that do and those that do not depend on the creation and establishment of human conventions. Although the conventions that establish justice arise originally from motives of self-interest, Hume is careful to emphasize the point that we regard these dispositions as *virtues* because of our natural sympathy with the public interest, and it is this that serves as the basis of our *moral* approval of these virtues.[31]

After he introduces the distinction between natural and artificial virtues and vices,[32] Hume offers another way of distinguishing and separating the virtues in terms of four particular "sources" of personal merit.

Every quality of mind is denominated virtuous, which gives pleasure by the mere survey; as every quality, which produces pain is call'd vicious. This pleasure and this pain may arise from four different sources. For we reap a pleasure from the view of character, which is naturally fitted to be useful to others, or to the person himself, or which is agreeable to others, or to the person himself.[33]

It is an important part of Hume's conception of virtue that he emphasizes that virtue has a self-regarding aspect and should not be considered solely with a view to benevolence.[34] Hume employs this fourfold set of distinctions to structure much of his anatomy of virtue, something that is particularly apparent in the second *Enquiry*. Among the qualities that are useful to ourselves are prudence, temperance, frugality, and industry.[35] With respect to qualities that are immediately agreeable to ourselves, he mentions cheerfulness, tranquility, and pride.[36] Qualities immediately agreeable to others include wit, eloquence, modesty (as opposed to impudence and arrogance), decency, and good manners.[37] Of the qualities useful to others the most obvious examples are benevolence and justice.[38] Throughout this analysis Hume is concerned to establish that the source of our approval of these virtues or qualities of mind is the sympathy we have for the utility or happiness which they secure for ourselves and our fellow human beings.[39]

Hume employs his "catalogue of virtues"[40] to portray several examples or "models" of virtuous characters. In the second *Enquiry* he presents the imaginary example of "Cleanthes," who is described as "a model of perfect virtue."[41] His review of Cleanthes' virtues presents him as possessing a full range of the various kinds of virtue that he has enumerated with respect to those that are immediately agreeable or useful to oneself or others. In other contexts, however, Hume cites real people taken from history – particularly the ancients.[42] One of the more interesting examples provided is the contrast drawn between Cato and Caesar.

The characters of Caesar and Cato...are both of them virtuous in the strictest sense of the word; but in a different way: Nor are the sentiments entirely the same, which arise from them. The one produces love; the other esteem: The one is amiable; the other awful.[43]

Hume's general point here is that virtuous individuals vary in the specific kinds of characters and qualities of mind that they may possess. There is no *single* model or exemplar of the virtuous person, as we find a wide range of types who may satisfy the relevant standard for judging this matter. We should expect, therefore, no convergence on one ideal life of virtue. In this sense Hume may be described as a "pluralist" about virtue, insofar as he rejects any single model or uniform ideal of the virtuous person. In another passage Hume describes the mixed character of Hannibal, where "great virtues [e.g. courage, confidence, prudence, etc.] were balanced by great vices [e.g. cruelty, dishonesty, etc.]."[44] As this example makes clear, some combination of virtues and vices is generally found in most individuals (i.e. most people possess some subset of the virtues in various degrees and in combination with some subset of the vices in various degrees).[45]

According to Hume's account experience shows us that there is not only great variation in the way that virtues and vices may be combined and integrated in the same person, there are also complexities and subtleties in the way the individual virtues and vices may manifest themselves in a given person and in particular circumstances. These complexities and subtleties suggest that in many cases there are no simple or sharp boundaries to be drawn between virtue and vice even with respect to *particular* qualities of mind. Hume notes, for example, with respect to the natural virtues, that "all kinds of virtue and vice run inevitably into each other, and may approach by such imperceptible degrees as will make it very difficult, if not absolutely impossible, to determine when one ends, and the other begins... "[46] He denies, however, that the same observation applies to the artificial virtues, where the rules and obligations involved "admit of no such inevitable gradation." Among the examples Hume offers of virtues that may become excessive and lead eventually to vice are charity and courage. A person, he notes, "is *too good*; when he exceeds his part in society, and carries his attention for others beyond the proper bounds."[47] Courage and ambition may take the form of "excessive bravery" or even "ferocity" and result in misery and ruin for all concerned – a weakness that the "military hero" is especially prone to.[48] "Courage and ambition," he says, "when not regulated by benevolence, are fit only to make a tyrant and public robber."[49] Even cheerfulness, he argues, may be excessive when it lacks any proper cause or occasion.[50] Although Hume is evidently aware of and sensitive to the issue of moderation and balance with respect to the virtues, he does not endorse a general doctrine of "the mean" of the kind that can be found in Aristotle's ethics.[51] It is, on the contrary, Hume's view that the issue of moderation and balance varies depending on the specific virtues concerned, and that some virtues more than others are liable to be corrupted or take an "excessive" form when not balanced with a relevant counterpart.[52]

Hume is also clear that the particular virtues we approve of and care about may vary considerably depending on the particular social and historical circumstances we are placed in. In this regard he contrasts the views of the ancients and the moderns concerning their different ideas of "perfect merit."[53] In a similar vein he also notes differences among nations on such matters,[54] as well as the importance of education and custom relating to this.[55] In different social and historical conditions, Hume maintains, different virtues will become more prominent and salient.

Particular customs and manners alter the usefulness of qualities: they also alter their merit. Particular situations and accidents have, in some degree, the same influence. He will always be more esteemed, who possesses those talents and accomplishments, which suit his station and profession, than he whom fortune has misplaced in the part which she has assigned him.[56]

In general, Hume emphasizes not only the variable and fragmented nature of virtue, but also its fragility and vulnerability to fortune and contingent circumstances.[57]

All these observations concerning the variation and fragmentation of virtue, as well as its vulnerability to circumstances and fortune, may encourage the view that Hume is a skeptic about virtue and rejects any fixed or reliable standard for identifying and approving of the diverse range of virtues that we encounter in the world and throughout history. Any conclusion of this kind, however, would be mistaken. One of Hume's fundamental concerns in his presentation of his moral philosophy, particularly in his two chief works on this subject, is to show how variation and diversity in our ideas of virtue are consistent with an underlying and universal standard by which we may reliably judge such matters. Although Hume is plainly skeptical about moral systems that aim to reduce the distinction between virtue and vice to a matter of reason alone, without reference to feeling and sentiment, he nevertheless emphatically rejects any skeptical suggestion that there is no "real distinction" for us to discern.[58] All moral evaluations, Hume maintains, must be made from "the general point of view."[59] Beyond this, our standard of morals, by means of which we may all recognize and distinguish between virtue and vice, depends on our capacity for sympathy and the importance all human beings naturally place on general considerations of utility.[60]

Sympathy, we shall allow, is much fainter than our concern for ourselves, and sympathy for persons remote from us much fainter than with persons near and contiguous; but for this very reason it is necessary for us, in our calm judgments and discourse concerning the characters of men, to neglect all these differences and render our sentiments more public and social ... The intercourse of sentiments, therefore, in society and conversation, makes us form some general unalterable standard, by which we may approve or disapprove of characters and manners.[61]

Granted that the general point of view enables us to form "calm judgments concerning the characters of men" about which we may reach agreement despite our diverse perspectives and interests, how can Hume account at the same time for "the wide difference" between peoples and nations with regard to their "sentiments of morals"?

Hume's answer to this question is that we must consider "the first principles" which are shared and common to different peoples, however much their particular practices and sentiments may vary. By way of analogy, he observes:

... the Rhine flows north, the Rhone south; yet both spring from the *same* mountain, and are also actuated, in their opposite directions, by the same principle of gravity. The different inclinations of the ground, on which they run, cause all the difference of their courses.[62]

In the same vein, while morals and manners in different times and among different nations no doubt vary, the basic principles which animate and govern them remain fixed and constant.

... the principles upon which men reason in morals are always the same; though the conclusions which they draw are often very different ... Though many ages have elapsed since the fall of Greece and Rome; though many changes have arrived in religion, language, laws, and customs; none of these revolutions have ever produced any considerable innovation in the primary sentiments of morals, more than in those of external beauty.[63]

On Hume's account, then, the skeptic is someone who denies that we have any relevant moral standard by which to distinguish virtue from vice. Hume clearly rejects any skepticism of this kind, since he is firmly committed to the existence of a universal standard of virtue and moral excellence grounded on human happiness and utility. Consistent with these commitments, however, Hume grants that in different social and historical circumstances there are (very) different ways of understanding which virtues and vices matter most to us and what sort of conduct or practices are consistent with this more general standard of virtue. Variation and disagreement at this higher level is not evidence, however, that there is no relevant common or shared moral standard.[64] In taking this line, Hume is able to accommodate some considerable degree of moral relativism consistent with his firm rejection of skepticism.[65]

While it is evident that Hume seeks to explain the foundation of virtue and our approval of it in terms of considerations of utility to the possessor and those who may deal with her, he avoids committing himself to any simple or straight correlation between happiness and a virtuous character. The issues involved are, on his account, more complex and problematic than this. Hume does maintain that "the happiest disposition of the mind is the virtuous."[66] Two overlapping mechanisms help to sustain this correlation. In the first place, as we have noted, virtue secures love and approval from others, and vice serves to secure the opposite. Through the operation of sympathy, the love and esteem secured by virtue has a "secondary" influence on our own mind and generates a strong concern for our reputation and good name in the world.[67]

By our continual and earnest pursuit of a character, a name, a reputation in the world, we bring our own deportment and conduct frequently under review, and consider how they appear in the eyes of those who approach and regard us.[68]

Nevertheless, while the opinion of others is important to us and influences our happiness,[69] every person's "peace and inward satisfaction" depends primarily on the mind's ability to "bear its own survey."[70] Even if vice goes undetected by others it will still generate misery and unhappiness for the person who discovers it in himself.

This constant habit of surveying ourselves, as it were, in reflection, keeps alive all the sentiments of right and wrong, and begets, in noble natures, a certain reverence for themselves as well as others, which is the surest guardian of every virtue.[71]

These observations concerning the operations of the passions in human nature, guided by the influence of sympathy and our sociable nature, support the claim that there exists a generally reliable correlation between virtue and happiness, and vice and misery.

Although Hume is committed to this broadly optimistic view about the benefits of virtue for those who possess it, he is careful, nevertheless, to qualify this optimistic outlook and indicate its significant limitations. While virtue, he says, is "undoubtably the best choice, when it is attainable; yet such is the disorder and confusion of human affairs, that no perfect or regular distribution of happiness and misery is ever, in this life to be expected."[72] In this context (i.e. his essay "The Sceptic") he proceeds to itemize various ways in which our happiness is vulnerable to considerations and factors independent of virtue and vice. He points out, for example, that our bodily health and our mental dispositions may subject us to grief and sadness, even though we may be perfectly virtuous. Beyond this, he acknowledges that we are naturally vulnerable to the negative assessments and hostile dispositions of others, even though these attitudes may not be justified. Moreover, our sympathy and concern for those we are close to (family, friends, etc.) make us vulnerable to sharing any grief or sadness that may befall them.[73] On the other side of things, Hume is similarly aware that the vicious individual (e.g. "the sensible knave") may escape the censure of others and may even escape any source of remorse or shame by failing to reflect on his own character and conduct.[74] There is no way to ensure the vicious will always be unhappy. In short, there is for Hume no perfect moral harmony to be expected in this life such that the virtuous can be insulated against the vagaries of fortune and the contingencies of human existence. Indeed, Hume firmly rejects any such outlook as illusory and plainly at odds with human experience. The correlations that exist between virtue and happiness and vice and misery are, nevertheless, tight enough to sustain and support moral practice and social life.

VIRTUE, VOLUNTARINESS, AND THE NATURAL ABILITIES

An important and controversial feature of Hume's account of virtue is his particular understanding of the relevance of voluntariness for virtue and vice. This aspect of Hume's account is, obviously, intimately connected with his views on the subject of free will and moral responsibility.[75] There are two basic issues that arise in this sphere that need to be carefully distinguished.

(1) Does Hume hold that all aspects of virtue for which a person is subject to moral evaluation (i.e. approval and disapproval) must be voluntarily *expressed*? That is to say, are virtues and vices to be assessed entirely on the basis of an agent's deliberate choices and intentional actions?

(2) Granted that virtues and vices are to be understood in terms of a person's pleasant or painful qualities of mind, to what extent are these traits of character voluntarily *acquired* (i.e. acquired through the agent's own will and choices)?

Hume's answer to both questions is clear. He denies that voluntary or intentional action is the sole basis on which we may assess a person's virtues and vices. Furthermore he also maintains that moral character is, for the most part, involuntarily acquired. The second claim does not, of course, commit him to the first. Nor does the first commit him to the second, since a person could voluntarily acquire traits that, once acquired, may be involuntarily expressed or manifest. Plainly the combination of claims that Hume embraces on this issue commits him to a position that radically deflates the significance and importance of voluntariness in relation to virtue – certainly in comparison with some familiar alternative accounts (e.g. as in Aristotle).

Let us consider, first, the relevance of voluntariness to the expression of character. As we have already noted, Hume does take the view that actions serve as the principal way in which we learn about a person's character.[76] Action is produced by the causal influence of our desires and willings. The interpretation and evaluation of action must, therefore, take note of the particular intention with which an action was undertaken. Failing this, we are liable to attribute character traits to the agent that he does not possess (and consequently unjustly praise or blame him).[77] Although intention and action do have a significant and important role to play in the assessment of moral character, Hume also maintains that there are other channels through which character may be expressed. More specifically, a virtuous or vicious character can be distinguished by reference to a person's "wishes and sentiments," as well as by the nature of the person's will.[78] Feelings, desires and sentiments manifest themselves in a wide variety of ways – not just through willing and acting. A person's "countenance and conversation,"[79] deportment or "carriage,"[80] gestures,[81] or simply her look and expression, may all serve as signs of character and qualities of mind that may be found to be pleasant or painful.[82] Although we may enjoy some limited degree of control over our desires and passions, as well as how they are expressed, for the most part our emotional states and attitudes arise in us involuntarily and may even be manifest or expressed *against* our will.

We may now turn to the further question concerning Hume's understanding of the way in which virtues and vices are acquired and, in particular, to what extent they are shaped and conditioned by our own choices. It is Hume's view that, by and large, our character is conditioned and determined by factors independent of our will. In the passages entitled "Of liberty and necessity"[83] he argues that not only do we observe how certain characters will act in specific circumstances, we also observe how circumstances condition character. Among the factors that determine character, he claims, are bodily condition, age, sex, occupation and social station, climate, religion, government, and education.[84] These various causal influences account for "the diversity of characters, prejudices, and opinions."[85] Any accurate moral philosophy, it is argued, must acknowledge and take note of the forces that "mould the human mind from its infancy" and which account for "the gradual change in our sentiments and inclinations" through time.[86] The general force of these observations is to establish that "the fabric and constitution of our mind no more depends on our choice, than that of our body."[87]

Critics of Hume's position on this subject will argue that if a person has little or no control over the factors that shapes her character then virtue and vice really would be, in these circumstances, matters of mere good or bad fortune and no more a basis for *moral* concern than bodily beauty or ugliness. If people are responsible *for* the characters their actions and feelings express, then they must have *acquired* that character voluntarily.[88] Hume's reply to this line of criticism is that we can perfectly well distinguish virtue and vice without making any reference to the way that character is acquired. Our moral sentiments are reactions or responses to the moral qualities and character traits that people manifest in their behavior and conduct, and thus need not be withdrawn simply because people do not choose or voluntarily acquire these moral characteristics. Hume does recognize, of course, that we do have some limited ability to amend and alter our character.[89] In particular, Hume acknowledges that we can cultivate and improve our moral character, in some measure, through self-criticism and self-understanding. Nevertheless, the points he emphasizes are that all such efforts are limited in their scope and effect and that, beyond this, "a man must be, before-hand, tolerably virtuous" for such efforts of "reformation" to be undertaken in the first place.[90]

Hume's views about the relationship between virtue and voluntariness do much to explain one of the most controversial aspects of his theory of virtue: his view that the natural abilities should be incorporated into the virtues and vices.[91] With respect to this issue he makes two key points. The first is that natural abilities (i.e. intelligence, imagination, memory, wit, etc.) and moral virtues more narrowly understood are "equally mental qualities."[92] Second, both of them "equally produce pleasure" and thus have "an equal tendency to produce the love and esteem of mankind."[93] In common life, people "naturally praise or blame whatever pleases or displeases them and thus regard penetration as much a virtue as justice."[94] Beyond all this, as already noted, any distinction between the natural abilities and moral virtues cannot be based on the consideration that the natural abilities are for the most part involuntarily acquired, since this also holds true for the moral virtues more narrowly conceived. It is, nevertheless, Hume's view that the voluntary/involuntary distinction helps to explain "why moralists have invented" the distinction between natural abilities and moral virtues. Unlike moral qualities, natural abilities "are almost invariable by any art or industry."[95] In contrast with this, moral qualities, "or at least, the actions that proceed from them, may be chang'd by the motives of rewards and punishments, praise and blame."[96] In this way, according to Hume, the significance of the voluntary/involuntary distinction is largely limited to our concern with the *regulation of conduct* in society. To confine our understanding of virtue and vice to these frontiers is, however, to distort and misrepresent its very nature and foundation in human life and experience.

MORAL SENSE, "MORAL BEAUTY," AND MORAL DEVELOPMENT

On the face of it, Hume's understanding of the relationship between virtue and moral sense (i.e. our ability to feel moral sentiments and draw moral distinctions on this basis)[97] seems straightforward. As we have noted, Hume defines virtue and vice as qualities of mind that give rise to moral sentiments of approval and disapproval.[98] Hume's account of virtue leans heavily on the analogy of "moral beauty."[99] The suggestion that virtue may be understood in terms of "moral beauty" presents a number of puzzles about how exactly Hume understands the relationship between virtue and moral sense. According to Hume's analysis, both beauty and virtue affect people pleasurably, and that pleasure gives rise to some form of love or approval. Clearly, however, a beautiful person need not herself have any sense of beauty or deformity in order to be beautiful or become an object of love produced by the pleasure she occasions. These observations raise the question of whether a person can be virtuous if they lack *moral sense*? That is, for a person to be capable of virtue must she possess moral sense? Surprisingly, Hume does not provide any clear statement about where he stands on this important issue.

This puzzle relates to another more general concern about identifying those individuals who may or may not be capable of virtue or vice (and who are appropriate objects of our moral sentiments). Hume points out that "animals have little or no sense of virtue and vice."[100] It does not follow from this, however, that animals lack pleasant or painful qualities of mind. Moreover, Hume makes clear that animals "are endow'd with thought and reason as well as men"[101] and that they are no less capable of sympathy and passions such as love and hate.[102] It cannot be Hume's view that animals are incapable of virtue and vice simply because they acquire their mental traits involuntarily, since Hume denies that voluntariness serves as a relevant basis for attributing virtues or vices. Finally, while it is true that human beings are superior to animals in respect of reason, Hume maintains that differences of this kind can also be found from one person to another.[103] In light of this we may also ask if Hume's account of virtue includes "mad-men"[104] and small children. These individuals are obviously people and, as such, according to Hume's principles, they too possess mental qualities that may be found pleasant or painful and could be regarded as legitimate objects of moral sentiment – however incapacitated or limited they may be in respect of reason, moral sense, and so on.

It may be argued, consistent with Hume's commitments, that there is more to be said about the absence of moral sense in animals, the insane and human infants as this relates to their incapacity for virtue. More specifically, it may be argued that there is a deeper and more intimate connection between virtue and moral sense than Hume's remarks appear to suggest. Our general capacity of moral sense (i.e. to generate and entertain moral sentiments of approval and disapproval) has an important role to play in the way that we *acquire* the virtues and *sustain* them. Hume's own remarks relating to the way in which the artificial virtues are established and maintained provides some basis for seeing why this may be so. As already noted, Hume describes in some detail how the conventions of justice arise through an original motive of self-interest and the way in which we come to *moralize* them. According to Hume, children quickly learn the advantages of following the established conventions of their society and the importance of their "reputation" for justice.[105] Children learn, through the influence of custom and education, to see any "violations as base and infamous."[106] It is, therefore, through the channel and mechanism of moral sentiment that the artificial virtues are established and secured.

Although Hume has less to say about the role of moral sentiment in relation to the natural virtues, similar observations would seem to apply. As a child grows up and matures, she is made aware that her mental qualities, as they affect others and herself, will inevitably give rise to moral sentiments in the people she comes into contact with. When a person is generous and benevolent, not only will she be treated well by others, she will become aware that she is being treated well *because* other people approve of her virtue. Through the influence of sympathy, the approval of others will itself become an independent source of her own happiness and provide further grounds for feeling proud or approving of herself. This entire process of becoming aware of the moral sentiments of others, and then "surveying ourselves as we appear to others," serves to develop the natural as well as the artificial virtues.[107] According to Hume this disposition to "survey ourselves" and seek our own "peace and satisfaction" is "the surest guardian of every virtue."[108] In light of these considerations, it may be argued that moral reflection, where we direct our moral sense at ourselves and review our own character and conduct from a general point of view, serves as a master virtue, whereby a person is able to cultivate and sustain other, more particular virtues. An agent who entirely lacks this disposition will be shameless and such a person will inevitably lack all those virtues that depend on moral reflection for their development and stability.[109]

Having established that there is an intimate relationship – we may describe it as an "internal" relationship – between virtue and moral sense, whereby the development and reliability of the former requires a capacity for the latter, we may now return to the question of why animals, the insane, and human infants are incapable of virtue and vice (and, as such, inappropriate objects of moral sentiment). If moral sense is required for the full development and stability of a virtuous character, we must ask what is required to develop and preserve moral sense. Although Hume is often read as presenting a "thin" account of moral sense, taking it to be constituted simply by pleasant and painful feelings of a peculiar kind,[110] this reading does not do justice to the full complexity and subtlety of his position.[111] In a number of contexts, most notably in the first section of the second *Enquiry*, Hume argues that the moral evaluation of character and conduct involves the activity of both reason and sentiment.

The final sentence, it is probable, which pronounces characters and actions amiable or odious, praiseworthy or blameable ... depends on some internal sense or feeling; which nature has made universal in the whole species ... But in order to pave the way for such sentiment, and give a proper discernment of its object, it is often necessary, we find, that much reasoning should precede, that nice distinctions should be made, just conclusions drawn, distinct comparisons formed, complicated relations examined, and general facts fixed and ascertained.[112]

Hume explains this feature of his moral system by returning to the analogy of "moral beauty."

The kind of beauty we associate with the "finer arts," in contrast with natural beauty where our approbation is immediately aroused without the aid of any reasoning, also requires a considerable amount of reasoning "in order to feel the proper sentiment; and a false relish may frequently be corrected by argument and reflection."[113] Hume argues that in a similar manner "moral beauty . . . demands the assistance of our intellectual faculties, in order to give it a suitable influence on the human mind."[114] The sort of "intellectual" activities required include, not only learning from experience the specific tendencies of certain kinds of conduct, as well as the ability to distinguish accurately among them, but also the ability to evaluate character and conduct from "some steady and general point of view."[115] Our ability to enter this general point of view and evaluate a person's character and conduct from this perspective, is essential, on Hume's account, if we are to be able to formulate a "standard of merit" that we can *all* share and refer to.[116]

The significance of this account of how our moral sense depends on the activity and influence of our "intellectual faculties" in relation to virtue is clear. Insofar as the cultivation and sustenance of virtue depends on moral sense, it follows that virtue also requires the intellectual qualities involved in the exercise of moral sense. An animal, an infant, or an insane person obviously lacks the ability to perform the intellectual tasks involved in producing moral sentiment. Such an individual will not be capable of acquiring those virtues that depend on moral sentiment. It follows that we cannot expect the virtues that are so dependent to be present when the relevant psychological capacities and mechanisms are absent, damaged, or underdeveloped.

The account provided of the relationship between virtue and moral sense, drawing from material provided by Hume, suggests a revision of his account of virtue is required. Virtues and vices should be understood not simply in terms of pleasurable and painful qualities of mind that arouse moral sentiments in the spectator, as this fails to explain the relevant dependency of virtue on moral sense (i.e. the genesis of virtue through the activity of moral sense). Among its failings, the broader account, as we have noted, requires Hume to include the natural abilities as being on "the same footing" as the moral virtues and leaves him unable to provide a plausible, principled distinction between those individuals who are or are not appropriate objects of our moral sentiments. A revised account of virtue would narrow its scope: virtues and vices are those pleasurable or painful qualities of mind that are capable of being cultivated or diminished, sustained, or inhibited, through the activity and exercise of moral reflection and moral sense. This way of delineating virtue and vice, and narrowing its scope, provides a principled way of distinguishing between natural abilities and moral virtues, as well as distinguishing between those individuals who are capable of virtue and vice and those who are not.[117]

The account provided of the disposition to moral reflection, considered as a "master virtue" and dependent on moral sense, fills what is otherwise a problematic gap in Hume's theory of virtue. It is often claimed that what is missing from Hume's theory is any plausible account of moral capacity along the lines of Aristotle's account of practical wisdom (itself understood as a master virtue). It may be argued, on the basis of the revised account that has been provided, that Hume's master virtue of moral reflection fills this gap. Using an analogy suggested by Aristotle, our moral sense, as Hume understands it, may be described as functioning like the rudder on a ship, which keeps us sailing in the direction of virtue, away from the rocks of vice.[118] This rudder, however, cannot guide us by means of either reason or feeling alone. On the contrary, for moral sense to guide us in the direction of virtue we must first exercise those "intellectual faculties" that "pave the way" for our sentiments of approval and disapproval. Our moral sense, therefore, operates effectively to promote and sustain virtue only through the *fusion* of reason and sentiment.

VIRTUE, VICE, AND SUPERSTITION: IRRELIGION AND PRACTICAL MORALITY

In the introduction, we noted Hume's concluding remarks in the *Treatise* where he suggests that his anatomy of virtue may be put to some practical use.[119] On the face of it, these remarks could be read as a straightforward part of his broadly "naturalistic" program and his project of a "science of man." On this reading, Hume believes that he has extended "the experimental method of reasoning into moral subjects" (as indicated by the subtitle of this work) and he is leaving it to others to put this advance in science to practical use in common life. Hume's anatomy of virtue, so interpreted, serves to place moral philosophy on scientific foundations that presuppose a necessitarian and wholly naturalistic understanding of human nature as a seamless part of the causal fabric of the world. A theory of virtue, constructed along these lines, has no need for a metaphysics of immaterial agents, governed by a transcendent being and laws of reason that operate and apply independently of the (mechanical) natural order. Nor does Hume's theory of virtue require a teleological conception of human nature that presupposes virtuous agents must acquire some rational insight into their essential nature or the ends or purposes that this may involve. Hume's naturalism, considered as a foundation for his account of virtue, is systematically skeptical about all metaphysical outlooks of these kinds.

While it is certainly true that Hume's theory of virtue should be placed in the wider context of his naturalistic ambitions, this raises the more general question of whether Hume's overall philosophical intentions throughout his philosophy should be read in these naturalistic terms (along with their related skeptical commitments). One important corollary of reading Hume in this way has been to take his concern with questions of religion as being of marginal or minor concern in his earlier work in the *Treatise*, becoming more pronounced and prominent only in his later works (i.e. particularly in the first *Enquiry* and the *Dialogues*). On this general reading, Hume's concern with the relationship between religion and morality is not central to his aims and objectives in the *Treatise* and remains of peripheral concern even in the second *Enquiry*. Clearly this way of reading Hume will encourage the view that his theory of virtue, although no doubt relevant to problems of religion, is nevertheless a matter that we can set aside as only of derivative interest – not part of Hume's main program.

While this is not the place to engage in a full examination of Hume's fundamental philosophical intentions, and how they evolved and developed over time, this general picture of Hume's philosophy as it relates to his theory of virtue should be challenged and questioned. I have argued elsewhere that the skeptical and naturalistic themes found in Hume's philosophy in the *Treatise*, as well as in his later works, must be understood and interpreted

with reference to his deeper irreligious or anti-Christian motivations and objectives.[120] What animates and structures Hume's arguments throughout the *Treatise*, I maintain, is his (skeptical) effort
to discredit the doctrines and dogmas of religion and to provide an
alternative secular, scientific account of moral and social life. These
irreligious features of Hume's *Treatise* also serve to guide and shape
the development and evolution of Hume's thought in his later works
(i.e. irreligious aims and ambitions serve to unify, structure, and
direct his thought not only in the *Treatise* but throughout all his
major philosophical works). According to this general interpretation
of Hume's philosophy, it is crucial that we consider his theory of
virtue in light of his core irreligious objectives and concerns.

In the most general terms, it is a basic aim of Hume's moral philosophy to strip away the metaphysical commitments and distortions of
theology and religious philosophy. Hume's specific views about the
virtues reflect these core concerns. Among the most significant of
the various observations and claims Hume makes along these lines
is his critique of the efforts of the Christian moralists and apologists
to present humility as a virtue and pride as a vice – a view that Hume
claims reverses the truth about this matter.[121] Related to this, Hume
employs his (constructive) account of virtue to criticize and ridicule
religious morality, presenting it as both corrupting and pernicious in
its influence. The natural and universal standard of morals, based on
considerations of utility, Hume claims, "will ever be received, where
men judge of things by their natural, unprejudiced reason, without
the delusive glosses of superstition and false religion."[122]

Celibacy, fasting, penance, mortification, self-denial, humility, silence, soli-
tude, and the whole train of monkish virtues; for what reason are they
everywhere rejected by men of sense, but because they serve to no manner
of purpose...[123]

These "monkish virtues," he continues, not only fail to serve any
of the desirable ends of virtue, they "stupefy the understanding and
harden the heart, obscure the fancy and sour the temper." Hume concludes these observations regarding the real effect of the "monkish
virtues" inspired by religion, by suggesting that we should "trans-
fer them to the opposite column, and place them in the catalogue
of vices."[124] Observations of this general kind, relating to the way

in which religion corrupts and distorts moral standards and moral practice, are laced throughout Hume's writings.[125]

While the pronounced tendency of religion is to corrupt and pervert morality, Hume makes clear that virtue is attainable without any support from superstition. He addresses this issue directly in the first *Enquiry*, where he allows "Epicurus" to speak on his behalf. Although Epicurus/Hume may well deny providence and the doctrine of a future state, he does not deny "the course itself of events, which lie open to every one's inquiry and examination." He continues:

I acknowledge, that, in the present order of things, virtue is attended with more peace of mind than vice, and meets with a more favorable reception from the world. I am sensible, that, according to the past experience of mankind, friendship is the chief source of joy in human life, and moderation the only source of tranquility and happiness. I never balance between the virtuous and vicious course of life; but I am sensible, that, to a well-disposed mind, every advantage is on the side of the former.[126]

It is, then, Hume's considered view that a careful anatomy of virtue, displaying its foundations in human sympathy and consideration of utility, can serve to guide our practice and structure our institutions in a manner that will free them of the corrupting and pernicious influence of superstition. To this extent it is indeed the case that Hume's "cold and unentertaining" dissection of virtue serves the purposes of a "practical morality" by discrediting religious morality and putting in its place a secular morality based on the secure and credible foundations of a proper understanding of human nature and the human condition.

NOTES

1 Abbreviations for references to Hume's works are
    D   *Dialogues concerning Natural Religion* (Hume [1779] 1993)
    Dial.   "A Dialogue" (published with *EM*)
    DP   *A Dissertation on the Passions* ([1757] 2007)
    EM   *Enquiry concerning the Principles of Morals* ([1751] 1998)
    ESY   *Essays: Moral, Political, and Literary* ([1777] 1985)
    EU   *An Enquiry Concerning Human Understanding* ([1748] 2000, ed. Beauchamp)
    LET   *The Letters of David Hume* (1932)

NHR *Natural History of Religion* ([1757] 1993)

T   *A Treatise of Human Nature* ([1739–40] 2000, ed. Norton and Norton)

TA   *An Abstract of A Treatise of Human Nature* ([1740] 2000). References are also provided to the Selby-Bigge/Nidditch editions of the *Treatise* (1978) and *Enquiries* (1975). Following the convention given in the Nortons' *Treatise* (and Beauchamp's *Enquiry*), citations are to book.part.section.paragraph, followed by *page* references to the Selby-Bigge/Nidditch editions. Thus *T* 1.2.3.4/34 will indicate *Treatise* bk. 1, pt. 2, §3, para. 4/Selby-Bigge/Nidditch p. 34. The citations of *EM* App. are by appendix number.section (e.g. *EM* App. 1.2, Appendix 1 §2); and those of *EM* Dial., by section – each followed by the corresponding Selby-Bigge/Nidditch page reference.

2 *T* Intro 4–10/xix–xxiii; *TA* 1/645; see also *LET* 1 13 (no. 3); *EM* 1.10, 517/174, 219.

3 *T* Intro 3/xviii; *T* 3.1.1.1/456; *EU* 1.1–2, 1.7/5–6, 9.

4 *T* 3.3.6.6/621, Hume's emphasis; cf. *TA* 1–2/645–6.

5 *T* 2.1.2.2, 2.1.5.3, 2.2.1.2, 2.2.1.6/277, 286, 329, 331.

6 *T* 2.1.2.5, 2.1.5.2/279, 285.

7 For further details relating to Hume's description of the indirect passions see Árdal 1966, chap. 2, and P. Russell 1995, chap. 4.

8 *T* 2.1.2.5, 2.1.7/279, 294–5.

9 *T* 3.3.1.3/575, Hume's emphasis; cf. *T* 3.1.2.5/473; *DP* 2.14–16, 3.1.

10 *T* 3.3.5.1/614. Hume takes the moral sentiments to be calm forms of love and hate. In support of this interpretation see Árdal 1966, chap. 6.

11 *DP* 6.19.

12 On Hume's views concerning the nature of character see Baier 1991, chap. 8, and Pitson 2002, chap. 5.

13 *T* 3.3.1.4/575.

14 E.g. *EU* 8.7/83, where ambition, avarice, self-love, vanity, etc., are described as "passions"; see also *EM* 9.5/271; *T* 3.3.3.3.3–8/603–4.

15 *T* 2.3.4.1/419.

16 Exactly how passions are understood to "endure" is a matter requiring some further interpretation and analysis. We need, for example, to distinguish "types" and "tokens" of a given passion. While Hume may be read as holding that specific *tokens* of the passions are more "durable" than other perceptions, on another interpretation he may be read as claiming that a person has a given character trait only insofar as a particular *type* of passion regularly appears in her mind and influences her behavior and conduct.

17 *T* 3.2.1.2/477: "'Tis evident that when we praise..."; see also *T* 2.2.3.4/348–9.

18 *T* 3.3.1.4/575, Hume's emphasis.

19 *T* 3.3.1.5/575, Hume's emphasis. See also Hume's remarks to Francis Hutcheson: *LET* 1 34. Earlier in the *Treatise* Hume claims that intentional action always reveals or manifests some durable principle of mind or a character trait of some kind (*T* 2.2.3.4/349). Although Hume provides little support for this claim, he does, as I explain, provide more substantial support for the (distinct) claim that only durable principles of mind give rise to moral sentiments. For a more detailed discussion of this point see P. Russell (1995), 98, 112–3.

20 See e.g. *T* 2.3.2.6/411.

21 *T* 2.1.6.3/291.

22 *T* 2.1.5.2/285; see also *T* 2.5.5.5, 2.2.1.7/286, 331.

23 *T* 2.1.6.4/293.

24 *T* 2.1.6.4/293; cf. *DP* 2.11, 2.42.

25 *T* 2.2.3.6, 2.3.2.6, 3.3.1.4/349, 411, 575.

26 For more detailed accounts of this distinction see e.g. Ballie 2000 and Cohon 2006.

27 *T* 3.1.2.9/474–5.

28 *T* 3.3.1.12/579.

29 *EM* 3.44–6/202–3.

30 *EM* App. 3.5/305.

31 *T* 3.2.2.23–4, 3.3.1.12/498–500, 579–80.

32 *T* 3.2.

33 *T* 3.3.1.30/591; cf. *T* 3.3.2.16/601.

34 In this respect Hume's system contrasts sharply with that of his (Scots-Irish) contemporary Francis Hutcheson (Hutcheson [1726] 2004, II §§ii–vii).

35 *T* 3.3.1.24/587; *EM* 9.2/269.

36 *EM* 9.2/269–70.

37 *EM* 9.2/269.

38 See Beauchamp for a more extensive list of Hume's catalogue of the virtues (*EM* editor's introduction, pp. 30–7). In a letter to Hutcheson Hume remarks that he takes his "Catalogue of Virtues from *Cicero's Offices*, not from the *Whole Duty of Man*." (*Whole Duty of Man* was a seventeenth-century Calvinist tract, which is discussed relation to Hume in Kemp Smith 1947, pp. 4–6.) Among other possible sources for Hume's views about character is Theophrastus' *Characters*, and also French writers such as La Bruyère (who translated Theophrastus' *Characters*).

39 *T* 3.3.6.2/618–9; *EM* App. 1.18, Dial. 37/293, 336. Hume acknowledges
    that this analysis may suggest that the ultimate source for our approval
    of virtuous characters is no different from what we experience when
    we contemplate a house, furniture and other such inanimate objects
    (*T* 3.3.1.20, 2.2.5.6/584, 617; *EM* 2.10, 5.1/179, 212). He maintains,
    however, that while the general source may be the same (i.e. consider-
    ations of utility) the specific feelings involved (i.e. the felt sentiments
    in our mind) are not (*T* 3.3.5.6/617; *EM* 5.1 n. 17/213 n.). For a criticism
    of this aspect of Hume's system see A. Smith [1790] 1976, pp. 188, 327.
40 *T* 3.3.4.2/607.
41 *EM* 9.2/269–70; cf. *T* 3.3.3.9/606.
42 Hume's *History of England* is another good source of examples of
    virtues and vices as they appear throughout history. Dees (1997) dis-
    cusses several illuminating examples taken from this source.
43 *T* 3.3.4.2/607–8; *EM* App. 4.6/316.
44 *EM* App. 4.17/320.
45 *ESY* 594. Hume's observations and examples relating to models of
    virtue suggest that he is committed to two distinct but closely related
    claims: (1) pluralism – where this is understood as the view that there
    exists a wide variety of models of a virtuous person and that virtuous
    individuals may possess very different combinations of virtue and lead
    very different kinds of life; and (2) fragmentation – where this is under-
    stood as the observation that few, if any, individuals are wholly virtu-
    ous or wholly vicious, since almost everyone possesses some mixture
    or combination of virtues and vices. These two claims (pluralism and
    fragmentation) lend some support to what may be described as Hume's
    tacit "anti-perfectionism." Understood this way, Hume is resistant to
    the (optimistic) ideal that suggests that all the virtues may coexist
    in one individual who is free of any taint of vice. Hume's examples
    and observations suggest that the virtues and vices are so related to
    each other that any ideal of this kind is not just difficult to attain,
    but illusory or impossible. For the purposes of human ethical life, and
    its associated limitations, we are better served by (credible) examples
    such as Caesar and Cato than by any ideal "perfect being" (e.g. Jesus
    Christ).
46 *T* 3.2.6.7/529.
47 *EM* 7.22/258, Hume's emphasis; cf. *EM* 2.18, 6.12/180, 238.
48 *T* 3.3.2.15/600–1, *EM* 2.3, 7.24/177, 258.
49 *T* 3.3.3.3/604.
50 *EM* 258 n.
51 Aristotle, *Nicomachean Ethics* (cited as *NE*) II.6. For present pur-
    poses, I take the Aristotelian doctrine of "the mean" to be

understood as claiming that all the virtues are traits of character that lie between two extremes of excess and defect, on each side of which we find a corresponding vice. On this reading, the virtues must be interpreted and understood in relation to the relevant vices that they fall between. (There are, of course, significant ambiguities in Aristotle's remarks concerning this doctrine and interpretations of his views vary.)

52 For Hume "moderation" is primarily a matter of the calm as opposed to violent passions governing our conduct and disposition and, related to this, acquiring "strength of mind," whereby (violent) passions and desires, aroused by a present or nearby object, are restrained with a view to longer term interests and concerns (T 2.3.4.1/417; EM 6.15/239–40; DP 5.4). There is a sense in which people with dispositions and traits of these kinds may be described as possessing the general virtue of "reasonableness," consistent with Hume's basic principles. On Hume's views about calm passions and "strength of mind" see Árdal 1966, chap. 5; and also Árdal 1976.

53 EM 6.19, 6.26 n. 31, App. 4.11, Dial. 25/241, 245 n., 318, 321, 333.

54 EM 6.35/248–9; see also his essay "Of National Characters."

55 EM 5.3/214.

56 EM 6.20/242; see also Hume's remarks about Fabius and Scipio at EM 6.9/237.

57 There is a degree of instability or an unsettled tension in Hume's overall position on this matter. On one side, Hume wants to argue that when evaluating a person or character we should exclude "external circumstances" that may frustrate or obstruct the full beneficial effect or influence of a given trait in producing happiness (T 3.3.1.20/584–5; see in particular his remarks about "virtue in rags . . . "). On the other hand, Hume also wants to insist that a virtuous person must be one whose character is in fact suitable to his particular circumstances and social conditions (EM 6.9, 6.20/237, 241–2). On the second interpretation, a person whose character is ill-suited to his historical circumstances and social station will be found wanting from the point of view of virtue, even when considered from a more disinterested and distant point of view. See P. Russell 1995, pp. 130–3.

58 T 3.3.1.15–23, 3.3.1.30, 3.3.3.2, 3.3.6.3/581–7, 591, 603, 619; EM 1.2, 5.39, App. 1.3/169–75, 225–9, 286.

59 T 3.3.1.15–8/581–4; EM 5.39–42/225–9.

60 T 3.3.6.1–3/618–9; EM 5.42 n. 25, App. 1.10/229 n., 289.

61 EM 5.42/229; see also T 3.3.1.18, 3.3.1.30, 3.3.3.2/583–4, 591, 603.

62 EM, Dial. 26/333.

63 *EM*, Dial. 36/335. Hume, of course, emphasizes throughout his writings the parallels that hold between morals and aesthetics. I return to this analogy further below.

64 See, in particular, Hume's various remarks and observations about incest, suicide, adultery, infanticide, homosexuality, dueling, and other such matters of moral disagreement and divergence in his "A Dialogue."

65 While it is evident that Hume rests his (universal) standard of morals on the general foundation of utility, there is some debate about the precise nature and extent of his "utilitarian" commitments as they relate to his virtue theory. See e.g. Crisp 2005 and Swanton 2007a. Suffice it to note that Hume does not embrace utilitarianism insofar as this is understood in terms of a requirement to *maximize* this good (in contrast with Hutcheson [1726] 2004, II §3, no. 8).

66 *ESY* 168.

67 *T* 2.1.11.1, 2.2.5.21/316, 365.

68 *EM* 9.10/276; see also *T* 3.2.2.26/500–1.

69 *T* 2.1.11.1, 2.1.11.9, 2.2.1.9/316, 320, 331–2.

70 *T* 3.3.6.6/620; *EM* 9.23/283.

71 *EM* 9.10/276; cf. *EM* 9.23/283; and also *T* 2.1.11.1, 3.3.5.4, 3.3.6.6/316, 615, 620.

72 *ESY* 178.

73 From Hume's perspective we have no more reason to assume that the virtuous must always be happy than we have reason to expect that the beautiful or rich will always be happy. Nevertheless, while there are multiple factors that influence the happiness or misery of every individual, virtue remains an especially weighty factor in securing and preserving our happiness.

74 *EM* 9.22/282–3.

75 A full examination of this aspect of Hume's philosophy is presented in P. Russell 1995.

76 *T* 3.3.1.5/575.

77 For Hume, behavior that is not caused by an agent's will and is wholly involuntary is not, strictly speaking, action at all. If a person's behavior is produced by external causes then it does not reflect on the mind of the person and cannot serve as a basis for moral assessment with respect to virtue and vice. However, what matters here is not simply that the behavior in question is involuntary but that it does not reflect on the person's qualities of mind or character.

78 *T* 3.3.1.5/575.

79 *T* 2.1.11.3/317.

80 *EU* 8.15/88.

81 *EU* 8.9/85.

82 Hume observes, for example, that a person may conduct himself in a wholly honorable way, and with "great integrity," and yet still have a gloomy and melancholy disposition which is "to our sentiments, a vice or imperfection" (*ESY* 179).

83 *T* 2.3.1–2; *EU* 8.

84 *T* 2.3.1.5–10/401–3; *EU* 8.7–15/83–8; see esp. *EU* 8.11/85–6: "Are the manners..."

85 *EU* 8.10/85. See also Hume's essay "Of National Characters," where he distinguishes between physical and moral causes (*ESY* 198).

86 *EU* 8.11/86.

87 *ESY* 168; see also *T* 3.3.4.3/608; *ESY* 140, 160, 579.

88 See Reid 1969, p. 261: "What was, by an ancient author, said of Cato, might indeed be said of him. *He was good because he could not be otherwise.* But this saying, if understood literally and strictly, is not praise of Cato, but of his constitution, which was no more the work of Cato, than his existence" (Reid's emphasis).

89 He takes up this issue at some length in his essay "The Sceptic," where he emphasizes the limits of philosophy in promoting virtue (*ESY* 168–80).

90 *ESY* 169.

91 *T* 3.3.4; *EM* App. 4.

92 *T* 3.3.4.1/606.

93 *T* 3.3.4.1/606–7.

94 *T* 3.3.4.4/609. See Hume's sardonic observation at *EM* App. 4.5/315: "It is hard to tell..." See Vitz 2009 for a discussion of Hume's rejection of the (Aristotelian) distinction between intellectual and moral virtues.

95 *T* 3.3.4.4/609.

96 *T* 3.3.4.4/609.

97 *T* 2.3.2/470–6; *EM* 1/169–75.

98 *T* 3.1.2.5, 3.3.1.3, 3.3.5.1/473, 575, 614; *EM* 8.1 n. 50, App. 1.10/261 n., 289.

99 *T* 2.1.7.7, 2.1.8, 3.2.2.1, 3.3.1.15, 3.3.1.27, 3.3.6.1/297, 298–303, 484, 576–7, 589–90, 618; *EM* 1.9, 6.24, App. 1.13/173, 244, 291; *ESY* 153. This analogy is prominent in Shaftesbury ([1711] 1964) and Hutcheson ([1726] 2004). The analogy between beauty and virtue has a deep basis in the details of Hume's system. With reference to the individuals who are the objects of evaluation, both beauty and virtue are pleasurable qualities and, as such, engage the general mechanism of the indirect passions (as described above). With regard to those evaluating beauty or virtue, in both cases the relevant standard of evaluation presupposes a judge with the requisite experience and discrimination required for

reliable evaluation. These structural similarities are fundamental to Hume's understanding of "moral beauty."

100   *T* 2.1.12.5/326.

101   *T* 1.3.16.1/176.

102   *T* 2.2.5.15, 2.2.12, 2.3.9.32/363, 397–8, 448; *EM* App. 2.13/302.

103   *T* 3.3.4.5/610.

104   *T* 2.3.1.13/404.

105   *T* 3.2.2.4, 3.2.2.26, 3.2.6.11/486, 500–1, 533–4; *EM* 3.21/192.

106   *T* 3.2.2.26/500–1.

107   *T* 3.3.1.8, 3.3.1.26, 3.3.1.30, 3.3.6.6/576–7, 589, 591, 620; *EM* 9.10, App. 4.3/276, 314.

108   *EM* 9.10/276.

109   The presence of moral sense, and the associated master virtue of moral reflection, is not a *perfect* guarantor that a person will always act in a morally admirable manner. It is, however, a reliable sign that this person will be strongly motivated to virtue, and that whenever she departs from this standard she will aim to reform her conduct accordingly.

110   *T* 3.1.2.4/472.

111   Hume's presentation in the *Treatise* does differ in emphasis in that he places greater weight on "moral taste" in contrast with "reason" (*T* 3.3.1.15, 3.3.1.27/581, 589).

112   *EM* 1.9/172–3.

113   *EM* 1.9/173. On this see Hume's essay "The Standard of Taste."

114   *EM* 1.9/173.

115   *T* 3.3.1.15/581–2; *EM* 5.41–2/227–8.

116   *T* 3.3.1.18, 3.3.3.2/583, 603.

117   On this account of the "internal" relationship between virtue and moral sense it is not only a matter of the former depending on the latter for its development or production, moral sense is also required for the exercise and operation of virtue. More specifically, (a) the virtuous person is one who recognizes and appreciates relevant moral considerations or reasons as having a certain salience and significance, and thereby possessing motivational weight; and (b) the virtuous person is someone who has appropriate (emotional) responses to character and conduct (i.e. his own as well as others'). In both these aspects moral sense is essential to the exercise and operation of virtue – it is not just an extrinsic or "external" feature of the virtuous person. (In contrast with this the natural abilities lack this "internal" relationship with moral sense and are *insensitive* to its operation and exercise.)

118   Aristotle, *NE* x.1, 1172a21. For further elaboration on this theme see P. Russell 2006.

119 *T* 3.3.6.6/621.
120 P. Russell 2008.
121 *T* 3.3.2.13/599–600; *EM* 8.11, App. 2.12/265–6, 301; *ESY* 86. Hume's views on this subject allow for some important qualifications concerning the extent to which we may manifest or show our pride or sense of self-worth, consistent with due regard for the feelings of others. Nevertheless, the meek and humble person is not one whom Hume finds admirable, in contrast with the evident dignity of the duly proud person.
122 *EM* 9.3/270.
123 *EM* 9.3/270.
124 *EM* 9.3/270.
125 See e.g. *EM* 5.3, App. 4.21/214, 322; *D* 123–5; *NHR*, chap. 14.
126 *EU* 11.20/140.

6 The historic decline of virtue ethics

INTRODUCTION: AFTER VIRTUE?

It may seem somewhat outdated to use Alasdair MacIntyre's depiction of the decline in *After Virtue* as a foil for this chapter, given that it appeared as long ago as 1981 and has been extensively discussed. The much more nuanced views that have emerged from detailed studies of the philosophy of the Renaissance and early modernity in recent decades would seem to make it unnecessary to take up, once again, the old stereotype that that age is characterized by "shaking off the yoke of Aristotelianism." So why flog that horse again? The reason to start with MacIntyre's provocative thesis lies in its simplicity, concerning both the depiction of the history of virtue ethics and the diagnosis of what went wrong. His reconstruction of the moral history of humankind from Homer to the end of the Middle Ages presents a coherent and overall harmonious picture. The coherence of this development was based on a "shared view of a satisfactory human life," a life well defined by one's social role and the general narrative that represented the cultural tradition throughout the ages. Such a shared view, according to MacIntyre, existed from the Homeric hero on, via the Athenian gentleman to the medieval wayfarer from life on earth to life in heaven. Virtue had a crucial role in that shared view, because it constituted the essential condition of the good life. What at first started as the simple practice of specific social roles was gradually transformed into a narrative of a meaningful order of human life, and finally became the established moral tradition for centuries to come.

That this overall coherent worldview came to an end represents, for MacIntyre, the "silent catastrophe of the modern age," because it meant the loss of the reliable moral system in the special form that had prevailed from the High Middle Ages on, as a combination of Aristotelian ethics and Christian religion.[1] MacIntyre himself presents a succinct and memorable summary of his point of view: (1) there is the fundamental contrast between (a) man-as-he-happens-to-be and (b) man-as-he-should-be-if-he-realized-his-essential-nature; (2) ethics is the discipline that enables humans to make the transition from state (a) to state (b).[2] The virtues are the dispositions that determine our actions in the way that accords with our proper human nature, while vices do the opposite. Given this grounding in human nature, there is no room for the notorious is/ought problem and the "naturalistic fallacy." From the very fact that humans have a function or role to fulfill, a definitive set of "oughts" follows, namely all those actions and reactions that are characteristic functions of "man-as-he-should-be." Aristotle was not the inventor, but only a prominent spokesman of the conception of human beings as entities with functions. It was deeply embedded in all those societies that assign to each member particular roles: as a member of a family, as a citizen, as a soldier, as a servant. To call a citizen, a father, a servant, or a soldier "good" is therefore a factual statement concerning their conduct, a statement that is either true or false, depending on how well they fulfill their functions.

Of this once coherent system, according to MacIntyre, all that is left are shadow images of the old tradition and the remnants of a vocabulary that has lost its coherence. That situation explains, then, why contemporary ethical debates are a cacophony of divergent discussions without a common basis, without a common direction, and without criteria for acceptable decisions. Neither rationalistic ethics à la Kant nor emotivist ethics in the wake of Hume nor the utilitarian conceptions after Bentham and Mill are able to provide a proper basis for a fruitful discussion of morality. Worse: it is quite unclear what distinction there is between moral and nonmoral problems, questions, and decisions.[3] That this predicament did not become obvious to the protagonists of ethics in modern times is attributed by MacIntyre to the preservation of some remnants of the old moral system and its values.

What is of central interest to this chapter is one undeniable feature that MacIntyre's interpretation aptly singles out, namely the disappearance of 'virtue,' not only from the center of moral discourse, but from ordinary language as well. A concept that had been the focus of moral discussion for over 2,500 years has become all but unintelligible. As everyone who ever taught a course in ancient philosophy to first-year students will know, it is hard work to make them even understand what the Greeks meant by 'virtue.' Nothing attests better to that fact than the replacement of 'virtue' by 'excellence' in updated versions of Ross' translation of Aristotle's *Nicomachean Ethics*. Whether this replacement makes the text more accessible is questionable, but this is not our concern. What does concern us is the disappearance of virtue and the virtues. In a short chapter, only a perfunctory sketch of the decline of Aristotle's virtue ethics can be given. In anticipation of its results it should be said that it was not a "silent catastrophe" that caused this development. There were in fact several catastrophes, and quite audible ones, and if they led to the disappearance of virtue as a central concept in ethics and in popular morality, it is not because early modern philosophers became inordinately preoccupied with the power of human reason, as MacIntyre would have it, but because of the consequences of those catastrophes.

Aristotle's virtue ethics

Virtue – *aretē* – in Greek, like its Latin counterpart *virtus*, originally designated any kind of outstanding ability or talent, whether it was of a physical, moral, or intellectual kind. Thus a winner in the Olympic Games displayed virtue just as did an outstanding fighter like Achilles or an eminent statesman like Solon. The philosophers of the classical age, starting with Socrates, gradually gave a more specific sense to this broad concept in their reflections on the conditions of a worthwhile human life, reflections that partly agreed with and partly aimed to reform the values received from tradition. Aristotle puts particular emphasis on the social aspect of this concept, for he advocates the view of man as an animal "born for citizenship" (*zōon politikon*) in the sense that he finds fulfillment in a community that guarantees a self-sufficient life to its members. A closer look would show, however, that Aristotle's conception of the good life far exceeds the traditional view of the nature of man. His ideal of a good man must unite two different kinds of virtues: (i) practical wisdom (*phronēsis*), the intellectual virtue necessary for conceiving of the right decisions and of the means and ways to carry them out, and (ii) the moral or character virtues (*ēthikē aretē*), the habitually acquired, appropriate emotional attitudes towards acting and being affected. The character or ethical virtues became the hallmark of Aristotelian ethics because it treats the right "moral taste," i.e. loving what is noble and hating what is disgraceful, as the most important incentive of human actions.[4] The "good man" is therefore the well-tempered individual, characterized by the right moral inclinations, acting in accordance with the injunctions of practical wisdom.

The advantage of Aristotelian virtue ethics should be obvious: virtuous persons need no further incentive to act in the right way, because they enjoy doing the right actions with respect, not only to their own good, but also to that of their friends and fellow citizens. External sanctions and enforcement are therefore superfluous, except in the case of less well turned out individuals, as Aristotle mentions in passing.[5] Furthermore, it is an "ethics for everyone," because under the right circumstances everybody can acquire a decent character; no special insights or complex philosophical reflections are required.[6] There are therefore no higher authorities in Aristotelian virtue ethics, neither of a religious kind nor of a transcendent intelligence like that of Plato's philosopher king. If Aristotle assigns the "master science of life" to the statesman in his function as legislator, he does so only because legislators are supposed to possess practical wisdom to a higher degree than the ordinary citizen so that they recognize the order and laws required for the common good.[7] The good life ("happiness") consists in nothing but the development and deployment of the best human capacities or talents, and the enlightened citizen will realize that the common good is therefore his own good, because it allows him to develop and exercise his best potential.[8] The lawgiver's task is therefore to provide the legal conditions of such a life for its citizens, including their moral and intellectual education and the material provisions that make such a life possible. For Aristotle is quite clear about the essential condition of his ethical system: the best in human nature can only be realized in a state whose constitution is the best by nature.[9]

The naturalistic approach of Aristotelian ethics explains why it survived antiquity and played a central role from the High Middle Ages on. Its resurrection was not just due to the enormous influence of Aristotelian philosophy after the rediscovery of his major works, but also to the flexibility of his ethical system that allows for adjustment to different social conditions. That it finally lost its attractiveness in the modern age has therefore often been attributed to the rebellion against Aristotelian philosophy in the early modern age. That this simple attribution to the general decline and fall of Aristotelianism is false, when it comes to his ethics, has been common knowledge among specialists for a long time. The disappearance of virtue ethics had little to do with the rejection of the basic principles of Aristotelian physics and metaphysics in the early modern age. For Aristotle's ethics remained an integral part of the curriculum of the universities long after modern natural science had gone its own way.

But before turning to the explanation of virtue ethics' decline it is necessary to take a closer look at the actual influence exerted by Aristotelian ethics in history. Because antiquity and the Middle Ages are not the topic of this chapter, this part of the story can be kept short. First of all, one has to resist the temptation of oversimplification.[10] Particular philosophical doctrines do not speak to all comers equally, and therefore it should come as no surprise that Aristotle's ethics was far from dominating the field in antiquity. Though the representatives of the four most influential schools, the Platonists, the Aristotelians, the Stoics, and the Epicureans each held that happiness, *eudaimonia*, is the highest aim of human beings, with virtue as an essential condition, this conviction is all that the four schools had in common. For, there was agreement neither on the nature of the good life nor on the nature and function of the virtues necessary to attain it.[11] 'Virtue,' to state it once again, was not narrowly confined to a set of character traits. What is crucial about human nature was a much fought over question between the different schools, as the relevant texts would show. Plato's view about the best state attainable to human beings was quite different from Aristotle's, and the same is true of the Stoics and the Epicureans.[12] Aristotle and his dichotomy of virtues of character and intellectual virtues never dominated the field, and it has to be emphasized that during the Hellenistic age the central features of his ethics received little attention. Though the renaissance of Aristotelian philosophy that started in the first century BCE is evidenced by the impressive corpus of commentaries written on his work, ethics played only a minor role in that revival of his philosophy, in comparison with logic, meta-physics, and natural philosophy.[13] That there are very few Greek commentaries on his ethics is no accident of history.[14] The situation in the vast Roman Empire was very different from that in the small Greek city state (*polis*) of the classical age, and the Neoplatonic ethical doctrine in late antiquity relied on Plato rather than on Aristotle.[15] In the reception of Greek ethics in early Christianity, Stoicism was more influential than Aristotelian virtue ethics, because its conception of a universal natural law was more congenial to the divine law that was at the center of the Judeo-Christian tradition. In any case, the reception of Greek ethics by the early Christian theologians was far from unanimous. Some treated Greek ethics not only as consistent but as an improvement of Christian moral convictions, because it provides an explication and systematization of their implicit presuppositions. Others regarded the Greek moral theories as incompatible with revealed truth of Christianity, because they had their basis in the natural power of human reason. Others were indifferent to Greek ethics, for the relation to God does not depend on the agent's moral attitude, but rather on the forgiveness of sins due to divine grace.[16] Finally, even those with a positive attitude to the morality of the pagan philosophers treated earthly happiness and its values as subordinate to heavenly happiness after resurrection.[17]

Aristotle's virtue ethics in the Middle Ages

A similar ambiguity towards the Greco-Roman traditions of moral philosophy prevailed throughout the Middle Ages. Even for the adherents of Aristotelian ethics the transformation of what fits the "Athenian gentleman" to what is suitable to the Christian wayfarer, the *viator* through life on earth to life in heaven, remained problematic. For the concern for earthly happiness had to be subordinate to that for happiness after death, and the virtues that determine life here on earth, and interactions with others were therefore subordinate to the Christian virtues of faith, hope, and charity. Aristotelian virtue ethics therefore played only a secondary role. How to turn "man-as-he-happens-to-be" into "man-as-he-should-be-if-he-realized-his-essential-nature" had become the domain of the religious authorities, not of philosophy.

For these reasons, it would also be wrong to assume that at least within the boundaries of philosophy of the High and Late Middle Ages Aristotelian ethics was predominant, once the *Corpus Aristotelicum* had become the mainstay of teaching at the universities. Though most of the prominent schoolmen were Aristotelians there were considerable differences between Aquinas, Duns Scotus, Ockham, and their adherents.[18] Moreover, the basic assumptions of Aristotelian anthropology do not really fit well with Christian creed. For Aristotle presupposes not only that well-educated individuals in well-ordered communities are able to achieve the highest form of happiness but that they can do so by their own devices. This is a doctrine that no Christian theologian could accept. This applies even to faithful Aristotelians like Aquinas. When it comes to happiness, *beatitudo*, he disagrees with THE PHILOSOPHER: true happiness can be obtained only after death. That is why Aquinas treats Aristotle's *eudaimonia* as a second-best that is limited to earthly happiness. St. Thomas' authoritative text in ethical questions is therefore not his commentary on Aristotle's *Nicomachean Ethics*, but his theological work.[19]

For such reasons, which could be expanded much further than space permits here, there was no unitary ethical system in the Middle Ages, and Aristotelian virtue ethics was far from playing a dominant role. Aristotle's ethics was treated at best as the basis of the regulation of worldly affairs. Theologians who looked at the highest form of happiness in Aristotle with favorable eyes did so because they identified the contemplative form of life recommended in *NE* x.6–8 with the contemplation of God. Otherwise, ethics indeed was treated as an *ancilla theologiae*. If Aristotle's ethics obtained a firm place in the curricula of the universities, this was due to the fact that it provided the most systematic treatment of its subject.[20] It is not a sign that Aristotelian virtue ethics had supreme authority, let alone a monopoly.

Aristotle and Christian spirituality

In the Renaissance the relation between theology and ethics did not at first change much. Christian faith itself was not at issue.[21] But there was a marked increase of dissent on all sides, and the picture of human nature became even more fluid. This is witnessed by views of

all provenances, both theological and humanist, on the character of
the world and on the place of humans in it.[22] On the one hand there
was a host of *contemptus mundi* literature, wallowing in vivid depic-
tions of the degraded state of human beings here on earth. Others, by
contrast, emphasized the fact that God created man in his own image
and made him lord over all other creatures. Thus, during the Renaissance the idea that man can both lower himself to the level of beasts
and become like God had quite some attraction.[23] But this elevation
of humans was regarded as a gift of God's grace – and this aspect has
no counterpart in Aristotle at all. The spiritual character of Platonism had therefore never entirely lost its influence, and important
theologians and philosophers in the Renaissance regarded Platonic
ethics as much more akin to Christian creed than Aristotle's. Thus,
Marsilio Ficino, the founder of Neoplatonism in Florence, hails the
famous goal of "becoming like god" in Plato's *Theaetetus* (176b) as
the *summum bonum*.[24] In Ficino's eyes, the approximation to God
consists in reflection on God's nature.[25]

That true happiness comes only after death remained, however,
a conviction that practically all philosophers of the Renaissance
shared with their medieval predecessors. On earth there is at best
an *imperfecta beatitudo* or *felicitas*.[26] The tension this fact had
already caused for the medieval Aristotelians increased during the
Renaissance, especially for those who defended the compatibility
of Aristotelian ethics and Christian theology. One solution was to
draw the borders of ethics precisely at the point where Christian
creed begins, so that salvation is dependent on the personal relationship with God. But as indicated before, such "inwardness" and
the hope of God's grace are quite alien to Aristotle's ethics. For
that very reason not only theologians but also many of the human-
ists simply rejected Aristotelian ethics as "thoroughly pagan."[27]
Others, like Philipp Melanchthon, transferred the two-kingdom theory to ethics: human reason is quite capable of working out the
right rules of behavior in worldly affairs. Biblical revelation, by contrast, is in charge of questions of faith. Hence these are separate
issues. As Melanchthon put it: "Christ did not come on earth to
teach the rules of morals that were known to human reason before-
hand, but to release us from our sins and to send the Holy Spirit to
those who believe in him."[28] Melanchthon therefore treated Aristotelian ethics as the first step, a step that is necessary for human

communal life, just as is legislation, but which must not interfere with the higher insights of faith. In this spirit classical ethics continued to be treated as a basic discipline among humanist Protestants, and it was not given up in favor of a Christian moral doctrine based on biblical texts alone. But as it had done in the Middle Ages, this compromise solution in the Renaissance represented an *Aristoteles dimidiatus*, as far as his ethics is concerned.

In addition, Aristotle was not the only master in the field of ethics, nor did he share it just with Plato. For in early modernity the Stoics and Epicureans received their fair share of attention. They had never been entirely absent in the Middle Ages either, thanks to Cicero, Seneca, and certain fathers of the church, most of all Augustine.[29] To be sure, in the instruction at the universities the *Nicomachean Ethics* remained the basic text. This was so in the universities of countries where the Catholic faith prevailed, strengthened by the work of Francisco Suarez, the towering figure in late scholasticism.[30] But the same was true of Protestant countries after the Reformation. The model of the arch-Protestant university at Wittenberg dominated all Protestant universities from Tübingen to Königsberg. This, however, is not necessarily a sign of a dominant influence of Aristotelian ethics as such but again reflects the fact that his work, because of its systematic order, was regarded as a suitable basic text for instruction. For this reason the medieval commentaries on the *Nicomachean Ethics* also remained in use, most of all the commentary of Thomas Aquinas, as its many reprints into the seventeenth century show. In addition, new commentaries, paraphrases and summaries continued to appear, and even many philosophers, who otherwise prided themselves on their intellectual independence, relied largely on those texts.[31]

There was, however, great disagreement among the clerical as well as among the worldly authorities with respect to central points of the Aristotelian ethics. This disagreement concerned above all the notion that human beings have a *function* whose fulfillment at the same time is the fulfillment of their nature and sufficient for happiness. It also concerns the separation of character virtues from the intellectual virtues and their cooperation. A further bone of contention was that Aristotle, in contradistinction to Plato and the Stoics, treated as indispensable a sufficient supply of external goods for the development and actualization of human nature. This point was totally unacceptable to ascetic religious thinkers. A further point of disagreement was Aristotle's notion that pure intellectual activity is the highest, best, and most happy-making form of life. That he identifies this activity with scientific contemplative thought was welcome to some, but unwelcome to others. Similarly, there was disagreement concerning Aristotle's theory of the "right mean," i.e. that virtue is the intermediate between excess and defect. This doctrine had its admirers, but it also met with harsh criticism. Especially the question of the "right measure" was a much debated issue, in view of the difficulties with quantification and the fact that Aristotle provides little instruction for its application. In addition, some objected that there cannot be two opposites of every virtue; instead of a median good they recommended extreme goodness, in view of the condemnation of lukewarmness in scripture.[32]

But the fundamental problem remained the overall compatibility of Aristotelian ethics with Christian doctrine. Thus his adherents were eager to show that, appearances to the contrary notwithstanding, his thought was compatible with personal immortality. Just as in the Middle Ages, the major positive evidence consisted in Aristotle's praise of the godlike status of the activity of contemplation. But while some authorities welcomed such a rapprochement to Christian doctrine, others rejected it. One of Aristotle's most implacable foes was, of course, Martin Luther: "Almost the entire Aristotelian ethics is fundamentally evil and an enemy of grace."[33] Luther's judgment was not due to ignorance, quite the reverse: he had used the *Nicomachean Ethics* as a textbook in his lectures as a young professor at the university of Wittenberg, before he turned reformer. Later on Luther came to accept Melanchthon's separation of the two kingdoms, the worldly and the heavenly, so that Aristotle's ethics could once again become part of Protestant higher education.[34] But this was due largely to Melanchthon's exertions.

The rejection of Aristotle

Melanchthon's special role in the reception of the Aristotelian philosophy is a symptom of his time and age. As a very young man – in the case of this child prodigy that means as a teenager – he had been an enthusiastic adherent of Aristotle and had planned a new edition

of his works together with Reuchlin and other eminent human-
ists. But after meeting Luther, he was turned by this overwhelming
religious powerhouse into a fierce opponent of Aristotelian philosophy for some years. Hence he declared that Protestant universities
should do without Aristotle altogether, and engaged in a veritable
campaign against Aristotelianism. But his opposition was not going
to last. He realized that the schwärmerei and the mental anarchy
among the adherents of Luther made it necessary to design a new
schema of general and clerical education. Its conclusion was that
there was nothing that provided a clearer structure, method, and
content for university instruction than the Aristotelian writings
and their respective commentaries. Melanchthon's task of restor-
ing the curriculum was made easier by the fact that Luther himself
was well aware of the difference between Aristotle and medieval
Aristotelianism and was therefore not opposed to a return to the
"genuine Aristotle" of antiquity. Subsequently, Melanchthon was
the major force in the continuation of the Aristotelian tradition in
the Protestant universities by providing compendia and handbooks.
All this shows that in the Renaissance and in early modern philosophy Aristotelian ethics had not been swept aside, as had been his
physics and metaphysics.

But as before, Aristotle's ethics never held the field alone. Certain Protestants continued to reject a compromise between the
Aristotelian and Christian doctrines, and the same attitude existed
also on the side of Catholic theologians. Thus Juan Luis Vives, the
humanist and friend of Erasmus, regarded Aristotle's conception of
happiness as incompatible with Christian salvation: "Aristotle looks
for happiness in this life and leaves none to the other."[35] In addition, Vives regarded Aristotle's detailed conditions of the good life as
objectionable. This applies most of all to the virtue of magnanimity,
the quest for the highest honors. According to Vives, such values
conflict with the spirit of the Sermon of the Mount. Vives was not
alone in his condemnation. In the sixteenth century there were many
theologians who treated Aristotle's conception of happiness and the
value of external goods as inimical to Christian faith. Aristotle's dec-
laration that no one who is poor, ugly, and of low birth can become
truly happy is not at all in agreement with the in-principle egalitarian spirit of Christianity. For such reasons theologians pointed out
that the Aristotelian virtues of character are incompatible with the

Christian virtues of faith, hope, and charity. After all, the character
virtues are achieved by habituation only, while the Christian virtues
are a gift of the Holy Spirit.

Other philosophers, by contrast, attempted to reform Aristotle's philosophy. Thus the Dutch Reformist theologian Antonius
de Waele rejects both the attempts of the scholastics to adjust theology to Aristotelian philosophy and Melanchthon's policy of simply ignoring ill-fitting details in Aristotle's text. Instead, de Waele
corrects Aristotle where he sees him as incompatible with Christian doctrine.[36] Another way of dealing with Aristotle consisted in
illustrating his ethics by examples from the Bible and from church
history. Thus the martyrs were presented as examples of superhuman courage and self-control. This justified the contention that Aristotelian ethics is fit to provide the lower steps of the ladder to heaven,
while Christian doctrine represents the topmost steps. This mot-
ley crowd of opinions bears witness not only to a lively interest in
Aristotelian ethics throughout the sixteenth century, but also to an
intensive study of his text itself.[37]

So far we have concentrated only on the disagreement concerning
Aristotle's *ethics* from the religious perspective. A long list could
also be drawn up concerning points of disagreement with respect to
the close connection between ethics and *politics*, which is essential
to Aristotelian thought. While the foundation of ethics in a community that presupposes the participation of all able citizens had been
welcomed by all those medieval thinkers who were leaning towards
republicanism, encouraged by the political situation in some Italian
city states, others were leaning towards a monarchical rule, both in
clerical and in worldly affairs. Furthermore, while Thomas Aquinas
attributed to Aristotle a foundation of ethics in a theory of natural
law that owes quite a lot to Stoic doctrine via Cicero, other philosophers disagreed on this point. We shall have to forego the opportunity
to give a review of the reception of Aristotle's politics in the Renaissance and early modern age. Suffice it to say that it was as varied
and controversial as that of his ethics.

Pessimism, politics, and ethics

Was it, then, this continued squabbling among theologians and
humanist philosophers concerning the role of Aristotelian virtue

ethics, in general, that led to its ultimate demise? Though such disagreement may have contributed to the disaffection with an ethics that can be used and abused in so many ways, it seems that the decisive factors were the very real catastrophes that marked the end of the Renaissance and the beginning of the early modern era. The devastation of the politico-religious wars, wars that were fought with great brutality in various European countries for decades, if not centuries, and the ensuing political situation had a lasting impact. Why the historical circumstances played a crucial role becomes obvious if we realize that there is a further condition of Aristotelian ethics, not made explicit by MacIntyre. The essential condition for humans to become as-they-should-be-if-they-realized-their-essential-nature is that they live in a state-as-it-is-at-its-best. The latter factor played no very prominent role among the Aristotelians in the Middle Ages, because there was a general reliance on God as the guarantor of a naturally right order, including the political order of Christian societies. But once the trust in that foundation had given way to a pessimistic outlook, the Aristotelian ethico-political system lost its plausibility. The onset of such pessimism is witnessed by the skepticism concerning man as a political animal, naturally fit for a life in peace, order, and self-restraint. Montaigne's carefully voiced skeptical attitude and Hobbes' view that the state of nature consists in the war of all against all are indicators of a fundamental change in that respect. Moreover and more importantly, the century-long conflicts resulted in the absolutist rule of "divinely appointed princes" in both state and church that came to dominate over virtually all of Europe. These long-lasting catastrophes changed the intellectual climate in a much more profound way than the continued philosophical debates about the suitability of Aristotelian ethics in post-Reformation Europe would let one suspect.

Against the stark experience of continued insecurity, violence, religious persecution, and political suppression the teleological outlook of a unified state of human perfection no longer seemed feasible. There had, of course, been wars, cruelty, persecution, and suppression throughout the Middle Ages. But at least the ideal of a functioning government with the common good as its aim was alive, as expressed by Thomas Aquinas: "The provinces or states that are ruled by one king enjoy peace, justice, and the affluence of goods."[38] If such a "shared view" of life in good communities ever existed in Christianity, despite all stress and strain throughout the centuries, the disintegration of even the appearance of a united Christendom put an end to that view. The disruption of civic life by continued wars, the permanent religious rifts, and the absolutist regimes that resulted from them were no mere unfortunate incidents in the history of moral philosophy, as MacIntyre seems to presuppose.[39] They had a lasting impact that drastically changed the moral and political outlook. There is, of course, always a gap between ideal and reality, but there is a point where ideals can no longer be aspired to, because they are beyond the possibility of realization. The conviction that the princely rulers, both worldly and clerical, should be models of virtue, which the scholastic and humanist philosophers had expressed in their rich mirror-of-princes literature, was no longer alive. If ever there had been MacIntyre's "shared view" of the human individual as of a wayfarer through life on earth to life in heaven, that view had been shattered. To be sure, there was no explicit break with the tradition of the past – i.e. none of the promoters of early modern moral philosophy, from Hobbes and Grotius on, explicitly asserted that it was the great political and religious crises that caused them to look elsewhere for a foundation of moral philosophy. But the very fact that they looked at scholastic ethics from quite a distance shows that the tradition was no longer regarded as viable.[40] The loss of faith in a community that provides the opportunity to live the best life went hand in hand with the increasing unpopularity of eudaimonism as the basis of ethics, and that loss was never replaced by a unanimously accepted foundation.

New bases of morality

As we have seen, the Aristotelian conception of man-as-he-is-at-his-best as the master of a satisfactory life here on earth had been in a precarious state throughout the Middle Ages and the Renaissance, so the conception of earthly happiness as the result of the exercise of human virtues had at best a secondary role to play. Ethics, like all of philosophy, served as the "handmaiden of theology." But even this relatively stable relationship was undermined, once theology spoke in different tongues and thereby lost the (by and large) unquestioned authority it had enjoyed throughout the religious strains and struggles that characterize the age from high scholasticism to the Reformation. The philosophers and political thinkers of the early modern age therefore started to look for a different basis of morality. That a worldly state of the type proposed in Aristotle's *Politics* could provide such a basis was not taken into serious consideration by any of the influential theorists.

In the wake of the Hobbesian theory that only rational self-interest provides the necessary motive to prefer a life in society to the war of all against all in a state of nature, thinkers like Grotius and Pufendorf regarded the seemingly marginal role of the natural law in Aristotle as a serious drawback. Pufendorf's friend and disciple Thomasius saw in Aristotle's ethics no more than a collection of "rules of prudence for the nobility at the court of Alexander the Great." This judgment was later accepted in Brucker's *History of Philosophy* and exerted quite some influence over the reception of Aristotelian ethics in the eighteenth century, when Humanism and its emphasis on "*Graecitas*" went out of fashion anyway.[41]

It would, however, be quite misleading to claim that the earth-shattering political and religious upheavals immediately led to the demise of the virtues in philosophy. Quite the opposite is true. Many philosophers were concerned with the concept of virtue and with particular virtues, and they continued to assign a central role to them, from Shaftesbury and the British sentimentalists to Hume, Adam Smith, and Rousseau. But each of them held different views about the virtues, their nature, their origin, and their functions, either with or without a religious or legalistic basis.[42] The very plurality of such theories, with different principles and justifications, constituted the main problem: there was much less agreement about the concept and function of the virtues in moral philosophy than there had ever been in antiquity. That philosophers and political thinkers assigned increased importance to the "autonomy of the individual" was, then, not due to a sudden faddish fascination of intellectuals with "individualism" as MacIntyre contends. It also was not due to a reckless dismissal of the old tradition. Instead, it was due to the disappearance of a unified tradition. The drastic change of the conditions of life no longer provided a basis for agreement on the right form of life, either public or private.[43]

THE MISFORTUNES OF VIRTUE

An overview of the different philosophers' treatment of the concept of virtue in the seventeenth and eighteenth century would exceed the limits of this chapter. Instead, a discussion of the main points of contention in Schneewind's (1990) depiction of "The Misfortunes of Virtue" must suffice by way of a conclusion. Unlike the novel by de Sade with the same title, Schneewind's article does not describe the cruel misuse of a naive faith in virtue by a vicious world. Instead, it gives a sketch of the stages by which virtue-centered moral philosophy lost its leading position and became subordinate to its act- and rule-centered competitors, based on a theory of natural law.

The rise of rules

While Thomas Aquinas had initially conceived of natural law as the basis of his Aristotelian virtue ethics, the demise of Aristotelian tele-ology (man-as-he-is-if-he-realizes-his-best-potential) gradually led to a focus on the legalistic aspect of morality. In the hands of the most famous proponents of natural law in early modern times, Grotius and Pufendorf, moral virtues became subordinate to explicit rules and laws. This change of emphasis clearly had its roots in the reli-gious and political upheavals that led to an increasing secularization of moral thought. For, though Grotius and Pufendorf still retained the belief in the divine origin of those laws, the aim of their theories was entirely worldly: strict laws were the necessary conditions of the very existence of a society that would guarantee life in peace. Virtues were conceived as dispositions to obey the laws and to stay within the realm of what is permissible where there is room for choice. This distinction between laws and virtues is mirrored in the separation of perfect and imperfect duties, accepted by the nat-ural law theorists. Perfect duties are those required by law, while imperfect duties are meritorious; they ameliorate the quality of life because they support those social relations that are not regulated by law. Thus, as Schneewind points out, the natural law theorists were not an unmitigated misfortune for virtue, for charity became the secularized form of the Christian virtue that served to improve social life.[44]

The distinction between perfect and imperfect duties had a great influence on the further development of moral philosophy, as witnessed by Hume's differentiation of artificial and natural virtues. He acknowledged the clarity of the artificial virtues: justice, fidelity to contracts and to the government, and their observance was necessary for the very existence of society. Hume could therefore dispense with divine sanctions as the foundation of the law, as still maintained by Grotius and Pufendorf. In contradistinction to the artificial virtues the natural virtues are based on mutual sympathy and emerge from the human character. Thus to some degree Hume's moral theory upheld the ancient tradition. But it also inherited its weakness: not only does it not set clear rules and borders but it tends to run together the aims of the different virtues that ameliorate human life. In addition, the theory failed to convince adherents of an act-centered juridical approach to morality, such as Adam Smith, because it could not provide clear-cut directives for moral conduct.[45] That the latter became a matter of concern shows that moral theory had become less a guide for individual conduct than for public policy. Both concerns had been an integral part of the Aristotelian tradition, but once they came to be treated as separate issues the demand for universal validity and clear demarcations assumed primary importance.

The rise of duty

Kant's ethics represents the last stage of the "misfortunes of virtue" in Schneewind's discussion.[46] Like Hume's distinction between artificial and natural virtues, Kant's distinction between perfect and imperfect duties is indebted to the natural law tradition. This distinction first appears, albeit briefly, in the *Groundwork of the Metaphysics of Morals*.[47] As an example of an imperfect duty Kant cites that of mutual help in need. While for Kant the maxims that contradict perfect duties cannot even be thought, a maxim that rejects mutual help can be thought without self-contradiction; but it cannot be willed, because a life without mutual beneficence is not desirable. A major problem with this distinction is that Kant fails to explain the motivation to perform imperfect duties, i.e. what determines when to perform them and when not. A clearer distinction with respect to the different kinds of duties is contained in the second part of Kant's late work *The Metaphysics of Morals*.[48] He distinguishes there between "duties of law" and "duties of virtue," and extensively discusses the metaphysical origins of a doctrine of virtue in that work's second part. As he makes clear there, the virtues are an important element of the inner attitude towards duty that leads to happiness, because that attitude constitutes one's own perfection and contributes to the happiness of others.[49] But Kant, like Hume in that respect, admits that precision is possible only in the case of duties of law. Concerning the duties of virtue there are no fixed rules, but only "pragmatic rules of prudence." Despite the fact that Kant is quite explicit about the importance of the duties of virtue because they contribute to the good of others, the *Metaphysics of Morals* had little impact in comparison with the *Groundwork* and the *Critique of Practical Reason*. In the later reception of Kant's ethics the preoccupation with the categorical imperative and the conditions of its application left little room for his late concern for virtue.[50]

In the nineteenth century, ethical debate became dominated by a rationalist ethics of duty – in the wake of Kant – on the one side and by utilitarianism on the other. The question of a meaningful human life on the basis of virtue was therefore no longer at issue in philosophical discussion, so that virtue's further decline became inevitable, because its use and misuse was then left to popular morality. Virtue had become "homeless," philosophically speaking. It would require an extensive project by sociolinguists to trace the decline of the use of 'virtue' in ordinary language in the Western world, especially in the Victorian age and its aftermath. For the purpose of this chapter the observation must suffice that over the many centuries the role of the virtues in general consciousness had already been narrowed down in a significant way. Because sexuality had for centuries been treated as *the* vice par excellence, virtue became almost exclusively identified with sexual abstemiousness. And since that was expected from women much more than from men, it finally became the domain of women, together with other Christian virtues such as unselfishness, humility, obsequiousness, etc. This narrow confinement more than other factors is responsible for the obsolescence of "virtue" as a topic in public discourse, so that the very term has become obsolete, if not unintelligible.

The decline of virtue as a central concept in morality went hand in hand with that of the conception of happiness as the good, worthwhile life. The two concepts that had originally been intimately connected have drifted so far apart that common consciousness nowadays regards them as all but antithetical. If virtue is associated with self-abnegation and abstemiousness, the claim that virtue is the condition of happiness does not make sense any more. Happiness, it seems, never made it quite back to earth so as to resume its former sense of "living well" after its centuries-long association with heavenly bliss. Happiness nowadays is usually associated with a subjective elated or euphoric state, but not with an objectively worthwhile life. "The good life," in turn, is generally identified with material well-being and comfort and far removed from considerations of virtue. Once these three concepts – virtue, happiness, and the good life – have drifted apart it seems that all the king's horses and all the king's men cannot get them together again. It is therefore hardly an accident that the existence of virtue ethics and its connection with happiness have attracted little attention even among the educated public, despite the fact that neo-Aristotelian virtue ethics has been around for several decades by now.

Schneewind's critique

In addition to this difficulty, there is Schneewind's ultimate challenge that the friends of the virtues should show that it was not virtue's own weakness that brought its misfortunes down on its head.[51] There are several difficulties that virtue ethics in an Aristotelian spirit would have to meet:[52]

(1) How can the morally sound agent, the *phronimos*, convince others, except by educating them all over?

(2) What criteria are there for the settlement of serious disagreements, and for a separation of the virtuous from the nonvirtuous agent?

(3) Does serious moral disagreement not presuppose that one of the parties is morally defective?

Schneewind's critical questions presuppose that there are no clear laws or rules in Aristotelian ethics, except very simple ones for the education of the young that grown-ups no longer need. As mentioned before, it is a distortion of Aristotelian ethics to disregard its emphasis on the need for laws and standards, provided by lawgivers and enforced in public education and in the regulation of public life. Appeal to those standards should work in a similar way for all rational agents, unless they are indeed defective either with respect to their rational capacities or to their character, or both. But this is true for all ethical discourse: it presupposes not only the acceptance of certain basic principles but also moral maturity among the discussants, be they utilitarians or deontologists. Furthermore, though Aristotle does not emphasize disagreement between two *phronimoi*, there is, nevertheless, sufficient room for serious disagreement when it comes to deliberation and decision, i.e. whether the aim is properly identified, and the ways and means adequately chosen. That Aristotle pays little attention to conflicts, even between the ultimate aims of the different virtues, is due to his focus on ideal rather than real conditions. But his awareness of the possibility of serious conflicts is indicated, for instance, in his discussion of "mixed cases" of voluntary actions.[53] They concern cases where an agent is forced, for instance, by a tyrant to commit a shameful act in order to save family or friends. This could mean the violation of justice in favor of friendship or vice versa. Serious disagreement about which violation is worse would not mean that one of the two parties must be morally defective. Aristotelian virtue ethics is, therefore, quite resilient with respect to Schneewind's critical questions.

That virtue ethics of an Aristotelian pedigree has had many supporters in recent decades is in part due to the fact that act-centered and rule-governed ethics also suffers from grave problems, be they of utilitarian or deontological character. The problems do not just concern the principles of laws and the applications of laws to particular cases, as witnessed by the discussion of ever new examples and counterexamples in academic debates. The problems also concern the principles of legislation and the public attitude towards laws. If citizens are supposed to obey the laws without constant surveillance and coercion, should they not do so under the expectation that they serve humans-as-they-should-be-if-they-realized-their-essential-nature, in a state that aims for peace and the well-being of its citizens? And can we do without such an ideal, especially at a time and age where all loopholes are exploited and the trust in the enforcement of laws and rules as the mainstay of society is seriously undermined? The deficiencies of modern societies in that respect explain the attractiveness of a "return to virtue ethics" by philosophers in recent decades.

The evaluation of these attempts is the topic of other chapters in this volume (chapters 1, 7, and 8). Suffice it to admit that neo-Aristotelians face an uphill fight concerning the definition and justification of virtues and the determination of the good life. It is an uphill fight because "pluralism" is not only a characteristic of the present age, but also its pride and joy, at least in the Western world. It is therefore hard to envisage a unified conception of human nature, of the good life that suits it, and of the society that makes it possible. For, it is much easier to agree on what we do *not* want than on what we *do* want. Thus, while no one would deny that certain character traits should be regarded as desirable around the globe, when we come to draw up a list there are difficulties as soon as we go beyond a minimalist point of view.[54] In a world that is full of cultural and religious clashes there is little chance of agreement. Moreover, the question of how to achieve desirable character traits, even if they could be agreed upon, leaves us in a worse quandary. Once upon a time it was expected that family, school, and church would provide the requisite education. Not only has the influence of these sources declined in contemporary Western societies, but there are also good reasons to doubt that they were really effective before. The horrendous crimes of the first half of the twentieth century were to a great extent committed by persons with a "proper" upbringing and the requisite cultural background. Moral education seems to have provided no better safeguard in those cases than it did in the case of the famous Athenian miscreants, the Thirty Tyrants. And if a small city state cannot guarantee the achieving of desirable character traits, how should this be provided by modern mass societies, fragmented as they are? It remains an open question how Aristotle in fact judged the situation in Greece when he composed the *Nicomachean Ethics*. Our best guess seems to be that he assumed that his conception of the good life, based on virtue ethics, ought to be at work in a well-construed *polis, if* it is supposed to last. And he may have left it at that hypothesis.

NOTES

1 The analysis of this integrated view includes Judaism, thanks to Maimonides, and Islamic philosophy, thanks to Averroes; MacIntyre 1981, pp. 51, 111 *et passim.*

2 MacIntyre 1981, p. 50. If this chapter uses largely the male form it is not only because that was still customary at the time when that work was written, but because it was the form used in our philosophical sources until the twentieth century.

3 MacIntyre's critique of the chaotic situation has been anticipated by Elizabeth Anscombe's (1958) diagnosis of the deficits of contemporary ethics. She purports to show that moral debates, mainly in Oxford and Cambridge in the late nineteenth and in the first half of the twentieth century, were without foundation, because crucial terms such as 'moral obligation,' 'duty,' and 'ought' in a moral sense were mere survivals from an earlier conception of ethics that was no longer understood. See Timothy Chappell's chapter in this volume for discussion.

4 See *Nicomachean Ethics* (cited as *NE*) II.1, 1103a14–18. The adjective *ēthikē* that became the traditional name of the discipline seems to be Aristotle's creation; but 'ethics' was taken over by the other schools that no longer gave preponderance to character virtues. The Latin translation *moralis* is due to Cicero's translation of the Greek term (*De fato* 1).

5 *NE* x.9, 1179b10–20.

6 At least this is so if the thorny problem is left aside of how to integrate the "divine life" spent in philosophical pursuits, according to *NE* x.6–8.

7 See *NE* I.2, 1094a26–b11. The treatment of Aristotle as a particularist overlooks the importance of the laws' provision of the universal standards and rules of life. Such oversight is due to Aristotle's emphasis on the necessary imprecision of these standards (*NE* I.3, 1094b11–27 *et passim*) and on the need to make adjustments in every particular decision with respect to the person of the agent, the person acted on, the ways and means, the occasion etc. (II.6, 1106b21–3 *et passim*). But these adjustments clearly presuppose universal standards; they don't make them superfluous.

8 That Aristotle's ethics has the purpose of making its audience good is stated in unmistakable terms in *NE* II.2, 1103b26–9. Throughout *Nicomachean Ethics* Aristotle refers to the legislator as the main originator

of this work, and the discussion of the future legislator's education is the conclusion of the *Nicomachean Ethics* and the transition to the *Politics*. On the unity of ethics and politics in Aristotle see Schofield 2006.

9   See the distinction between justice by nature and justice by convention and its analogue in political constitutions, *NE* v.7.

10 For a detailed survey see Irwin 2007, chaps. 5–13 and Jean Porter's chapter in this volume.

11 On this issue see Annas 1993, p. 322: "the notion of happiness involved is a very weak and flexible one, capable of accommodating widely divergent claims from morality and from the interest of others."

12 Though MacIntyre 1981, pp. 111–13, sometimes acknowledges such disagreement, his overall reconstruction of "the classical tradition" and "the classical view of man" brushes it aside on the ground that "it always sets itself in a relationship of dialogue with Aristotle," p. 154.

13 The twenty-three heavy volumes of *Commentaria in Aristotelem Graeca* (ed. H. Diels) contain only a fraction of the once extant commentaries on Aristotle's works.

14 Apart from the early commentary by Aspasius in the second century CE there are only two very late commentaries, an anonymous commentary of the tenth century CE, and Eustratius' in the twelfth century. It is unclear whether there had been a commentary by Alexander of Aphrodisias on *Nicomachean Ethics*, the most renowned commentator in antiquity.

15 The blending of Christian belief with the inherited culture of Greece and Rome resulted in a preference of the more spiritual picture of the otherworldly Platonism from the third century on.

16 On this issue see Irwin 2008, chap. 14: "Christian Theology and Moral Philosophy."

17 Augustine pursues this distinction at great length in his doctrine of "two cities," the earthly and the heavenly city, in *The City of God*.

18 MacIntyre 1981, pp. 154ff. acknowledges conflicts – even the conflict of too many ideals in the Middle Ages, due to the Christianization of formerly quite disparate, pagan cultures. He also recognizes the conflict imparted by the difference between the Stoic view and the Aristotelian view in the Middle Ages, p. 158, but overall he holds that the medieval framework of morality was shaped by the Aristotelians, despite his admission that Aquinas' attempt to reconcile Christian doctrine and Aristotelian morality made him a highly deviant figure even in his own time, pp. 162–8.

19 See the later reaction in Suarez, *De fine hominis* iv.3.

20 For a rich overview see Lines 2002.

21 See Kraye 1991, pp. 317–19.

22 Kraye 1991, pp. 306–16.

23 Giovanni Pico della Mirandola 1942, pp. 104–6.

24 Marsilio Ficino 2001–6, XIII, 3; see also Allen 1984.

25 The main point of contention among the Platonists of the early Renaissance was whether it is the pure intellect or the will that leads to happiness, because it is the will that pulls the intellect towards God. But this is a controversy we shall leave aside, for the question of voluntarism is not central to our topic.

26 Kraye 1991, p. 318.

27 Guillaume Budé 1775, I, 227. Similarly Valla 1972 and Vives 1785, VI, 120.

28 Melanchthon 1850, vol. 16, col. 281. See also Luther 1523.

29 See Kraye 1991, pp. 360–4. In view of the high demands of the Stoics and their low estimation of the necessary goods, their doctrine was, on the whole, regarded as too austere and narrow. Epicurus owed his resurrection mainly to the Latin translation of Diogenes Laertius in 1420 and to the rediscovery of Lucretius in 1417.

30 On Suarez and his influence see Irwin 2008, chaps. 30–2.

31 See Petersen 1921, p. 124; Wollgast 1988; Kraye 1996, pp. 142–60.

32 Valla 1972, pp. 95–7; 1982, p. 80.

33 Luther 1883, vol. 1, p. 226, sententia 41: "Tota fere Aristotelis Ethica pessima et gratiae inimica est."

34 Luther's and Melanchthon's judgment on Plato's philosophy was even more negative: If mistakes are caused by ignorance and remedied by knowledge this is incompatible with the forgiveness of sin by grace alone. In addition, Melanchthon regarded the systematic character of Aristotle's procedure as an advantage over Plato's ambiguously expressed doctrines (Melanchthon 1843, vol. 11, col. 348).

35 Vives 1785, VI, 211: "Aristoteles in vita hac quaerit beatitudinem, alteri nihil relinquit."

36 de Waele 1620, col. 7: "Nos conati sumus . . . materias ab Aristotele in Ethicis ad Nicomachum praecipue tractatas . . . eodem fere ordine compendiose proponere, et errores in eis observatos ad veritatis Christianae normam corrigere."

37 The *Margarita philosophica* by G. Reisch (1512) is a witness to this fact. Besides the Trivium and Quadrivium it also contains Aristotle's natural philosophy and ethics. This work was reprinted for a century and an Italian translation appeared as late as 1599; see Park 1988, p. 465.

38 Aquinas 1973, I.4, p. 260: "provinciae vel civitates quae sub uno rege reguntur, pace gaudent, iustitia florent et affluentia rerum laetantur."

39 MacIntyre 1981, p. 220, grants not only the defeat of Aristotle's science but also the "disfigurement" of his politics by the doctrine of absolute despotism, both in the state and in the church.

40 Schneewind 1997, esp. pp. 70–81, discusses the problems that the experience of the wars caused for both the defenders of a natural law theory and the realization of the insufficiency of virtue as a unitary basis for the reconstruction of morality. Irwin 2008 does his level best to show that the secular moralists were not as alien to the tradition as is often thought, but his careful studies do not show that such was their intention.

41 Brucker 1743, p. 835.

42 See esp. Schneewind 1997, chap. 14: "The Recovery of Virtue."

43 Schneewind 1990, 61–2. at least in part agrees with this diagnosis when he attributes to the natural law theorists the motive to cope with difficulties arising from disagreement: "disagreement involving nations, religious sects, parties to legal disputes . . ."

44 Schneewind 1990, pp. 48–51.

45 See Schneewind 1990, pp. 54–8.

46 Schneewind 1990.

47 Kant 1785.

48 Kant 1797.

49 In recent years this aspect has received quite some scholarly attention; see Engstrom and Whiting 1996; Sherman 1997.

50 Schneewind 1990, p. 61.

51 Schneewind 1990, p. 63.

52 Schneewind 1990, p. 62.

53 *NE* III.1, 1110a4–26.

54 The efforts of the United Nations concerning human rights since 1946 are a good example. What virtues are presupposed by those rights would require a study of its own.

7 Virtue ethics in the twentieth century

VIRTUE ETHICS IN THE TWENTIETH CENTURY: WHERE DID IT COME FROM?

It is so fatally easy to think that past philosophers were missing something *obvious*. And from there it is a short step to the conclusion that those past philosophers can't have been much good. Virtue ethics – an account of the practically normative that begins from admirable dispositions of character like justice, kindness, courage, wisdom, and so on – looks so obviously possible, now that it is actual, that we may wonder why the luminaries of early twentieth-century Anglophone philosophy apparently just did not see the possibility. How could they have missed it?

Yet in the commonest thumbnail history of twentieth-century ethics up to (say) 1958, that is just what happened. We have, it is supposed, two familiar foundational questions about action:

> "What maxim can I, rationally, act on here?" (the Kantian/
> deontological question)
> "What action would maximize utility here?" (the utilitarian
> question),

and alongside these there is – says the usual story – a third foundational question we can equally well ask about any proposal for action:

"What kind of action would accord with the virtues here?" (the virtue ethical or Aristotelian question).

For their comments and help I am grateful to Sarah Broadie, Christopher Coope, Roger Crisp, Miranda Fricker, Brad Hooker, Simon Kirchin, Kelvin Knight, Adrian Moore, and Daniel C. Russell.

Until 1958, allegedly, people just blundered about not even seeing the possibility of this third approach. Then Elizabeth Anscombe published "Modern Moral Philosophy" (1958) and Philippa Foot published "Moral Arguments" (1978a) and "Moral Beliefs" (1978b) – and enlightenment dawned at once.

Those three papers were indeed revolutionary (nothing equally revolutionary has followed them in virtue ethics since); so revolutionary that I shall devote a good proportion of this chapter simply to expounding them. Still, there is something wrong, something thin and Whiggish, in this standard story about where twentieth-century virtue ethics came from, and it leaves some interesting questions unanswered. For one thing, we should ask whether the turn to virtue ethics was really that radical a change: wasn't it anticipated by other things that had already happened in Anglophone philosophy? Dewey, Royce, and Bradley are obvious starting points for this line of inquiry. Or we might ask why modern virtue ethics emerged in Oxford particularly: perhaps the intensive undergraduate teaching of Aristotle's *Ethics* in Oxford eventually had this effect? (We might wonder, too, why so many of virtue ethics' first exponents were women, and why women philosophers continue to be so much better represented in virtue ethics than in most other areas of ethics even, never mind philosophy. Some may want to offer a Gilligan-style explanation, appealing to alleged facts about the two genders' different ethical "voices" or styles, and women's tendency to be more empathetic and less coldly or detachedly rational [Gilligan 1982]. No one who knew Anscombe or Foot could have any doubt what *they* would think of such appeals.)

The usual story also crucially assumes that utilitarians, Kantians, and virtue ethicists alike – and presumably all other schools of moral theory too – are trying to answer the same question. All seek a *definition of morally right action*, something to fill in the dots in "An action is morally right iff... "[1] And the competition to be run between their different ways of filling in those dots is a game of example and counterexample. It is a matter of seeing which of the three theories comes closest to giving a convincingly exceptionless, yet also substantive, formula which defines morally right action. This competition to furnish a formula may be rather prominent in a lot of contemporary debate about normative ethics. But there were good reasons why such competitions were of no interest to either of the founding fathers of ancient virtue ethics, Plato and Aristotle. Nor, come to that, were they of much interest to Kant or the original utilitarians. I suggest that they are not what should interest us either.

As far as *right* goes, Plato and Aristotle are certainly interested in that, but in many other things too: good character, right emotion, overall well-being, and the social embodiment of individual excellence in a civil and political order. They have no very concentrated focus on the right at all, and no ambition whatever to offer a compact definition of it. Plato has a rather endearing habit of destroying compact definitions almost everywhere he meets them, and famously endorses (or at least takes very seriously) the thesis that there is no knowing what is right until we have definitions of the relevant virtues; he then goes out of his way to demonstrate that no definitions of the virtues are available, not at least to just anyone. Rather similarly Aristotle will talk about "right practical reasoning" (*orthos logos*), but almost always accompanies this talk with an insistence that only a practically wise person, a *phronimos*, can tell what counts as *orthos logos*, and why.

As for *morally*, we must observe at once – again following Anscombe – that Plato and Aristotle, having no word for "moral," could not even form a phrase equivalent to "morally right." The Greek *ēthikē aretē* means "excellence of character," not "moral virtue";[2] Cicero's *virtus moralis*, from which the English phrase descends directly, is simply the Latin for *ēthikē aretē*. This is not the lexical fallacy; it is not just that the *word* 'moral' was missing. The whole idea of a special category called "the moral" was missing. Strictly speaking, the Aristotelian phrase *ta ēthika* is simply a generalizing substantive formed on *ēthē*, "characteristic behaviors," just as the Ciceronian *moralia* is formed on *mores*. To be fully correct – admittedly it would be a bit cumbersome – we should talk not of Aristotle's *Nicomachean Ethics* but of his *Studies-of-our-characteristic-behaviors Edited-by-Nicomachus*.[3]

Plato and Aristotle were interested – especially Plato – in the question how the more stringent demands of a good disposition like justice or temperance or courage could be *reasonable* demands, demands that it made sense to obey even at extreme cost. It never occurred to them, as it naturally does to moderns, to suggest that these demands were to be obeyed simply because they were demands of a special, magically compulsive sort: *moral* demands. Their answer was always that, to show that we have reason to obey the strong demands that can emerge from our good dispositions, we must show that what they demand is in some way a necessary means to or part of human well-being (*eudaimonia*). If it must be classified under the misconceived modern distinction between "the moral" and "the prudential," this answer clearly falls into the prudential category.[4] When modern readers who have been brought up on our moral/prudential distinction see Plato's and Aristotle's insistence on rooting the reasons that the virtues give us in the notion of well-being, they regularly classify both as "moral egoists." But that is a misapplication to them of a distinction that they were right not to recognize.

When we turn from the Greeks to Kant and the classical utilitarians, we may doubt whether they shared the modern interest in finding a neat definition of the "morally right" any more than Plato or Aristotle did. Kant proposed, at most, a *necessary* (not necessary and sufficient) condition on *rationally permissible* (not morally right[5]) action for an individual agent – and had even greater than his usual difficulty expressing this condition at all pithily. The utilitarians often were more interested in jurisprudence than in individual action, and where they addressed the latter – as J. S. Mill often does, but Bentham usually does not – tended, in the interests of long-term utility, to stick remarkably close to the deliverances of that version of "common-sense morality" that was recognized by high-minded Victorian liberals like themselves. When Kant and the utilitarians disagreed, it was not about the question "What are the necessary and sufficient conditions of morally right action?" They weren't even asking that question.

So how come we ask it? How did the logically precise demarcation of the morally right come to be so central to early twentieth-century ethics? Partly because, quite generally, the logically precise demarcation of concepts had come to seem the main, perhaps the only, contribution that philosophy could offer to understanding: whatever could be said at all could be said clearly.[6] It was just a specific application of this program of conceptual analysis to see what it could deliver in ethics. So then some particular ethical concept(s) had to be selected as the key one(s) to analyze. And here the choice of "morally right," "morally ought," "moral obligation," "moral duty," as analysanda seemed close to automatic because of a second factor, a change in emphasis that had come about between Sidgwick and G. E. Moore. Though his tendency to reductiveness increased markedly as his career progressed, Sidgwick at least started out with quite a rich and varied theoretical vocabulary. But – so Moore groundbreakingly argued – one that was shot through with conceptual confusion. Moore contended against Sidgwick that the moral (as he calls it, "the good") was essentially something quite different from the beneficial or the felicific or the pleasurable or any other "natural property." Moral concepts were definitionally irreducible to nonmoral concepts; to think otherwise was "the naturalistic fallacy." (The perennial temptation to think that the older generation has foolishly missed something blindingly obvious is one that Moore and his disciples were always happy to yield to in the case of Sidgwick.)[7] No doubt "the morally right" might lie where a calculation of the felicific consequences might be expected to locate it; Moore too was a sort of consequentialist. But if so, that was always an a posteriori discovery, not something that could be deduced a priori simply from the concept of "the good." Hence the true business of ethics could not lie in *listing* the merely contingent facts about where "the good" was to be found. In line with Moore's more general approach, which he himself called "ordinary language philosophy," the real research program of ethics could only lie in intuitive reflection on or conceptual clarification of the notion of the good itself.

Further constraints on what such a conceptual clarification of "the good" or "the right" could be came from the massive intellectual pressure exerted on early twentieth-century philosophy by logical positivism. Central to logical positivism was the absolute distinction between facts and values, *is*es and *ought*s (a distinction inherited from Hume, and echoed in Moore's "natural/nonnatural" contrast, which logical positivism did little more than update). If values could not be facts, could not be parts of the objective world, that did not leave much for them to be except attitudes, preferences, or desires. Moore took values to be aspects of a single, mysteriously "nonnatural" property of goodness. But in subsequent writers such as Ayer, Moore's mysteries were fairly quickly tidied up into the positivistically acceptable notion of attitude expression: to call something good or right was not to predicate a property of it, but to express an attitude of commendation or approval towards it. Where this attitude was universalizable, the approval in question became distinctively *moral* approval.

Early twentieth-century philosophy was dominated by this sort of quasi-Wittgensteinian research program, the program of linguistic analysis as it is sometimes called, championed by such philosophers as Austin and Ryle.[8] In ethics it reached its logical terminus in Richard Hare's "universal prescriptivism." Hare saw all moral language as analyzable in terms of one basic concept, that of obligation or "ought," and analyzed even this single concept in a way that revealed its nature as basically not descriptive or nonevaluative, but *pre*scriptive and evaluative: "oughts" did not say anything about the way the world was, they merely embodied the speaker's universalized preferences. First all moral values were analyzed down to one thing, along lines suggested by Sidgwick and Moore; then even this one thing was proved not to be a *thing* at all, but an attitude to things. And so the ethical world was made safe for value-free scientific naturalism.

A PALACE COUP: FOOT AND ANSCOMBE

This reductive, streamlining, and antidescriptive approach to ethics is about as entirely opposed to virtue ethics as any approach could be; if early twentieth-century Anglophone ethics did not see the possibility of a virtue ethics, perhaps this was because it was looking 180° the opposite way. (Quite a lot of Anglophone ethics still is.) Foot's and Anscombe's breakthrough, in their 1958 articles, was to show how the reductive and streamlining tendencies of linguistic analysis could be resisted and indeed reversed.

Their attack on the moral philosophy of linguistic analysis was a palace coup: 1950s Oxford, where Anscombe and Foot were tutors and had recently been pupils, was also the Oxford of Austin, Ryle, Hare, and Ayer. But their work was internally subversive in more than a merely institutional sense; they themselves (particularly Foot) were practitioners of the method of linguistic analysis. Their principal complaint was not that others had attended closely to language, but that they had not attended closely enough. J. L. Austin himself was famously "not interested in isms," and Wittgenstein nearly used "I'll teach you differences" (*King Lear* i.iv) as the epigraph for *Philosophical Investigations*. Anscombe and Foot simply pointed out how

Wittgenstein's and Austin's insistence on close attention to the fine detail of ordinary language might have prevented the sweeping generalizations about the language of morals that dominated the 1950s orthodoxy.

Elizabeth Anscombe

Hence the famous opening salvo of Anscombe's "Modern Moral Philosophy":

> I will begin by stating three theses which I present in this chapter. The first is that it is not profitable for us at present to do moral philosophy; that should be laid aside at any rate until we have an adequate philosophy of psychology, in which we are conspicuously lacking. The second is that the concepts of obligation, and duty – *moral* obligation and *moral* duty, that is to say – and of what is *morally* right and wrong, and of the *moral* sense of "ought," ought to be jettisoned if this is psychologically possible; because they are survivals, or derivatives from survivals, from an earlier conception of ethics which no longer generally survives, and are only harmful without it. My third thesis is that the differences between the well-known English writers on moral philosophy from Sidgwick to the present day are of little importance. (Anscombe 1958, p. 195)

It is not even useless, Anscombe suggests, to fixate on the supposed logical grammar of the special sense of 'moral,' or 'ought,' or 'good,' and try and derive an entire ethics from them alone. It is worse than useless, because it hides from us all the questions that really need attention. To ask what these words mean, as if they were words without a history or a psychology behind them, is not to "do linguistic analysis" – unless perhaps it is to do incompetent linguistic analysis. It is to assume that there is some one fixed and universal thing that they and their translations mean in every language and culture. And it is to assume that no substantive question could arise about how, once understood, such words are involved in motivation. (Hare takes it that to understand moral terms is *eo ipso* to feel their motivating force, which for him is a matter of the meanings of the words involved. Surely part of what Anscombe meant by calling for new work in "philosophy of psychology" was to reject this reduction of a complex problem in philosophy of mind to a matter of seeing the implications of one's own terminology.)

Anscombe also calls for more careful and historically sensitive thought about the origins – in Nietzschean terms, the genealogy – of our moral concepts and language. Like Nietzsche, she thinks that key parts of our moral language, and in particular our notion of obligation, derives from the Judeo-Christian *"law* conception of ethics":

> ... if such a conception is dominant for many centuries, and then is given up, it is a natural result that the concepts of "obligation," of being bound or required as by a law, should remain though they had lost their root; and if the word "ought" has become invested in certain contexts with the sense of "obligation," it too will remain to be spoken with a special emphasis and special feeling in these contexts. (Anscombe 1958, p. 176)

It follows from this history that our current moral concepts are incoherent:

> It is as if the notion "criminal" were to remain when criminal law and criminal courts had been abolished and forgotten ... The situation, if I am right, was the interesting one of the survival of a concept outside the framework of thought that made it a really intelligible one. (Anscombe 1958, p. 176)

Hence the peculiar futility of setting out to look, by the methods of linguistic analysis, for the timeless essence of the notion of obligation. There is no such timeless essence, and if we want to arrive at a satisfactory understanding of ethics, we need to think more historically. A very similar conclusion is reached, by a different route and mainly in reaction to Kant, both in Hegel and – as already mentioned – in Nietzsche.

I have suggested that part of what Anscombe is calling for, when she calls for a "philosophy of psychology," is a more satisfactory account of motivation than e.g. Hare's prescriptivism provides. This suggestion is borne out, later on in "Modern Moral Philosophy," by her reflections on the connections between justice and goodness, and between both notions and motivation. Before that, she also says this:

> Is it not clear that there are several concepts that need investigating simply as part of the philosophy of psychology and, as I should recommend – banishing *ethics totally* from our minds? Namely – to begin with: "action," "intention," "pleasure," "wanting." More will probably turn up if we start with these. Eventually it might be possible to advance to considering the

concept "virtue"; with which, I suppose, we should be beginning some sort
of a study of ethics. (Anscombe 1958, p. 188)

One major contribution to this latter research program had already
been published by 1958: this was Anscombe's own *Intention* (1957).
That famous little book's dense and sometimes decidedly nonlinear
argument almost defies summary, but central to it is Anscombe's
neo-Thomist thesis that the intention in an action is typically the
correct answer to the question "Why are you, the agent, doing this?"
When the agent knows the answer to this, she knows it directly and
nonobservationally; yet she can be wrong about it – she is not incor-
rigibly authoritative about her own intentions. What she intends,
therefore, is a matter of fact, but that fact is not completely fixed
either by any verbal avowal of self-knowledge (however sincerely
made), or by any behavior that she may produce: the Cartesian and
the behaviorist are *both* mistaken about intention.

We might wonder how these conclusions could help us with moral
philosophy – a question which Anscombe both repels (by saying as
above that we should "banish *ethics totally* from our minds" and
just do the philosophy of psychology) and also attracts (by implying
as quoted above that this philosophy of psychology is a key prole-
gomenon to ethics). I offer three answers.

The first (given by Anscombe herself later in her paper) is that
a correct understanding of intention is crucial to the evaluation of
particular difficult cases, such as those to which the doctrine of
double effect and the action/omission distinction have been applied
("casuistry").

The second (which Anscombe develops in *Intention*) is that we
learn much of ethical importance by considering what are, and what
can be, the goods that actions can intelligibly be aimed at. She argues,
contrary to much opinion in 1957/8, that not just anything can be
intelligibly taken as an end:

But is not anything wantable, or at least perhaps any attainable thing? It
will be instructive to anyone who thinks this to approach someone and say
"I want a saucer of mud" or "I want a twig of mountain ash". He is likely
to be asked what for; to which let him reply that he does not want it *for*
anything, he just wants it. It is likely that the other will then perceive that a
philosophical example is all that is in question, and will pursue the matter
no further; but supposing that he did not realise this, yet did not dismiss

our man as a dull babbling loon, would he not try to find out in what aspect
the object is desirable?...Now if the reply is: "Philosophers have taught
that anything can be an object of desire; so there can be no need for me to
characterise these objects as somehow desirable; it merely so happens that
I want them," then this is fair nonsense. (Anscombe 1957, pp. 70–1)

The third answer to the question how philosophy of psychology helps with ethics is that the sheer *variety* of the concepts that
Anscombe suggests we look at as fruitful preambles to our moral
studies shows the antireductive and antistreamlining tendency of
virtue ethics at work. More illustrations of this third answer – and
also more material on our second answer, about the necessary unin-
telligibility of some proposed answers to questions about what it is
possible to value – appear as we turn from Anscombe to the other
main protagonist of the "ethical revolution" of 1958: Philippa Foot.

Philippa Foot

Foot's key thesis in "Moral Arguments" is, in Rai Gaita's words,
that "we cannot unilaterally make something intelligible" (Gaita
1991, p. 161). It was an implication of the prescriptivist orthodoxy
that any preference or approving attitude at all could serve as a
moral principle, provided we apply it consistently. As Hare often
said in debate, the man whose attitude is that all Jews should be
gassed says nothing *logically* wrong, provided he agrees that, should
he himself turn out to be a Jew, then he too should be gassed. But
Foot, like Anscombe, sees something deeply unintelligible in this
voluntarism about the possible objects of preference or approval.
The problem with such "moral attitudes" is not that they must
be logically inconsistent. The problem is rather that, when we cut
away the ideas of *approving, thinking good,* and *duty* from their
connections with everything that normally gives them sense except
the notion of desire/preference, then what remains, even if it is still
universalizable, is simply not an intelligible notion of approval or
thinking good or duty (1978a, pp. 105–6):

Anyone who uses moral terms at all, whether to assert or deny a moral proposition, must abide by the rules for their use, including the rules about what
shall count as evidence for or against the moral judgement concerned...I
do not know what could be meant by saying that it was someone's duty to

do something unless there was an attempt to show why it mattered if this sort of thing was not done . . . How exactly the concepts of harm, advantage, benefit, importance, etc. are related to the different moral concepts, such as rightness, obligation, goodness, duty, and virtue is something that needs the most patient investigation, but that they are so related seems undeniable, and it follows that a man cannot make his own personal decision about the considerations which are to count as evidence in morals.

And it is not just *moral* that has a logical grammar that, Foot argues, necessarily roots intelligible uses of the word and its cognates in our notion of human well-being. The same is true of all our central ethical terms, and, more widely, of most of the terms that we use in social/practical life. *Rude* is one example that Foot discusses in "Moral Arguments" (1978a, pp. 103–5); in "Moral Beliefs" Foot discusses *pride, fear, dismay, danger, warning, harm,* and *injury.*

The characteristic object of pride is something seen (a) as in some way a man's own, and (b) as some sort of achievement or advantage; without this object pride cannot be described. (Foot 1978b, pp. 113–14)

Fear is not just trembling, and running, and turning pale; without the thought of some menacing evil no amount of this will add up to fear. Nor could anyone be said to feel dismay about something he did not see as bad . . . (Foot 1978b, p. 114)

Suppose that philosophers, puzzled about the property of dangerousness, decided that the word did not stand for a property at all, but was essentially an . . . action-guiding term, used for *warning* . . . [so then] a man whose application of the term was different from ours throughout might say that the oddest things were dangerous without fear of disproof . . . [But] this is nonsense because without its proper object *warning*, like *being dangerous*, will not be there. It is logically impossible to warn about anything not thought of as threatening evil, and for danger we need a particular kind of serious evil such as injury or death. (Foot 1978b, pp. 114–15)

If someone tries to use *dangerous* in an odd way (e.g. "That dictionary is dangerous"), the natural question is "How do you mean?" Maybe the answer is "It's very heavy, and it's teetering on the edge of a high shelf," or "It defines *poison* as 'nutritious food,'" etc. Such answers make this use of "dangerous" intelligible. But suppose the reply is "I say it's dangerous because it is something that I believe we must shun." This reply gets nowhere near making such a use of *dangerous* intelligible. *Why* do we need to shun the dictionary? Until this is answered, we have no idea what the speaker means.

Similarly, we cannot make sense of moral utterance as the prescriptivists and logical positivists wished to – simply as universalizable commendation of whatever one happens to find commendable. As a matter of logical grammar, not just anything can be intelligibly commended (even in a single case, never mind universalizably). We need to understand what is meant by suggesting that something is commendable; and to show what is meant by that suggestion, we have to find a way of linking the commendation back to notions of human well-being and harm.

DEVELOPMENTS AFTER FOOT AND ANSCOMBE

Thick concepts

Appreciating the latter point fully might have prevented a certain turn in the argument that recurs in contemporary debates about the "thick concepts." The term 'thick concepts' – popularized by Bernard Williams in *Ethics and the Limits of Philosophy*, and derived from Gilbert Ryle's work via John Rawls and the American sociologist Stewart Goetz – is a label for just the sort of phenomena that Foot is describing. Typically, where an ethical concept is "thick," as (to take Williams' examples; Williams 1985, p. 129) *treachery*, *promise*, *brutality*, *courage*, are thick, that will mean that we use the concept both to "describe" and to "prescribe": uses of it may express moral commendation or condemnation or the like, but will also be unintelligible without an understanding of the social context that determines what counts as treachery or a promise, brutality or courage. Moral realists from Searle onwards have frequently argued that such concepts constitute a bridge between the natural and the ethical; moral irrealists have as frequently rejoined that thick concepts can be "disentangled" into their descriptive and prescriptive components, and so pose no threat to the familiar fact–value gap. Current debate about the thick concepts tends, under the influence of John McDowell (McDowell 1979), to focus on the question of whether this disentangling is feasible, given that the thick properties (and in particular the virtue properties) typically do not align neatly with any descriptive properties, so it is itself an achievement of virtue to see exactly where the thick concepts are instantiated.

A look back at Foot's and Anscombe's treatments of the issue suggests that this is not necessarily progress. The point, for them, was never whether it is logically possible to adopt a commending or condemning attitude to just anything. (Of course it is; all sorts of nonsense is *possible*.) Their point was rather that it cannot be *intelligible* to commend or condemn just anything, because the basis for all intelligibility (in this sense) lies in our shared conception of human well-being. Hence moral irrealists who point out, as e.g. Blackburn and Lenman have, that there is no logical reason why we could not generally commend murder and generally condemn friendship are saying nothing that Foot or Anscombe deny. The irrealist *is* controverting Foot and Anscombe if he goes on to say that there is no such thing as a shared conception of human well-being on which to base such further explanation, or that, though there is such a shared conception, there are no limits whatever on how further explanations appealing to it might go; more about those claims below (pp. 163–6).

This is the sense in which, if Foot and Anscombe are right, the program of linguistic analysis in ethics collapses: because, at least as developed in prescriptivism, it is too sweepingly general. Where previous linguistic analysis had pointed us towards a simple, streamlined, ahistorical, nonnaturalistic approach to ethics, Foot's and Anscombe's new variants of it point us in the opposite direction – towards a case-by-case naturalism which looks at each ethical phenomenon that it finds in our life in its own right, takes that phenomenon's history seriously in trying to understand it, and makes no assumptions about whether it can be neatly reduced to or fitted in under any broader patterns. "Theory typically uses the assumption that we probably have too many ethical ideas, some of which may well turn out to be mere prejudices. Our major problem now is actually that we have not too many but too few, and we need to cherish as many as we can" (Williams 1985, p. 117).

It is no denigration of the best work in virtue ethics since Anscombe and Foot to say that it has largely just filled out the research program that they outlined in these three revolutionary articles of 1958 (that's why I have spent so much time on them). So, for example, Bernard Williams' brilliant and far-ranging *Ethics and the Limits of Philosophy* is an extended reflection on the question of what may follow if we take seriously Anscombe's almost Nietzschean pessimism about the future of the conception of the normative that our largely secular age has inherited from Protestant Christianity, and take seriously her advice to abandon the idea that "the moral" can be used as a unitary frame for every practical question. And Charles Taylor's (1989) marvelous *Sources of the Self* contributes to "philosophy of psychology" (and many other things) by treating our notion of the person, the agent, in neo-Hegelian style as something with a long history and a complicated sociology inscribed in it, and by trying to understand that history better.

Alasdair MacIntyre

A third example is Alasdair MacIntyre's finest book, *After Virtue* (1984). MacIntyre's project in *After Virtue* – and in his two subsequent books, *Whose Justice? Which Rationality?* (1988) and *Three Rival Versions of Moral Inquiry* (1991) – is to develop and deepen the history of our ethical thought précised in a couple of pages in "Modern Moral Philosophy," to show exactly how and in what sense we have got to a historical position where our moral concepts are afflicted, as Anscombe said, by deep and pervasive incoherence.[9] It is also his project, insofar as this can be done, to propose a cure for this incoherence. MacIntyre's diagnosis is that, in the wake of what he calls "the Enlightenment project" of founding ethics upon "reason," we have lost our grip on any clear notion of the human *telos* – of the kind of picture of human well-being that furnishes ethical life with its objective and, as above, its intelligibility:

[The key thinkers of the Enlightenment] all reject any teleological view of human nature, any view of man as having an essence which defines his true end. But to understand this is to understand why their project of finding a basis for morality had to fail. The moral scheme which forms the historical background to their thought had...a structure which required three elements: untutored human nature, man-as-he-could-be-if-he-realised-his-*telos*, and the moral precepts which enable him to pass from one state to the other. But the joint effect of the secular rejection of both Protestant and Catholic theology and the scientific and philosophical rejection of Aristotelianism was to eliminate any notion of man-as-he-could-be-if-he-realised-his-*telos*... the abandonment of any notion of a *telos* leaves behind a moral scheme composed of two remaining elements whose relationship becomes quite unclear. (MacIntyre 1984, pp. 54–5)

MacIntyre's cure for this malady is that we should seek to rebuild the kind of community within which, according to him, that notion of the human *telos* receives its clearest and most compelling articulations:

> What matters at this stage is the construction of local forms of community within which civility and the intellectual and moral life can be sustained through the new dark ages which are already upon us. And if the tradition of the virtues was able to survive the last dark ages, we are not entirely without grounds for hope. This time however the barbarians are not waiting beyond the frontiers; they have already been governing us for some time. (MacIntyre 1984, p. 263)

MacIntyre's picture raises queries. For one thing, we might wonder if it is even possible to reconstruct such communities of virtue; MacIntyre has often had to ward off the accusation that his view boils down to an unrealistic historical nostalgia. That question is especially pressing if this reconstruction is (as seems inevitable) to be done self-consciously: in the biting words of al-Ghazali (quoted in Dodds 1951, p. 206), "the essential condition in the holder of a traditional faith is that he should not know he is a traditionalist." (This epigram exposes a difficulty that might worry us at other points too in our thinking about the virtues, some of which, modesty and innocence for example, seem as constitutively dependent as traditionalism upon a lack of self-consciousness.)[10]

Again, MacIntyre seems wrong to claim that "the key Enlightenment thinkers" abandoned teleology as a basis for ethics. If anyone deserves to be called "key Enlightenment thinkers" Rousseau and Locke do – both of whom present political theories based wholly on the notion of the natural. Curiously, MacIntyre mentions neither Rousseau nor Locke at this point in his argument. But even the thinkers he does mention here – Pascal, Kant, Hume, Diderot, Adam Smith, Kierkegaard – are not uncontroversially nonteleological ethicists.[11]

Bernard Williams

Apart from these objections to the details of MacIntyre's historical account, we should not miss the deeper and more important question that it raises. This is the question whether any conception of the human *telos* can survive the replacement of Aristotelianism by modern evolutionary science:

> [I]n Aristotle's teleological universe, every human being... has a kind of inner nisus towards a life of at least civic virtue, and Aristotle does not say enough about how this is frustrated by poor upbringing, to make it clear exactly how, after that upbringing, it is still in this man's real interest to be other than he is. If Aristotle, with his strong assumptions about the nisus of each natural kind of thing towards its own perfection, cannot firmly deliver this result, there is not much reason to think we can. Evolutionary biology, which gives us our best understanding of the facts that Aristotle represented in terms of a metaphysical teleology... is not at all directly concerned with the well-being of the individual, but with fitness, which is the likelihood of that individual's leaving offspring... Aristotle saw a certain kind of ethical, cultural, and indeed political life as a harmonious culmination of human potentialities, recoverable from an absolute understanding of nature. We have no reason to believe in that. (Williams 1985, pp. 44, 52)

The rise of evolutionary science in the mid-nineteenth century has profoundly affected all thought since – so it can hardly have failed to influence moral thought. We may speculate that a new interest in the category of the natural as a basis for ethics and politics, and a revival of curiosity about the true nature of human well-being, were among the effects of evolutionary thought that may have stimulated the twentieth-century reemergence of virtue ethics. But while evolution may have spurred people to start thinking again in more eudaimonistic ways, many philosophers, such as Williams in this passage, have serious doubts as to whether, properly understood, modern evolutionary theory is in any deeper way an ally of virtue ethics, or even compatible with it. Certainly if virtue ethics depends upon the idea that there is an unchanging human essence which immutably dictates what, as a matter of science, human beings are meant to do and be – their *telos* – then virtue ethics seems doomed. For this notion of the *telos*, if it was indeed the notion that Aristotle was using in his ethics, is not just *historically* out of reach for us, as MacIntyre argues some notions of the *telos* are in *After Virtue*. It is out of reach full stop, because the theory of evolution has refuted it.

If it was Aristotle's notion of the *telos* in his ethics. That can be questioned, of course, and perhaps should be. Even if the sort of teleology that Williams targets is indefensible, it might well be that that sort of teleology is not to be found in Aristotle. In fact it is controversial whether the notion of *telos* is to be understood even in Aristotle's science as the notion of what Williams calls an "inner nisus" in things. But even if Aristotle did use such a notion in his scientific writings, it would not follow that Aristotle is using *telos* in the same sense in his ethical writings – for example in *Nicomachean Ethics* I, where *telos* rather seems to mean simply a goal, in particular a goal that makes sense of practical reasoning. Some commentators see little reason to think that Aristotle in his ethics is thinking of human well-being in any "extraethical" sense at all: in the modern literature, the work of John McDowell (especially McDowell 1980) is the *locus classicus* for this reading.

Be this as it may, the naturalistic reading of Aristotle's notion of the *telos* persists, and continues to create a fundamental discomfort in a lot of virtue ethicists, including Philippa Foot herself in her later writings, most notably *Natural Goodness* (2001). As James Lenman rightly notes, many virtue ethicists seem – like Foot – to be keen to expound a basically zoological conception of the good life for humans, while at the same time being remarkably *unkeen* to talk about the best science we have for discussing zoology, neo-Darwinism:

[I]t seems extraordinary... that Foot in the course of the whole argument of *Natural Goodness* does not mention Darwin once... The whole modern Darwinian synthesis of evolutionary theory and genetics is similarly off the page in a paper by Michael Thompson from which Foot, McDowell and Hursthouse all draw inspiration. Thompson does briefly consider that it might be relevant to advancing our understanding of what life is to make some reference to DNA but dismisses this as doing no more to advance our understanding than "pointing to a few gorillas and turnips" (Thompson 1995, pp. 256–257). Surely this remark is *wildly* ill-judged. It is as if a proposal that we might grow in understanding of what proteins are by saying something about amino-acids were dismissed as of no more value than pointing to a few sausages. (Lenman 2005, p. 47, citing Thompson 1995)

"So virtue ethics cannot be based on an Aristotelian notion of the human *telos*. Does that mean it cannot be based on *any* notion of the human *telos*?" A resolute neo-Darwinian may insist that this is exactly what it means:

to say this is to reiterate what Williams, in a passage discussed by Hursthouse (1999, p. 256), calls the "first and hardest lesson of Darwinism", that there is simply no teleology in nature (Williams 1995b, pp. 109–110). The lesson is hard because it is so natural to think of the natural world as if there were . . . [W]e know, after Darwin, how shallow and reducible this teleology is. The teleological explanation, Species X has property P because it serves function F, is legitimate only as shorthand for a longer explanation in terms of processes of natural selection that are altogether blind and purposeless. (Lenman 2005, p. 47, citing Hursthouse 1999 and Williams 1995b)

It is actually rather surprising that either Lenman or Williams should sign up for full-on reductionism at this point. Both are basically Humeans – and Hume, as I point out in note 11, can easily be read as a teleological thinker, provided one understands his teleology as something intersubjectively constructed. Similarly some Darwinians might take a more eirenic line than Lenman and Williams, and accept that the kind of teleology that matters to neo-Aristotelianism is not mere shorthand for some more basic level of explanation to which it can ultimately be reduced. Like many other human phenomena, it is real (in some appropriate sense of "real") in its own right, and *emergent* from those more basic levels.

WHERE TO FROM HERE?

If that more eirenic approach can be sustained, then what sort of question will "What is happiness for humans?" become, and what sort of answers to it will be good answers? I cannot fully discuss these difficult issues here.[12] Briefly, "What is happiness for humans?" is a question for empirically informed philosophical reflection, and good answers to it are answers which are well supported by human experience and humane wisdom. But to look for any scientific or quasi-scientific vindication of this sort of reflection or wisdom, as Foot does in *Natural Goodness*, is to look in altogether the wrong direction; we would do better to draw answers to such questions from novels and poems and other works of art. (An approach not unknown in recent virtue ethics: consider Martha Nussbaum's work.)

Foot's "Aristotle" seems quite wrong to think that science can help us much with the notion of the *telos* – and not merely because of developments in science since the fourth century BCE. In Plato's *Gorgias* Callicles describes at length the possible advantages of injustice, and in Book 1 of Plato's *Republic* Thrasymachus observes that

if a just ruler is really to be compared in Homeric style to a shep-
herd, then we should see nothing unjust about his fleecing his subjects. In these two dialogues, which were clearly intimately known
to the actual Aristotle, we can already see the basic problem with
quasi-scientific appeals to human nature, which is simply that such
appeals either lack genuine scientific foundations, or else underde-
termine the good.[13] For any such appeal, there may be paradigms of
beautiful character and happy saintliness that it suggests, but "there
is also the figure, rarer perhaps than Callicles supposed, but real,
who is horrible enough and not miserable at all but, by any etholog-
ical standard of the bright eye and the gleaming coat, dangerously
flourishing" (Williams 1985, p. 46).[14]

The notion of the human *telos* that we need for ethics is not
a notion drawn from science, but from what Wittgenstein calls
"the shared customary behaviour of mankind [*die gemeinsame men-
schliche Handlungsweise*]" (*Philosophical Investigations* 1, §206) –
indeed from what Aristotle himself would have called *ta ēthē*. By
looking in that direction we may lose our grip on the later Foot's
ambition to root a naturalistic ethics at least partly in science rather
than in "ordinary life." But that prospect was always a mirage anyway, and if in shedding it we can shed what Kant would have called
the "heteronomy" of this sort of Aristotelian view as well – its tendency to impose on us a natural goal of life that leaves us little or no
room for choice or self-creation – then so much the better.

Here points from which Aristotle's influence has perhaps dis-
tracted us can be made clear with the help of a very different influence, Wittgenstein's – a philosopher who is often and perhaps under-
standably taken not to be an ethicist at all, though in fact, I think,
he is easily the most important ethicist of the twentieth century.
His influence has been mediated into virtue ethics by the work of
such diverse authors as Peter Winch, Roy Holland, David Wiggins,
John McDowell, Rai Gaita, Martha Nussbaum, Stephen Mulhall,
and Stanley Cavell – as well as by Anscombe herself and at least
the younger Philippa Foot. Few outside the Vatican now seriously
expect a neo-Aristotelian virtue ethics to provide us with a quasi-
scientific account of human nature and the human *telos* from which
we can simply read off that such-and-such behavior is natural or
unnatural. To help us understand the human *telos* and, hence, the
nature of *eudaimonia*, virtue ethics can explore the detail and the

texture of what we, at our clearest-headed, think already about what is good fortune and bad fortune, admirable or despicable, virtuous or vicious; about what is already implicit in the loosely woven socially and culturally defined network of hopes, expectations, ambitions, attitudes, and dispositions that we already – not necessarily uncritically – inhabit. Understanding the human *telos* is understanding *this*, and what kinds of well-being it makes possible – not propounding a hypothesis in experimental science.[15]

I don't mean this just as a point about how virtue ethicists should think of the human *telos* and *eudaimonia*. I mean it as a recommendation about how to do virtue ethics, and indeed ethics, overall. The best future for twenty-first-century virtue ethics is surely not for it to join in with the currently popular research program that investigates which of the leading moral theories can give an explanatory basis for the maximum number of moral platitudes with the minimum number of epicycles – a (mostly) harmless parlor game that you would have thought even academics would tire of sooner than they apparently have. Nor can there be much future in accounts of virtue ethics that take it (as, fortunately, not all do) to be all about a particular practical deliberative question. To think that I can settle every deliberative problem simply by asking myself "What would the virtuous person do?" is as hopeless as thinking that I can do it simply by asking "What would maximize utility?" or "What do universalizable principles dictate?" (It is especially futile as guidance to myself if I *am* the virtuous person, which is not usually supposed to be an impossibility.) Nor does the situation improve much if we put a theoretical gap of a familiar sort between our deliberative question and our criterion of rightness; for then we face some well-known and to my mind insoluble problems about how to cross this gap once we have opened it up. Virtue ethicists do better not to think of themselves, or anyone else, as working with basically just *one* deliberative question, or criterion of rightness, in the first place: as before, the great thing about virtue ethics is the variety of ethical thoughts that it allows us to have. In fact virtue ethics need not think of itself as a moral *theory*, in the sense of a systematizing enterprise, at all – and is well advised not to.

What contemporary virtue ethics *can* usefully take as its agenda for future research is the phenomenology of our ordinary life, and in particular of the place in that life of our ideas of well-being and excellence. This is a descriptive and exploratory enterprise; it is about bringing out "what we think." But it is also a critical and prescriptive one: it is also about exposing what we only think we think (Williams 1993, pp. 7, 91), locating contradictions between things that we do think but cannot keep together coherently, and getting rid altogether of those things that we think that we had better *stop* thinking – the "spectacles that we never think to remove," our prejudices.

Such a moral phenomenology – which may or may not deserve to be called "the philosophy of psychology" – is naturally a highly complex task, involving many subtasks. The good news is that virtue ethicists are already engaged in pursuing a wide range of them. The question of what human well-being is, and how the truth about that both relates and does not relate to the truths of science, we have already explored at some length. The questions of which dispositions are virtues or excellences, and what a disposition is; of whether, as a matter of empirically verifiable fact, we *have* anything worth calling dispositions;[16] and of what it is *like* to see the world from the standpoint of (a) virtue – are on this agenda too. Again, it has already proved very fruitful to engage anew, as Aquinas and others once did, in close phenomenological studies of particular virtues and other ethically important phenomena – justice, courage, love, friendship, faith, modesty, hope, glory – in order to understand what they are, how they relate to each other, how they motivate, and what kind of ideals they might set up for us to contemplate and pursue.[17] Correspondingly there is a need – already partly satisfied – for good analyses of the vices that are opposite to the virtues – pride, lust, hatred, anger, greed, jealousy, sloth and the rest (G. Taylor 1985, 2006). Further, the study of the virtues and vices cannot be well pursued – as Aristotle himself points out – without close investigation of the emotions and of the concept of pleasure; nor, to come back in a way to Anscombe, can we get very far in understanding the virtues without a good appreciation of notions like intention and motivation.

In all these ways and others "virtue ethics" fertilizes not just one progressive research program, but a whole range of them. Insofar as this gives virtue ethics an advantage over other, less fruitful approaches to normative ethics, it has to be a tactical blunder for virtue ethics to get drawn into debates about "which moral theory is the best one" which in practice are always conducted on those other approaches' singularly barren terms.

NOTES

1   For this assumption see e.g. Hursthouse 1999, chap. 1. For recent criticism of the assumption, see Coope 2007, to whom my discussion here is much indebted.

2   Our word 'virtue' too is infected by magical-sense-of-moral connotations which are not there in *aretē*, which is why it would be better to use 'excellence' or 'admirable trait' if we could. But it is now impossible to do this consistently. 'Virtue' is simply too well embedded in the relevant vocabulary – particularly, in the phrase 'virtue ethics' itself. So, with some reluctance, I shall mostly follow the usual practice and use 'virtue' rather than 'excellence.'

3   For Aristotle's remarks on *ēthos* and its close relative *ethos*, "habit," see *Nicomachean Ethics* (cited as *NE*) II.1, 1103a17.

4   An *obviously* misconceived distinction when you reflect that *prudentia* is the name of what, since Cicero and Aquinas called it a *virtus moralis*, we tend to call a moral virtue.

5   Not per se morally right. Certainly the moral turns out to be identical with the rational for Kant. But it is the rational that he primarily focuses on, and the identification of this with the moral is a philosophical discovery which epistemically at least "could have gone otherwise."

6   Wittgenstein, *Tractatus Logico-Philosophicus* 4.116. The meaning of "said" in this saying is unclear, as is the meaning of "clearly."

7   J. M. Keynes, in a 1906 letter to Lytton Strachey quoted by Williams 1995b, p. 155: "It is *impossible* to exaggerate the wonder and *originality* of Moore; people are already beginning to talk as if he were only a kind of logic-chopping eclectic. Oh why can't they see! How amazing to think that we and only we know the rudiments of a true theory of ethic; for nothing can be more certain than that the broad outline is true. What is the world doing? It does damned well bring it home to read books written before *PE* [Moore's *Principia Ethica*]. I even begin to agree with Moore about Sidgwick – that he was a wicked edifactious person."

8   "Quasi": Austin himself was quite negative (as was Ryle) about Wittgenstein. He saw more connections between his work and G. E. Moore's ordinary language philosophy.

9   The bibliography to *After Virtue* is remarkably short. For alphabetical reasons "Modern Moral Philosophy" is the first item in it. And aptly so.

10 Cf. Driver 1989, and Simone Weil: "Le contentement de soi après une bonne action (ou un oeuvre d'art) est une dégradation d'énergie supérieure. C'est pourquoi la main droite doit ignorer... toute forme de récompense (*misthos*) constitue une dégradation d'énergie" (Weil 2006, p. 354).

11 Pascal, Kant, and Kierkegaard all have a clear and prominent notion of an objective human *telos*, and their idea of the *telos* is pretty much the same as, say, Aquinas's: it is the Christian notion of salvation. Hume and Smith may well have no *objective* notion of a *telos*, but they certainly have an intersubjective constructed notion of that *telos*. Even Diderot is no more genuinely without any conception of human nature and the human good than, say, Karl Marx.

12 For good discussions see Lenman 2005, Williams 1985 and "Evolution, Ethics, and the Representation Problem," in Williams 1995b, and Hursthouse 1999, esp. pp. 256ff.

13 Watson 1990, p. 462: "Either the theory's pivotal account of human nature will be morally indeterminate, or it will not be objectively well-founded."

14 Rai Gaita notes, in rather similar vein, that Aristotelian virtue ethics has a tendency to be rather weak on *pity*, and contrasts e.g. Simone Weil's attitudes: see Gaita 1991, pp. 193–5. What we may call the Christian virtues are often surprisingly sidelined in virtue ethics, insofar as it is authentically Aristotelian: cf. Coope's (2007) tendency to downplay charity/benevolence, and upgrade justice.

15 Williams calls this sort of move "the Wittgensteinian cop-out" (1995b, p. 103): "the idea that the central concept for gaining insight into human activities is that of a 'language-game'... suggests an autonomy of the human, under a defining idea of linguistic and conceptual consciousness, which tends to put a stop to any interesting questions of the biological kind before they even start." Williams' charge unfairly conflates two questions that "Wittgensteinians" need not conflate: a synchronic one, about how a language game works now, and a diachronic one, about the history of a language game, how it arose and may have changed over time. Undoubtedly *Philosophical Investigations* is mainly interested in the former question. That does not mean that Wittgensteinians cannot pursue the latter.

16 Doris 1998, Harman 1998. For replies see Merritt 2000, Miller 2003.

17 Geach 1977, Williams 1980, Chappell 1993, 2011, Zagzebski 2007.

8 Virtue ethics and right action

It seems reasonable to claim that every normative theory should say something about right (and wrong) action. An account of right action is supposed to answer questions such as: "What, if anything, do all right actions have in common?" and "What makes an action right?" It is commonly thought that what distinguishes one normative theory from another, what makes it a form of consequentialism rather than deontology, say, is its answer to these questions. In addition, an account of right action is thought to have a practical purpose. If we can discover what all right actions have in common, it seems, we will be able to answer questions such as "Did the agent perform a right action?" and "What ought I to do in this situation?"

Unfortunately things are not quite so simple. Although we can legitimately expect an ethical theory to give some sort of answer to all of these questions, we cannot realistically expect these answers to be contained in a single criterion of right action. To begin with, we should note that "What do all right actions have in common?" is not the same question as "What makes an action right?" By answering the first question a theory provides what is sometimes referred to as a substantive account of right action. Such an account allows us to correctly identify and assess certain actions as right. By contrast, the latter question calls for an explanatory account of right action, that is, an explanation of what the rightness of an action consists in. Roger Crisp demonstrates the difference by noting that a particular normative theory could hold that all right actions have in common the fact that they promote the best consequences. However, when it comes to explaining what makes such actions right, the same theory could give a different answer, for example, "...because it is in accordance with the correct moral rule."[1] When we examine a particular account of right action, then, we have to make sure whether it is meant to be explanatory or merely substantive.

A second complication is that not all ethicists use the term 'right action' in the same way. Deontologists and consequentialists typically use "right" to mean either permissible or obligatory, whereas "wrong" is understood as synonymous with "impermissible." Many deontologists, as well as a few consequentialists, reserve a special category – that of the *supererogatory* – for actions that go "beyond the call of duty," and that deserve special praise and recognition. Right action is further distinguished from good action, by which is meant an act that is well motivated. By contrast, virtue ethicists primarily think in terms of acting well, of what is noble or ignoble, admirable or deplorable, good or bad. Some virtue ethicists dispense with deontic notions (such as right, wrong, obligatory, and permissible) altogether, on the grounds that these terms presuppose the existence of a supreme lawgiver.[2] Others provide a virtue ethical account of right action, but some of them use the term in the sense of acting well, thus blurring the distinction between rightness and goodness of action.

Thirdly, we should take note of an important distinction between action guidance and action assessment. The statement, "*X* is a (or the) right action," is sometimes used to provide guidance, as a response to the question, "What ought one to do?" At other times, however, it is used to assess or evaluate an action. Deontologists and consequentialists tend to think of these two functions as two sides of the same coin: when an agent does what he ought to do, he ends up performing a right action. As we shall see, however, some virtue ethicists argue that action guidance and action assessment can come apart, that is, that it is possible for an agent to do what he ought to do without thereby performing a right action. An account of right action should therefore include an account of both action guidance and action assessment.

A final complication is that one should not necessarily expect a criterion of right action, one that provides either an explanatory or substantive account of right action, to also be a useful decision-making procedure. In recent years many ethicists – and not all of them virtue ethicists – have questioned whether it is reasonable, given the complexity of moral decision-making, to expect a normative theory to come up with a decision-making procedure that can be applied by anyone to render the correct result. Some utilitarians have argued, for example, that while the principle of utility identifies an act as right if it maximizes utility, using that principle as a decision-making tool might well prevent us from maximizing utility. In an emergency situation the most reliable way of achieving the best outcome for everyone involved could well be to follow a set of rules or instructions, rather than consciously aiming at the overall good.[3] Similarly, virtue ethicists argue that it is unrealistic to expect there to be such a thing as a "theory of right action" which will tell us which actions are right and why they are right, and that can be used by anyone, at any stage of moral development, as a kind of decision procedure. Instead, they tend to emphasize the importance of acquiring the virtues, most notably practical wisdom, in allowing us to deal with real-life problems.

In what follows I discuss three virtue ethical accounts of right action, namely a qualified-agent account, an agent-based account, and a target-centered account. In examining each of these it will be helpful to consider (1) whether it is a substantive or an explanatory account of right action, (2) the sense in which it uses the term 'right action,' and (3) whether it distinguishes between making the right decision (action guidance) and performing a right action (action assessment). Although virtue ethicists have made an important contribution to applied ethics, my focus in this chapter is on normative theory. I shall therefore set aside practical questions such as, "How do I go about performing actions that are right?"

A QUALIFIED-AGENT ACCOUNT

The most familiar attempt by virtue ethicists to provide a theory of right action is to appeal to the idea of what would be done by the virtuous person. This involves thinking about what is important in one's current situation, which virtues are called for, and what acting virtuously involves in this situation. These theories are referred to as "qualified-agent accounts," and in this section I will focus on the version provided by Rosalind Hursthouse.[4]

In response to the question, "How can virtue ethics give an account of right action in such a way as to provide action guidance?," Hursthouse gives the following criterion:

(V) An action is right iff it is what a virtuous agent would characteristically do in the circumstances.[5]

She goes on to define a virtuous agent as one who has and exercises the virtues, and a virtue as a character trait a human being needs to flourish or live well.

One thing to note about this criterion is that it is a substantive, rather than an explanatory account of right action. It does not hold that an act is right *because* it is what a virtuous person would do. The virtuous person chooses a certain action for reasons that are independent of the fact that this kind of action is what virtuous agents characteristically do in those circumstances, and we would expect that it is these reasons, rather than the fact that she acts upon them, that make her action right. Supporters of qualified-agent theories deny that there is a single right-making feature that all right acts have in common. Instead, they hold a pluralistic view, akin to the view held by deontologists such as W. D. Ross, namely that what makes an action right could be any of a number of things, for example that it satisfies an important need, or that it gives someone their share, or that it consists of telling the truth, etc.[6] It is for this reason that they emphasize the role of practical reasoning, understood as the capacity to appreciate or discern what is right or appropriate conduct in particular situations.

Despite this similarity there are important differences between qualified-agent accounts and deontology, which can be demonstrated by comparing their treatment of moral dilemmas, specifically tragic dilemmas.[7] According to Hursthouse, an agent finds herself in a tragic dilemma when he is forced to make a choice between two or more terrible actions, "terrible" in the sense that they involve, for example, causing a great amount of suffering, breaking a promise or killing someone. She mentions Bernard Williams' well-known case of Jim and Pedro as a possible example.[8] Whether Jim kills one peasant, or refuses and allows the twenty to be killed, he would be doing something that can only be described as "terrible." But is he forced to do something terribly *wrong*? Consider (W), which is the corollary of (V):

(W) An act is wrong iff it is what a vicious agent would characteristically do in the circumstances.

Now, it looks like Hursthouse will have to say that Jim acts
wrongly, whatever he does. However, she resists this conclusion
by denying that a statement such as "Jim kills a peasant" provides
an accurate description of what the agent does. The way in which
he acts, his feelings, attitudes, and motives are all part of his action.
This allows Hursthouse to say that although the virtuous agent is
forced to make a choice between two terrible actions, and cannot
therefore emerge with his life unmarred, he is not forced to act
wrongly, for he does not act indifferently or gladly, as the vicious do,
but with immense regret and pain.[9]

The next question that arises is whether the virtuous agent can
perform a right action in a tragic dilemma. Hursthouse claims that
some tragic dilemmas are resolvable; the virtuous agent will see that
one alternative is preferable to the other. In such cases a Rossian
deontologist claims that the agent is faced with a conflict between
prima facie duties, but if he chooses to act in accordance with
whichever duty is overriding in this situation, he ends up acting
rightly. A straightforward application of (V) gives a similar result:
if the agent acts in a way that is characteristic of a virtuous agent
(by resolving the dilemma correctly, acting with immense regret and
pain, etc.) he performs a right action. Somewhat surprisingly, however, Hursthouse thinks this is the wrong result; it is a mistake to
give "this terrible deed, the doing of which mars the virtuous agent's
life, a tick of approval, as a good deed."[10] So she allows that the
virtuous agent can make the right decision (or resolve the dilemma
correctly), but denies that he thereby performs a right action.

But how can this be? Isn't "performing a right action" simply
equivalent to "doing what one ought to do" or "making the right
decision"? According to Hursthouse, this is not necessarily the case.
She distinguishes between two ways in which the term 'right action'
can be used. A statement such as "You ought to do X" or "X would
be right" gives action guidance; it tells us that the right decision
would be to do X. By contrast, the statement "X is a right action"
involves assessing or evaluating it, giving it a "tick of approval" as
a good or excellent action. Sometimes doing what one ought to do
results in a right action, but not always. Tragic dilemmas are one
type of case where action guidance and action assessment can come
apart, where we can say that an agent did what he ought to have
done, but his action was not a right action. A right action, then, is

not equivalent to "what ought to be done" but is "an act that merits praise rather than blame, an act that an agent can take pride in doing rather than feel unhappy about, the sort of act that decent, virtuous agents do and seek out occasions for doing."[11]

Once we see that Hursthouse has a different understanding of what the term 'right action' means, it becomes clear why she believes a virtuous agent cannot perform a right action when faced with a tragic dilemma. She therefore adds a qualification to her original specification of right action (V), namely: "... except for tragic dilemmas, in which a decision is right iff it is what [a virtuous] agent would decide, but the action decided upon may be too terrible to be called 'right' or 'good.'"[12] She hereby acknowledges that human beings are vulnerable to moral luck, insofar as they can, through no fault of their own, find themselves in situations where they are unable to do anything that could count as right.

Some people find this view unattractive. A simpler, more straightforward solution would be to hold that a virtuous agent who finds herself in a tragic dilemma through no fault of her own, who chooses the action because it is the least bad of those available to her, and who acts with immense regret and pain, performs a right action.[13] This view is supported by theories that judge the rightness of action solely on the basis of the agent's motive, and I will discuss an example of such a theory in the following section. At this stage it is worth noting that for Hursthouse, acting from a virtuous motive is necessary but not sufficient for right action. In her view, an action that is well-motivated but has a terrible outcome cannot be right, even if it constitutes the "lesser of two evils." This is her way of accepting that virtue ethics must address our serious practical concerns about outcomes and consequences.[14]

Let us now look at a different kind of moral dilemma, which is probably more common, namely where an agent finds himself in the situation because of some character defect or past wrongdoing. Hursthouse's example is of a man who has impregnated two women, A and B, and can now marry and support only one. Imagine that B finds another suitor who is happy to support both her and the child, so that it would clearly be worse to abandon A.[15] If he marries A, will he perform a right action? Some critics object that (V) does not apply to this kind of case, simply because a virtuous agent would not find himself in this situation in the first place.[16] Hursthouse responds that (V) does allow for action assessment; it tells us that it is impossible for the philanderer to perform a right action. If we keep in mind that "right action" is not equivalent to "what one ought to do" but instead is an act that warrants a "tick of approval," then this may be a satisfactory response. "Marrying A is not a right action" does not imply "He ought not to marry A." It simply means that he does not do a good deed, or as Hursthouse puts it, a satisfactory review of his conduct is not for him.[17]

This response has not completely satisfied her critics, however. Robert Johnson argues that it is intuitively plausible that a nonvirtuous agent can perform a right action even if he cannot do what a virtuous agent would do. He gives the example of a chronic liar who wants to improve his character, and tries to do so by following the advice of his therapist to write down all his lies, reminding himself why telling the truth is important, and so on. Johnson argues that (V) gives the wrong result – namely that his action cannot be right, because he cannot do what a virtuous person would do in this situation, since no virtuous person would find himself in this situation in the first place. Yet, in his view, there can be "something truly excellent in a moral respect about the reformations of the liar."[18]

Some virtue ethicists respond to this objection by revising (V), for example by defining right action in terms of what the virtuous agent would advise one to do, or would approve of one doing.[19] A different approach is to retain (V) and to hold that the reforming liar does not perform a right action. His actions can be described as resembling the actions of courageous and determined agents, and so in this sense it accounts for our intuition that there is *something* truly excellent about his behavior. However, the central virtue in question here is honesty, and by writing down his lies etc., the reforming liar does not (yet) act in a way that is characteristic of a virtuous (honest) person. Applying a qualified-agent criterion of wrong action, (W), we can say that his actions are no longer characteristic of the vicious, and so it is appropriate to reward him with some praise and encouragement. Whereas traditional theories tend to think of right and wrong action as exclusive, virtue ethics allows for a range of actions that lie somewhere on the continuum between right (characteristic of the virtuous) and wrong (characteristic of the vicious). There are ways in which the habitual liar's actions are beginning to resemble those of an honest person, most notably the fact that he is beginning to see the value of telling the truth, but they are not yet characteristic of an honest person.[20]

Let us now return to the matter of action guidance. The objection still stands that the philanderer and the habitual liar cannot get guidance from (V), since a virtuous agent will not find himself in these kinds of situations in the first place. One way to respond to this objection is to admit that (V), as a criterion of *right* (good, excellent) action, is not an action-guiding principle; it does not tell us what we *ought* to do. Now of course, one can derive a positive action-guiding principle from (V), namely "Do what a virtuous agent would characteristically do in the circumstances" (AG+), as well as a list of more specific virtue rules, such as "Do what is charitable" and "Do what is honest."[21] In some cases, where nothing the agent can do will count as characteristic of the virtuous, (AG+) and the virtue rules will not provide guidance. But now remember that we also have (W), from which we can derive another action-guiding principle, "Do not do what a vicious agent would characteristically do in the circumstances" (AG−). This generates a list of more specific vice rules, namely "Do not do what is dishonest, uncharitable, mean, etc.," that does provide action guidance to nonvirtuous agents. Thus our philanderer has at least three options: (1) to abandon both women, (2) to abandon A and pursue B, ignoring the fact that B is no longer interested in him, and (3) to abandon B and marry A. Now, all three of these actions are characteristic of a vicious (selfish, unreliable, irresponsible) agent, since they involve abandoning a woman one has impregnated. However, by choosing option (1) or (2), an agent will manifest the further vice of being insensitive to an important difference between the two women, namely that B will be looked after even if he abandons her, whereas A won't. The rule, "Do not do what is uncaring or indifferent" thus points to option (3) as the correct one.

A further point that can be made in this regard is that by choosing to do (3) the philanderer will take the first step on the road to becoming a more responsible (and thereby more virtuous) person. In much the same way, in the case of the compulsive liar one could argue that he should perform a set of remedial actions if he is to avoid continuing to act in the way that vicious (dishonest) people characteristically do. It is worth noting that in this respect virtue ethics has an important advantage over traditional moral theories, which tend to focus exclusively on current-time-slice analyses of choices and actions. Virtue ethics does allow these kinds of analyses, but it also, and more importantly, is about the development of virtuous agents over time.[22] In the case of the philanderer, for example, it tells him not only to marry A, but also to become a loyal, caring and responsible husband and father, with all that that entails.

We have seen that Hursthouse's qualified-agent theory provides an account of right action not in the sense of what is permissible or obligatory but in the sense of what is good or excellent. It is an ideal, and as such it is one that may not be realized all the time. Some kinds of situations, such as tragic dilemmas and dilemmas that are a result of previous acts of wrongdoing, will not allow for the doing of right actions. But Hursthouse also argues that for an act to be right, it must be motivated by the right reasons. Consider, for example, the case of an agent who gives to charity to impress a friend. Such actions are commonly described as "doing the right thing for the wrong reason," but Hursthouse thinks this phrase is misleading for it obscures the fact that, in one way, the agent is not "doing the right thing" but instead is trying to impress a friend.[23] She writes:

What you *do* does not count as right unless it is what the virtuous agent would *do*, say, "tell the truth, after much painful thought, for the right reasons, feeling deep regret, having put in place all that can be done to support the person on the receiving end afterwards." Only if you get all of that right are you entitled to the satisfactory review of your own conduct ... [S]imply making the right decision and telling the truth is not good enough to merit approval.[24]

Acting virtuously requires that the agent knows what she is doing (rather than her acting accidentally or unintentionally), that she acts for a reason and, moreover, for the right reason (rather than from an ulterior motive), and that she has the appropriate feeling(s) or attitude(s) when she acts. Hursthouse notes an interesting difference between terms such as 'acting morally' (or 'acting rightly') and 'acting well,' namely that the former is not open to such qualifications as "quite," "fairly," "very," or "perfectly," whereas the latter is. We can act "fairly well," "quite well," or, if all the conditions for acting well are met, "perfectly" or "excellently."[25] This is one of the reasons why Hursthouse notes that virtue ethics is not happy with the term 'right action,' with its suggestion of uniqueness, and its implication of "if not right then wrong," and instead prefers talking in terms of "good action" or "acting well."[26]

In what follows I shall discuss an agent-based account of right action, which treats the rightness of an act as strictly dependent on virtuous motivation. Agent-based virtue ethics differs in an important respect from qualified-agent theories, in that it provides an explanatory account of right action, that is, it tells us that an action is right *because* it comes from a certain motive. By contrast, we have seen, qualified-agent theories provide a substantive account of right action, allowing us to fix the properties of right and wrong to their proper object, but without thereby telling us what makes an action right or wrong.

AGENT-BASED VIRTUE ETHICS

In *Morals from Motives* Michael Slote develops an agent-based virtue ethics which is inspired by the sentimentalism of Hume and Hutcheson as well as James Martineau. It gives the following account of right action:

(A) An act is right (morally acceptable) if and only if it comes from good or virtuous motivation involving benevolence or caring (about the well-being of others) or at least doesn't come from bad or inferior motivation involving malice or indifference to humanity.[27]

Like consequentialism, agent-based virtue ethics denies that an action can be right or wrong in itself. But whereas consequentialism claims that rightness depends on consequences, agent-based virtue ethics holds that what makes an action right is the fact that it proceeds from a nonvicious motive. (A) is therefore an explanatory account of right action, and applied to the case of the promiscuous lover it says that he performs a right action if (and because) his marrying A and abandoning B is motivated by a concern for their welfare, say, rather than his own good.

Another feature of agent-based virtue ethics which is worth mentioning is that it claims that virtue is fundamental, in the sense that the admirability of a virtue is not dependent on any further properties, such as its consequences or its being needed for flourishing. Slote distinguishes agent-*based* theories from those that are agent-*prior*. The latter do not derive rightness wholly from virtuous motives, and neither do they make virtue fundamental.[28]

Many people find agent-based virtue ethics intuitively plausible, and I suspect that the reason for this is that it seems to avoid the problem of moral luck. Their reasoning might go something as follows:

> If rightness depended on the actual consequences of an action, then an action could be right or wrong quite by accident, for we cannot fully control the consequences of our actions.[29] Agent-based virtue ethics has an advantage in that it holds that a fully benevolent agent – one who makes every effort to find out relevant facts and is careful in acting – cannot be criticized as acting immorally if she fails to help the people she seeks to help, or praised as acting morally if she helps people without seeking to do so.[30]

Upon closer examination, however, it is not all that obvious that this is an advantage, for consequentialism has a ready response to this objection:

> Consequentialism does allow luck to play a role in rightness, but this is not a weakness. When assessing an action as wrong we are not thereby blaming or criticizing the agent. We are simply saying that he shouldn't have done what he did. To be sure, an evaluation of an act as wrong is often *accompanied* by criticism of the agent, given that people who act wrongly usually do so intentionally or from some character flaw or weakness. But this need not be the case. We can judge a specific action as wrong, as something that ought not to have been done, while at the same time acknowledging that the agent is not to blame. Equally, we can judge an act as right and still criticize the agent for acting from a bad motive.

It appears, then, that agent-based virtue ethics does not have an advantage over consequentialism when it comes to the problem of moral luck. To the contrary, the above discussion serves to highlight an important problem for agent-based virtue ethics, namely that it does not allow us to make this very distinction between doing the right (or wrong) thing, and doing it for a good (or bad) reason, and to this extent the theory seems counterintuitive.[31] Now of course, the mere fact that a theory conflicts with some of our intuitions is not sufficient to discount it, for our intuitions may well be mistaken. So we have to examine more closely the kinds of cases where our evaluation of the action and evaluation of the motive appear to diverge, to see whether there really is a problem.

Let us begin by considering what looks like an example of "blame-less wrongdoing":

Alex intends to help Tessa but ends up, not merely failing to help but actually harming her.

Slote handles this kind of case by noting, first, that the agent may not manifest true benevolence at all, so the act may not be entirely blameless. He explains: "benevolence...isn't benevolence in the fullest sense unless one cares about who exactly is needy and to what extent they are needy, and such care, in turn, essentially involves wanting and making efforts to know relevant facts, so that one's benevolence can be really useful."[32] But it doesn't necessarily follow that Alex's action will be assessed as wrong. Slote's version of agent-based virtue ethics does not hold that an action has to be motivated by benevolence in its fullest sense for it to be right. Instead, as we have seen, it states that an action is right if it exhibits or expresses an admirable motive, *or at least does not exhibit or express a deplorable motive*. It would therefore judge the agent who protests that she "meant only to help" as having acted wrongly only if her action manifests a deplorable character trait, such as careless-ness or insensitivity. So, part of the response to the objection that an agent-based theory fails to account for the intuition that there can be examples of blameless wrongdoing, then, is that some such actions are not blameless at all, and therefore wrong according to an agent-based view.

But what does it say about cases where a fully benevolent agent ends up, through no fault of her own, harming those she seeks to help? Consider the following case as a possible example of blameless wrongdoing:

John gives a thirsty person a drink, but unbeknownst to him the drink is poisonous and the person dies.

Most people would agree with Slote that John cannot be blamed or criticized, but is the action nevertheless wrong? Intuitions on this vary. Some people claim that John acted wrongly, that he ought not to have offered the drink, given the bad consequences. Others would say that it is right to give a thirsty person what you have good reason to believe is a drink of water. So on this score, it seems, an agent-based view is not obviously counterintuitive. But the very fact that intuitions can diverge so much may give rise to the suspicion that the parties do not hold the same *conception* of right and wrong action. Slote sometimes uses the term 'right' as interchangeable with "good," "fine," or "morally acceptable," and as we have seen, he assumes that assessing an action as wrong amounts to criticizing the agent. By contrast, those who hold a more legalistic conception of rightness insist that assessing an action as right or wrong is a separate matter to assessing a person's praise- or blameworthiness.[33]

Let us now consider a different kind of case, namely where a poorly motivated agent performs an action that appears to be intuitively right. Slote discusses the following example:

A prosecutor does his duty by trying to convict a defendant whom he believes to be guilty, but is motivated by malice rather than by concern for the public good.

This case raises significant difficulties for agent-based virtue ethics. The standard consequentialist view is that although the act is right (if it has a good outcome), the motive is bad.[34] Similarly, Kantians would claim that although he acts in accordance with duty and therefore rightly, he does not act from duty, with the result that his action has no moral worth. By contrast, according to agent-based virtue ethics, the prosecutor acts wrongly because he acts from malice. Now, one reason why this appears counterintuitive is that it seems to suggest that he does not have a duty to prosecute, or that he ought not to prosecute. But Slote is quick to deny this implication. He argues that if the agent does not prosecute it will also manifest a bad motive – lack of concern for the public good – and hence be wrong. Let us assume, for the sake of simplicity, that the prosecutor does not have the option of recusing himself and letting someone else prosecute. If his only choice is between prosecuting maliciously and letting the accused go free, then it seems that whatever he does would be wrong. The malicious prosecutor, it appears, finds himself in an irresolvable moral dilemma: he ought to prosecute and not let the accused go free, and he ought not to prosecute from malice, but he cannot do both.

One difficulty that faces theories that are committed to the view that there can be genuine moral dilemmas is, as Slote puts it, that it "seems to contravene the maxim that 'ought' implies 'can,' for if badly motivated people have obligations but everything such people can do counts as wrong, they have obligations that they are unable to fulfill."[35] Slote tries to avoid this problem by arguing that one is never forced to perform a wrong action, for there is always the following sort of option:

> Presumably, one cannot change one's motives or character at will. But a thoroughly malevolent individual who sees a person he can hurt may still have it within his power to refrain from hurting that person, even if we can be sure he won't in fact exercise that power. And the act of refraining would fail to express or reflect his malevolence and would therefore not count as wrong.[36]

According to Slote, then, the malicious prosecutor has it in his power to prosecute the defendant while also refraining from expressing his malice, from which he concludes that agent-basing is consistent with "ought implies can." But this response is inadequate, for as Daniel Jacobson argues, although it is sometimes possible to avoid expressing poor motivation by refraining from acting in a certain way, this need not be the case on any given occasion. Even though our actions are volitional, our motives may not be, and Slote himself accepts that one cannot change one's character or motives at will.[37] So it seems that Slote might well have to accept that an agent can sometimes have obligations which he is unable to fulfill.

Another, more fundamental difficulty for Slote is to explain how an agent-based theory can provide action guidance: on what grounds can it claim that the malicious prosecutor has a duty to prosecute in the first place? Slote answers this question by claiming that if he doesn't prosecute his motivation will also be bad. He writes:

> Imagine that, horrified by his own malice, he ends up not prosecuting and unwilling even to think about letting someone else do so. This action too will come from an inner state that is morally criticizable, namely, one involving (among other things) insufficient concern for the public (or general human) good or for being useful to society.[38]

According to Michael Brady, Slote here violates a central tenet of his theory, namely that the moral status of an action depends on the status of the agent's motives. Slote defines the prosecutor's duty independently of his actual motives, namely, in terms of the motives which would be expressed if he failed to prosecute. Brady also notes a further problem that arises when trying to provide a motive-based account of moral duty, namely that the agent's motives in prosecuting seem to *change* what he has a duty to do:

> [I]f he has a duty to prosecute, because a failure to do so would express a bad motive, then his doing his duty from a malicious motive means that it would be wrong for him to prosecute, and thus means that he doesn't have a duty to prosecute after all. Instead, given his malicious motive, our prosecutor has a duty not to prosecute.[39]

These kinds of problems point to an important inconsistency in Slote's reasoning. On the one hand, he claims that a failure to prosecute will come from a bad motive and therefore be wrong, and from this he concludes that the agent has a duty to prosecute. This reasoning is in line with traditional usage, which takes a statement such as "Not-*X* is wrong" as implying that "*X* is right" or "The agent has a duty to *X*." On the other hand, as noted above, Slote also denies that the claim, "Prosecuting from malice is wrong," implies that the agent does not have a duty to prosecute. But Slote cannot have it both ways: a claim about the wrongness of an action either does or does not support a claim about what one has a duty to do. If we accept that claims about wrongness do support claims about duty, we end up with a contradiction, namely that the agent has a duty to prosecute (because not prosecuting would be poorly motivated and therefore wrong) *and* that he does not have a duty to prosecute (because prosecuting from malice would be wrong). If, instead, we accept that claims about wrongness do not support claims about duty, then Slote has not yet provided an answer to the question of how a duty to prosecute can be understood in agent-based terms. All he has shown is that a failure to prosecute would be wrong if it comes from a lack of concern for the public good.

The latter alternative seems preferable, and indeed, it is suggested by Slote himself when he claims that an agent-based approach can distinguish between "doing one's duty for the right reasons and thus acting rightly, on the one hand, and doing one's duty for the wrong reasons and thus acting wrongly."[40] This suggests a distinction between action guidance and action assessment, similar to the one Hursthouse draws. In this view, action-guiding statements like "He ought to *X*" or "He has a duty to *X*" do not necessarily imply that an agent who does *X* will thereby act rightly.[41] The advantage of making this distinction is that it allows an agent-based theory to say, in the case of the malicious prosecutor, that even though it may be true that he cannot perform a right action, given his malicious motives, it does not necessarily follow that he finds himself in an irresolvable dilemma, for what he ought to do (or has a duty to do) is to prosecute the defendant. In this way it also avoids the "ought implies can" problem: the agent can do what he ought to do (namely, to prosecute); what he may not be able to do is to act rightly (by prosecuting from a good motive).

Now, if the central tenet of agent-based virtue ethics, namely that the moral status of an action depends on motive, is seen as a claim about rightness and wrongness, rather than about duty or obligation, the question arises as to how it can account for obligation. There appear to be various ways in which such a theory can be developed. One possibility is to give an account of obligation in terms of the motives of the hypothetical virtuous agent.[42] Another is to derive a list of action-guiding rules or duties from the virtues, such as "Do what is benevolent" and "Do not do what is malicious." Of course, it is questionable whether such an approach will still be purely agent based, but that may well be a price worth paying.[43]

A TARGET-CENTERED ACCOUNT

As we have seen, some supporters of qualified-agent approaches claim that an agent who acts from a poor motive fails to perform a right action. Agent-based virtue ethics gives motive an even more central place, insofar as it holds that acting from a nonvirtuous motive is both necessary and sufficient for right action. By contrast, Christine Swanton develops a target-centered account of right action which takes the focus off of motivations.[44] She begins by considering Aristotle's distinction between *acting from virtue* and a *virtuous act*:

...virtuous acts are not done in a just or temperate way merely because *they* have a certain quality, but only if the agent also acts in a certain state, viz. (1) if he knows what he is doing, (2) if he chooses it, and chooses it for its own sake, and (3) if he does it from a fixed and permanent disposition.[45]

This distinction allows Aristotle to say that a nonvirtuous agent (who does not act from a fixed and permanent state of virtue) can nevertheless act virtuously. But how exactly is this possible? Swanton's answer is that the agent can hit the target of a virtue.[46] Consider the virtue of benevolence, which has as its target "promoting the good of others." An act that succeeds in promoting the good of others is a benevolent act. Assuming that benevolence is the only relevant virtue in the situation, such an act is right, but without the agent necessarily being motivated by benevolence. Conversely, a fully benevolent agent can miss the target of benevolence, thus failing to act rightly, but without thereby being blameworthy. Swanton notes that the requirements for acting from (a state of) virtue and acting virtuously are demanding in different ways. Acting from virtue requires "fine motivation (including having fine ends), fine emotions, practical wisdom, and the possession of a stable *disposition* of fine emotions, feelings, and other affective states."[47] Acting virtuously requires successfully hitting the target of a virtue, and one may fail to do so through sheer bad luck or incomplete knowledge, for instance when one gives a thirsty person a poisonous drink under the impression that it is water.

A target-centered account of right action has two central premises:

(T1) An action is virtuous in respect V (e.g. benevolent, generous) if and only if it hits the target of virtue V (e.g. benevolence, generosity).

(T2) An action is right if and only if it is overall virtuous.

This account is structurally similar to consequentialism, in that it offers an explanation of what makes an action right in terms of success in action, which is not entirely reducible to inner properties of a virtuous agent. In this way Swanton's account draws a distinction between rightness and praiseworthiness, and between wrongness and blameworthiness.[48] A frequent objection to consequentialism in virtue of this structure is that it oversimplifies our relations to others. W. D. Ross writes, for example, that it suggests that "the only morally significant relation in which my neighbours stand to me is that of being possible beneficiaries by my action."[49] Swanton's theory avoids this objection by providing a more nuanced account of what counts as success in action.

The first point to note in this regard is that hitting the target of virtue may involve several modes of moral response. Swanton uses Iris Murdoch's example of the friendly or benevolent treatment of a daughter-in-law to illustrate. In this example benevolence requires the agent to see her daughter-in-law in the right way (through a loving rather than a hostile gaze, by thinking of her via honorific rather than pejorative concepts), displaying respect in promoting her good (by not lying to, manipulating, or coercing her), and expressing appropriate forms of closeness so as not to appear cold and unfeeling.[50] Second, Swanton notes that whereas the target of some virtues is external, the target of others is entirely internal. For example, the virtue of determination or mental strength involves trying hard in a sustained way, and this target may be reached even if the agent fails rather consistently in her endeavors. It would therefore be a mistake to think that Swanton offers a purely "external" criterion of right action, one that a person is able to meet no matter what kind of motives, disposition, or character they act from.[51] Third, some virtues have more than one target. For example, hitting the target of courage involves both an internal target (controlling one's fear) and an external target (handling a dangerous or threatening situation successfully). Fourth, targets may vary with context. Swanton uses the example of poisoning opossums with cyanide to protect indigenous forests. Focusing only on the effect on the opossums, some people would describe the act as cruel. However, someone who is aware of the poisoner's mental anguish might deny this, despite the fact that it hurts the opossums. Finally, some targets of virtue are to avoid things. For example, the target of modesty is to avoid drawing attention to oneself, talking about oneself excessively, boasting and so on.[52]

Now that we have a better idea of what it means to hit the target of a virtue, the question arises as to how stringently (T1) should be applied. Must the act be the best one possible, or need it only be "good enough" in order to hit the target? The first view makes the target of a virtue very stringent, whereas the latter view allows for a range, from the truly splendid and admirable to acts that are "all right." A target-centered approach can accommodate either of these views, but Swanton opts for the first, for she finds it natural to think of the targets of a virtue as best acts (relative to the virtue). She distinguishes between actions that are right (overall virtuous, which entails the best action possible in the circumstances), wrong (overall vicious) and "all right" (not overall vicious).[53]

One feature of a target-centered account that distinguishes it from the other virtue ethical approaches discussed here is that it can accommodate traditional deontic notions such as "obligation" and "prohibition." As we have seen, Hursthouse and (arguably) Slote use "right action" in the sense of an action that is good or virtuous, rather than in the sense of what ought to be done. By contrast, Swanton makes a clear distinction between an action that is virtuous and one that is done from a virtuous motive, and then ties rightness to virtuous action rather than action from virtue; an act is right if and only if it hits the target of all the contextually appropriate virtue(s). Swanton goes on to distinguish between right actions that are obligatory (or that ought to be done), and right actions that are desirable or admirable but not obligatory. The latter includes supererogatory actions that are excessively demanding, as well as undemanding actions such as returning a minor favor. She also distinguishes between wrong actions that are prohibited, and wrong actions that are undesirable only, such as relatively minor rudeness or inconsiderateness.[54]

This gives her approach an advantage over some other virtue ethical approaches, namely that it does not encounter the same kind of difficulty of having to explain away counterintuitive results. To see this, let us consider the case of the malicious prosecutor again. As we have seen, agent-based and qualified-agent approaches support the view that if he acts from malice, he fails to perform a right action (even though he does what he ought to do). By contrast, a target-centered approach tells us that although the prosecutor does not act from virtue, his action will be right if he manages to hit the target of justice (by giving the defendant a fair trial). This fits with the intuition that many people have when it comes to assessing the prosecutor's action, namely that what is important is whether the prosecutor succeeds in giving the defendant a fair trial, regardless of the prosecutor's motives.

Applying a target-centered account to the case of the promiscuous man similarly gives a plausible result. The promiscuous man, having impregnated two women, finds himself in an irresolvable dilemma, for he can, at best, only hit the target of the relevant virtues (such as loyalty, care and concern) with respect to his treatment of one of them. Whether he marries *A* or *B*, his action will fail to be virtuous overall. Fortunately for him, however, when *B* makes it clear that she no longer needs nor wants his support, she "lets him off the hook," in the sense that he no longer has an obligation to marry and support her, and is now able to do the right thing by *A*. It is important to note, then, that in contrast to Hursthouse's qualified-agent account, a target-centered account of right action accepts that it is possible for an agent to perform a right action despite finding himself in the situation through past wrongdoing. This is because assessing the act as right does not amount to claiming that he can take pride in his conduct but simply to saying that he does what is either permissible or obligatory. A target-centered account can also explain why we might be skeptical about whether the promiscuous man will in fact succeed in acting rightly. The simple act of marrying *A* is not going to be sufficient for right action; in the context of marriage and parenthood, hitting the targets of the relevant virtues – loyalty, benevolence, care, trustworthiness, etc. – is neither simple nor easy, and given his past conduct, we may doubt that the character of the promiscuous man is such as to allow him to get it right and keep on getting it right.

Swanton argues that a target-centered approach allows us to admit the possibility of right action in tragic dilemmas, where an agent is faced with alternatives all of which are extremely repugnant. This is because virtue-based evaluations allow us to think of "actions" as embracing demeanor, motivation, thought processes, reactions and attitudes. In the Jim and Pedro case, for example, it is possible for Jim to act virtuously overall, that is, if his demeanor, motivation, thought processes, and reactions can be described as strong, courageous, anguished, etc. rather than as arrogant, callous, light minded, etc.[55] A possible objection to this view is that, in genuinely tragic dilemmas, it may be impossible for the agent to hit the target of some virtues. In Jim's case, what presumably motivates him to kill a villager is benevolence or concern for the welfare of other villagers. However, it may be thought odd to claim that the act of killing an innocent man hits the target of benevolence, even if we accept Swanton's claim that what is considered to be the appropriate target of a virtue depends on context. It seems that the agent's benevolence must be frustrated in this case. As Daniel Russell puts it:

"benevolence does not do in this case what one, *qua* benevolent, has a *pro tanto* reason to do."[56] Now, if this is correct, then target-centered virtue ethics will once again have the difficulty of explaining why killing one villager can nevertheless be the right thing to do in these circumstances.

Another difficulty for target-centered virtue ethics is to answer the question of where exactly to draw the line between right actions that are obligatory and those that are desirable but not obligatory, and between wrong actions that are prohibited and those that are merely undesirable but not prohibited. Swanton notes that her approach is neutral on this issue, and that some target-centered virtue ethicists will support a more demanding version of the theory than others. Still, it may be claimed that we need some kind of nontrivial reason for distinguishing between cases where hitting the target of the relevant virtues is obligatory, and when doing so is desirable or admirable but not obligatory. A possible answer would be to say that acting rightly cannot be obligatory in cases where hitting the target(s) is excessively demanding, for example in cases involving extreme generosity, where the agent is asked to make a significant sacrifice. However, we also want to say that undemanding actions, such as returning a minor favor, are not obligatory either but merely admirable. So it seems that whether a right action is obligatory or admirable depends on more than just how demanding it is. It may also depend on factors such as whether the action will make a significant difference to another person, whether a promise was made, and whether someone has a right to be treated in a certain way. The challenge, then, is for target-centered virtue ethicists to distinguish between obligatory and desirable actions (and between undesirable and forbidden actions) in a way that is nontrivial and also consistent with the central tenets of the theory.[57]

CONCLUSION

In this chapter I examined three virtue-ethical accounts of right action, together with some of the difficulties faced by each. Hursthouse's version of qualified-agent virtue ethics provides a substantive account of right action in the form of (V): an action is right if and only if it is what a virtuous agent would characteristically do in the circumstances. "Right" is here used in the sense of what is good or admirable rather than in the sense of what ought to be done. Action guidance comes in the form of the "V-rules," which are derived from (V) and its corollary, (W). A challenge for qualified-agent approaches is to explain what makes an action right, or, if no such explanation is forthcoming, at least to provide a reason why answering the explanatory question is not important.[58] By contrast, Slote's agent-based virtue ethics gives an explanatory account of right action, according to which an action is right if (and because) it is motivated by a non-vicious motive. A significant problem for agent-based virtue ethics is to provide an account of moral obligation in terms of motivation. Finally, according to Swanton's target-centered approach what makes an action right is that it hits the target(s) of the contextually appropriate virtue(s). Arguably, this account of right action is more conventional than the other two insofar as it does not separate action guidance from action assessment: a right action is one that is either obligatory or desirable. The result is that this approach does not encounter the same degree of difficulty with having to explain away counterintuitive results. However, certain aspects of this approach still need to be further developed, for example, determining what counts as the appropriate targets of a virtue in a given context, and explaining when a right action is obligatory and when it is merely desirable.

I mentioned in my introductory remarks that we should not expect an account of right action to serve as a decision-making tool in everyday life, and it should now be clear why this is the case. Consider, for example, an agent-based criterion of rightness. Someone who consciously sets out to act from a certain motive, say benevolence, will fail to do so, for what will motivate him to act is not benevolence itself, but rather a desire to act from a benevolent motive. Hence Slote writes: "The morally good person isn't guided by a theory or (agent-based) moral principle or even a sense of rightness as much as by a good heart that seeks to do good for and by people."[59] Swanton similarly accepts that a target-centered account of right action is not to be used as an action-guiding tool. Instead, she answers the question of how a virtuous agent should approach problem-solving by emphasizing the importance of dialogue together with what she calls the "virtues of practice." These include virtues such as wisdom, sensitivity, creativity, discipline, and commitment to valid information, and the aim of exercising these virtues is to get things right, that is, to act virtuously overall, in solving practical problems.[60]

NOTES

1   Crisp 2010, pp. 23–4.
2   See, for example, R. Taylor 2002 and Hacker-Wright 2010.
3   See, for example, Railton 1984, pp. 137–71.
4   Hursthouse 1999, chap. 1. For alternative qualified-agent accounts see Zagzebski 1996, pp. 232–54, and Annas 2011, pp. 16–51.
5   Hursthouse 1999, p. 28.
6   Hursthouse does not make this point herself, but it is consistent with what she argues in Hursthouse 1995a. For further discussion see Kawall 2009 and Svensson 2011.
7   For a discussion of the differences between virtue ethics and deontology, see van Hooft 2006, chap. 1.
8   See Williams, in Williams and Smart 1973, pp. 97ff.
9   Hursthouse 1999, pp. 73–4.
10 Hursthouse 1999, p. 78.
11 Hursthouse 1999, p. 46.
12 Hursthouse 1999, p. 78.
13 See van Zyl 2007.
14 See D. Russell 2009, chap. 2.
15 Hursthouse 1999, pp. 50ff.
16 See Harman 2001, pp. 120–1.
17 Hursthouse 1999, p. 50.
18 Johnson 2003, pp. 810–34.
19 See, for example, Kawall 2002 and Tiberius 2006. For a critical discussion of some of the variations on (V), see Svensson 2010.
20 I discuss this response in more detail in van Zyl 2011a. See also D. Russell 2008, pp. 308–11.
21 See Hursthouse 1999, pp. 36–9.
22 See Merritt 2000 for a discussion of this point.
23 Hursthouse 1999, p. 125.
24 Hursthouse 2006b, pp. 108–9.
25 Hursthouse 1999, pp. 123–6.
26 Hursthouse 1999, p. 69.
27 Slote 2001, p. 38.
28 See Slote 2001, chap. 1 and D. Russell 2009, chap. 3.

29 Slote (2001, p. 39) hints at this objection to consequentialism when he writes: "if we judge the actions of ourselves or others simply by their effects in the world, we end up unable to distinguish accidentally or ironically useful actions (or slips on banana peels) from actions that we actually morally admire and that are morally good and praiseworthy."

30 See Slote 2001, pp. 34ff.

31 See, for example, Jacobson 2002 and Brady 2004.

32 Slote 2001, p. 18.

33 I discuss Slote's use of the term "right action" in more detail in van Zyl 2011b.

34 We can, of course, imagine a case where a consequentialist would agree that the act in question is wrong, for example where the agent's malice interferes with his performance to such an extent that the outcome is worse than what it would have been had he not prosecuted at all. We need not consider these kinds of cases because the agent-based view is that prosecuting from malice is always wrong, regardless of the outcome.

35 Slote 2001, pp. 15–6.

36 Slote 2001, p. 17.

37 Jacobson 2002, pp. 57–62. See also Hurka 2001, p. 227, and Doviak 2011.

38 Slote 2001, p. 14.

39 Brady 2004, p. 6.

40 Slote 2001, p. 15.

41 See D. Russell 2008, pp. 311ff.

42 For a discussion of a hypothetical agent-based virtue ethics, see Gelfand 2000.

43 For further discussion of agent-based virtue ethics see Brady 2004, Das 2003, Doviak 2011, Jacobson 2002, D. Russell 2009, van Zyl 2009 and 2011b.

44 Swanton 2001 and 2003. For an application of this approach, see Sandler 2007.

45 *Nicomachean Ethics* II.4, 1105a9–b2, trans. J. A. K. Thomson (see Aristotle 1976).

46 Swanton here develops an idea proposed by Audi 1997, p. 180.

47 Swanton 2003, p. 238.

48 Swanton 2001, pp. 32–3.

49 Ross 1930, p. 19.

50 Swanton 2003, p. 234. See Murdoch 1970, pp. 16ff.

51 For a discussion of the difference between internal and external criteria, see Oakley and Cocking 2001, pp. 10–11.

52   See Swanton 2003, pp. 234–8.
53   Swanton 2003, pp. 239–40.
54   Swanton 2003, pp. 240–1.
55   See Swanton 2003, pp. 247–8.
56   D. Russell 2009, p. 69.
57   For further discussion of Swanton's account of right action, see Das 2003 and D. Russell 2009.
58   See Svensson 2011.
59   Slote 2001, p. 42.
60   See Swanton 2003, chaps. 12 and 13.

9 Virtue ethics and bioethics

Between Elizabeth Anscombe's 1958 rallying call for moral philosophy to return to the virtues and philosophers taking up this challenge two decades later, the field of bioethics emerged in the wake of debates about environmental degradation, sexual morality, civil rights, and the morality of war. What began initially as a critique of medical paternalism and of science's trampling on the rights of research subjects, soon diversified into ethical discussion of a great variety of issues in clinical practice and beyond, including abortion, infanticide, euthanasia, and assisted reproduction. But while moral philosophers began responding to Anscombe's call in new work on moral psychology and the virtues from the late 1970s onwards, these ideas made their way into bioethical discussions only gradually. Of course, clinicians, scientists, and laypersons had often used various virtue terms in thinking about a range of issues which subsequently came to be seen under the heading of bioethics, such as blood and organ donation, withdrawal of life support, and experimentation on humans. For instance, in his influential 1966 article on the ethics of clinical research, Harvard medical researcher Professor Henry Beecher (1966) argued that "the presence of an intelligent, informed, conscientious, compassionate, responsible investigator" is a reliable safeguard against unethical research on human subjects (p. 372). And so when virtue concepts began to enter and shape bioethical debates from the mid-1980s and virtue ethical approaches to issues in bioethics started gathering pace in the 1990s, philosophers were in a way catching up with what many outside philosophy already regarded as important considerations in these debates.

Bioethics has been at the forefront of the applied ethics revolution in academic philosophy since the early 1970s. Some of the earliest examples of applications of virtue ethics were in the context of bioethics, and Aristotelian forms of virtue ethics have been the dominant substantive accounts informing these applications. Significant virtue-oriented discussions of issues in bioethics began with Philippa Foot's 1977 article on euthanasia and Stephen R. L. Clark's book on the moral status of animals later that year. These were followed by the development of accounts of virtues for physicians and other health professionals, by writers such as Gregory Pence (1980), Edmund Pellegrino, and David Thomasma (Pellegrino and Thomasma 1981).[1] The late 1980s and early 1990s saw virtue ethical analyses extended to abortion and assisted reproduction, particularly in the work of philosophers such as Rosalind Hursthouse, and the first decade of the twenty-first century has seen more theoretically developed forms of virtue ethics applied to a variety of health professional roles, prebirth testing and other issues in reproductive ethics. The dissatisfaction with utilitarian and rights-based approaches to ethics that helped prompt the renewal of philosophers' interest in virtue ethics also had a corresponding effect in the context of bioethics, and work on feminist approaches to ethics and bioethics created further interest in virtue ethics.

A major concern expressed about the emergence of virtue ethics was whether the approach could be genuinely action guiding. Given that bioethics is by its nature a practical discipline, worries about the practicality of virtue ethics itself might seem to be magnified in this context. However, if anything, the reverse has turned out to be the case, as virtue ethical approaches to bioethics have provided some very practical conclusions, which have shed much light on the issues involved.[2] Indeed, not only has virtue ethics illuminated a range of bioethical issues, but its applications to bioethics have, in turn, arguably helped to develop virtue ethics as an approach more generally. For these applications to a range of issues and cases in bioethics have helped meet concerns about the impracticality of virtue ethics, and have reinforced the idea that acting rightly is not simply a matter of acting from good motives but involves acting in accordance with the relevant standard of excellence that one is normatively disposed to uphold, or "getting things right" (see Hursthouse 1999, p. 12). The complexity of issues faced in professional life has also shown the importance of virtue ethics' emphasis on an irreducible and rich plurality of values (see Oakley 1996),

and has thereby reminded us of the importance of phronesis for living well (see D. Russell 2009; Annas 2011). And some of the deep
and urgent questions raised by applications of virtue ethics to (e.g.)
questions of abortion and euthanasia have prompted further developments in Aristotelian accounts of the good and human flourishing.
These applications have also helped to flesh out more fully what
is involved in having various familiar virtues, such as beneficence
(which requires a deeper understanding of a person's well-being than
simply avoiding short-term alarm in passing on bad news to, say,
patients with cancer), and have brought out *new* virtues relevant to
particular domains, such as psychiatry and parenting. Virtue ethical
approaches to the roles of health professionals have also shown how
its emphasis on partiality, here in clinician–patient relationships,
is actually a strength rather than a weakness, compared with other
ethical perspectives. Further, in showing new ways in which rights
can be exercised well or badly, discussions of topics such as abortion
from a virtue ethical perspective have revealed further limitations
in rights-based approaches. And the familiar idea of role differentiation has been found to reinforce the plausibility of virtue ethics'
teleological approach, particularly in its account of the notion of
professional integrity.

EUTHANASIA

The earliest contribution to bioethics from a secular virtue ethical
perspective that I am aware of is Philippa Foot's 1977 article on the
nature and morality of euthanasia.[3] Major advances in life-sustaining
technologies in the 1960s and 1970s, along with rising challenges
to entrenched medical paternalism, generated much debate about
when such support can be withdrawn, and about whether active
means of bringing about death are ethically justifiable. Foot's subtle
and important discussion gave an early indication of how thinking
about such practical issues in virtue terms can enrich philosophical debates, and can reflect more accurately the sorts of ethical
considerations that people in such circumstances actually wonder
about and agonize over, than do familiar utilitarian and rights-based
approaches.

Central to Foot's analysis is her reminder that euthanasia is, by
definition, a death that is for the good of the person who dies, and

she defines an act of euthanasia as "inducing or otherwise opting for death for the sake of the one who dies" (1977, p. 87). As she later puts it, "An act of euthanasia, whether literally act or rather omission, is attributed to an agent who opts for the death of another because in his case life seems to be an evil rather than a good" (p. 96). This definition frames the scope of Foot's discussion, and so rules out from euthanasia those cases (which she acknowledges lay discussions of this topic often include) where a competent person asks to die, but where – as they may themselves recognize – the condition of their life is not currently such that death would be a good to them in the circumstances. In such cases, Foot argues that while it would be compatible with the virtue of justice to accede to their request, it would nevertheless be contrary to the virtue of charity or benevolence to do so: "charity might require us to hold our hand where justice did not" (p. 106). Thus, in reminding us that euthanasia is death brought about *for the good of* the person who dies rather than merely at the request of the person (competent or otherwise) who dies, Foot is able to bring out the relevance of the virtue of charity to the question of when acts of euthanasia are ethically justifiable. Where a competent person asks to die and their death would benefit (or be a good for) them, Foot argues that bringing about that person's death is justifiable only if one acts *for that purpose*, of benefiting them, or for their sake, rather than bringing about their death for some other purpose while simply *noticing* that it is also for their own good. The goal of such an act is therefore crucial to its ethical justifiability. Thus a genuine act of voluntary euthanasia would be right only if it is done for the good of the one who dies – and by one who has a sound grasp of what is that person's good, as someone acting with the virtue of charity must have. In this way, Foot links acting from the relevant virtues directly to the rightness of what one does here.[4] (As we will see shortly, this link between right action and the patient's good is also important for virtue ethics analyses of *doctors'* involvement in assisted suicide and voluntary euthanasia.)

In explicating when death can be a good to the person who dies, Foot draws on an Aristotelian account of a good life in terms of human flourishing. Foot argues that life is still a good to the person living it when it has a minimum of basic goods such as a level of autonomy, relationships with others, moral support from them, and justice, even if various bad features, such as significant disability and suffering, are also present. But death would be a good when these sorts of basic goods are not present, even minimally, in one's life:

> On *any* view of the goods and evils that life can contain, it seems that a life with more evil than good could still itself be a *good*...It is not the mere state of being alive that can determine, or itself count as, a good, but rather life coming up to some standard of normality...Ordinary human lives, even very hard lives, contain a minimum of basic goods, but when these are absent the idea of life is no longer linked to that of good. (1977, pp. 94–5)

Thus, Foot suggests that it is possible for someone to have a rational desire to die, and yet for death to be a bad for them, because their life still has at least a modicum of basic goods. Conversely, Foot also recognizes that even in circumstances where these basic goods are absent (as they often were, for instance, for prisoners in Stalin's labor camps), some people may nevertheless still want to live, and here it would be contrary to the virtue of justice to bring about their death: "there is nothing unintelligible in the idea that a man might cling to life though he knew those facts about the future which would make any charitable man wish that he might die" (p. 90). Foot argues that considering end-of-life decisions from a virtue perspective can reveal a significant moral difference between killing and letting die (which more familiar rights-based analyses or utilitarian approaches tend to overlook). Justice and charity would converge in allowing one to comply with a competent person's request to be killed, where their life lacks a minimum of basic goods. However, these virtues would diverge where a competent person in such circumstances demands *not* to be killed but prefers to be left to die – here, justice prohibits us from performing the act of killing that charity would normally permit, and the person must be allowed to die as they wish.[5]

Foot also considers examples of passive euthanasia, where decisions are made not to prolong life in certain circumstances (which she recognizes is commonly practiced by doctors, and is widely accepted under certain conditions), and she argues that "charity does not always dictate that life should be prolonged where a man's own wishes, hypothetical or actual, are not known" (1977, p. 107). And, in discussing some questions regarding acts of euthanasia involving severely disabled infants, Foot cautions against hasty assumptions that the lives of such infants can no longer be a good to them (pp. 109–10). In demonstrating that charity might forbid the killing of a person who has clearly waived their right to life and others' duties of noninterference, Foot's pioneering article brought out an important limitation of rights-based approaches here (a point subsequently taken up by Rosalind Hursthouse in her virtue ethical analysis of abortion, as we see later), and she helped show that the application of the relevant virtues is contextual. Foot's article was also significant in applying an Aristotelian account of when life – and so also death – can be a good, thus going beyond desire-based accounts of those questions, but without endorsing widespread medical paternalism in end-of-life decision-making.[6]

An important subsequent virtue ethical approach to euthanasia is provided by Liezl van Zyl (2000), who emphasizes the virtues of compassion, benevolence, and respectfulness, as medical virtues that are particularly important in end-of-life decision-making, and provides a set of rules to help decide the moral justifiability of deliberately terminating or shortening a patient's life. One of the key ethical objections against doctors performing voluntary euthanasia is that this is incompatible with their role as healers (see e.g. Kass 1989). But while the idea of doctors as healers has been influential in contemporary virtue ethical discussions of medical practice, this objection seems to rest on the mistaken assumption that ending a patient's life at their autonomous request can never be in their interests and so could never be a healing act. The broad sense in which this objection uses the notion of "healing" as "making whole" enables a good death to be understood as the completion or making whole the life of a patient, in certain circumstances (see Oakley and Cocking 2001, pp. 83–4; see also van Zyl 2000, pp. 210–12).

HEALTH-CARE PRACTICE

Many of those who have recently investigated virtues and virtue ethics in the context of health-care practice remarked that biomedical ethics had wrongly neglected the virtues in its formative years. Oaths and codes of medical ethics in ancient Greece and various Asian cultures emphasized the importance of physicians having certain virtuous character traits. Medical virtues figured prominently in Thomas Percival's important 1803 book on medical ethics, which heavily influenced the development of the American Medical Association's (AMA's) inaugural code of ethics in 1847, where doctors were advised to develop traits such as tenderness, firmness, and fidelity.[7] However, the rise of scientific medicine in the latter part of the nineteenth century and the declining influence of religion on medical practice shifted the emphasis away from these virtuous character traits in conceptions of what it meant to be an ethical physician, and in successive versions of the AMA Codes (see Imber 2008; Beauchamp and Childress 2009, p. 35). Also, during the first two decades of the newly recognized field of bioethics from 1970 onwards, with its moves towards more patient-centered principles of medical ethics, the role of virtues in ethical medical practice was shunned, partly, it seems, due to a perceived association with an unjustified medical paternalism.

Soon after this, however, bioethicists began to turn their attention to developing accounts of virtues in medicine and other health-care professions. A significant influence, particularly on these initial developments, was Alasdair MacIntyre's notion of a virtue as a trait that enables one to achieve the goods internal to a practice. Drawing on his extensive historical study, MacIntyre (1981, p. 178) argued that "A virtue is an acquired human quality the possession and exercise of which tends to enable us to achieve those goods which are internal to practices and the lack of which effectively prevents us from achieving any such goods," and he cites justice, courage, and honesty as examples of traits that would count as virtues across a range of practices. Clearly medicine counts as a practice, on this account, although MacIntyre mentions medicine only in passing, and he does not talk in detail about professional virtues or the goals of professions. Edmund Pellegrino and David Thomasma (1993) subsequently developed a detailed account of virtues such as compassion, fortitude, courage, and justice in medical practice. These and other character traits count as virtues in this context, Pellegrino and Thomasma argue, because they help doctors to achieve the ends of medicine. So on this approach, what counts as virtue in a medical context is importantly determined by the ends or goals of medicine, and thus by the nature or philosophy of medicine as a practice.[8] Other bioethicists also provided accounts of important virtues in medical practice (see Pence 1980; Shelp 1985; Drane 1988, pp. 43–62; W. F. May 1994; and Jansen 2000). Tom Beauchamp and

James Childress' highly influential textbook, *Principles of Biomedical Ethics*, first published in 1978, gave more prominence to virtues in successive editions, and they now discuss five "focal virtues" of compassion, discernment, trustworthiness, integrity, and conscientiousness, along with care, respectfulness, nonmalevolence, benevolence, justice, truthfulness, and faithfulness (2009, pp. 38–46).[9] As Roger Higgs (2007) explains, what the virtue of truthfulness or honesty demands of a doctor is not to be someone "who as a reflex reveals all," or someone who "dump[s] complex information on the patient's side of the table and leav[es] them 'to clear up because it's their business'" (p. 336), but rather to be someone who carefully and sensitively helps a patient understand the information about their condition that they wish to know.

These were important advances for virtue theory in medicine, and provided a more comprehensive picture of what the ethical practice of medicine involves. This renewed attention to virtues was also fueled by moves to revive a distinctive medical ethic, in response to the shortcomings of broad-based ethical theories like Kantian and utilitarian approaches here. Thus, Larry Churchill (1989) argued that doctors should be guided in their professional behavior by a sense of what it is right for them, *qua doctor*, to do in the circumstances, considering the distinctive values and goals of medicine – such as doctors' commitments to act in their patients' best interests. Indeed, being a virtuous doctor seems to require that one aspire to uphold certain medical ideals, such that one may be disposed to provide benefits to patients that may go beyond what they could plausibly be thought to have a right to (see Blum 1990). These ideas about role-differentiated standards and values (sometimes expressed in terms of the "internal morality of medicine") also echoed wider challenges to impartialist ethical theories to take partiality and personal relationships such as friendship more seriously.

But while these discussions helped demonstrate the indispensability of virtuous character traits to good medical practice, such accounts were offered as necessary practical supplements to rights-based or utilitarian perspectives on medical ethics, rather than as stand-alone virtue *ethical* approaches to medical practice. Explaining the importance of various virtuous character traits for addressing ethical questions in medicine was indeed a constructive and distinctive contribution to discussions of those questions, but these accounts tended to be somewhat disengaged from concurrent moves in ethical theory to develop utilitarian and Kantian conceptions of virtuous character, and so it remained unclear how a stand-alone virtue ethical approach to medical practice was to be spelled out, and how it would differ from accounts of virtuous medical character traits given by more familiar ethical theories.

In *Virtue Ethics and Professional Roles* (Oakley and Cocking 2001), Dean Cocking and I provided a more detailed account of how a stand-alone Aristotelian virtue ethics could be applied to a range of ethical concerns in medical and legal practice. Cocking and I took up the virtue ethics criterion of right action developed by Hursthouse (1991), whereby an action is right if and only if it is what an agent with a virtuous character would do in the circumstances, and we demonstrated how virtue ethics differs from and improves upon utilitarian and Kantian accounts of the character traits needed by ethical doctors. Because of its teleological structure, Aristotelian virtue ethics provides a natural basis for developing an ethical theory of professional roles. Which character traits count as virtues in everyday life is determined by their connections with *eudaimonia*, the overarching goal of a good human life. Virtues in the context of professional roles can be derived through a similar teleological structure. That is, Cocking and I (Oakley and Cocking 2001, pp. 74-5) argued that good professional roles must be part of a good profession, and a good profession is one which involves a commitment to a key human good, without which humans cannot flourish.[10] For example, *health* is clearly a central goal of medicine – as Aristotle (1980) put it at the beginning of *The Nicomachean Ethics* (1094a7), "the end of the medical art is health" – and given the importance of health for human flourishing, medicine would clearly count as a good profession on this approach. And which of a doctor's character traits count as medical virtues are those which help them serve the goal of patient health. Medical beneficence qualifies as a virtue because it focuses doctors on their patients' interests and blocks inclinations towards the unnecessary interventions of defensive medicine. Similarly, trustworthiness aids effective diagnosis and treatment by helping patients feel comfortable about disclosing intimate information, while medical courage helps doctors work towards healing patients by facing risks of serious infection when necessary, without rashly disregarding proper precautions against

becoming infected themselves (Oakley and Cocking 2001, p. 93).
On this approach, a doctor ought to tell a patient the truth about the
patient's condition, not because patients have a right to know this, or
because telling the truth maximizes utility, but because this is part
of having the virtue of truthfulness, and a disposition to be truth-
ful to patients serves the medical goal of health, without breaching
the constraint (which applies to doctors qua professionals) against
violating their patients' autonomy. Thus, in generating a defensible
professional ethic the norms of the profession in question cannot be
taken as given, but must be shown to reflect a commitment to an
important substantive human good which is partly constitutive of a
flourishing human life. One of the strengths of an approach which
takes the moral status of professional roles to depend importantly on
their links with key human goods is that it fits naturally with a central feature of any occupation's claim to be a profession in the first
place.

On Cocking's and my account, every virtue can be understood
as incorporating a *regulative ideal*, involving the internalization of
a certain conception of excellence such that one is able to adjust
one's motivation and conduct so that they conform to that standard.
For example, a virtuous doctor would regulate their relationships
with patients according to an ideal of serving their patients' health,
and this ideal will also govern when such relationships are properly established and terminated – e.g. a doctor–patient relationship
can legitimately be concluded when the patient is healed. Differences in these governing conditions enable clear distinctions to be
drawn between different sorts of professional–client relationships,
and between professional and personal relationships (Oakley and
Cocking 2001, pp. 48–54). Cocking and I also brought out differences between the regulative ideals of doctors whose characters were
guided by utilitarian or Kantian approaches, and the regulative ideals of doctors whose characters were guided by virtue ethics. This
marked a departure from the prevalent tendency to construe virtue
ethics approaches to medical ethics as distinguished simply by their
emphasis on character in approaching ethical issues in medical practice. This was also a time when there was starting to be greater
engagement and dialogue in ethical theory between the advocates of
virtue ethics, Kantian ethics, and utilitarianism (see e.g. Baron *et al.*
1997).

This approach draws a close connection between virtue ethics in a professional context and role morality. Although the idea of role morality is an old one and many of those who accept such an idea are not themselves virtue ethicists, Cocking and I linked virtue ethics in professional roles to the notion of role-differentiated virtues, whereby traits can count as virtues in professional life, even if they are neutral – or even perhaps, if they are vices – in ordinary life, so long as they help the practitioner serve the good that is needed for humans to flourish.[11] In the former case, for example, "a doctor's acute clinical judgment in making a correct diagnosis from a multitude of symptoms" (Oakley and Cocking 2001, p. 129) can count as a medical virtue, while in the latter case, moral indifference to another's shortcomings could conceivably count as a virtue for a criminal defense lawyer (pp. 146–7). This differed from earlier approaches to the virtues in medicine, which applied traits that are broad-based virtues in ordinary life to the professional role of doctors.

An advantage of this approach is its attractive analysis of the virtue of *professional* integrity, which involves having and acting with a commitment to serve the proper goals of one's profession. For example, doctors who cite professional integrity as a reason for refusing to provide a futile intervention for a dying patient can be understood as holding that such an intervention would be contrary to their overarching professional goal of acting in their patients' best interests. A doctor in this situation could legitimately tell the patient "I cannot with my doctor's hat on do this for you." This clearly differs from cases where doctors reject such interventions by appealing to ordinary morality, such as the idea that futile interventions are contrary to human rights or human dignity, and from cases where doctors reject a futile intervention because they have a personal, conscientious objection to using it (say, on religious grounds). The moral relevance of the goals of a profession to evaluating the conduct of individual professionals is also apparent when those goals are contravened. So, for example, one acts wrongly in torturing another, but it is even worse for a *doctor* to torture another person – doctors profess to be healers, and torturing is the opposite of healing.

This type of virtue ethical approach has also recently been extended to other health professions, including psychiatry, nursing, and social work.[12] For example, Jennifer Radden and John Sadler

(2010) argue that serving the proper psychiatric goals of mental health and healing requires psychiatrists to develop role-constituted virtues like self-knowledge, self-unity, and realism, along with "unselfing," which involves a "personally effaced yet acutely attentive and affectively attuned attitude toward the patient, the relationship, and its boundaries" (p. 132). Radden and Sadler argue that these and other virtues, such as integrity, are crucial in psychiatry, as patients are especially vulnerable to exploitation in this context. Alan Armstrong (2007, pp. 125–56) argues that compassion, courage, and respectfulness are role virtues in nursing practice (see also Brody 1988; van Hooft, 1999; Sellman 2011), and Sarah Banks and Ann Gallagher (2008) argue that justice and courage are among the important virtues needed by practitioners to serve the proper goals of social work. There has also been interesting work done on the idea that it is important for patients to, themselves, bring various virtues to the medical encounter, such as fortitude, prudence, and hope (see Lebacqz 1985). This work might be extended by drawing on the cross-fertilization now beginning to occur between virtue ethics and virtue epistemology (see e.g. Battaly 2010). For instance, perhaps an epistemically virtuous patient would have an ability to critically evaluate certain sorts of evidence provided by various complementary therapies, and would avoid the vice of credulousness.

ABORTION

In her 1991 article, "Virtue Theory and Abortion,"[13] Rosalind Hursthouse provided a ground-breaking analysis of abortion. Developing and extending points from her discussion of her "neo-Aristotelian" perspective on abortion in her 1987 book *Beginning Lives*, Hursthouse argues that the morality of an abortion depends importantly on the sort of character a woman manifests in her reasons for terminating her pregnancy.[14] She also outlines how a virtue ethical criterion of right action can be articulated in ways directly parallel to more familiar deontological and utilitarian accounts. Hursthouse's discussion of abortion was a major advance, as philosophers had already been showing considerable interest in the virtues and virtue ethics, but little attempt had thus far been made to develop virtue ethics in ways that provided a coherent criterion of right action independent of and yet clearly comparable to utilitarian and rights-based approaches, or to demonstrate how such an approach could be applied.

Rather than trying to "solve the problem of abortion," Hursthouse sought to enhance our understanding of virtue ethics by illustrating how it would have us think about a particular issue, and she saw abortion as an excellent case study because virtue ethics seems to radically alter existing discussions of this subject. Hursthouse found that the standard two-dimensional abortion discussions in terms of the competing rights of the mother and the fetus had reached an impasse, and she makes the striking claim that such debates are in any case beside the point: "virtue theory quite transforms the discussion of abortion by dismissing the two familiar dominating considerations as, in a way, fundamentally irrelevant" (1991, p. 234). An important element of Hursthouse's argument is her observation that rights can be exercised well or badly: "in exercising a moral right I can do something cruel, or callous, or selfish, light-minded, self-righteous, stupid, inconsiderate, disloyal, dishonest – that is, act viciously" (p. 235). Because abortion involves "the cutting off of a new human life, and thereby, like the procreation of a new human life, connects with all our thoughts about human life and death, parenthood, and family relationships" (p. 237), Hursthouse takes the central question for the morality of an abortion to be, not whether women have a right to terminate their pregnancies, but rather, "In having an abortion in these circumstances, would the agent be acting virtuously or viciously or neither?" (p. 235).

Having an abortion, Hursthouse suggests, can be a callous, self-centered, or cowardly act, or conversely, can demonstrate humility, depending on the circumstances in which a woman decides to terminate her pregnancy. For example,

to think of abortion as nothing but the killing of something that does not matter, or as nothing but the exercise of some right or rights one has, or as the incidental means to some desirable state of affairs, is to do something callous and light-minded, the sort of thing that no virtuous and wise person would do. It is to have the wrong attitude not only to fetuses, but more generally to human life and death, parenthood, and family relationships. (1991, pp. 237–8)[15]

For, as Hursthouse plausibly claims, "parenthood in general, and motherhood and childbearing in particular, are intrinsically worthwhile, [and] are among the things that can be correctly thought to be partially constitutive of a flourishing human life" (p. 241).[16] And terminating a pregnancy (unlike, say, having one's appendix removed) involves cutting off a new human life, which in most circumstances, Hursthouse argues, should be regarded as a morally serious matter (p. 237; see also Hursthouse 1987, pp. 16–25, 50–8, 204–17, 330–9). Nevertheless, an adolescent girl who falls pregnant "may quite properly say 'I am not ready for motherhood yet,' especially in our society, and, far from manifesting irresponsibility or light-mindedness, [may] show an appropriate modesty or humility, or a fearfulness that does not amount to cowardice" (1991, p. 242). Similarly, women who seek abortions due to their very poor health or unavoidably harsh employment conditions "cannot be described as self-indulgent, callous, irresponsible, or light-minded..., [rather] something is terribly amiss in the conditions of their lives, which make it so hard to recognize pregnancy and childbearing as the good that they can be" (p. 240). And, "a woman who has already had several children and fears that to have another will seriously affect her capacity to be a good mother to the ones she has... does not show a lack of appreciation of the intrinsic value of being a parent by opting for abortion" (p. 241). Broadly speaking, then, there are two sorts of reasons why, on this account, a woman might in certain circumstances act wrongly in having an abortion. First, she may be failing to appreciate the intrinsic value of parenthood, and its importance to a flourishing human life; and second, she may be taking the decision to cut off a new human life without due seriousness. Hursthouse (1987, pp. 72–9, 83–4, 214–16) also discusses briefly how these sorts of failings can be exhibited in decisions about allowing severely disabled infants to die, and in certain sorts of research on human embryos.[17]

Hursthouse recognizes that some of her conclusions about the morality of abortion might be found "startling," but she acknowledges that the virtue- and vice-related terms she uses "are difficult to apply correctly, and anyone might challenge my application of any one of them.... Any of these examples may be disputed, but what is at issue is, should these difficult terms be there, or should the discussion be couched in terms that all clever adolescents can apply correctly" (1991, p. 244). But whether or not one agrees with her examples of women acting virtuously or viciously in seeking an abortion, Hursthouse's analysis of the shortcomings of rights-based approaches has struck a chord, and her introduction of virtue and vice terms into contemporary abortion debates seemed to better match the concerns and experiences of many women (and men) considering whether to terminate a pregnancy. For many women who take themselves to have an overriding right to terminate their pregnancies nevertheless wonder about the sorts of considerations raised by Hursthouse when they are thinking about the moral justifiability of having an abortion in their current circumstances.[18] Hursthouse's discussion was thereby a welcome broadening of the terms of a well-worn debate where the protagonists were in a rut, and it helped answer oft-heard criticisms of virtue ethics as impractical, by showing how this approach can provide a distinctive and compelling analysis of an important and complex contemporary issue. Moreover, its systematic explanation of virtue ethics helped move theoretical discussions of the approach away from some perennial misguided objections and on to better-targeted criticisms that were more relevant to virtue ethicists' actual claims, and that turned out to be more constructive in developing the approach further. Hursthouse also indicated how virtue ethics can provide rules and principles (a theme she subsequently developed in more detail in her 1999 book *On Virtue Ethics*), and she dispels some misconceptions about conflicts between virtues, making some suggestive comments (later elaborated in *On Virtue Ethics*) about how some such conflicts might be resolved, or dissolved. Hursthouse also made some useful comments about fair terms for debates in comparative moral theory and about what it is reasonable to expect of a normative ethical theory, in any case, and in rectifying some common misunderstandings of virtue ethics, her article helped pave the way for further developments and applications of the approach.

PREBIRTH TESTING

Another area of reproductive ethics where virtue ethical approaches have produced major advances is the vigorously contested topic of prebirth testing and selective reproduction, where various techniques such as PGD (preimplantation genetic diagnosis) can enable prospective parents to make decisions about what characteristics their child will have. For instance, in a series of recent articles,

Rosalind McDougall (2005, 2007, 2009) provides an illuminating ethical analysis of embryo selection decisions made on the basis of sex and disability in terms of what a virtuous parent would do in the circumstances. Drawing on the Aristotelian approach of Hursthouse and others, McDougall argues that fulfilling the role of parent well towards one's existing children requires the development of several important virtues, and that it is wrong to engage in nonmedical sex selection, or to select an embryo that will be born deaf, because such actions are contrary to key parental virtues. McDougall develops an account of three central parental virtues, each of which helps parents to promote their child's flourishing, which she regards as the primary goal of parenting – "acceptingness," "committedness," and "future-agent-focus." Given the unpredictability of what may happen to one's child, acceptingness is an important parental virtue, because this trait involves an "embracing of the child regardless of his or her specific characteristics" (2005, p. 603), rather than a readiness to abandon the child if they develop, say, a chronic illness or disability.[19] The virtue of committedness involves a preparedness to nurture one's children to adulthood (2007, p. 186), which is important because of children's vulnerability and extreme level of dependence on their parents. And the virtue of future-agent-focus is a trait that motivates parents to behave in ways that "promote the development of children into good moral agents" in the future, in recognition of the fact (conceded rather reluctantly by some parents) that one's children "are not babies forever" (2007, p. 186).[20] McDougall then argues that these three traits are virtues not only in the context of those who are already parents, but also in circumstances where prospective parents are considering selective reproduction decisions.

Like a number of commentators on the ethics of selective reproduction, McDougall is critical of harm-based approaches as too narrow. According to familiar applications of harm-based perspectives, selective reproduction decisions are not wrong unless such decisions foreseeably harm the resulting child. And, in the context of decisions involving bringing someone into existence, the resulting child is commonly thought to be harmed by such a decision only where the conditions of their life are so dreadful that it would be rational for them to prefer not to exist at all, or (as it is often put) where their life is "not worth living."[21] But as McDougall points out, there are a range of selective reproduction decisions which people often find ethically contentious, even though the condition of the resulting child's life is clearly above such a low threshold; and an attractive feature of a virtue ethical perspective here is that it enables a wider range of ethical considerations to be brought to bear on such decisions, and so addresses what many find to be intuitively plausible concerns about such cases.

Broadly speaking, on McDougall's parental virtues analysis of selective reproduction, "an action is right if and only if it is what a virtuous parent would do in the circumstances" (2005, p. 602). On this approach, nonmedical sex selection is wrong, not due to any concerns about the welfare of the resulting child, but because it is contrary to the parental virtue of acceptance, or acceptingness (p. 601). If a child of the preferred sex happens to be loved and consequently fares well as a result, McDougall argues that this does not vindicate the act of sex selection that resulted in its existence in the first place: "Sex selection is wrong because it is not in accordance with the parental virtue of acceptance, regardless of the outcome for a specific child" (p. 604). McDougall goes on to suggest that this approach "provides a justificatory basis for a restrictive policy" in relation to sex selection, though she does not elaborate on the regulatory implications of her argument (p. 605).[22] McDougall (2007) also uses this framework to analyze decisions to select *for* deafness, as American deaf couple Sharon Duchesneau and Candy McCullough did in a much-discussed 2002 case. McDougall gives some reasons why selecting for deafness would seem to be contrary to both the parental virtues of acceptingness and future-agent-focus. But she acknowledges that the virtue of future-agent-focus could perhaps be construed as supporting the selection of a deaf child, if it is unlikely that the child would be raised outside a deaf community. So McDougall recognizes that on her application of virtue ethics, the justifiability of deliberately selecting an embryo with an impairment depends partly on whether the impairment is likely to be incompatible with the child's flourishing, and this in turn will be partly dependent on the environment in which the child is likely to be raised.

However, Carla Saenz (2010) finds that McDougall's account of how various parental virtues apply to selective reproduction

decisions sets an implausibly minimalist standard for virtuous parenting. McDougall holds that a virtuous parent would take an accepting attitude in their selection decisions towards traits that are compatible with their child's flourishing, but would not take such an
attitude towards traits that are incompatible with their child's flourishing. But Saenz argues that few traits are genuinely *incompatible*
with a child's flourishing, and that virtuous parenthood might be
more plausibly understood as involving a more demanding requirement, to bring about traits (or to accept the bringing about of traits)
that are *necessary for* the child's flourishing (pp. 504–6). On that standard, deliberately selecting an embryo that will become an impaired
child would be difficult to justify, as it is hard to see how a given
impairment could be necessary for a child's flourishing, and so bringing about an impairment in selective reproduction is not something
that a virtuous parent would do. Saenz also expresses concerns
about how conflicts between the parental virtues that McDougall
mentions might be settled. Questions have also been raised about
moves from what are plausibly seen as virtues of *actual* parents,
to claims about what would count as virtues of *prospective* parents
(see Wilkinson 2010, pp. 32–5). Nevertheless, McDougall's analysis clearly shows how virtue ethics has rich resources to provide a
new and attractive approach to these current issues in reproductive
ethics.

Virtue ethics has also been applied to a range of other issues in
bioethics, such as the moral status of animals and our treatment
of them (Walker 2007), xenotransplantation of organs and tissue
between animals and humans (Welchman 2003), and ethical questions arising in public health (Rogers 2004).[23] Further, biomedical
research has been argued to have distinctive goals, and accounts
of professional integrity and the role virtues of researchers which
enable them to serve the proper goals of research are also being
developed (see Litton and Miller 2005; Goldberg 2008).

FUTURE DIRECTIONS FOR VIRTUE ETHICAL
APPROACHES TO BIOETHICS

The boundaries of bioethics are frequently extended by new developments in science, medicine, and biotechnology, and virtue ethical
approaches are beginning to be applied to issues at the frontiers of

the field. One of the most hotly debated topics in contemporary bioethics is the ethics of human enhancement, and virtue ethicists have recently begun to provide distinctive perspectives on the issues raised here (see e.g. Farrelly 2007; Fröding 2011; Tonkens 2011; see also Buchanan 2009, 2011; Sparrow 2011, pp. 33–4). Virtue ethicists are also developing deeper and more empirically grounded accounts of various virtues, by drawing on important work in neuroscience and social psychology, which their philosophical colleagues have been examining in recent years, and so we can expect to see much future work in what might be called neuro-virtue ethics.[24] Indeed, given the reliance of virtue ethicists (particularly of the Aristotelian variety) on empirical claims to help support their arguments, recent advocates of virtue ethics in bioethics have been more inclined than earlier exponents to accept that it is incumbent on them to draw on relevant empirical research to substantiate those aspects of their arguments (which is in any case a widely shared expectation in bioethics). However, there has been relatively little work by virtue ethicists on various questions of justice in health care, including issues of health-care resource allocation, access to genetic testing, ethical concerns raised by infectious diseases and emerging pandemics, and access to affordable medicines by those in developing countries.[25] These sorts of issues are becoming increasingly important in bioethics, and virtue ethicists will need to see whether the approach has the resources to find promising ways of addressing them.

Another important contemporary issue in bioethics in which further work can be expected is the problem of medical conflicts of interest, due to the pervasive and often harmful influence of pharmaceutical companies on doctors' prescribing behavior. Ethical concerns about these conflicts are usually analyzed in terms of rights-based and utilitarian approaches, which see the wrongness of such conflicts in terms of violations of patients' rights to know about their doctor's industry links, or in terms of patients being harmed by receiving medication which is not in their best interests. However, virtue ethics seems particularly promising for addressing medical conflicts of interest, as the core ethical problem here concerns the appropriateness of the interest *influencing* or *guiding* one's decisions and actions. That is, in judging someone's action as wrong in a conflict of interest situation, we are essentially concerned with what interest *guided* the person to perform this action, and the ethical acceptability or otherwise of this influence is determined by reference to what interest should, according to the proper goals of this person's role, be guiding them in this context. Thus, a central question here would be, what sort of person do doctors show themselves to be when they prescribe drugs on the basis of self-interest, rather than according to the best interests of patients? In allowing pharmaceutical gifts and shares to influence their prescribing in such ways, doctors seem to be redefining themselves and their roles – as Epictetus said of the man who diminishes himself by stealing a lamp: "the man bought the lamp at this price: for a lamp he became a thief" (*Discourses*, Book 1, chap. 29 "On Constancy"). Also, reflection on how professionals make social commitments upon joining a profession to have a certain sort of character (in the priorities and reasons upon which they act in a professional context), and not simply to maximize expected utility or to uphold certain patient rights, can bring out another strength of virtue ethics, compared with other approaches.

Further work on virtue ethics approaches to public policy and regulation can also be expected, in the wake of existing applications of this approach to issues in personal and professional life, thus addressing challenges about whether virtue ethics has the resources to offer concrete advice on regulatory and policy interventions. One attempt to explicitly extend virtue ethics to public policy analysis and development focuses on what sort of person *regulators* show themselves to be when supporting a certain policy of legislative intervention (see Slote 2001, pp. 100–3). For example, Australia's policy of mandatory offshore detainment of asylum seekers could be characterized as morally wrong insofar as it expresses a xenophobic and uncaring attitude on the part of the legislators who supported it. This approach may lead to fruitful avenues for further research, but it would also be important to consider what sort of person *those who are regulated* show themselves to be when they comply with or resist a particular regulatory intervention, such as attempts by policymakers to influence doctors' prescribing behavior by providing them with financial or other incentives for prescribing in patients' best interests.

Another perspective, developed by Martha Nussbaum (1988, 1990a, 2006) and others, builds on Aristotle's approach in the

Politics, whereby the proper end of a polity cannot be determined without some substantive account of a good human life: "He who would duly inquire about the best form of a State ought first to determine which is the most choiceworthy life – for if this is unclear, the best form of political arrangement must remain unclear also" (1323a14–17; see also 1325a7–9). Nussbaum draws here on Aristotle's view that "the form of government is best in which every man, whoever he is, can act best and live happily" (*Politics* 1324a23–5), and argues that the proper goal of a polity is to provide the means or conditions which enable its citizens to have an equal chance of developing and exercising their capabilities to live flourishing human lives (Nussbaum 1988, esp. pp. 146–50, 160–72).[26] The capabilities in question here include those familiar to us from the *Nicomachean Ethics*, such as being able to understand the world, to engage in practical reasoning about our lives, and to form personal relationships with others. In a similar vein, Rosalind Hursthouse (2008) argues, in her account of what constitutes a good family, that a good society would support social policies which encourage and sustain good, loving families and would reject policies that tend to create dysfunctional families.

Overall, then, it seems clear that applications of virtue ethics to concerns in bioethics have not only shown the practicality of virtue ethics, but have also revealed further theoretical advantages of this approach compared with rights-based and utilitarian perspectives. Virtue ethics' emphasis on an irreducible plurality of goods has been important in debates about the value of life, and ideas about role-differentiated virtues have strengthened the plausibility of the teleological orientation of Aristotelian virtue ethics. Because of this reciprocal relationship between theory and practice, virtue ethics seems not only well placed to help resolve some of the difficult issues raised by bioethics, but such applications would seem to be indispensable to further developments of this approach itself.

NOTES

1 Earl Shelp 1985 was also an important milestone on the development of virtue approaches to medical ethics.
2 As with other ethical theories, there has sometimes been a time lag between conceptual and philosophical innovations in virtue ethics and

applications to bioethics and other areas of applied ethics. For instance, little of the recent philosophical debate about the adequacy of "do as the virtuous person would do" as a criterion of right action has found its way to bioethics, at this stage.

3   Later in 1977 saw the publication of Stephen R. L. Clark's influential book, *The Moral Status of Animals*, which also drew on Aristotelian ideas about flourishing and the virtues, in the context of how animals ought to be regarded and treated.

4   Note that Foot seems to think (1977, pp. 96–7, 102–3, 111) that there may be virtues other than justice or charity which would become relevant to the morality of terminating human life in other sorts of circumstances (including, perhaps, circumstances where life is still a good, or death may not necessarily be a bad, to the person who dies). As Hursthouse (1991, p. 234 n.) notes, Foot sees euthanasia as a special category, because the act must be done for the sake of the one who is to die.

5   Foot intends this part of her discussion to be a reply to James Rachels' (1975) famous critique of arguments that killing is intrinsically morally different to letting die. On related issues, see LeBar 2009, and Richards 1984.

6   Foot's article was one of the first in contemporary discussions to talk of species "flourishing" (p. 91), as a way of explaining what it is to benefit living things. Foot was using this term in relation to plants, in beginning her explanation of connections between the concepts of 'life' and 'good'.

7   See Thomas Percival 1803, and AMA 1847 Code of Ethics, in Post 2003, pp. 2657–62.

8   Pellegrino and Thomasma have provided such accounts in their 1981 and 1988. Pellegrino and Thomasma contrast their account with principle-based approaches, which were receiving increasing critical attention. But there is no incompatibility in virtue ethics between virtues and rules; and indeed, various rules can be very useful in clinical practice. I have always found this characterization of virtue ethics, in medicine and generally, in terms of a contrast with rule- or principle-based approaches misleading, and it has now been superseded.

9   Beauchamp and Childress now regard thinking in terms of virtues and rules as complementary perspectives that tend to converge in the advice each gives about how one should act in the context of ethical questions arising in clinical practice.

10 This Aristotelian approach differs from that of MacIntyre (1981), who did not require that those goods internal to practices which virtues enable us to achieve were necessary constituents of a flourishing human life.

11 See Aristotle, *Nicomachean Ethics* 1148b7–8: "we may describe as a bad doctor or a bad actor one whom we shall not call bad, simply . . . in this case we do not apply the term without qualification."

12 This approach has also been applied to emergency medicine (Girod and Beckman 2005), and to organizational ethics in health care (Kurlander and Danis 2007).

13 Hursthouse uses the terms 'virtue theory' and 'virtue ethics' in this article, but she clearly means to refer to what is now commonly known as 'virtue ethics'.

14 In "Virtue Theory and Abortion" (1991) Hursthouse reiterates and elaborates on points from her discussion of abortion at the end of *Beginning Lives* (1987), but she puts her points in the article more explicitly in terms of virtue ethics. This article seems to have had more impact on subsequent developments of virtue ethics than did the book.

15 Note that Hursthouse does not confine her evaluations of abortion decisions to girls and women: "No less than girls and women, boys and men can, in their actions, manifest self-centeredness, callousness, and light-mindedness about life and parenthood in relation to abortion. They can be self-centered or courageous about the possibility of disability in their offspring; they need to reflect on their sexual activity and their choices, or the lack of them, about their sexual partner and contraception; they need to grow up and take responsibility for their own actions and life in relation to fatherhood" (1991, p. 244).

16 Hursthouse cautions that it does not follow from this that people who choose to be childless are irresponsible or selfish, "for we are . . . in the happy position of there being more worthwhile things to do than can be fitted into one lifetime. Parenthood, and motherhood in particular, even if granted to be intrinsically worthwhile, undoubtedly take up a lot of one's adult life, leaving no room for some other worthwhile pursuits" (1991, p. 242).

17 R. J. Kornegay (2011, p. 54) raises the concern that Hursthouse's analysis could also be thought to extend to contraception decisions, where it might seem less plausible. But given Hursthouse's emphasis on cutting off a new human life as a crucial consideration, it is difficult to see how her account might be extended to the point before such a new human life actually begins. Nevertheless, Hursthouse's account could be thought to apply to the use of abortifacients (such as the drug RU-486), and such an application might already be thought to raise concerns that would need to be addressed. (Hursthouse 1987, esp. pp. 80–4, discusses the idea that embryos are potential human beings.) Kornegay goes on to argue that Hursthouse understates the role that her views on fetal

moral status play in her analysis of abortion (see also Hacker-Wright 2007, esp. pp. 457–9).

18 See Kristen Luker (1984), who explains, in her pioneering research on women's reasons for terminating a pregnancy, that few of the 600 women she interviewed at length "were 'casual' about having an abortion. Some were more conflicted about the abortion decision than others, but for all the women I interviewed, the decision to seek an abortion has been serious, thoughtful, and carefully considered" (p. 203 n.). See also Cannold 1998.

19 McDougall concedes that the parental virtue of acceptingness does not extend as far as accepting one's child's violence towards one, because having the *virtue* of acceptingness towards one's child requires that one is accepting to the right degree, on the right occasions, and so on. As with other more general virtues (such as generosity), the parental virtue of acceptingness steers an Aristotelian middle course between being too accepting of one's child and being not accepting enough towards them.

20 McDougall says this virtue captures the kernel of truth in well-known "right to an open future" arguments, without invoking any such right.

21 See Parfit 1984 on the nonidentity problem, and Feinberg 1986 on wrongful life.

22 Note that in cases of sex selection for *medical* reasons, McDougall argues that another parental virtue – "concern that the child's opportunities exceed a certain level" (2005, p. 604) – can override the requirements of acceptingness, and so justify selecting a boy or a girl to avoid having a child with a severe sex-linked genetic disorder.

23 See also Björkman 2006 on virtue ethics and organ transplantation more generally.

24 See also the University of Chicago's initiative, A New Science of Virtues: A Project of the University of Chicago, at: www.scienceofvirtues.org/.

25 An important foundation for work by Aristotelian virtue ethicists on such topics would be Martha Nussbaum (2006). See also Sideri 2008, and Oakley 1994.

26 See also Hursthouse 1993, Oakley 1994, and Holland 2011, p. 199. Holland argues that the common virtue ethical appeal to virtuous exemplars is unhelpful when it comes to formulating biomedical regulation and public policy, but he is nevertheless cautiously optimistic about the prospects for a virtue politics, and he sketches the beginnings of such approaches, along similar lines to Nussbaum. For further discussion of these and related proposals, see Mark LeBar's chapter in this volume.

10 Environmental virtue ethics
What it is and what it needs to be

ACT AND CHARACTER, PRINCIPLE, AND RULE

If we ask what makes an action right, one plausible answer is that the right action is the one that does as much good as possible. Roughly speaking, this is the theory known as consequentialism. The theory is most often associated with John Stuart Mill, and it is one of the simplest theories we have. An alternative theory: What makes an act right is not whether it *promotes* what is good so much as whether it *respects* what is good. Associated most often with Immanuel Kant, this theory is known as *deontology* and says, more specifically, that the only thing that is an unqualified good in itself is the good will of an autonomous person and therefore, an action is right if, but only if, it expresses respect for all persons as ends in themselves and therefore treats no person merely as a means to further ends.

Yet another alternative, *virtue ethics*, is so different it might be best to see it not as an alternative answer to the same question but as responding to a different question altogether. Often associated with Aristotle, but with roots in various traditions as discussed in this volume, virtue ethics tells us that what is right is to be a certain kind of person, a person of virtue: courageous, modest, honest, even-handed, industrious, wise. A virtuous person will, of course, express his or her virtue through action. But, for virtue ethics, the specification of rules of right action is largely a secondary matter – one that in many ways presupposes the kind of practical wisdom possessed by the person of virtue.

This chapter incorporates material from Zwolinski and Schmidtz 2005, and also from Schmidtz 2001a.

We wish we could settle which of these theories is right, then specify what that correct theory tells you to do. For better or worse, though, moral life is more complicated than that. The three theories just described are the main theories we discuss in introductory classes in moral philosophy, but most philosophy professors believe that none of them represents the single best way of capturing all that is true about morality. Morality is complex. It calls for creativity and judgment in the same way that chess does. You may come to the game of chess hoping to learn a simple algorithm that picks out the winning play no matter what the situation. For human players, though, there is no algorithm. There is no substitute for creativity and good judgment, for the ability to think ahead and expect the unexpected. Even something as simple as a game of chess is full of surprises, yet the complexity involved in playing chess is nothing compared to the complexity involved in being moral.

One could think, and we do think, that this way of understanding the challenge of being moral is most at home in a virtue ethical approach. Our students seem often to come to their first ethics course hoping to be given a list of rules or a code of professional conduct. Experience tells us, though, that when moral philosophers try to do applied ethics, there turns out to be something artificial and unhelpful about trying to interpret morality as a set of rules. Rules function in our reasoning as trump cards. If we have a rule, and can believe with complete confidence that the rule ought to be followed, and if we ascertain that a certain course of action is forbidden by the rule, that settles it. The rule trumps all further reasoning, so no further reasoning is necessary.

How comforting it would be to have such rules. And of course, sometimes the situation actually is rule governed. Not always, though. Often, there are reasons favoring an action, and reasons against, and neither trumps the other.

It may still be possible, however, to decide in a principled way. *Principles* are not like rules. Where rules function in our reasoning like trump cards, principles function like weights. If the applicable moral rule forbids X, then X is ruled out, so to speak. In contrast, principles can weigh against X without categorically ruling out X.

Consider an analogy. A home builder might say, in describing his or her philosophy about how to build houses, "You have to minimize ductwork." Question: Is that a rule or a principle? The answer is that, interpreted as a rule, it would be silly. As a rule, it would say, no matter what weighs in favor of more extensive ductwork, minimize ductwork, period. In other words, zero ductwork!

In fact, though, "minimize ductwork" is a good principle rather than a bad rule. As a principle, it tells home builders to be mindful of energy wasted and living space consumed when heated or cooled air is piped to remote parts of the house. Other things equal, get the air to where it has to go by the shortest available route. This principle will seldom outweigh the principle that the ceiling should be a minimum of seven feet above the floor. That is to say, it is not a trump, but it does have weight. A good builder designs houses with that principle in mind, but does not treat the principle as if it were a rule.

When students sign up for introductory courses in ethics, some of the most conscientious come in hoping to learn the moral rules. It is a shock when we say we have been teaching ethics for thirty years, but for the most part, we don't know the moral rules, and we suspect there are too few to give comprehensive guidance regarding how we ought to live.

When making real-world practical decisions, the considerations we bring to bear are more often principles than rules. So why, when we look to moral philosophy, would we hope to be given rules rather than principles? What is the attraction of rules? The idea of following a rule is comforting because it has the feel of relieving us of moral responsibility. If we follow the rules, it seems to guarantee our innocence. Unlike rules, principles offer no such escape. Rules are things we follow. Principles are things we apply. There is no illusion about principles being the kind of thing we can hide behind. Principles leave us with no doubt as to who is responsible for weighing them, for making choices, and for bearing the consequences.[1]

The upshot, and it is fundamental to understanding what being a moral agent is like in the real world: if you need to figure out what to do, don't look for rules; look for principles. Needless to say, this too is a principle, not a rule. It has exceptions. There are, after all, rules. Rules sometimes do trump all other considerations.

None of this, we believe, is exactly entailed by the virtue ethical approach, but neither is any of this contradicted by that approach.[2] Virtue ethics is about understanding the challenge of being moral as in the first instance a challenge of being a certain kind of agent, a certain kind of character. But part of being a moral character is being principled, and so too being a moral character involves being sensitive to and respectful of morally justified rules, and of principles, when they bear on what is required of a moral agent in the case at hand (Schmidtz 2001a).

REPUGNANT CONCLUSIONS: A FUNDAMENTAL CHALLENGE FOR ENVIRONMENTAL ETHICS

We have outlined a fairly expansive way of understanding virtue ethics, and it is on this ecumenical understanding that Thomas Hill, one of the trailblazing Kantians of our time, transformed the field of environmental ethics with an essay that inspired the emergence of what we now call environmental virtue ethics.[3]

In a classic article, Hill showed how traditional (rights-based) deontological and (utilitarian) teleological theories can fail to track our moral intuitions regarding environmental issues (Hill 2005). When Hill's neighbor cut down a beautiful old avocado tree and covered his yard with asphalt, Hill was indignant, but paused to wonder whether he had any theoretical justification for his indignation. The problem was not that trees have rights, or that Hill's neighbor had no right to cut down the tree. Hill's neighbor was depriving others of the enjoyment of the tree, but although this was consistent with Hill's indignation, it did not really account for it.

Ultimately, Hill concluded, the core question was not what was wrong with the act, but what was wrong with the person. "What sort of person," Hill asked, "would do a thing like that?" Hill's answer was that an admirable person would not do it. A person would have to be insensitive, and lacking in humility. Interestingly, the humility about which Hill was talking was recognizably an ecological humility. It is what Aldo Leopold meant when he spoke of our need to acknowledge and ultimately cherish our proper status as citizens (not conquerors) of the biotic community (Leopold 1966).

Like Tom Hill, many of us who are disturbed by the callous treatment of our natural environment would feel uncomfortable arguing that trees, brooks, or sand dollars have a *right* to be left alone. Also like Hill, though, neither is our discomfort grounded in a calculation of aggregate utility. The problem is that both deontological and consequentialist theories locate the source of our discomfort in the wrong sorts of considerations. As a result, they tend to give us false guidance in a variety of situations.

One particularly notorious example of this is Derek Parfit's Repugnant Conclusion (Parfit 1984). Parfit conceived his Repugnant Conclusion as a problem for one version of a utilitarian value theory, but in the sections that follow, we generalize Parfit's argument. We suggest, first, that all utilitarian theories of value face analogous problems, and second, that we cannot solve the problem (although we might be able to obscure it) by adopting a different kind of *act-centered* theory. Ultimately, Repugnant Conclusions suggest (we do not claim they entail) problems for the whole idea that moral theorizing should culminate in a simple formula for right action. We need a different sort of theory. We need not merely a better formula, but a better objective, such as is hinted at in Tom Hill's environmental virtue ethics.

The Repugnant Conclusion

Standard versions of the principle of utility say something like this: an act is right if and only if it maximizes happiness.

What does it mean to maximize happiness? First, the principle is referring to an aggregate: that is, the sum of everyone's happiness.[4] Second, the principle on its face is quantitative, referring to the kind of thing that can be maximized. Third, the quantity is most naturally thought of as a total sum, as opposed to an average. As Parfit notes, however, there is a problem with this seemingly innocuous third point.

Suppose we are deciding whether to have one or two children, and have no reason to doubt that the two children would each be about as happy as the one. If the two children would each be as happy as the one, then we conclude there is more total utility, indeed about twice as much, in having two children than in having one.

On its face, we seem to have utilitarian grounds for having two children rather than one. However, as Parfit points out, when we endorse the principle that the right act maximizes *total* happiness, we commit ourselves to the Repugnant Conclusion that

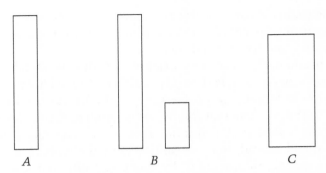

Figure 10.1 Population size and average quality of life. Population B differs from A only by the addition of a group of persons whose lives are less fortunate, but still worth living. C is the result of equalizing the well-being of the two groups in B by imposing a small cost on the better-off group for a large gain to the worse-off group. Width of the blocks = population size; height = average quality of life.

For any population of at least ten billion people, all with a very high quality of life, there must be some much larger imaginable population whose existence, if other things are equal, would be better, even though its members have lives that are barely worth living. (Parfit 1984, p. 388)

Here is how Parfit reaches that conclusion. Figure 10.1 illustrates three possible populations. The width of the blocks represents the number of people living; the height represents their average quality of life. In population A, people's lives are, on average, well worth living. Population B differs from population A only in that, in addition to the population of A, it contains an added group. These people's lives are worth living, too, though less so than the lives of the persons in population A. Let us stipulate that their existence does not affect the persons in population A at all – members of population A do not even know of this new group's existence. The question, then, is this: do we make a situation *worse* by moving from A to B – that is, by the mere addition of persons whose lives are worth living?

It's hard to imagine condemning such an addition. By hypothesis, no one's rights are violated, total utility is higher, and each new person is happy to be there.[5] At the very least, B seems *no worse* than A. How does B compare with C? In C, the better-off group from B has been made worse off. But their loss is smaller than the

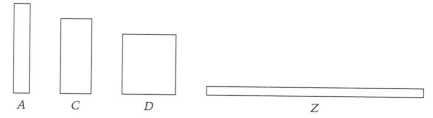

Figure 10.2 Quality of life and increasing population size. Repeating the sequences described in Figure 10.1 leads to a state of affairs Z that is much worse than the original (A). Width of the blocks = population size; height = average quality of life.

gain achieved by the worse-off group, so total utility has risen. The resulting distribution is superior on egalitarian grounds as well. On various grounds, then, C is at least as good as B.[6]

The problem, of course, arises in the repetition of this sequence, as illustrated in Figure 10.2. For if the move from A to C is justified, why not the move from C to D, and so on, all the way to Z? In other words, if a state of affairs is made better (or at least, not worse) than another by doubling the population while decreasing average utility by less than 50 percent, why not continue until we are left with an *enormous* number of people whose lives are, on average, only *barely* worth living?[7]

This is the Repugnant Conclusion. To people seeing this puzzle for the first time, the conclusion that Z is morally desirable, or even that it is merely no worse than A, sounds absurd. How could a society be superior to another simply in virtue of being so much larger, when average members are so much worse off that *one more* traffic jam, stubbed toe, or malfunctioning toilet will drive them to conclude that life is no longer worth living?

Generalizing: a problem for utilitarianism

Here is an easy response. Total utilitarianism works well enough in a world of fixed population, but in a world where population size is one of our choice variables, we need a more sophisticated metric. In this more complex world, the intuitive attraction of utilitarianism is better captured by *average* utilitarianism: the theory that an act is right if and only if it maximizes average utility. As Parfit was aware, though, average utilitarianism has its own version of the problem.

The Other Repugnant Conclusion: For any population of people with a quality of life more or less like ours, say, we can imagine a smaller population (in the limit, a single, godlike Utility Monster) that is on average so much happier that it would be better if our population were replaced by that smaller one.

Some environmentalists will not find this repugnant, but this is because they have other reasons to oppose overpopulation. To them, there are things in the world that matter more, maybe a lot more, than the happiness of persons. In other words, they are not utilitarians. To utilitarians, though, the *Other* Repugnant Conclusion is almost as big a problem as the original.

To summarize, the problem in its general form is that we have two kinds of mechanical measures of aggregate happiness: total or average. In practice it may be massively difficult, indeed impossible, truly to arrive at any such measure. But the problem suggested by our Repugnant Conclusions goes deeper: that is, we would not be able to trust a *number* even if it were easy to obtain, and even if its accuracy were indubitable. The fact would remain that neither version of a utilitarian number – that is, neither total nor average happiness – reliably tracks the intuitions that led us to find utilitarianism plausible in the first place.[8]

Generalizing further: a problem for all act-centered theories

The problem is more than a problem for utilitarianism. It is a problem for all *act-centered* theories: that is, moral theories that treat specifying action-guiding rules as their primary task. From an act-centered perspective, it is hard to explain *why* the Repugnant Conclusion is repugnant. We have already seen that utilitarian theories, which base their evaluation of actions on their tendency to produce desirable states of affairs, are left with little means of stopping once they accept the desirability of the initial moves from A to B, and B to C.

Deontological theories might appear to be in better shape. After all, they do not base their evaluation of an act's morality on its tendency to produce a certain state of affairs, so they can reject the move from A to B even if they judge B to be a better state of affairs. Nevertheless, it is an awkward response for a theory to bite the bullet and say (as the hardest forms of deontology do) that consequences should play *no* role in our evaluations of states of affairs. But that consequences should play some role is all that is needed to get Repugnant Conclusions off the ground. For if C is superior to A on *some* morally relevant grounds, then the burden of proof is on the deontologist to show that there are countervailing moral considerations that override the moral case for moving from A to C. And this seems unlikely. Who is being treated as a mere means in the course of moving from A to C? Where in the chain is the step that cannot be universalized? For that matter, what if anything is wrong with Z from a deontological perspective? Whose rights are being violated? More profoundly, whose rights are violated by the bare admission that Z is a better state of affairs? A theory might try to save face by insisting that the move from A to Z is for some reason impermissible, but quibbling about the propriety of the move would be too little too late. If a theory admits that Z is *better*, it has already embarrassed itself, regardless of whether it prohibits *moving* to Z.[9]

Deontological theories are more apt for considering how to treat currently existing people than for considering whether it would be good for an additional population to come into existence. Which is to say, deontological theories are less apt for a world where moral problems are increasingly taking on ecological dimensions.

Somehow, the initial utilitarian rationale for the move from A to C is spurious. In some way, a total utilitarian has the wrong idea, not about whether consequences are relevant, but about the way in which consequences are relevant.[10] At best, an average utilitarian does only a little better. We may hope for some escape from the problem once we factor in environmental considerations, but it is built into the problem that life in the larger population is, after all, worth living. So whatever loss of environmental amenities people face, average people nevertheless are eking out lives worth living, even if only barely.

An anthropocentric deontology likewise would seem not to solve the problem, as there is no particular reason to suppose members of this larger population are failing to treat each other as ends in themselves. A deontology expanded to embrace animal rights merely treats one symptom of a larger problem, because the problem goes beyond our treatment of other sentient creatures to the wanton destruction of trees and such. The larger concern is not animal rights; it is more fundamentally an ecological concern, perhaps with aesthetic overtones.[11]

IS THERE ANOTHER WAY OF DOING MORAL THEORY?

There would seem to be a more direct way of going to the heart of the problem, but it would involve giving up on standard act-centered moral theories. The heart of the task is at least in part to define ideals of human excellence – to define a conception of the good life for a person that makes sense as an ideal, with no presumption that the ideal must be adopted as a goal to be promoted. We have other ways of responding to ideals; simply respecting them comes to mind, an attitude perhaps more in keeping with intuitions that motivate deontology. Part of an ideal of human excellence could, in turn, incorporate forms of environmental sensitivity. Again, though, there is no assumption that environmental sensitivity must translate into an activist agenda – simply appreciating the beauty of nature is among the more admirable ways of being sensitive to it.[12]

Thomas Hill suggests that our discomfort with environmental exploitation is not wholly a product of our belief that environmental goods are being put to inefficient use, nor that those who exploit such goods are violating any rights in doing so. It is a mistake, he thinks, to suppose that "all moral questions are exclusively concerned with whether *acts* are right or wrong, and that this, in turn, is determined entirely by how the acts impinge on the rights and interests of those directly affected" (Hill 2005, p. 48). Instead, Hill suggests, we ought to ask "What sort of *person* would destroy the natural environment?" Approaching the issue from this perspective allows us to see that "even if there is no convincing way to show that the destructive acts are wrong (independently of human and animal use and enjoyment), we may find that the willingness to indulge in them reflects the absence of human traits that we admire and regard as morally important" (Hill 2005, p. 50). People who carve their initials in 100-year-old Saguaros might not be violating any rights, and the satisfaction they get might well outweigh the suffering caused to other sentient beings, but the fact remains that there is some defect in such people's characters. In Hill's language, they lack a kind of humility – an ability to appreciate their place in the natural order or to "see things as important apart from themselves and the limited groups they associate with" (Hill 2005, p. 51).

Hill's approach offers a natural, straight-to-the-point way of thinking about what Richard Routley called the "Last Man Argument." Routley's thought experiment presents you with a situation something like this: You are the last human being. You shall soon die. When you are gone, the only life remaining will be plants, microbes, invertebrates. For some reason, the following thought runs through your head: "Before I die, it sure would be nice to destroy the last remaining Redwood. Just for fun." What, if anything, would be *wrong* with destroying that Redwood? Destroying it won't hurt anyone, so what's the problem? The problem is, what kind of person would destroy that last Redwood? What kind of person would enjoy such wanton destruction of such a beautiful, majestic, living thing? Hill's question seems like exactly the right question.[13]

Indeed, for a number of philosophers Hill's question promises to transform the way we think about environmental ethics. The relatively recent field of environmental virtue ethics has developed in order to study the norms of character that ought to govern human interaction with the environment, and scholars such as Philip Cafaro, Jason Kawall, and Ronald Sandler are developing this field in a way that is yielding fruitful theoretical and practical results (Cafaro 2004; Kawall 2003; Sandler 2007). These scholars seek to characterize attitudes and dispositions that are constitutive of environmental virtue, and to explain the proper role of an ethic of character within a broader environmental ethic. And practically, scholars have focused both on the implications of and prerequisites of particular virtues such as benevolence or temperance, and also on the implications of a virtue ethics approach for specific practical problems such as consumerism and genetically modified crops.

Hill's approach also offers a way of dealing with Repugnant Conclusions. For even if we cannot provide a definitive account of the wrongness of preferring a society Z, of the sort described in the Repugnant Conclusion, there remains *something* wrong with being the kind of person who would prefer Z. That something could be hard to articulate, but no less real for that. In any case, Hill does provide some pertinent articulation. The sort of person who would prefer Z is the sort of person who does not possess the humility that would lead a more virtuous person to see value in human society playing an appropriately limited role in the biotic community, for nonanthropocentric as well as anthropocentric reasons.

It is difficult to make accurate judgments of character without setting the context in some detail. And it is difficult to imagine a context in which a person's expressed preference for Z is worthy of being taken seriously enough to merit a moral evaluation. In the next section, we will attempt to describe a situation in which it makes sense to speak of a person "choosing" to move from A to Z. For now, though, suppose that someone you know were offered the option of snapping their fingers and thereby popping into existence a population either like A or like Z in some far-off and (otherwise) causally isolated universe. Presumably, since no other values are at stake, a disposition to choose population Z in such circumstances is simply part of what it *means* to believe that Z is a superior state of affairs to A.

Given this fact, then, what are we to say about the character of a person who prefers Z to A? Bear in mind that Z is, in the end, a fairly miserable place. People's lives are, it is true, still worth living. But only barely so. Think of how much misery a person can endure while still believing that life is worth living. Now think of a whole world – a very *crowded* world – filled with such people. What kind of person would bring *that* kind of universe into existence when they could just as easily have produced a universe with a smaller number of very happy people? What would be the point? Intuitively, there is *no* point, contra total utilitarianism.

The most natural explanation for such a disposition seems to be a sort of obsession. It's normal to think that the happiness of particular other people is important. It's normal to generalize from this and think that happiness itself is important. It's *maniacal* to think that this abstraction translates into a reason to prefer, over A, the concrete misery of world Z. Like cases of obsession in general, what seems to have gone wrong here is an extreme inability to grasp the larger context. In this respect, it is not unlike a person who originally pursues cleanliness for the sake of health (and health for the sake of a long, enjoyable life), but ends up cleaning compulsively. What started off as a reasonable principle – be as clean as you can – has been transformed into a manifestly unreasonable rule that trumps all other aspects of a worthwhile life.

The compulsive pursuit of cleanliness thus ultimately undermines the very value that led them to pursue cleanliness to begin with. There is something similarly wrong in being a person who would think of maximizing a happiness number, as if, from an anthropocentric perspective, what matters most were *happiness* rather than persons themselves (or something about persons other than their happiness, such as whether they achieve excellence).

NOTE ON CONTRIBUTING TO OVERPOPULATION

In the real world, of course, populations are never the product of any individual's choice. Individuals and families do not choose populations; they choose whether or not to have children. Populations emerge only as a (typically unforeseen and unintended) consequence of the combination of many such decisions. The fact that we can raise questions about the character of one who holds a sincere preference for population Z might thus seem to have few implications for deciding what to say about people and policies which *actually move us* toward Z. Do character-centered ethics have anything to say about these more practical population-related questions?

Insofar as they are not the product of any single individual's choice, undesirable populations can be regarded as an externality along the lines of air pollution. No individual family's decision to limit the number of children they have significantly affects the size or well-being of the overall population, just as no commuter significantly affects the amount of smog in the air by choosing to ride their bicycle to work one day. In either case, however, the aggregate result of many individuals failing to make such decisions is tragic.

Suppose for argument's sake that adding large numbers to the existing population will contribute to an unsustainable (or undesirable) population growth. In that case, raising a large family would amount to a failure to contribute to a sort of public good.[14] If that were the case, achieving a desirable population would require a general policy of restraint on the part of most families, and having a large family in that situation would be to free-ride on the restraint of others. The irresponsibility here needn't be calculated – many families simply won't know (and won't bother to find out) the consequences of having more children than they can afford. The point, however, is that where act-centered theories fall short of explaining the indignation we sometimes feel (or explain it in an ad hoc, round-about, or otherwise unsatisfying way) when confronted with free-riding that does only minute harm, a character-centered theory provides a rich vocabulary for criticizing those who contribute to Repugnant Conclusions as short-sighted, irresponsible, weak-willed, selfish, and so on.

Does virtue ethics help to provide a specifically environmental perspective on what's wrong with people who contribute to over-population? (1) A utilitarian can say an act has bad environmental consequences, which counts for something. (2) A deontologist can say an act that has sufficiently bad environmental consequences will as a result be nonuniversalizable, and may also fail to treat other would-be users of the same environmental amenities as ends in themselves. (3) A virtue theorist can say an actor is a bad person qua member of the biotic community, which is something else. A virtue theorist can acknowledge that the third conclusion is true partly because the first one is, but can go on to say there is more to being a good person than to act in a way that has good conse-quences. A good person is considerate, and therefore *cares* about consequences. A good person is humble, in the sense of seeing him-self as a locus of value in a world where there are many loci of value, and recognizing that it is not only humans who can be worthy of appreciation.

INTUITION AND THEORY

One false ideal for moral theory is the idea that the right theory will be simple in the sense of being able to substitute for the wisdom of experience. Part of the point of the Repugnant Conclusion is that wise persons realize that the intuitions leading them to find utili-tarianism plausible are not in fact captured by the simple formulas utilitarians sometimes claim to offer.[15]

It is not as if theory is a radical alternative to intuition. A theory is an attempt to capture our intuitions with a simple formula. How could we expect to do that without losing some of morality's intu-itive nuance? Of course theories will have counterexamples! It is in our veins as philosophers to continue to test our theories against the intuitions we intend to be articulating with our theories, and of course those articulations will be an imperfect match.

Theories try to systematize our intuitions, but that is like trying to launch a ballistic missile in a direction such that its simple trajectory will track the more complex trajectory of a guided missile. Counterexamples take the form of showing where the ballistic missile deviates from the guided missile's more convoluted path. This is not to express skepticism about the whole project of moral theorizing, so much as about the more particular assumption that act-centered moral theorizing is the way to go. Act-centered theories are one way of trying to articulate. There is no reason to assume they are the best way. Nothing like that is guaranteed. What is more or less guaranteed – we see no counterexamples on the horizon! – is that act-centered theories will provide imperfect guidance.

We are not presenting this as a knockdown argument against act-centered theory. Our conclusion is that act-centered theory has a certain kind of value, not that it has no value. Virtue ethics reminds us that providing moral agents with a decision procedure covering all possible situations is not the main purpose of moral theories (if it is even a purpose at all). The people for whom moral theories are intended are people already in the midst of living their lives. They come to philosophy hoping it can help them reflect on their lives. A moral theory is successful if it provides that assistance; unsuccessful if it does not. Cases like the Repugnant Conclusion show us that an act-centered theory is not useful as a universal decision procedure. The proper lesson is not that act-centered theories are useless, though, but rather that we are better off treating act-centered theory as the sort of thing from which wise persons can gain insight that is useful, even if limited.

SUMMARY

There are times, as Tom Hill says, when the question is not what is wrong with the act, but what kind of person would do it. The Repugnant Conclusion seems to show that there are cases where the moral problem, even from an act-utilitarian perspective, is not straightforwardly a problem of how to maximize total utility. Our "Other Repugnant Conclusion" seems to show that average utilitarianism does not solve the problem; therefore, even by its own lights, act utilitarianism, the simplest, most mechanical of all moral decision procedures, is not reliable as a mechanical procedure even in principle. Moral decisions require *wisdom*, not mere computational power, and there is no simple recipe for wisdom.

It is mere appearance, and misleading appearance, that act-centered theories are better than agent-centered ones at converting moral decision-making from art into science. Prevailing act-centered theories incorporate theories of value that specify some of the considerations to which a wise moral agent will be sensitive. That is their contribution to moral wisdom. It is a significant contribution, but they have not done better than that, and probably never will.

Human rights matter, as do animal rights, whenever they are at stake. Interests matter, when they are at stake. Treating persons as ends in themselves matters, when persons and their ends are at stake. Perhaps universalizability matters in some independent way, but if it matters in some independent way, it probably matters in virtue of what it says about an agent's character. The idea is that to act in a way that you could will to be a universal law is arguably the essence of acting with integrity. That is, when we do that, we are acting from motives that we would not hesitate to make transparent, for all the world to see. If Kant was right, acting in accordance with what one could will to be a universal law was the essence of good will, which (although 'good will' is a notoriously technical notion in Kantian scholarship) appears to be a state of character. A virtue theory might not agree with Kant that good will is the only thing good in itself, but might readily agree that good will is basic, and that unless one gets one's character in order, the other good things in life become ashes.

Finally, talk of rights, interests, and treating persons as ends seems especially apt when we are talking about how to treat persons, or perhaps other sentient beings, and that is what we were talking about in the previous paragraph. But what if the issue concerns a person's relation to an insentient creature such as a Redwood, or to the biotic community as such? Intuitively, Tom Hill's question is *the* question.[16]

NOTES

1   If morality was really just (or even primarily) a system of rules, we might expect that very clever teenagers could become moral experts simply by reading about and mastering those rules. The fact that we

think that moral expertise is more a matter of wisdom and experience than memorization is one reason for thinking this view of morality to be mistaken. See Annas 2004, 2006, §A.3; Hursthouse 1999, pp. 59ff.

2 Indeed, as Dan Russell has noted in discussion, this is one point on which virtue ethicists such as Julia Annas, Elizabeth Anscombe, Rosalind Hursthouse, and Philippa Foot present a more or less united front.

3 See also Philip Cafaro's excellent work on Henry Thoreau as a forerunner of environmental virtue ethics (Cafaro 2004).

4 It must seem obvious we will have trouble contriving a number that reliably represents aggregate happiness, but utilitarians have little choice but to insist it can be done. Or, at least, to insist that the ideal of maximization can serve as a useful guide to moral deliberation even in the absence of reliable numbers. We accept the assumption for argument's sake. But see Schmidtz 1992.

5 The average utility of the entire population has, of course, decreased. But the average utility of the original group remains unchanged, and there are reasons to think this should be the relevant consideration. If we judged the morality of an action based on the average utility of the population which exists *ex post*, rather than *ex ante*, then average utility would seem to condone (secretly) killing off anybody who was less happy than average. Surely this is not the way to make the world a happier place.

6 This is not to deny that there are impermissible ways of moving from *B* to *C*, or even that a state of affairs which would otherwise be desirable can be rendered condemnable by being brought about in an impermissible way. So long as we assume this is *not* the case, *C* looks preferable to *B*.

7 What does it mean to say that a life is only barely worth living? On its face, this description is compatible with a life's being pretty miserable. This, at any rate, is the interpretation we operate with for the purposes of this chapter. On reflection, however, the judgment that a life is worth living might be one to which it is difficult to assign any concrete interpretation in the absence of a particular perspective. A person who is *already living that life* might be more disposed to sincerely believe that their life is worth living than a person who is observing the world from the outside, deciding whether or not it would be worth it to live that life (rather than remain in their current state of oblivion). Perhaps there are psychological forces which impel the person living their life to convince themselves that it is worthwhile. Or perhaps the fact that they are situated in a particular point in time is relevant (costs in the past are sunk, and there's always hope for the future). Are these

reasons to discount the preference expressed by actual individuals? What's the alternative?

8   Michael Huemer (2008) has likewise argued that the Repugnant Conclusion is inescapable within any utilitarian framework, although he treats this as a reason for accepting the Repugnant Conclusion rather than a reason for leaving utilitarianism behind.

9   In the case of what we call the Other Repugnant Conclusion, the deontological prohibition of the crimes that would be involved in making most of humanity disappear is straightforward. Here too, however, we see a problem with using the language of universalizability or respect for persons to explain what is wrong with the kind of environmentalist who thinks the world would be better if virtually all of humanity were to disappear.

10 One other possibility would be to handle consequentialist issues in contractarian fashion, that is, by saying that the utilities in question are not fungible. It is true that for any given person, more utility is better for that person, but it is not true that anyone's utility can be traded for anyone else's in such a way as to produce a higher aggregate. Such a theory would reject what otherwise seems to be a utilitarian case for moving from A to Z, but at a cost of refusing to entertain comparisons at all, and thus also refusing to acknowledge that A is preferable to Z in some agent-neutral way. For discussion of nonaggregative forms of utilitarianism, see Coons, forthcoming.

11 For related arguments that recast the question as one about the right thing to do rather than reasons for preferring, see Narveson 1967. See also Booin-Vail 1996.

12 Matthews (2001) argues that militant environmentalists make the same mistake as everyone else who seeks to conquer the biotic community: failing to embrace a truly ecological ethos of "letting it be."

13 This paragraph borrows from Schmidtz and Willott's "The Last Man and the Search for Objective Value," chap. 2 of their 2001.

14 To be clear, we do not accept the premise, but it nicely illustrates how indignation over minute harms can often be better explained in terms of universalizability than in terms of utility, and even better, in terms of what such behavior says about the characters of people who free-ride at other people's expense.

15 One of the many features that made Mill a great moral philosopher was his refusal to place more weight on the simple formula of utilitarianism than it was meant to bear. Readers of *Utilitarianism* will find nothing like an algorithm at work in Mill's thoughtful and nuanced moral analysis.

16 Schmidtz (2001b) argues that we can respect nature without being
    species egalitarians. Indeed, the view that potatoes and chimpanzees
    have equal moral standing is incompatible with genuine respect for
    nature. Genuine respect acknowledges what living things have in com-
    mon, but also acknowledges differences.

11 The virtue approach to business ethics

The first influential critique of business from the point of view of virtue ethics was that of Alasdair MacIntyre ([1981] 1984). But while many business ethicists have read and discussed MacIntyre's argument that the profit motive in business undermines virtue, few have agreed with him. Nearly all business ethicists believe, not surprisingly, that there is such a thing as business ethics. MacIntyre does not. Robert Solomon's *Ethics and Excellence* (1992), explicitly indebted to Aristotle, was more influential, perhaps because Solomon argued that there could be virtue in business.

In part as a result of the influence of Solomon and MacIntyre, the virtue approach in the field is predominantly Aristotelian. Adam Smith and Hume are cited far less.[1] Solomon and MacIntyre both appear to accept a form of eudaimonism, the characteristically Aristotelian notion that ethics is primarily about the good life for the person of good character; so it matters what effect business activities have on one's character. This view not only suggests something about the nature of the good life but also offers reasons for being ethical. For businesspeople and business students that is a major issue.

But the virtue approach is not widely accepted in the field. One reason for this is the influence of scholars in organization theory, which is, roughly, the study of organizational systems and structures and their effect on corporate performance. Because these scholars typically try to identify principles of effective management, they can see the point of ethical principles as well. Even so, most organization theorists want to be scientific (so Ghoshal 2005); they see

I thank the editor of this volume for many useful suggestions.

themselves as seeking causal relations among readily observable and quantifiable variables as natural scientists do. Business ethicists trained primarily in organization theory see ethics as a subdiscipline of that field. They focus on the variables that are conducive to ethics, where ethics is usually cashed out as a reputation for ethics or infrequency of problems with the law or some similar measurable variable. Although moral philosophers in business ethics do not believe that ethics is scientific, they must converse with organization theorists, who outnumber and outvote them. It is difficult enough to make the case for ethical judgment; the difficulty increases if one must defend the apparent vagueness of virtue ethics and the view that there is no single metric in ethics, so that ethics differs from cost–benefit analysis. This helps explain why the virtue approach does not seem attractive to many business ethicists.

I shall argue that the views of organization theorists, and of many economists as well, are based on a facile utilitarianism, which is in turn based on an oversimplified and misleading conception of human motivation and rationality. An Aristotelian view offers a subtler and more persuasive view, which applies more usefully in a business context than does an approach based on principles. So I disagree with MacIntyre, who believes that capitalism is inimical to virtue in organizations.

AN ECONOMIC VIEW OF ETHICS

Organization theory, and therefore business ethics, is influenced by economics and by the view of human motivation that economists typically offer. Insofar as economists are hospitable to ethics, they usually favor utilitarianism. Psychological traits, attitudes, and beliefs are important only insofar as they lead to good or bad acts. Organizational behavior theory, which differs from organization theory in that it focuses more on human behavior and psychology, takes these items more seriously but tends to operationalize them. Organization theory owes more to sociology than to psychology. Economists take a reductionist view of these entities. So business ethicists who regard virtues as more than mere dispositions face skeptical colleagues.

Furthermore, most business ethicists today have considerable faith in markets. There is indeed much to be said for markets in

which there is strong competition and participants have the information required to maximize their interests by their purchases.
Such a market will be highly productive. It will enable positive-sum
exchanges. It will be just, too, in the sense that what a participant
gets out of the market will depend on what he or she contributes to
it. It will respect negative rights, in that all deals will be voluntary
and there will be a broad range of choices.[2]

From this view one might infer that ethics in highly competitive
markets is to a significant degree a matter of competing successfully, that the virtue of a firm is effectiveness, and that the virtue
of its employees is to do their jobs well. In a well-managed firm the
employees will be compensated according to their contributions; so
the self-interested employee will act ethically. From here it is no
great distance to Milton Friedman's (1970) well-known claim that
the moral responsibility of corporate managers is to compete successfully and make profits.

Not all markets are highly competitive, however, and market
imperfections and failures, especially failures of knowledge, will create ethical problems.

BUSINESS ETHICS AND UTILITARIANISM

Most business ethicists reject Friedman's view, but they usually take
utilitarian considerations seriously even when they are not praising
markets. Advocates of corporate social responsibility (Carroll 1981,
for example) believe that corporations often can and should act in
ways that benefit society, particularly when the corporation is in
a uniquely good position to do so, as when Merck manufactured
and distributed their patented medication Mectizan to over 200 mil-
lion Africans suffering from or exposed to river blindness. The benefits more than justified the cost, according to Merck management.
Stakeholder theorists (for example, Freeman et al. 2007) argue that
the interests of stakeholders other than stockholders create obligations for corporations, which ought to seek win–win situations with
them. Their examples suggest that the winning that they have in
mind is largely financial.

Nearly all business ethicists believe that business can be an ethical enterprise, and other things being equal they favor organizations
that are effective, hence productive. To the question "Why should

I be moral?" the standard answer is that I should be moral because the business system can be productive if and only if people like me act honestly, work responsibly, and otherwise contribute to productivity. Everyone fares better if everyone acts ethically than if everyone acts unethically, though I do very well if everyone but me acts ethically.[3]

Business ethicists and organization theorists are often called upon to say whether good ethics is good business. An affirmative response typically rests on evidence that something like having a corporate ethics statement correlates with higher than average profits (so Burke 1985, pp. 325–31). One can also claim that a reputation for trustworthiness is a business asset. Rarely do business ethicists dismiss the question by arguing that ethical obligation is not contingent on corporate effectiveness. Being of more practical orientation than most moral philosophers, they do not care to present business ethics as impractical or an impediment to effectiveness. To accept the view that business ethics is an oxymoron would leave them with little or nothing to say to businesspeople, whose thinking they do want to influence.

Business ethicists like to point to the evidence (for example, that collected by Collins and Porras 2002) that the most profitable companies are those whose strategies and policies are driven by a prosocial corporate mission. So Johnson and Johnson, for example, aims to satisfy its customers first, then its employees, then the communities in which it operates, and its stockholders only fourth. But corporate management has long believed that the stockholders are best served if the other three stakeholder groups are given priority. So, happily for all concerned, profit and ethics coincide (Johnson& Johnson 1940).

Although intrinsic goods of the kind that virtue ethicists consider important are not so prominent in the field, they are not entirely ignored. Along with the utilitarian focus there has been some attention to issues like meaningful work and freedom from sexual harassment, but scholars of organizational ethics are usually respectful of the point that one may quit an unsatisfactory job and that employers have economic reasons for not treating their employees badly. Scholarship on ethics in international business often justifies multinational enterprise as an engine of eventual prosperity for all. Even critical analyses of sweatshops usually acknowledge that they provide relatively good economic opportunities to people in developing countries, and can be a first step towards a strong economy.

There are, however, at least two problems with this view of ethics and good business. First, many individual companies succeed by being unethical – by selling bad products, by competing unfairly or eliminating competition, by exploiting vulnerable workers, by taking irresponsible risks, sometimes under pressure from investors. Second, the lesson that we are being invited to draw from Johnson & Johnson is that one should do well by one's stakeholders because that is the best way to competitive success. That makes ethics a strategy, not a free-standing obligation.

MacIntyre, Solomon, and others who take the virtue approach to business ethics emphatically deny that the right thing is whatever contributes to effectiveness and therefore productivity. They argue that one can contribute to productivity while being a person of bad character, or while becoming bad by habitually acting badly. Being a person of good character is of value in itself; doing the right thing is neither more important nor more praiseworthy than being a good person, and doing the wrong thing is compatible with, and not redeemed by, good results. So the question remains whether a successful businessperson can be a good person. If not, there is no place for virtue ethics in business, or in business school. MacIntyre and Solomon give opposite answers to the question, but they both avoid some bad assumptions about human motivation.

HOMO ECONOMICUS AND INTERESTS

It is widely assumed that success in business is in one's best interests, and that the great issue is whether self-interest conflicts with ethics. From the point of view of virtue ethics this assumption suggests a simple and questionable view of self-interest, and therefore of the relationship between self-interest and ethics.

At least for the purposes of prediction, many economists and in particular rational choice theorists assume that every human being is a *Homo economicus*, a rational maximizer of his or her own interests. One's interests amount to the satisfaction of one's desires, which are, as in the Humean account, neither rational nor irrational. Typically what is desired can be bought, and the strength of one's desire is a matter of what one is willing to pay. So utility is the satisfaction of any old desire.[4]

There is reason to believe that a productive market requires the kind of selfishness characteristic of *Homo economicus*. As Adam Smith famously observed, the general welfare is typically served when all participants in the market work to benefit themselves. It may seem to follow that, as business is fundamentally a competitive enterprise, I shall be better off if and only if my competitor is worse off. If so, then selfishness is a prerequisite for business success. To contribute to everyone's welfare or, for that matter, to act so that justice is done or protected would at least sometimes be a losing competitive strategy.[5]

But this is not right, for reasons that many virtue ethicists would offer. If we are to begin to understand the relationship among ethics, self-interest, and success in business, we must see that, contrary to the *Homo economicus* model, one's interests are not simple and not set in stone. Here Aristotle is especially instructive. He claims that character is a matter of what you enjoy: good things if you are a good person, bad if bad (*NE* II.3, 1104b5ff.). So he disagrees with Hume: reason is not the slave of the passions, for a passion can be rational or irrational. Achieving a good character entails developing rational desires and emotions rather than irrational ones. As his account of *akrasia* (weakness of will) shows, Aristotle is aware that one may have certain desires that one would prefer not to have. Acting on one's rationally preferred desires rather than on those by which one does not want to be motivated calls on the virtue of self-control. But if you are a fully virtuous person, a person of practical wisdom (*phronēsis*), you have no wayward desires. Your second-order desires – to use language made popular by Frankfurt (1981) – are in accord with your first-order desires. Your character is strong. You have what Adam Smith called self-command.

A reflective businessperson, or anyone else, might ask this: Why is it in my interest to be a person of kindly character rather than a rapacious person? It may be true that all will be better off if all are honest and considerate, but then the best strategy for me will be rapacity no matter what others do. If character is a matter of what one enjoys, as Aristotle claims, then this is a wrongheaded question. We should instead ask this one: Given that you want to serve your own interests, *what do you want your interests to be?*

What do you want to enjoy? Do you want to be the sort of person who can enjoy only overwhelming financial success? Or instead the sort of person who enjoys a life in which work plays an important but not overwhelming role and offers challenge, fun, intellectual development, association with stimulating people, and compensation that supports a comfortable life? When I consider what would be a good life for me, I should ask myself not only what I prefer, but *what I would choose to prefer* if I could choose thoughtfully and rationally. That question cannot be readily answered by reference to self-interest.

Yet there is a wise answer to that question if, as is probable, most people who give the second answer are happier in the end than those who give the first.[6] Great wealth is hard to come by, and those who aim at it will probably be disappointed. And if you do succeed in becoming rich, there is a good chance that you will not be very content, because you will always be comparing yourself to those who make more.[7] As Adam Smith observed, greed is insatiable.

According to positive psychologists, people of moderate but sufficient means are happier than very poor people on the whole, but extremely rich people are not much happier than those who are moderately well off.[8] We are made happy, these psychologists say – and Aristotle would agree – by our associations. The happiest people enjoy a close family and many good friends. But even for reflective people it is not short work to develop preferences that are achievable and sustainable and will support a good life. Building character takes a few decades, Aristotle claims. And time is a necessary condition, not a sufficient one.

RATIONALITY AND INTEGRITY

In Aristotle's view, good character essentially involves rationality, in this sense: a person of good character has good values and therefore wants to desire good things, and is able to achieve those good things. So Aristotle needs to say what is truly desirable, desirable to a rational person. A fully rational person can figure out what is best in the very long run – what sort of life will be happiest – and then find a way to live such a life. Aristotle claims that *eudaimonia*, which we usually translate as *flourishing*, is about the very long run: it is not a passing condition (*NE* 1.10, 1101a9ff.).[9]

The good life is based on two essential human characteristics. First, we are communal creatures, and cannot live well without supportive family, friends, and community. Second, we are rational creatures. We want to have desires that form a coherent whole at any time and through time, rather than those that contradict each other or violate our values or change constantly. Aristotle claims that your personal identity is at stake here, that maintaining your character is tantamount to continuing your life (*NE* IX.4, 1066a13–29, b7–14).[10]

Without this sort of integrity you will sometimes desire, and may get, what you do not value. Valuing courage, you wish that you looked forward to the crucial negotiations or did not fear disagreeing with the boss, but you find that you are less courageous than you would like to be. You are better off, as well as more virtuous, if your values and desires are consistent throughout. Most of us, alas, are not always like that. Valuing good health and attractiveness, we nonetheless find the pastry tempting. Valuing success, we nonetheless shrink from the required challenges and are not eager to work hard.

As integrity is a matter of having and acting on coherent values over time and at a time, it will not do to have one set of values and desires for your job and another outside work. In a complex and turbulent world we find it difficult to maintain a single set of values, but the alternative is to lose sight of what matters most. We may forget that money is a means to *eudaimonia* and not identical with it. So Aristotle says (*NE* I.5, 1096a5–7), and suggests that moneymakers fall short of the good life because they make money their end.[11]

Integrity is more than coherence, however. We may achieve coherence on the cheap, by rearranging our values to rationalize our actions.[12] Integrity requires developing values rationally, maintaining them, and then acting on them. Unfortunately, as social psychologists have demonstrated, we often reason in the wrong direction. Instead of acting on the basis of our values, we do what is easy and then concoct some plausible value that we claim motivates us. Afraid to confront the boss, I tell myself that I am being diplomatic. Being greedy, I tell myself that the derivatives that I am selling help allocate capital effectively. One of the most important functions of education, and moral education in particular, is to teach us to reason in the right direction. But that too is a life's work.

Aristotle argues that you cannot be a bad person and still lead a happy life. If you are rapacious and you sometimes act nicely for strategic reasons, as when people are watching, you will often find yourself doing things that you do not enjoy. You will be acting inconsistently with your values and with your desires (*NE* ix.4, 1066b7–14). In any case, to repeat, you are a communal being, and your happiness depends in part on your being a productive and congenial member of a community. Desires that are at odds with this fact about us are not going to lead us to happiness. So vicious behavior puts you at war with yourself and with your community, and you are supposed to be a rational and communal creature.

Aristotle is clear about the importance of a good community to support virtuous people. We may wonder whether business offers adequate support for virtue. Aristotle seems to believe that it does not, and he is not alone in that view.

BUSINESS VIRTUES

Some (Sennett 1998, for example) believe that business tends to undermine integrity. Business may impart bad values, or it may put one in a situation in which one has competing values, and a kind of fragmentation results. I shall argue that this does not always happen.

When we evaluate an action in business, we need to attend to the context that makes it what it is – say, paying a bill. We might say that there are special context-cognizant rules and virtues for business. For example, while friendship is important, it should not normally be the basis of a decision to hire or promote someone. One can sometimes justifiably withhold information from employees as well as competitors. One may fool a competitor, just as in baseball one may steal a base or throw a curve. These policies and actions are justified by the need for the corporation to compete effectively.

An example illustrates the problem that these considerations do not solve. Cassandra, a manager, has been told by senior executives of the firm that corporate headquarters are about to be moved and that some managers, including her subordinate Myron, with whom she has a friendly relationship, will be fired. Cassandra works under a general agreement not to tell employees about major corporate strategic initiatives, and she is reminded that her agreement does not permit her to tell Myron or anyone else about the firings. Cassandra then learns that Myron is about to close on a new house, which will be a great financial burden once he loses his job. Should Cassandra say anything to Myron? Considerations of long-term effectiveness do not alter our impression that this is a case in which Cassandra's job-related obligation makes her a bad friend.

One's role as a manager does bring some obligations with it, as does one's role as a parent or a soldier. Parents and soldiers are obligated to do things that are not obligatory for people generally, and may even be forbidden to them. (See Alzola, forthcoming.) Conflicting prima facie moral claims are a fact of ordinary life, but there is a special problem about virtues. Virtues begin as habits: we act virtuously, and over time we develop an understanding of what a particular virtue demands and some level of comfort and satisfaction in acting virtuously. But an organization can cause one to develop bad habits that run contrary to one's virtues and may undermine one's integrity.

No doubt one can behave ruthlessly at the office and at the same time kindly to one's neighbor. Consider the doctors who performed extraordinarily cruel "experiments" for the Nazis but otherwise acted as responsible professionals. But these doctors were not in fact good people who found it necessary to perform some hard tasks for their nation's sake. They were bad and weak. A person of good character will have the sort of integrity not found among the Nazi doctors, whose professionalism was shallow and vulnerable, not a real virtue. An evil regime can weaken people's character. So, it would seem, can an evil organization.

It does not follow, nor is it true, that people of good character will always ignore the prima facie obligations associated with their roles or jobs. Those obligations must be considered, but there is never an algorithm available to determine their weight. One might argue that that is a sign of weakness of virtue ethics, which seems nebulous in practice, especially in comparison to principle-based ethics, and most especially in cases of ethical conflict.

A case will show that that inference is not justified.

A FACT-BASED CASE

An American consulting firm decides to send one of its consultants to Japan to assist some of its consultants and their clients in doing business-related research. The obvious person to send is Debra, who spent some years managing the strategy research office before becoming a consultant.[13] The alternative is Jon, a male consultant with a significant background in research, but not primarily business research. Some senior managers are reluctant to send Debra because, they say, the Japanese will not work with a woman.

A senior consultant, Greg, decides to send Jon. But then Hank, a general partner of the firm, learns of the assignment and asks whether, as he expects, Debra is going to do it. No, he is told; the Japanese won't work with a woman. Hank responds by demanding that Debra be sent. And so Debra goes off to Tokyo, where she performs brilliantly and is asked to stay longer than originally intended.

Debra's success proves no more than any other anecdote. She might have failed. The story is not meant to show that standing up to sexism always leads to a good outcome, or is always the right thing to do. But justice counts for something; in fact, it may be just to do something that decreases the probability of success. Yet while it is typically unjust to discriminate against someone on the basis of gender, that principle may not be straightforwardly applicable to this case. If the Japanese cannot work with a woman no matter what she has to offer, they are being unjust, but does it follow that it is unjust to accede to their wishes in a case like this? Is Greg being just to Debra if he sends her off a cliff to make a point? And how do we deal with the fiduciary duty to the firm's partners?

The story illustrates the problems in calling a decision good if it is made in accordance with certain ethical principles. Business ethicists who are moral philosophers pay particular attention to intermediate principles that reflect special obligations, such as managers' fiduciary duties to owners or the requirement that merchants be honest with customers. The problem is that, as the story shows, even those less lofty moral principles can conflict, and there is no algorithm for weighing them where they do.

In situations of this sort, consultants and other businesspeople often argue for the priority of principles that support their initial intuitions, which in turn are often related to their interests. In this respect businesspeople are not unusual. So in many organizations it would be impossible to have a conversation that would lead to consensus on how to prioritize principles in a case like this, which people see from the point of view of their own perceived interests or some other questionable standpoint, and rationalize accordingly.

Worse, many businesspeople prefer not to talk about moral principles at all. This is business, they say, not Sunday school; so we should think about the success of the business rather than about moral principles. But whatever discomfort businesspeople may feel in discussing moral principles, they usually want to think of themselves as courageous, responsible, honest, and so on. Tell them that they have violated some ethical principle and they may say something dismissive of ethical principles. But tell them that they have shown themselves to be cowards or liars or bullies or unprofessional and they will react negatively indeed. They take some satisfaction in thinking of themselves as people of strong and good character. Perhaps this is because they think and speak of courage and honesty, for example, as real psychological states that explain behavior. And so they are, though the language in which they have their home is normative as well as psychological.[14]

The advice that an ethics consultant would give Greg in this case would not differ very much from that of a highly professional human resources consultant. Neither would suggest doing what would bring about the greatest good for the greatest number, or treating the people involved as ends rather than merely as means. Both would look closely at the facts of the case and try to make a very practical decision. Both might remind Greg that he too is a professional, and must be respectful of the clients' needs without being subservient, and loyal (but not slavishly so) to the partners of the firm. Both would urge Greg not to make the decision out of inordinate fear that it will go wrong.[15]

A good ethical decision is not always a good business decision. It is true, however, that in some cases business considerations impinge on ethical decisions because utilitarian considerations do (for example, the consequences of Debra's failure would hurt the firm and her and help no one) and because considerations of rights do (for example, there is an obligation not to waste the partners' money). Both consequentialists and deontologists will acknowledge that treating consultants fairly is correct from a business point of view. These are *ceteris paribus* considerations; some of the *cetera* look more like business considerations, others look more like ethical considerations. When a professional is making the decision, considerations of the interests of one's stakeholders will typically be taken more seriously, and will make it look more like an ethical decision.

A virtue ethicist, and perhaps a human resources consultant as well, might follow Aristotle in saying that one should look at a situation like this from several different points of view, not limited to that of fiduciary duty, and try to notice and take proper account of the salient features of a situation. This is what Aristotle seems to mean when he claims that if you are a person of good character, you perceive a situation rightly. That is, you are morally responsible for framing the act rightly. If you get it wrong – if you fail to grasp the ethically essential features of the situation – that is a sign that you have a character flaw.[16] A good person will perceive that a certain act is courageous rather than foolhardy, generous rather than vainglorious, and will act accordingly.

Part of correct framing is having the appropriate emotional reaction. Aristotle notes that an irascible person will take offense too readily, and a phlegmatic person will not be angry even when anger is appropriate (*NE* iv.5, 1125b26–1126a3). Perhaps Hank had something like the gut reaction that a seasoned and successful strategist has when contemplating options. From Aristotle to Robert H. Frank (1988), philosophers and others have argued that we should have the *right* emotions and intuitions, rather than none at all. Without them one may be no more than a clever rationalizer, and at worst a sociopath.

CORPORATE CULTURE

Corporate culture affects ethical deliberation, and framing in particular. Corporate culture – the set of norms that affect how people in the organization act, think, and talk, and how they frame certain kinds of situation – can determine or strongly influence what counts locally as a virtue or a vice. Some cultures encourage conflict; others demand consensus. Some cultures are macho, and women are viewed accordingly. Often a culture's norms are not explicit, and employees may not be entirely conscious of them, or of the power of the role models that embody them. In some organizations the prevailing culture encourages prejudice against women and minorities and others who "just don't fit in."

Living for a time in a strong culture may influence how you talk, what you do, and what you want; in some cases it influences the kind of person you want to be. You may want to have the desires and emotions that you see in the leading local role models. You may enjoy being tough, and may be embarrassed to find yourself being accommodating. You may find yourself relishing competition and rolling your eyes when you are asked to compromise or cooperate.

In some cases your higher-order desires will be ineffective. The Milgram experiment (see Milgram 1974) shows that people who had claimed with apparent sincerity that they would never harm an innocent person showed that they were prepared to do so immediately: they tortured innocent people, as they thought, by administering increasingly painful electric shocks in response to wrong answers. Doris (2002) and others have claimed on the basis of this and similar experiments that there really is no such thing as character as we understand it: there is only the immediate environment. Perhaps a safer inference would be that the character of many people is weak; for a significant number of the participants in the experiment refused to cooperate beyond a certain point, presumably because they did have strong character.[17]

What is beyond dispute is how easily one's immediate environment can influence one's framing. The subjects of the Milgram experiment may have seen their actions as *helping Professor Milgram with his important experiment* rather than as torturing anyone. Think of those who framed their actions as *only following orders*. These are fairly simple cases: they show framing that was obviously morally inadequate.[18] One hopes that in situations like these we would see the suffering of innocent people as a central feature. But if it is so difficult to get it right in the obvious cases, we can infer that it will be very difficult indeed to get it right in complex cases about which thoughtful people will disagree.

How, then, does a person of good character make a decision in a complex situation? The right kind of experience and the right kind of education will likely impart good values and fairly useful prima facie principles. One's reasoning about specific issues will be better because one is better at noticing and evaluating aspects of the situation that people of lesser character do not handle so well. One will notice the influence of the ambient culture.

A similar faculty is at work in developing strategy (Rosenzweig 2007, esp. chap. 10). Skilled strategists are aware of the data that analysts can gather; they know many techniques for using the numbers in assessing the prospects of strategic business units. But beyond the numbers they can *just see* that this option is a potential bonanza and that that option is a black hole. Their track records show their ability. But according to Rosenzweig, as important as analytical skill is character: a manager must resist the pressure to do what is safe and standard, what worked last time, what will not expose him or her to criticism if things do not work out.

If a strong organizational culture can affect one's character, then the choice of an employer is a most important one. It will in effect be choosing which desires to cultivate – a form of adaptive preference formation – hence choosing a character. If you go to work for a rapacious Wall Street firm that demands your whole life and pays you a lot, you may well turn out to want to be an overworked shark. If you go to work for Google, it will not be long before you want to be and are the sort of person who enjoys working in a Google-like culture.

It takes wisdom born of experience to be aware of the influence of one's environment on how one assesses situations where the culture is strong, and strength of character to act on the basis of one's values. It is much easier to give in to the pressure and then rationalize. So it is important for managers to create organizations whose culture is hospitable to virtue, as it is important for holders of public office to create communities that encourage virtue, as Aristotle claims. In a bad organization virtue may be overwhelmed, and the employee whose good and strong character is not overwhelmed will likely be unsuccessful.

However, MacIntyre argues, in effect, that all profit-seeking organizations are bad.

MACINTYRE'S CRITIQUE: PRACTICES AND INSTITUTIONS

That some virtues may turn out to be useful in business does not impress MacIntyre. He has offered the most influential critique of business from a virtue ethics point of view in arguing that corporations breed vice and suppress virtue. Concern for profit undermines virtue within corporations and in markets. Internally it perverts the cooperative virtues; externally it encourages the competitive vices. If he is right, then business ethics really is an oxymoron.

Central to MacIntyre's critique of business is the notion of a *practice*, a "coherent and complex form of socially established cooperative human activity" (1984, p. 187). The activities are performed according to "standards of excellence." Virtue – that is, excellence – in practices creates goods internal to the practice. Cooperative work on a practice requires and so cultivates not only technical skill but also trustworthiness, honesty, sensitivity, pride in one's work, loyalty to the group, unselfishness, and so on. The practice may generate external rewards like money and prestige, but the internal goods are more important.

External goods like money and prestige are typically owned by individuals rather than shared, and are "subjects of competition in which there must be losers as well as winners" (MacIntyre 1984, pp. 189–91). Markets, on this view, are zero-sum games. Internal goods are shared; achieving them is a win–win situation, as in the cases of trustworthiness and honesty, for example.

Practices require institutions to support and protect them, to hire and pay the practitioners, marshal them, and give them an organizational home. Corporate institutions must aim at profits and market share, hence at high productivity and low costs; so managers focus on external goods, whether or not they are the result of practices. In particular, managers typically think of profit as the overriding end of their work, and employees only as means to that end. Aiming at maximizing profits undermines the intrinsic satisfaction of gaining the internal goods that one might find in cooperative activity in an organization.

MacIntyre echoes Aristotle's claim about moneymakers: that they mistakenly consider money an end rather than a means. They would be right if rationality were a feature only of the relationship between means and ends, if any old end were as rational as any other, if any old desire were as worthy of being fulfilled, if *Homo economicus* were a good model.

But surely managing can itself be like a practice: it can be done excellently, and can create internal goods of its own (G. Moore 2002, 2005a, 2005b, 2008, 2009). Managers can protect the practices while ensuring that they provide the organization with the external goods necessary for it to compete successfully. Those managers do not fit MacIntyre's caricature.

Perhaps more important, external objectives need not undermine virtue. Aristotle allows that a soldier in a national army not only develops military virtues but also benefits his nation by fighting for its defense. Surely the goal of national defense does not undermine the development and exercise of courage, duty, and honor. *Esprit de corps* contributes to victory. But then how does the overriding purpose of winning the war differ with respect to internal goods from the (supposed) overriding purpose of making a profit?

Internal goods are necessarily connected with external ones because, although virtues are internally good states of the soul, virtuous people characteristically and essentially generate external goods. Consider courage, for example. It would not be a virtue if courageous soldiers and politicians did not benefit the state. Consider craftsmanship. One who works skillfully and conscientiously according to standards of excellence is acting virtuously in MacIntyre's sense if not in Aristotle's. But in acting this way a craftsman makes a product, which is supposed to be a good product. A would-be virtuoso creator of a product that is useless in all respects cannot be credited with true craftsmanship. A group of investment bankers who enjoy working in an atmosphere of trust and cooperation to create a financial instrument that is far riskier than it appears to potential customers are not acting virtuously, whatever internal goods characterize their *praxis*.

Furthermore, internal goods in MacIntyre's sense may be a success factor for an organization. Employees' excellence in what MacIntyre calls their "socially established cooperative . . . activity" characteristically generates social capital and so helps preserve the commons in organizations.[19]

However, many organization theorists advocate just the sort of management that MacIntyre criticizes. Ghoshal (2005) attacks the influential scholars Jensen and Mechling (1976) and Williamson (1975) for claiming that close supervision and individual financial incentives will make employees productive. It appears that their claim is based on the view that people are typically motivated as *Homo economicus* is.[20] If managers do manage this way, then they probably will ignore or discourage trust and trustworthiness, cooperativeness, and other collective virtues, which are crucial to success in many organizations, and which MacIntyre underestimates. Trust and trustworthiness in particular are of vital importance in most organizations, and they generate internal goods not unlike those of friendship.[21]

Not all successful organizations are managed the way MacIntyre, Jensen, and Mechling think that competitive success requires. Some managers are aware that they need to create mutually beneficial cooperation to preserve the commons in the organization: that is, they need to create social capital. One way to do this is to persuade employees that the mission of the organization has its own importance and that it confers value on their jobs. Being proud of the quality of the products or services they create may motivate employees, contrary to the *Homo economicus* assumption. Wanting the organization to do well, the employees will not act on what they take to be their narrow interests and be free-riding slackers. They are counterexamples to the *Homo economicus* model in that they develop and hold in common new interests that are not selfish. In such cases employees' trust that other employees are pulling their weight will be true because self-fulfilling. Thus a good external mission strengthens internal social capital.[22] Firms like Johnson & Johnson undermine MacIntyre's claim that profit is inimical to virtue.

MacIntyre also claims that competitive markets are zero-sum games, and he implies that there is no room for social capital in the competitive arena. Initially this seems more plausible than his claims about organizations, but I argue now that it too is false.

EXTERNAL VIRTUES AND STAKEHOLDER RELATIONS

According to the standard theory of the firm, usually attributed to Coase (1937), organizations exist because they reduce transaction costs relative to market relationships. The latter are fraught with uncertainty that no contract can eliminate; so the parties must undertake research, negotiation, and other costly means to reduce risk. The relationship may fail because of mutual distrust, to the disadvantage of both parties. By acquiring the supplying firm the buyer can preserve the economies that would otherwise be lost, but that is not always possible. When it is not, social capital becomes important.

Unexpected events may place a party to a contract in a difficult situation, and demanding fulfillment may put that party in jeopardy and harm the other in the longer run. What is preferable is the kind of flexibility that permits the supplier to ask for a higher price than contracted for, as a result of an increase in materials costs, for example, on the understanding that the next time materials costs are less than anticipated, the supplier will return the favor. Trust allows that kind of flexibility; sticking to the letter of the contract could put one party or the other out of business and/or enrich some lawyers.

MacIntyre believes that competition undermines the virtues. In the sort of case we are discussing, however, the very possibility of competition puts pressure on firms not to exploit, but to create social capital with stakeholders in the supply chain and elsewhere. Creating high-quality goods and services at prices determined in competition is a formula for success that enhances a firm's reputation for trustworthiness, which surely is a cardinal corporate virtue. It helps develop social capital with one's stakeholders and rallies employees around the corporate mission. Social capital and profit are mutually supportive, and social capital is a good thing in itself.

There are, as MacIntyre says, winners and losers in competition. Competition in a particular area may be a zero-sum game from the point of view of the competitors, but the market as a whole is not zero-sum but highly productive. But that is not all I am claiming. Markets can also create what MacIntyre calls internal goods. From Adam Smith onwards, some philosophers have argued that competitive markets demand such virtues as honesty and trustworthiness; others have argued in the other direction. (See Hirschman 1982 on this controversy.) The least we can say is that MacIntyre has not made his case, and that it is possible to have competition that does not undermine virtue. Smith does not claim that the invisible hand guarantees that the very structure of a free market will force its participants to be virtuous; in fact, businesspeople will take every opportunity to fix prices and otherwise avoid competition.

We create productive markets and avoid commons problems as businesspeople compete on the basis of quality and price, and stakeholders respect – though they do not always serve – one another's interests. Competition is never perfect, however: customers may not fully understand the products on offer, or exactly what they need. Barriers to entry and exit stifle competition. Where the markets cannot be perfected, the solution is for businesspeople to be like professionals. Physicians, lawyers, and other true professionals are obligated to attend to the needs of their patients or clients. People engage professionals precisely because the assumption of perfect knowledge is clearly false. So professionals have a particular obligation to their patients or clients even if, as in the case of attorneys, the general welfare is not immediately served. A doctor should not undertake an expensive procedure when an inexpensive one would benefit the patient as much. Businesspeople often have a similar advantage in knowledge of the customer's needs. So professionalism is appropriate for an auto repair shop, for example: it is wrong to replace a customer's muffler when only a clamp is needed, even if the customer asks for a new muffler under the mistaken impression that it is necessary.

Since almost all companies are sellers as well as customers and in other respects stakeholders themselves, it should be possible for them to work out how to create market relationships of the right sort, though trial and error will inevitably be part of that process.[23] The right sort of market will encourage businesspeople to enjoy what they do insofar as it teaches and exercises some virtues that make for *eudaimonia*: intelligence emotional and rational; courage; sensitivity; cooperativeness; respect for excellence; patience and, when appropriate, impatience; conscientiousness; thrift; ability to postpone gratification; honesty; self-command.

We find the right sort of market more often in some businesses than in others. In particular, it is not so hard to see the financial services industry as a zero-sum game. Even if we assume that all investment advisers are honest and competent professionals, every successful investment is someone's opportunity cost. And it would be optimistic to assume that honesty and professionalism prevail among those who trade in arcane derivatives, as opposed to arcane electronic technologies. There MacIntyre's strictures may apply better. It is a cause for worry that an increasing number of the ablest educated college students are taking positions in financial services, where their skills cancel each other out to a significant degree.[24]

Let me summarize the argument against MacIntyre. It is a necessary but not sufficient condition of a business activity being a virtuous practice, or part of one, that it generates some external good.

But not everything that meets a demand is good, because desire-satisfaction utilitarianism is wrong. Two related adjustments are therefore required. First, to make up for market inefficiencies, the purveyor of goods or services ought to have a professional stance, and so succeed by actually adding value rather than by exploitation or rent-seeking. Second, within the organization there must be some satisfaction associated with creating goods and services that are actually good and are demanded for that reason. Under those circumstances virtuous and successful business is possible.

But we may wonder whether that sort of professionalism can be taught, and whether a business school is the right place to teach it.

EXPERIENCE AND CASE STUDIES

Not all businesspeople aspire to the satisfactions of a virtuous life. Some of them want a lot of money to spend on toys. According to Aristotle and most virtue ethicists, that is not a good life. But it may not be possible to convince these businesspeople that their lives would be better if they were virtuous. So there are many who doubt that ethics courses help business students become more ethical.

Most teachers of business ethics do not claim to make their students more ethical. Typically a course in business ethics gives students tools – usually principles – for making ethical decisions. Students familiar with cost–benefit analysis will grasp utilitarian theories without difficulty. They will understand justice and negative rights pretty well. But they may still not be convinced that they have good reasons to be ethical. So one might say that a course in business ethics does not make a student ethical any more than a course in finance makes a student greedy.

Ethics taught from a virtue perspective, on the other hand, ought to recommend itself to students. Virtue ethics in the Aristotelian tradition takes the position that ethics is about the good life, a life which one has good reason to live. To take virtue ethics seriously is to understand why one should be ethical. In that respect a course in virtue ethics will be more ambitious than a course that just considers principles. But according to Aristotle and many others, becoming ethical is a long process, which begins in childhood. How much can be accomplished in one semester?

The case study method suits business ethics as it suits strategy.[25] In a typical strategy course the students read a text and then consider case studies that invite them to apply the principles in the text. This is the beginning of the process of developing their intuitions about strategy. In real-life corporate strategy, there is much to be said for trusting the intuitions of an intelligent and experienced person with a good track record. When a manager makes decisions about the strategies for certain business units, there will be some easy cases. Where the market is growing and the unit is dominant, reinvesting for growth is the obvious strategy. But there are nonobvious cases, as when a group of weak units can together achieve economies of scale or use slack resources. There is seldom any algorithm for inferring the correct strategy from the available numbers, but some managers are consistently better than others at knowing which description of a strategic situation is the salient one. Their record of success is evidence of their skill.

Case studies exercise students' moral judgment about particulars, as when justice and economic efficiency conflict. In looking at a case and considering what its salient features are, students are developing moral imagination and thus practical wisdom and thus good character. They are then less likely to become *Homines economici*.

There is some encouraging evidence that students can learn to recognize the warning signs of rationalization and ethical anesthesia, so that when they join an organization that is an ongoing Milgram experiment there will be a spark of recognition. Beaman *et al.* (1978) show that people taught about social pressure will be better able to resist it thereafter. Lieberman (2000) offers evidence that continued discussion in an appropriate environment can make a positive difference.

Here an ethicist with a background in organization theory might add that students can be taught how to create organizations hospitable to virtue without being inhospitable to profit. So even if Doris is right about the lack of character, people can get into the habit of acting virtuously and develop an interest in doing so.[26]

A course in strategy teaches students how to choose appropriate long-term objectives for an organization and then to marshal the necessary resources and organize them to move in that direction. A course in ethics can help students to think about their own lives in that way. It can raise questions about why someone would want to pursue a certain sort of career or join a certain sort of firm. So it may help expose the reasons given as incoherent or based on self-ignorance or peer pressure. As Rosenzweig suggests, success in achieving corporate as well as personal objectives requires an array of virtues.

The objective is to help students learn to answer the question, "What shall I do?" in part by asking them to address the question, "What shall I be?" Choosing the long-term objectives of one's life is no easy task under any circumstances. One cannot readily choose which desires to have: many people are tempted by doughnuts, some by dishonesty. Students can, however, reflect on what is most important to them and how to protect it. They can surely come to understand how facile and misguided it is to say that ethics is opposed to their interests, and how they can have something to say about what their interests will be.

IN CONCLUSION

Aristotle does not admire businesspeople, but I have argued from a largely Aristotelian perspective that it is possible to find a good life in a corporate environment. Success in a good company requires and therefore teaches virtues that drive the kind of competition and cooperation that creates a productive and fair business system. The sort of person that we admiringly call a professional will thrive in such an environment.

NOTES

1   A distinguished exception is Werhane 1991.
2   McCloskey (1996), who considers herself a virtue ethicist, is eloquent on these issues.
3   In discussing the commons and other collective action issues, economists and some ethicists assume that the agents are narrowly self-interested. Virtue ethicists do not usually make this assumption.
4   The theory seems to imply that psychological egoism is trivially true.
5   Posner (1983), a rational choice theorist, claims that the notion of justice has no content. Sen (2009 and elsewhere) differs, and attacks rational choice theory as a whole. Smith himself is closer to Sen than most commentators have realized; so Werhane 1991.

6 See Haidt 2001.
7 See, for example, Frank 2004, chap. 8.
8 See Gilbert 2005, pp. 217–20 and Haidt 2006, chaps. 5, 6, and 11.
9 See Daniel Russell's Chapter 1 of this volume.
10 Just as a substance is not a mere pile of stuff but has a certain form and purpose, as Aristotle argues in the *Metaphysics*, so a life is more than just a succession of experiences. In this he is echoed by psychologists like Festinger (1957) and Chaiken *et al.* (1996).
11 He does not condemn the desire for wealth, however (*Nicomachean Ethics* [cited as *NE*] VII.4, 1148a25).
12 So Luban 2003.
13 Names and some minor details have been altered. The actual incident happened more than thirty years ago.
14 Martin (2006) discusses the relationship between virtues and psychological, including pathological, states.
15 These considerations support Freeman's (1994) argument against what he calls the separation thesis, which holds that business and ethical decisions are clearly separable.
16 *NE* III.5, 1114a32–b3. See also *NE* VII.3, 1147a18–35, where Aristotle suggests that weakness of the will can be a matter of perceiving a prospective action as eating something sweet (rather than as eating something fattening), so that one ought to eat the thing. I shall argue that the corporate environment may influence one's framing. On framing in business and business ethics see Werhane 1999.
17 For a thorough treatment of this issue, see Alzola 2008.
18 Ross and Nisbett (1991) note that some of Milgram's subjects were uncomfortable because they could not frame the situation in a way that they found clear and acceptable. Others had no such problems. (I thank the editor for directing me to this point.)
19 For a thorough account of how this can be done, see G. Moore, 2012.
20 Ghoshal attributes their simplifications and reductions to a misguided desire to make organization theory a science. Ghoshal appears to take the Aristotelian view that it is a mistake to demand more precision than is appropriate to the subject matter.
21 We might suppose that the friendship that preserves the commons in an organization is the utilitarian kind, which Aristotle ranks lower than the sort of friendship that considers the friend's interest one's own (*EN* VIII.3). But the commons will be more easily preserved if all agents care about or share one another's interests.
22 There is nothing in Aristotle that corresponds exactly to the notion of social capital, but the importance of social capital does support Aristotle's views about community.

23 Rawls (1971) famously defines his conception of justice by imagining a group of people who must create laws for their community without knowing any of their personal characteristics or the roles they will play in the community. Stakeholders really do play many roles in the business system, and will therefore presumably not want to grant undue advantages to, say, buyers rather than suppliers, because they are both.

24 Perhaps the compensation scheme in a typical investment bank validates the *Homo economicus* view; more likely, as Ghoshal seems to believe, it encourages that view.

25 For a more detailed account see Hartman 2008 and 2006.

26 Chen *et al.* 1997 suggest as much.

12 Virtue and politics

In this chapter I explore the relationship between virtue and politics. There are of course many interesting and important questions about what virtue is and what kind of virtue is important; similarly, there are many different questions we could ask about "politics," so that the question of their relation is hopelessly broad. To be useful at all, an exploration will have to have a narrower focus. Here, this narrowing will take two forms.

First, of all the possible views of virtue, I will confine my attention to a particular genus, namely the kind of view of virtue and its importance we have inherited from the ancient Greek philosophers, notably Plato, Aristotle, and the Stoics. Even here there is diversity of opinion as to what a modern descendent of that tradition must consist in, but I hope that that diversity will be both fecund and tractable, in ways I shall explain.

Second, I will focus on one question about politics that is germane to much modern political theory, and that is how a political order may be *justified* in the exercise of its authority. My discussion will focus on the connection between the kinds of virtue a virtue ethical theory allows or requires and consequent justifications for political authority. I will argue that a certain *liberal* conception of political authority – what is sometimes called "justificatory liberalism" – is something virtue ethical theories have reason to endorse. At the same time, extant theories treating the connection between virtue and politics struggle, I claim, with its requirements, though there is a way forward.

I thank Kevin Vallier, Doug Rasmussen, Doug Den Uyl, and the editor of this volume for their very helpful comments on earlier drafts of this chapter.

My plan is as follows. In the first section ("Political Authority and Its Justification"), I introduce the features of political orders which motivate our inquiry. In the second section ("Virtue Ethical Theories and Justification of Political Order"), I consider as prototypes for the connection between virtue ethics and politics the models offered by Plato and Aristotle, and in the third ("Theories of Virtue and Politics") I survey some of their modern heirs. In the fourth section ("Virtue Justifications for Political Authority") I argue that these modern theories fail to meet a constraint on political action that virtue ethical theories should endorse, and in the last section ("Virtue and Liberal Justification") I suggest how they might be augmented in order to succeed in doing so.

POLITICAL AUTHORITY AND ITS JUSTIFICATION

We begin, as indicated, with a quality that seems to distinguish political institutions from other kinds of social institutions: their distinctive claim to *authority*. Authority is not to be confused with power; it is a kind of moral standing – a power to create and change what is morally obligatory and permissible. This authority takes two forms, both of which are asserted by modern nation states as well as by subsidiary political institutions.

1

They claim the unilateral right to coerce those under their authority (typically all those within their particular territorial limits).[1] On their determination, those subject to their authority may permissibly be compelled to perform any number of tasks (including taking up arms), be dispossessed of their property, imprisoned, or even executed.

2

They claim to be able to *obligate* those under their authority. If they say turning right on a red light is not permitted, then one is *ipso facto* obligated not to turn right on red. This isn't merely *political* obligation but *moral*. If they determine that those subject to their authority owe a certain amount in taxes, then it is not merely the case that those subjects may be coercively compelled to pay those taxes: they are *morally obligated* to do so, whether compelled or not.

It is possible to theorize about only one, rather than both, of these claims for political institutions, but both are typically made on behalf of modern liberal political institutions, and both are necessary to count as *authority* in the sense in which we generally use it.[2] These forms of authority are, on the received view of political authority, held uniquely by political authorities. The coercive measures of which they may legitimately avail themselves are available to no other human individual or group (except of course under the auspices of some political authority or another). And no other individual or group is thought to have the capacity *unilaterally* to obligate others. Of course, we may *obligate ourselves* in all sorts of ways through what we do, but the power unilaterally to obligate *others* is reserved to political authorities.

How do these bodies come to have this authority? That question is one of the *justification* of political authority: the case that can be or is made to those under some political authority that its decrees really are authoritative. At some times and places, that question has been thought to have an obvious answer. Political authority has been thought to arise from sheer power, or by vestiture by God, or superiority of birth, or otherwise. But none of these is obvious any longer.

VIRTUE ETHICAL THEORIES AND JUSTIFICATION OF POLITICAL ORDER

Virtue ethical accounts are in the business of characterizing the nature of the reasons morality gives us. They are distinct from other moral theories in part in their focus on character traits, virtues, as central to the project of understanding moral reasons.[3] The virtues are traits that we exhibit in most or every element of life. One natural question for virtue ethical theories, therefore, is what their accounts of moral reasons imply or suggest about political orders and the authority they claim.

Broadly speaking, the question of the justification of political authority has a centrality for us that it did not have for ancient virtue ethicists. However, these thinkers were very interested in modeling the basic structures that legitimate political orders might take, and modern virtue ethicists have often found these models helpful for thinking about what might make political orders legitimate. Consider for example Plato's *Republic*. We might see the point of considering rightness (*dikaiosunē*) both in the individual and in the polis, as Plato does there, as in effect making a case for a certain aim or end for the polis, namely the propagation of virtue in those who live there.[4] We might be able to read off a *direct* inference to a justification of political authority from this aim in either of two ways. First, and more simply, the polis might take as its aim the production of inhabitants that are virtuous, as virtue is specified for individuals. Its authority would then be justified by the service of this end.[5] Or, second, the structure of the polis itself might "mirror" the internal structure of individual virtue, in something like the way Plato explores.[6] Plato develops the idea of individual justice or virtue, "each having and doing his own work," by developing a model of a just polis in an isomorphic way.[7] To the extent a political authority has this sort of structure, its exercise of authority would be justified. The point here is not that either of these is Plato's notion of political authority, since that does not seem to have been a question to which he sought an answer. Rather, the point is that we can see these ways of answering this question as represented in the account of the polis he offers.

Aristotle, by way of contrast, maintains that the end or purpose of political community is to allow its citizens to live a good life, which (he argues in his ethical works) is the life of virtue; this is nearer to an explicit account of political authority.[8] Of course, the first of our Platonic models suggested something similar, but without the explicit appeal to the connection between virtue and flourishing, which here is doing important work. Political institutions are devoted to making more virtuous both those exercising political authority and those subject to it, in each case for the sake of the contribution of that virtue to living well;[9] political authority to coerce and obligate derives from this end. Thus, virtue grounds political justification here too, but only *indirectly*: it does its justificatory work via its contribution to the primary end which justifies political authority, namely the good lives of citizens.

These are three different examples of the ways virtue ethicists might think about the implications for political authority of the virtue ethic they espouse, but there is nothing limiting the

inferential relations to these patterns. And of course modern political theorizing must take on board more and different frameworks
for political authority than the ancients considered. Let us turn to
how some prominent modern virtue ethical theorists build on the
models the ancients left us.

THEORIES OF VIRTUE AND POLITICS

Though it is natural to ask about political implications of virtue
ethical theories, not all virtue ethicists do so.[10] Moreover, some theorists who draw on deep virtue ethical roots are nevertheless more
concerned about political theory. So our survey will be a bit ad hoc,
in order to embrace those who have made significant contributions
to the issue from either direction.

Slote

Michael Slote has been a prominent virtue ethicist whose account
of virtue has evolved over the years, and whose account of political authority has also emerged as an increasingly significant part
of his view. Slote originally attempted to derive an account of
virtue by beginning with a nonmoral but "aretaic" conception of
the admirable, but this account was not extended to derive political conclusions.[11] His first foray into thinking about political justification instead drew on a conception of "self-reliance" or "self-
sufficiency," drawn from the Stoic notion of *autarkeia*.[12] A society
is just, he argued, just to the extent that its people are self-sufficient
or self-reliant.[13] He did not represent self-sufficiency as a complete
account of virtue, but did believe it can have implications both for
one's capacity to meet material needs and for one's capacity to form
beliefs and opinions so as to act on the world. The virtue of self-
sufficiency is thus of central interest to social life and to political
organization. In this early work we can interpret Slote as offering an
example of the first and simplest sort of direct model for justifying
political authority: since a polity is just in virtue of being populated
with self-sufficient citizens, political authority arises from the aim
of producing precisely such citizens.

   In more recent years, however, Slote's basic account of virtue has
shifted significantly, and with it some of the details of justification

of political authority.[14] Slote's focus for his account of virtue has drawn more on the eighteenth-century "sentimentalist" tradition of David Hume and Adam Smith than on the virtue ethics of the ancient Greeks. His account of virtue now focuses on *compassion* as a motivation that is of basic value, and correspondingly on *universal benevolence* as the focal element of social relationships, through *empathic concern* for others.[15] An agent is virtuous if she is motivated by these values.[16]

The political account that grows out of this focus on empathy can be seen as either of the two direct models represented in Plato. Slote speaks of social institutions such as laws and customs as standing to a society in "something like" the way actions stand to individual agents, in reflecting motives of benevolence or caring.[17] We might read him here as thinking there is an "internal structure" to empathy or benevolent motivation in virtuous individuals, and that there is some sort of isomorphic structure in social institutions, in virtue of which we can judge them just (and their authority justified).[18] Alternatively (perhaps more plausibly), Slote may have in mind the simpler of the direct structures, whereby political authorities act justly, and are justified, to the extent that their conduct is driven by individuals whose motives are empathetic and benevolent.[19] Here, however, unlike the structure in *Republic*, where authority is justified on account of the virtue it cultivates in its citizens, the justification would arise from the *virtuous motives* of those responsible for the conduct of political institutions. The justificatory relation from virtue to political authority is still direct and immediate, but (unlike Plato's model) the focus is on virtue as a *cause* rather than as a *result*.

This sort of direct justificatory relation is not as common among contemporary virtue ethicists as is some variety of the strategy we saw in Aristotle of *indirect* justification. Our first examples of this strategy we may see in the work of Martha Nussbaum and Rosalind Hursthouse.

Nussbaum and Hursthouse

Nussbaum's political conception is deeply inspired by Aristotle's own political theory, and because her focus is on that element of Aristotle rather than his account of virtue, the justificatory path from virtue to political authority is not direct in the way Slote's is. Nussbaum's claim is that the end or task of a polity is to enable (so far as is possible) its citizens to make choices that conduce to or constitute a good human life.[20] So the fundamental linkage for the legitimating principle of political authority in Nussbaum's view is to the good human life, and only indirectly to virtue. To understand how the Aristotelian account of virtue contributes to the justification of political authority, therefore, we need to grasp two steps: the connection between virtue and the good human life, and the connection between the good human life and political authority.

Nussbaum does not belabor the first of these connections in her writings on politics, partly because she seems to adopt the connection Aristotle himself sees between these, and partly because her focus is the second of the connections. But she does emphasize a central Aristotelian point: the good human life is one directed by virtue generally, and this means – in light of the central role in virtue of practical wisdom – that the good life must be lived at the direction of practical wisdom.[21] This has important implications for her view of the task of the polis, since (we might say) the conditions for living well cannot just be handed to one on a silver platter: they must (as she puts it) be *chosen*.

The second connection, then, is one that licenses political authority just to the degree that it establishes the *capabilities* of its citizens to make such choices. Nussbaum argues that this licensure is *distributive* in two distinct senses. First, she resists a view on which a polity is good in virtue of exemplifying *collectively* some feature or features of a good life, as the second of our readings of the justifying story in *Republic* would have it.[22] It would not suffice to have a polity in which some were (say) courageous but not wise, others wise but not healthy, etc. The requirements that the polis produce the conditions necessary for good lives are to be understood distributively, as applied to each and every person subject to its authority.[23]

The conception is distributive in a second sense, in that it is concerned focally with the distribution of the essential resources and opportunities needed for the development of the capacities necessary for good human life. This would include such obvious concerns for distributive justice as things like wealth, but it also includes less obvious distributive concerns, such as the provision of public education and opportunity for political office. Nussbaum emphasizes the variation and specificity of the capabilities in each person; this means that the "resources" we ought to be concerned with must be tailored to the specific conditions in which the citizens need to develop their capabilities.

How are we to construe the sort of justification that Nussbaum's account allows for political authority? The linchpin of justification on Nussbaum's view is the "task" or end of the polity in establishing conditions in which citizens can choose good lives: "What we are aiming to secure to people are precisely the conditions in which each of them, as individuals, will be able to exercise choice and to function according to their own practical reason."[24] Although she does not belabor the point, Nussbaum's emphasis on the work of wisdom and choice in establishing a good life seems to require considerable latitude left open to citizens to make such choices. The kind of justification Nussbaum offers is in one sense *perfectionist*: it depends for its force on its commitment to a particular conception of human good. But it is a weak form of perfectionism, in that political authority is presumably not justified in prohibiting many instances of bad choice. It's not clear, for example, that political authority would be justified in preventing citizens from harming themselves or exposing themselves to risk in ways that are patently harmful. Nussbaum does not seem to endorse imposing wise or virtuous choices on citizens when they themselves would choose otherwise.

Although she has not been as expansive on this topic, Rosalind Hursthouse also seems to take political authority to be constrained by the requirements of virtuous life and agency. Hursthouse's comprehensive treatment of virtue ethics, *On Virtue Ethics*, does not discuss political implications. But in earlier work, Hursthouse explicitly acknowledges a "continuity" between ethical and political sciences.[25] One way this continuity is reflected is that virtue imposes a necessary constraint on the exercise of political authority: "If a just law, determining a right, cannot, as things stand, be implemented in a particular society, without necessitating that some members of the society act wickedly or wrongly, then it cannot, as things stand, be implemented."[26]

This is actually a significant constraint on political authority, and one which is easily overlooked if we confine our attention to the structure of political institutions themselves. Whatever justification for law or policy there may be, Hursthouse claims, it cannot require wicked action of its citizens. There is thus a limit on the treatment of others that political authority may demand.[27] Call this Hursthouse's Constraint. This is an important issue for any virtue ethic worthy of the name, and it is one to which we shall return.

Perhaps it may at best be honored in the breach in Nussbaum's account. Nussbaum believes that the public nature of the ideals which wisdom and virtue recognize requires their deployment not just by legislators but also by judges.[28] Partly this is a reflection of the fact that codified rules (however wisely crafted) do not interpret themselves, and need interpretation in particular cases. Here Nussbaum follows Aristotle, who characterizes the "equitable" as a necessary form of "corrective" to legal justice, required because "all law is universal but about some things it is not possible to make a universal statement which will be correct."[29]

Now, Aristotle's point is relatively unproblematic for cases of disputes between citizens. It is a different matter, however, if it is a matter of extending judicial authority over the lives of citizens, directing them in accordance with the judge's conception of the good – the "wise supplementing of the generalities of written law by a judge," as Nussbaum has it.[30] To the extent that this sort of "supplementing" – on the part of either the judge or the legislator – supplants the exercise of practical rationality and choice on the part of citizens, it would (one might think) amount to the usurpation of the agency of those citizens, and thus run afoul of Hursthouse's Constraint, by Nussbaum's own lights.

One way for Nussbaum to reply would be to reject Hursthouse's Constraint. She could insist that service of the social end justifies its servants doing what is required to serve it, even in vicious action.[31] More plausibly, she might claim that we must understand the requirements of virtue in light of the requirements of political life, so that a judicial "supplementation" really is an *exercise* of virtue. Now, the plausibility of such a response depends on the details of an account of virtue. Since Nussbaum does not offer such an account, it is not clear whether she would endorse this or some other strategy in reply. By way of contrast Hursthouse's later extended defense of neo-Aristotelian virtue ethics seems to vindicate Hursthouse's Constraint and give theoretical primacy to individual virtue. Such an account might provide a significant challenge to a conception of virtuous action on which political ends take pride of theoretical place. We return to take up this question in more depth after considering the last of our modern exemplar theories.

Rasmussen and Den Uyl

Douglas Rasmussen and Douglas Den Uyl (hereafter RDU) begin with a conception of the good human life, understood along (roughly) Aristotelian lines, like Nussbaum and Hursthouse. Moreover, they agree that the crucial element in such a life is the exercise of choice and practical wisdom to direct one's life. In fact, their view is premised upon the idea that political authority ought to provide conditions for the possibility of a self-directed life.

Their construal of the upshot of this point differs sharply from Nussbaum's, however, and takes them far from the implications Aristotle drew from our interest in living well. The significance of self-direction (the activity of *phronēsis*, or practical wisdom) for human flourishing means that political authority is to secure a space protected by *rights* in which to exercise this capacity. Instead of identifying crucial capabilities which it is the task of politics to identify and promote among its citizens, RDU focus on rights to life, liberty, and property as "metanormative" principles which secure the context in which individual self-direction is possible.[32] Saying that these principles are metanormative is to say that they do not prescribe specific ends to individuals in their choices as to how to live; instead, they provide a social framework in which individuals may take normative direction of their own conception of the good life.

Why the emphasis on rights as opposed to capabilities, as on Nussbaum's view? Partly this is because there is no general account of *what* "generic goods" must be distributed *where* to guide such a political function: the value of these goods, RDU claim, is unique to each person.[33] Individual variability in the resources required for self-direction makes resources "not useful when it comes to determining fundamental political/legal principles."[34] However, as we have seen, this is a point Nussbaum can and would willingly embrace.

A point with more bite is that rights make possible a kind of self-direction that is suitable for metanormativity, in a way in which (presumably) commitments to capabilities do not. For Nussbaum's view is compatible with the idea that the value of capabilities, even tailored to the needs of specific individuals, exists independently of the recognition of that value by those individuals. RDU argue (deeply in the spirit of the ancient Greeks) to the contrary, that there is no genuine value to such goods absent the self-directed agency of the person for whom they are good.[35] We might think of the contrast this way: self-direction is what establishes a flourishing life for an individual, in a way which makes the distributive resources necessary for the development of capabilities valuable in the first place. Self-direction is the *sine qua non* of the good life; it plays a *directive* role, as Daniel Russell has put it.[36] By way of contrast, the capabilities Nussbaum focuses on to fix the end of political authority on the "distributive" conception seem to be valuable in their own right.

RDU are explicit that their conception of rights as metanorms, arising from the necessary conditions for the possibility of self-direction and thus human flourishing, is not merely compatible with but constitutes a sound justification for a liberal order:

Liberalism is a political philosophy of metanorms. It seeks not to guide individual conduct in moral activity, but rather to regulate conduct so that conditions might be obtained where moral action can take place.[37]

Saying that rights are matters of metanorms does not mean they are not normative, nor that they do not imply obligations. They are "metalevel" norms in the sense specified earlier: their role is to secure the conditions in which it is *possible* for individuals to be virtuous and to flourish, in any of the innumerable ways in which human flourishing is possible.

RDU are clear *both* that the political conditions that rights sustain are neutral between competing conceptions of flourishing (and, moreover, that they secure the "right to do wrong," or to live badly),[38] *and* that nevertheless their view does not endorse "neutralism" in the justification of political authority.[39] That is, they do not pretend that their case for justified political authority will appeal to persons who reject their grounding notion of the good human life and the role of the exercise of phronesis in it. They defend a form of "comprehensive liberalism" in which the justification for political arrangements are situated as part of a "deeper ethical vision," amid "philosophical doctrines that have something to say in general about what is valuable or best for human beings to pursue or embrace."[40] But this very commitment is what gives rise to a tension within their theory, as well as within Nussbaum's. It is to the nature of that challenge that we now turn.

VIRTUE JUSTIFICATIONS FOR POLITICAL AUTHORITY

In what way do the virtue ethical justifications we have considered justify the use of political authority? Consider the perspective of those on whom political authority is to be exercised, and who do not accept the conception of virtue or human flourishing these views have on offer. In their view the justification will come up short, because it will be seen as depending on a view that is false (or at the very least not persuasive). They will see the authority exercised against them, not as authority, but as sheer power or force.

Is this a problem? This is a difficult question. There are some to whom *no* justification will be satisfactory: a psychopath may well be unlikely to accept *anything* as justifying his imprisonment, but that hardly entails that no justification is adequate. On the other hand, the mere thought that one is in possession of the truth is by itself surely too weak a standard.

However, we do not need extreme cases to see that there is a real concern here. Consider the fact that the three broad virtue ethical approaches we have surveyed differ in their prescriptions for the exercise of coercive control. For example, Slote invites us to imagine the mother of an adult (fully competent) son who wishes to ride his motorcycle without a helmet. Slote claims that she would be justified in intervening in such a way as to "coerce him into riding with a helmet" if she were able to do so.[41] RDU presumably would disagree. No doubt there would be similar disagreements between Slote and Nussbaum, or between Nussbaum and RDU, especially in light of the sharp contrast between the latter two in what they believe are the requirements of flourishing. In each case, the party on the "receiving end" of the coercive authority would regard it as unwarranted by an adequate or correct conception of the justifying

aim of political authority. While it cannot be the case that all three
of these views are correct, it is manifest that each is a view which
can be and is held by an intelligent person, trying to think carefully
about the legitimate grounds of political authority, and attempting
to arrive at morally permissible grounds for construing political relations, indeed along lines that give primacy of concern to virtue. Yet
in each case the justification offered will be seen as unacceptable.

This should especially worry defenders of virtue ethics. It is not
a problem to see the accounts in question as providing a satisfactory justification when we consider the resulting political theory
in the abstract. It is much more difficult to do so when we take
up the question Hursthouse invited us to consider, which is what
the recommended policy will require of agents carrying it out. (Here
think about not just police, judges, and legislators, but voters who
see themselves as installing or exercising political authority.) Can
they do so in good conscience, knowing that those upon whom their
coercive authority will be exercised will see it as unjustified and
unwarranted? It is one thing to console yourself with the thought
that nothing would satisfy the subject of your authority when he is a
psychopath; it is another when it is a person of good faith and intelligence aspiring to live cooperatively and peacefully with you, as we
may take the case to be for each of our theorists. Hursthouse's Constraint should have real bite when we think about virtuous people
exercising coercive authority in a political order.

Now, our theorists can mitigate the force of this worry by claiming
that their views are compatible with a *weak* form of liberal neutrality. That is, they can argue that despite the roots of a favored virtue
ethical account in a specific account of human flourishing, a form
of liberal neutrality can still be present in the political institutions
endorsed by that account. Christine Swanton makes this case explicitly, arguing that while a strong form of liberal neutrality (understood
as the nonpromotion of any specific conception of the good) is out of
reach for an Aristotelian virtue ethicist, a weak form (understood as
the nonprohibition of practices incompatible with that conception)
is not only possible but very likely required by Aristotelian virtues
properly understood.[42] The Aristotelian virtue ethicist can argue for
a weakly liberal state which engages in education and encourages
a favored conception of human flourishing via e.g. tax and subsidy
policies, so long as it does not engage in "legal moralism": barring

practices just because they fail to satisfy or promote that conception. Nussbaum and RDU may make an even stronger case, since each of them is prescribing a liberal state in which there is wide room for adhering to and living out a variety of conceptions of the good.

But that is not quite the point. The issue is not one of how much latitude one has in choosing the terms of one's own life. Instead, it is *who gets to decide* what that latitude is. Hursthouse's Constraint brings that point out with force. On Swanton's, Nussbaum's, and RDU's theory, as on Slote's, just as on many illiberal views, the answer to that question is unilateral: the theorist in possession of the best theory (or the most power, in illiberal cases) is entitled to impose his or her favored policies – those he or she takes to be entailed by the true ethical/political theory – on others, including those who reject theory and policy alike.

Consider a petty despot, running his small country with an iron hand, dictating virtually every aspect of the lives of its citizens (obviously a deeply illiberal political arrangement). Now suppose he reads Nussbaum's or RDU's theory, and is deeply impressed by it. "It is monstrous for me to exercise this degree of control," he decides, and immediately implements a wide variety of liberalizing measures. If he has read Nussbaum, he immediately takes up the question of ensuring resources to enable the development of the capabilities her view identifies as crucial. If he has read RDU, he immediately institutes a legal system that secures rights of the sort they endorse, so that the conditions for the possibility of self-direction and self-perfection are established. In both cases, the result would be a vastly more liberal state, but in both cases nevertheless there is still something awry: the citizens are still living *at the whim of the despot*. If he changes his mind tomorrow, conditions will change again. Yet it isn't just this instability that is at issue, for even if he were as constant at heart as a despot can be, there would still be something wrong with the authority exercised by his regime. An Aristotelian virtue ethic can claim, as Hursthouse would, that he is still treating his subjects wickedly in subjecting them to his will in this way. That injustice is bad for both the despot and his subjects.

The point is that the conditions specified in these theories are missing something crucial about the *justification* for political authority – something that a virtue ethic focusing on practical wisdom and self-direction ought to care deeply about. We get a succinct summary of what that "something" is from Locke. He claims that we are "naturally" (that is, outside the moral constraints of political institutions) in a moral state of equality such that

all the power and jurisdiction is reciprocal, no one having more than another; there being nothing more evident, than that the creatures of the same species and rank, promiscuously born to all the same advantages of nature, and the use of the same faculties, should also be equal one amongst another without subordination or subjection.[43]

Our petty despot obviously does not grant "reciprocal power and jurisdiction" to his subjects. From the perspective afforded by Locke's position, we could say that in cases of conflicts between our virtue ethical views of political authority, the justificatory account offered by those theories claims "power and jurisdiction" that it denies to parties with other normative accounts, in virtue of its favored apprehension of the justifying end of political authority. It does so just in virtue of the fact that it sees its own apprehension of that end as justifying the coercive authority, while denying that the coerced party's apprehension of that end has similar justificatory force.

This is hardly a novel problem. It is the problem that arises from what John Rawls calls "reasonable pluralism": the fact that there is a diversity of reasonable views about the justification of political authority.[44] It is a driving feature of Rawls' conception of "political liberalism," or what Gerald Gaus calls "justificatory liberalism":[45] liberal conceptions of political authority that require the justification of that authority to each individual subject to it. As Gaus characterizes this outlook:

Justificatory liberalism rests on a conception of members of the public as free and equal. To say that each individual is free implies that each has a fundamental claim to determine what are her obligations and duties. To say that each is equal is to insist that members of the public are symmetrically placed insofar as no one has a natural or innate right to command others or to impose obligations on them.[46]

The weaker form of liberalism characterized by Swanton is compatible with unequal authority exercised; our despot's society is a liberal one in this first-order sense. It is not, however, liberal in the sense that Locke, or Gaus, calls for, in the stronger, *who-gets-to-decide*, sense – a sort of *second-order* liberalism.[47]

Now, the fact that the weak liberal justifications of political authority offered by the modern virtue ethical accounts run straight into the second-order concerns that animate justificatory liberalism might, of course, offer good reason for the virtue ethicist to reject justificatory liberalism. Certainly there is no general consensus that liberalism at the second-order level is even possible, or desirable if it is possible.[48] But our virtue ethical accounts themselves give reasons for discomfort with this easy way out.

Consider Slote's empathy-based account. The complaints of those subordinated to an alien conception of the good will generally produce a tension in the empathic agent, even an empathic agent certain of the good that she is promoting. In his discussion of the paternalistic (?) mother who makes her adult son wear a motorcycle helmet, Slote maintains that if she is really caring, she will recognize that she has thereby damaged the relationship (even if by doing the right thing), and will take steps to reestablish it.[49] If this is the case in a one-off instance of riding helmetless, it would seem to be even more strongly and persistently the case in which the autonomy (as Slote thinks of it, the "capacity to think and decide things oneself")[50] of those subordinated amounts to a comprehensive shaping of the conditions of social life and individual choice, as is the case with political authority.

The problem is clearer in the case of the views rooted in Aristotle and human flourishing, as these accounts give central importance to the exercise of practical wisdom, in the direction of one's own life.[51] This is something that Nussbaum explicitly acknowledges. She ascribes to Aristotle the recognition that compelling results, especially coercively, cannot come without cost to good human functioning.[52] In her most recent work, in fact, Nussbaum has pressed just the point at issue here against "perfectionist" forms of liberalism that advocate political institutions that are driven by a conception of the human good. These views fail to show an adequate respect for persons, she argues, which is a different matter from showing respect for doctrines.[53] To demand respect for political institutions on the grounds of some particular doctrine is to demand that people respect laws and institutions in light of views they do not hold, and fails to respect them as persons. We "show respect for persons by creating and protecting spaces in which they can live according to their own views."[54] But Nussbaum has not recognized that the capabilities she espouses in her earlier work run up against precisely this problem in the justification it offers for liberal political institutions. Those, like RDU, who take the basic tenets of human flourishing to require different political structures will find themselves at best "second-class citizens" in virtue of living under institutions that in all conscience they cannot endorse.[55]

This is an equally significant point for RDU, who see their view as a form of liberal political theory, in virtue of its defense of rights and constraints on coercion, as we have seen. But they are explicit that the justification for the political authority they espouse is rooted in a "full-blown moral theory."[56] The liberalism they defend is couched in a distinction between different kinds of norms and obligations: the "difference between norms that directly regulate moral conduct and those that regulate the conditions under which such conduct could take place."[57] But the very respect for self-direction which grounds their account will produce a bind when one's self-direction requires constraint by the lights of a "full-blown theory" one does not accept. That constraint will not be experienced as self-direction at all. Those who do not endorse the favored conception – whether on virtue ethical or other grounds – will find only limited solace in not being prohibited from engaging in activities they believe will promote their own flourishing, and that of their children, while being forced to divert their time and resources into supporting enterprises they do not believe in.[58] Education in particular, being so central to any plausible form of human flourishing, will inevitably be a subject of deep disagreement, and the coercive imposition of an alien conception of flourishing on the lives of those one cares about will be deeply resented. Moreover, the bases for this sort of resentment are ones that the virtue ethicist will be ill-served to deny ought to move the virtuous agent.[59] That is precisely where Hursthouse's Constraint comes in. Weak neutrality may alleviate, but it will not remove, the internal sources of tension that arise from the issue of political justification for the liberal virtue ethicist.

What is virtue ethics to make, then, of the demands of a stronger, justificatory form of liberalism?

VIRTUE AND LIBERAL JUSTIFICATION

Might it be possible to take on board the concerns of justificatory liberalism *within* a virtue ethical account itself? At least within the neo-Aristotelian virtue framework that grounds the accounts offered by Nussbaum and RDU, I believe it is. Recall that in both of these accounts political authority is vindicated by the demands of human flourishing, and it is human flourishing that establishes what traits count as virtues. It is the leverage afforded by human flourishing that allows us to see how those concerns might be embraced.

Both of those accounts recognize the significance of our *sociality* for our flourishing. Nussbaum emphasizes this in focusing on Aristotle's own testimony to the significance of "political" life: "The good human life is a life with and toward others: membership in a polis is an important part of one's other-directed activity."[60]

Nussbaum follows Aristotle in not distinguishing the social from the political, but we can and should.[61] RDU recognize that distinction, and indeed lay the very groundwork necessary to sustain justificatory liberalism:

The open-ended character of human sociality is important. It reveals the need for a perspective that is broad enough to explain how the possible relationships among persons who as yet share no common values and are strangers to each other can, nonetheless, coexist ethically, that is, be "composible."[62]

RDU take this point to indicate the need for a "metanormative principle" to regulate these social relations. To some extent, that inference reflects the fact that developing an ethic of virtue is not their primary concern.[63] Moreover, as we shall see they do not regard their view as sustaining or vindicating "justificatory neutralism," so it is not clear they would endorse the moves I now propose. Still, they have indicated that what we seek is an *ethical* story about how individuals with little overlap in values can coexist peacefully. They must accept Hursthouse's Constraint.

One way to do so is to include in our account of the virtues a virtue consisting in standing in just the sort of justificatory relation with others that justificatory liberalism requires. That virtue would require that we see others as Locke maintained we "by nature" should: as capable of obligating us in precisely the ways and to the degree that we take ourselves to be obligating them.

We can flesh out the idea of this virtue by drawing on recent insights from the contractualist ethical tradition. It is congruent, for example, with the moral justifiability condition T. M. Scanlon claims is an essential feature of our social relations with others:

> The contractualist ideal of acting in accord with principles that others (similarly motivated) could not reasonably reject is meant to characterize the relation with others the value and appeal of which underlies our reasons to do what morality requires. This relation, much less personal than friendship, might be called a relation of *mutual recognition*. Standing in this relation to others is appealing in itself – worth seeking for its own sake.[64]

Scanlon's thought is one that is directly relevant to the proposal I make here. There are several points to be made about how it can contribute to a virtue ethical approach to justificatory liberalism.

First, Scanlon makes his point in the course of defending an account of a particular dimension of morality, namely "what we owe to each other." He is not making a claim as to *political* justifiability. But this means that this narrow point – as a matter of moral requirements in the exercise of coercive political authority – may hold even if his broader contractualist account is not persuasive as a matter of moral requirement. Certainly his point captures something important about the spirit behind justificatory forms of liberalism: the thought that others are owed justifications of the use of coercive force against them in terms they themselves accept, or at least cannot reject at the cost of reasonability.

Second, as Scanlon develops the point, the relation of "mutual recognition" ought not to be seen as some sort of free-standing feature of human relations. Instead, it provides a framework within which *all* sorts of other human relations take hold.[65] He offers an example to show that any plausible account of *friendship* must incorporate this sort of relation as well,[66] but the point is really extensible to any social connection that a plausible virtue ethic will espouse. It is what our nature as rational *social* animals – the nature of selves featured in neo-Aristotelian virtue ethics, grounding its conception of human flourishing – will require.

Finally, although Scanlon does not present standing in this relation as a virtue or anything like it, it is a short step to thinking that seeing others in the way it requires is plausibly a virtue, or enough like a virtue, to augment a neo-Aristotelian theory of what the virtues consist in.[67] It amounts to a disposition to see ourselves as related to others in such a way that when we propose to exercise the kind of authority constitutive of political authority – that is, authority backed by coercive force – we see ourselves as beholden to them to justify our doing so in terms that are compelling not merely to us, but to them as well. This is a way of giving Hursthouse's Constraint explicit traction in the deployment of political authority.[68] As Locke would argue, we must not see ourselves as entitled to obligate others (as the exercise of political authority claims to do) in some way that cannot be reciprocated. If this disposition is a virtue, then it will be vicious to exercise political authority in a way that cannot be justified reciprocally, and that will violate Hursthouse's Constraint. That sort of equality or reciprocity in capacity to obligate is plausibly necessary for a virtue theory that takes our sociality – and our social relationships as embedded in patterns of mutual obligation – seriously.

Of the accounts we have considered, RDU's account seems the closest to embracing this point. For they recognize what they call a "metanorm of justice," which consists in a requirement on the conditions of social life, such that "morally significant action can take place."[69] And they insist that this is a norm that is required for human flourishing. If we think not about the norm itself, but about the character of the virtuous agent, and in particular think of that character as so disposed to see and treat others in ways that the norm expresses, we have something very like this proposed virtue, which it is within the reach of a neo-Aristotelian virtue ethic to incorporate.[70]

However, they are committed to a point that is incompatible with this thought, which is that the *rights* that justice requires are not matters of duties to the rights-holders (and thus do not reflect the obligations of mutual recognition), but concomitants of commitment to human flourishing, or to conditions necessary for joint action.[71] Now, this view of rights is not plausible: it entails that when I violate your right, I have wronged not you but my commitment to human flourishing. That is an implication it is hard to imagine RDU wish to embrace.[72] Some elements of their account of rights as metanorms would therefore need to give way to embrace the proposal I advocate, but it is not clear that these elements are fundamental.

The point, then, is that a virtue ethical theory – in particular, one grounded in neo-Aristotelian convictions about human flourishing – has open to it the possibility of taking on board a particular virtue which would sustain a second-order, justificatory form of liberalism, with the embrace of equal standing to obligate that that entails. RDU (approvingly) quote Friedrich Hayek's criticism of "conservatism":

When I say that the conservative lacks principles, I do not mean to suggest that he lacks moral conviction. The typical conservative is indeed usually a man of very strong moral convictions. What I mean is that he has no political principles which enable him to work with people whose moral values differ from his own for a political order in which both can obey their convictions.[73]

Hayek's complaint about "conservatives" is precisely the problem for virtue ethical theories framed as those we have examined here are framed. Arguably it is something that a plausible virtue ethical theory should aspire to overcome.

NOTES

1   See Weber, who defines "state" in these terms (Weber 1994, pp. 310–11).
2   There are skeptics about the idea that political authority entails an obligation to obey the law (point 2 above); see for example Edmudson 1998, chap. 2. But this remains the received view.
3   See Hursthouse 1999, p. 1.
4   I do not say that this is Plato's idea, or anything like it. Officially, the thought experiment of the ideal polis is set out for its *epistemic* advantages over the ideally virtuous individual: it is, Socrates claims, easier to see rightness in the larger body than in the smaller (*Republic* 369a). Nothing about the ideal polis he arrives at seems directed toward the aim of producing virtuous citizens per se.
5   Nussbaum calls a weak version of this view the "whole–part conception" of the end of the polity, and sees support for it in Aristotle at *Politics* VII.9, 1329a19 (Nussbaum 1988, p. 156). It is weak in that it might be the case that the polis is good if its inhabitants are virtuous, without their virtue being the "task" of the polity. This is important if

the lives of some inhabitants of the polis (e.g. "mechanics") cannot be virtuous for some reason.

6   Nussbaum calls this the "holistic conception" of the end of the polity, and points to *Politics* VII.1, 1323b33 as its manifestation in Aristotle (Nussbaum 1988, p. 156).

7   *Republic* 434a–435e.

8   *Politics* I.2, 1252b30, II.1, 1260b25, III.6, 1278b24; *Nicomachean Ethics* (cited as *NE*) I.13, 1102a5. I abstract away from the notoriously problematic ways in which Aristotle restricts citizenship, as well as disputes about Aristotle's settled view on what is the good human life.

9   *Politics* II.2, 1261a32.

10 For examples of prominent virtue ethicists who are not primarily concerned with questions of politics, see Hursthouse 1999 and Annas 2011. (Hursthouse does take up the relationship to some degree in Hursthouse 1990–91; we shall take up some of Hursthouse's observations from the latter work below.)

11 Slote 1992. The idea of the "aretaic" here draws from the Greek *aretē*, which we might translate as "excellence." In Slote's hands, the excellence in question is not however to be construed as *moral* excellence.

12 Slote 1993, p. 6. In this respect Slote counts as a virtue ethicist who draws on the tradition of the ancient Greek theorists, although his more recent work has departed from these foundations.

13 Slote 1993, p. 16.

14 Slote has not (to my knowledge anyway) explained his shift away from the earlier account of virtue.

15 Slote 1998b, pp. 186ff.; 2001, pp. 23–5; 2007, chap. 1.

16 In Slote 2010, Slote offers a semantics of 'good' grounded in "agential warmth" and empathy as the referent for axiological terms.

17 Slote 1998b, p. 186; 2001, p. 99; 2007, p. 94; 2010, p. 125.

18 See Slote 2007, p. 94.

19 Slote 1998b, p. 187; 2001, p. 101; 2007, p. 95.

20 Nussbaum 1988, p. 147. In this, Nussbaum articulates a conception that is either advocated or developed as an expression of Aristotle's own view in e.g. Gottlieb 2009, chap. 10.

21 Nussbaum 1988, p. 179.

22 Nussbaum 1988, p. 158.

23 Nussbaum devotes considerable energy to showing that Aristotle's exclusion of these distributive considerations from application to women, slaves, and mechanics is not really justifiable by Aristotle's own lights (Nussbaum 1988, pp. 164–6).

24 Nussbaum 1988, p. 153. Richard Kraut endorses this aim, and claims
   that it is in fact the operating justification for the "modern state," in
   Kraut 1999.
25 Hursthouse 1990–91, p. 229.
26 Hursthouse 1990–91, p. 242.
27 In this sense, Hursthouse says, ethics is prior to politics (Hursthouse
   1990–91, p. 236).
28 Nussbaum 1990b, pp. 97ff.
29 *NE* v.10, 1137b12, trans. Ross/Ackrill/Urmson [Aristotle 1980]).
30 Nussbaum 1990b, p. 100.
31 Nussbaum would surely reject a strong form of this claim. She follows
   Aristotle in rejecting institutions that block people from exercising their
   own capacities to realize their ends: "Aristotle makes it clear . . . that if a
   'right' result (say, giving to others) is accomplished by a coercive strategy
   rather than by personal choice, a part of good human functioning will
   have been lost" (Nussbaum 1988, p. 163).
32 Rasmussen and Den Uyl 2005, p. 78.
33 Rasmussen and Den Uyl 2005, p. 80.
34 Rasmussen and Den Uyl 2005, p. 306.
35 Rasmussen and Den Uyl 2005, pp. 172, 274.
36 D. Russell 2005, chap. 1.
37 Rasmussen and Den Uyl 2005, p. 34.
38 Rasmussen and Den Uyl 1991, p. 109; 2005, pp. 36, 38, 63, 269, 287.
39 Rasmussen and Den Uyl 2005, pp. 38–9, 56–9, 268.
40 Rasmussen and Den Uyl 2005, pp. 268, 56.
41 Slote 2010, pp. 120–1.
42 Swanton 1993, p. 47.
43 Locke, *Second Treatise of Government*, §4.
44 Rawls 1993.
45 Gaus 1996.
46 Gaus 2010, p. 234.
47 David Schmidtz remarks, "In effect, there are two ways to agree: We
   agree on what is correct, or on who has jurisdiction – who gets to
   decide . . . Isn't it odd that our greatest successes in learning how to live
   together stem not from agreeing on what is correct but from agreeing
   to let people decide for themselves?" (Schmidtz 2006, p. 6).
48 For especially critical views among the virtue ethicists we have considered, see Kraut 1999 and Rasmussen and Den Uyl 2005, p. 59.
49 Slote 2010, p. 122.
50 Slote 2010, p. 117.
51 Nussbaum 1988, p. 153; Rasmussen and Den Uyl 2005, chap. 4.

52   Nussbaum 1988, p. 163. In much the same spirit, Christine Swanton, in commenting on Slote 1993, observes that it is "not at all clear that the sole or even major response to a value (such as self sufficiency) should be to promote it, let alone promote it by enforcement" (Swanton 1993, p. 46).

53   Nussbaum 2011, p. 33.

54   Nussbaum 2011, p. 36.

55   Nussbaum 2011, p. 35.

56   Rasmussen and Den Uyl 2005, p. 38.

57   Rasmussen and Den Uyl 2005, p. 39.

58   Nussbaum cites James Madison in defense of the claim that such policies violate the "basic equality of citizens" (Nussbaum 2011, pp. 35, 43). This complaint would hit squarely the "weak liberalism" proposed by Swanton.

59   After all, as Aristotle says, "the law in its ordaining of what is good is not burdensome" (*NE* x.9, 1180a24, trans. Ross/Ackrill/Urmson [Aristotle 1980]).

60   Nussbaum 1990b, p. 98.

61   This in two ways, as Rasmussen and Den Uyl (2005, p. 142) observe. First, we may and typically do have many forms of social relationship that are at levels smaller than any political organization. Second, we can and do typically have *cosmopolitan* social relationships that are more expansive than the bounds of any political organization.

62   Rasmussen and Den Uyl 2005, p. 83. See pp. 141–52 for a fuller discussion of their commitment to the place of sociality in human flourishing.

63   At the same time, it is clear that they intend to incorporate a roughly Aristotelian account of the virtues – with the virtue of practical wisdom taking center stage – in their account. See 2005, pp. 146ff. and esp. p. 172.

64   Scanlon 1998, p. 162; italics added.

65   This might be a reason for thinking that what I treat here as a distinct virtue is really a structural feature of other virtues, perhaps along the lines of the way practical wisdom is at work in all virtues of character in Aristotle. I know of no reason to resist that way of thinking except for ease of exposition.

66   Scanlon 1998, p. 166.

67   In LeBar 2009 (pp. 654ff.) I make a similar point for occupying what Stephen Darwall calls "the second-person standpoint," which is one in which we see ourselves as embedded in accountability relations with others. See Darwall 2006.

68   Of course, if one does not have a model of the virtues on which they cannot conflict, this virtue might come into conflict with others. Here

I assume, as the ancients did, that the virtues do not conflict; indeed, they are "reciprocal" – one cannot have one without having the others as well. I thank Kevin Vallier for raising this point.

69 Rasmussen and Den Uyl 2005, p. 162.

70 On the other hand, they insist that they "do not think ... there is some deontic or non-agent-relative reason for constraining our conduct" in a way which might ground this sort of requirement (Rasmussen and Den Uyl 2005, p. 221). This is because they think such requirements "cannot be understood in terms of normative ethics alone." I do not see that there need be anything "non-agent-relative" about the norm in question, and in fact very likely the focus on the virtue will be a matter of agent-relative reasons. But the constraint is, or appears to be, deontic by its nature: the virtue is one which sees others as providing reasons for constraint, in the way deontic requirements are typically thought to provide reasons.

71 Rasmussen and Den Uyl 1991, p. 106; 2005, pp. 266 n., 289, 291.

72 On this point and its significance for the nature of rights, see Feinberg 1972. It is not clear why RDU insist on this point, except for wanting to maintain the distinction between metanorms and other norms. However, that distinction would not seem to depend on making this claim about rights, since the recognition that rights essentially involve duties and accountability to others is compatible with thinking that recognition of them need not be for the aim of flourishing, nor indeed for any particular end.

73 Hayek 1978, p. 401.

13 The situationist critique of virtue ethics

Traditional philosophical theories of virtue define a "virtue" as a species of character trait. Many contemporary philosophical theories of virtue follow suit, though not all do. Adopting this traditional definition exposes a theory of virtue to what has come to be known as the "situationist" critique of virtue ethics. To explain this critique, and to keep track of the ensuing debate, it helps to distinguish philosophical situationism from psychological situationism (compare Snow 2010).

Psychological situationists are not philosophers and they make no philosophical claims. Rather, they belong to a particular experimental tradition within social psychology, a tradition that is opposed to traditional personality theory or "personology" (for an accessible introduction, see Ross and Nisbett 1991). Since they are the original situationists, I shall henceforth refer to psychological situationists as "situationists" *tout court*. Philosophical situationists – principally, Gilbert Harman (1999, 2000) and John Doris (1998, 2002) – reject theories of virtue that employ the traditional philosophical definition of 'virtue.' Specifically, they claim that such theories are "empirically inadequate" and their argument for this claim centrally appeals to the experimental results of situationism. It is *their* argument that constitutes the "situationist critique."

The philosophical situationists' argument can be framed as a pair of inferences, which take us from the original situationist data to their own bottom-line conclusion. Their bottom-line conclusion is that traditional theories of virtue are "empirically inadequate."

For helpful comments on a previous draft, I am grateful to Daniel C. Russell and Christian Miller.

According to philosophical situationism, the experimental results of situationism demonstrate that most people do not have any character traits. On this basis, philosophical situationists first infer that most people do not have any virtues, as traditionally defined. They then infer, second, that not enough people have any virtues so defined (i.e. not enough for traditional virtue theory to be empirically adequate).

Naturally, this framing of their critique needs some refinement. In particular, we need to specify what kind of character trait is at issue and also to determine how many people are supposed, by traditional virtue theory, to have virtues in the first place (and hence, how many people lacking virtue are "enough" to expose that theory as empirically inadequate). Let us make a start on the first task, postponing the second task for the moment.

At a minimum, we can understand a *character trait* to be a reliable disposition a person has to behave in certain characteristic ways. While plainly requiring further articulation, this initial specification has the merit of satisfying a crucial condition of dialectical adequacy: namely, that specifications of "character trait" be univocal across the philosophical situationists' first inference. For if the specification of "character trait" under which situationism demonstrates that most people do not have any "character traits" differs from the specification under which a virtue is defined as a species of "character trait," the philosophical situationists' critique will fail by equivocation. Later we shall encounter grounds for concluding that their critique does fail in this way.

Situationists actually distinguish two dimensions along which someone's disposition to behave in some characteristic way may be "reliable." One dimension they call "temporal stability," while the other they call "cross-situational consistency." A person has a temporally stable behavioral disposition when she behaves in the same specific way in response to repeated encounters with the same fairly specific situation: for example, when she copies from an answer key on a classroom test in the summer and then copies from an answer key on a classroom test again in the winter. A person has a cross-situationally consistent behavioral disposition when she behaves in the same characteristic way – as distinct, that is, from the same specific way – in response to encounters with a diversity of specific situations, each of which is nevertheless relevant to the characteristic behavior in question. For example, someone's disposition to dishonesty is cross-situationally consistent when she not only copies from an answer key on a classroom test, but also pockets some stray change she finds on a classroom desk – assuming, at least, that cheating and stealing are both characteristic of "dishonesty."[1]

When traditional theorists of virtue define a virtue as a species of character trait, their definition entails that a virtue includes a reliable disposition to behave in certain characteristic ways.[2] Thus, the virtue of courage includes a reliable disposition to behave courageously, the virtue of compassion includes a reliable disposition to behave compassionately, and so on. Of course, not any old reliable disposition to behave (say) courageously will express or evidence the virtue of courage. A reliable behavioral disposition is only a necessary condition of the relevant character trait, not also a sufficient condition.

What further conditions a person's reliable behavioral disposition has to satisfy in order to qualify as a virtue depends on the particular theory of virtue. For example, most theories will not qualify a reliable disposition to behave "courageously" as a virtue unless the agent's "courageous" acts are performed *for the right reasons*.[3] Some theories will not so qualify that disposition unless the agent's "courageous" acts are performed *wholeheartedly*. Other theories will not so qualify that disposition unless the agent also *has all of the other virtues*. Aristotle's theory of virtue imposes all three of these further conditions, but some are more controversial than others.

So traditional theorists of virtue accept that having a reliable behavioral disposition is a necessary condition of having a virtue. More specifically, the behavioral disposition they require has to be reliable along *both* of the dimensions situationists distinguish. In other words, a person's reliable disposition to behave (say) compassionately has to be temporally stable *and* cross-situationally consistent. As we shall see, the focus of the debate between philosophical situationists and traditional theorists of virtue concerns the cross-situational consistency of the relevant behavioral dispositions. Philosophical situationism's fundamental empirical claim is that most people do not have any cross-situationally consistent behavioral dispositions. If most people lack any cross-situationally consistent disposition to behave compassionately, it certainly follows that most people lack the virtue of compassion, as tradi-tional theorists of virtue define it.

We should notice a final preliminary point about the meaning of "character trait." In principle, a behavioral "disposition" is impor-tantly distinct from a mere behavioral "regularity." Among other things, the former goes beyond the latter in offering a particular explanation for it. If someone copies from an answer key on a class-room test every week, his behavior exhibits a certain regularity – specifically, a temporally stable regularity. Strictly speaking, how-ever, this regularity is not sufficient to establish that the person has a temporally stable behavioral disposition. For, in itself, a temporally stable behavioral regularity is consistent with various explanations, whereas a temporally stable *disposition* entails that the correspond-ing regularity is explained, in particular, by features of the person's individual psychology (rather, say, than by factors *external* to his psychology – e.g. the company he keeps). Since a "character trait" is specified in terms of a reliable behavioral disposition, understood in this more robust sense, attributions of character traits inherit that additional explanatory burden.

In practice, though, the distinction between behavioral regular-ities and behavioral dispositions has not played a prominent role in the debate because what situationists really deny is the more basic proposition that most people's behavior exhibits any cross-situational regularity. If that were true, there would be nothing for any cross-situationally consistent disposition to explain.

PHILOSOPHICAL SITUATIONISM'S BEST DATA

Let us now consider the evidence philosophical situationists adduce for their fundamental empirical claim that most people lack any cross-situationally consistent character trait. The best place to begin is with Hartshorne and May's (1928) famous study of honesty in chil-dren. Hartshorne and May observed how thousands of school chil-dren behaved in various specific "honesty-relevant" situations. For example, their observations included a "stealing" situation (some change has been left on a table in an empty classroom and there is an opportunity to take it); a "lying" situation (another child is going to get in trouble and there is an opportunity to avert this by making a false report); and a "cheating" situation (one is correcting one's own test sheet in class and there is an opportunity to amend one's answers first with the benefit of the answer key). These situations are relevant to the assessment of someone's honesty because we ordinarily expect that an honest person can be relied upon not to steal, not to lie, and not to cheat. In particular, then, we might expect an honest subject in Hartshorne and May's experiment not to pocket the change *and* not to make a false report *and* not to amend her answers from the key.

What Hartshorne and May found, however, was that the average correlation between their subjects' not pocketing the change and their not making a false report was only 0.13;[4] the average correlation between not pocketing the change and not copying from the answer key was also only 0.13; and the average correlation between not making a false report and not copying from the answer key was only 0.31. Overall, the average correlation between any two of Hartshorne and May's behavioral measures of honesty was only 0.23. By contrast, the average correlation between not copying from the answer key on one occasion and not copying from another answer key six months later was 0.79.

In other words, not much cross-situationally consistent honest behavior was observed among Hartshorne and May's subjects, at least not as far as the performances of their "average subject" were concerned. On the other hand, *within* a given "honesty-relevant situation" (such as the cheating situation), there was a good deal of temporally stable honest behavior. To put their findings yet another way, *few* of Hartshorne and May's subjects turned out to be cross-situationally consistently honest, even though many of them exhibited temporally stable behavior in some or other sub-subdepartment of honesty (not even "not cheating," e.g., but only "not copying from an answer key").

Hartshorne and May's data are the best place for us to begin a review of the situationist evidence for three main reasons. First, their study investigates a character trait that plainly counts as a standard virtue, unlike many other traits of interest to social psychologists, such as talkativeness or dependency.

Second, and most important, the quantitative values they report are perfectly representative of the findings of other explicit investigations of cross-situational consistency. By an "explicit investigation of cross-situational consistency," I mean an experiment in which subjects are placed in a *plurality* of *different* specific situations, each of which is designed to elicit a manifestation of the same character trait. Summarizing this experimental literature, Ross and Nisbett (1991, p. 95) declare that

> the average correlation between different behavioral measures specifically designed to tap the same personality trait (for example, impulsivity, honesty, dependency, or the like) was typically in the range between .10 and .20, and often was even lower... Virtually no coefficients, either between individual pairs of behavioral measures or between personality scale scores and individual behavioral measures, exceeded the .30 "barrier."

This correlational "barrier" represents the heart of the situationist's empirical case.

Third, as a bonus, Hartshorne and May also placed their subjects in iterations of the *same* specific situation, which is what allowed them to collect explicit data on temporal stability. While the correlation of 0.79 for their cheating situation seems to be at the high end of the typical range for stability correlations – Ross and Nisbett describe this range as "often exceed[ing] .40, sometimes reaching much higher" (1991, p. 101) – what remains representative about Hartshorne and May's data is the markedly unfavorable contrast between consistency correlations and stability correlations. This contrast is the reason why situationists focus their skepticism on the cross-situational consistency of behavior, rather than on the reliability of behavioral dispositions quite generally.

WHAT IS THE SCOPE OF A THEORY OF VIRTUE?

So the heart of situationism's empirical case consists in the low ceiling on correlations reported from explicit investigations of cross-situational consistency. Later we shall have occasion to consider the rest of the case. But let us first examine what follows from its heart, focusing again on Hartshorne and May's honesty study.

Hartshorne and May found that most of their subjects were *not* cross-situationally consistent across their behavioral measures of honesty. As we have seen, two inferences lie between this observation and the philosophical situationist's bottom-line conclusion. Each of them turns out to be objectionable. But let us begin with the second inference. Suppose that most of Hartshorne and May's sub-jects (therefore) lacked the virtue of honesty and that their findings are widely replicable.[5] Does it follow that "not enough people have the virtue of honesty," as the philosophical situationists' critique requires?

To examine this question, we have to return to the task we left trailing earlier, concerning the number of people who are supposed, by traditional virtue theory, to have any given virtue, such as hon-esty. In effect, this is a question about the scope of the theory. To whom does a theory of virtue apply (and *how* does it apply to them)? To license her inference from "most people lack the virtue of hon-esty" to "not enough people have that virtue," the philosophical situ-ationist has to interpret traditional virtue theory as applying to *most* people *and* as applying to them by claiming, among other things, that *they have* the virtue of honesty. However, as many defenders of traditional virtue theory have pointed out, this interpretation is tendentious. To illustrate, let me discuss two alternative interpre-tations of a traditional theory's scope. One is more subtle than the other, but on neither does it follow that "not enough people have the virtue of honesty." Moreover, these alternatives are consistent, so the virtue theorist does not have to choose between them.

On the first interpretation, virtue theory applies to "most" people (indeed, to everyone), but no claim is made that most people *actually have* the virtue of honesty. Instead, the traditional virtue theorist's claim will be that everyone *should* have that virtue. Her claim will be normative, rather than descriptive. Of course, even this norma-tive claim has at least one empirical presupposition – namely, that for any given person it is possible that he or she can have the virtue of honesty. On the face of it, however, this presupposition is fully consistent with the "fact" that most people lack the virtue of hon-esty. Indeed, it is arguably consistent with a state of affairs in which no one actually has the virtue of honesty.

Doris and Stich (2005, §2) concede that the empirical evidence does not show that the acquisition of virtue is impossible. They reply that it is possible that the acquisition of virtue is psycholog-ically impossible and that the onus is now on the virtue theorist to demonstrate that it is psychologically possible. If "psychologi-cally possible" means "possible for a real human being [as distinct from merely logically possible]," this is a curious reply. For, as we shall elaborate next, Hartshorne and May's data are consistent with *some* people's actually having the virtue of honesty (see Adams 2006, p. 116); and from the fact that some people actually have the virtue, it follows that it is possible for a real human being to have the virtue.

But perhaps "psychologically possible" is meant to gesture at some more demanding empirical constraint on an ethical ideal's having normative purchase on the average human being – more demanding, that is, than mere "possibility for a real human being." Perhaps, for example, it is meant to suggest that an ideal of virtuous character has normative purchase *only if* the average human being has a fighting chance of actually acquiring the relevant character trait (compare Doris 1998, p. 525 n. 41). To vindicate this suggestion, and thereby turn the gesture into a reply, would require two arguments, each anchored in the same construal of the average person's "fighting chance." One argument is needed to show that the low ceiling on cross-situational consistency correlations deprives the average person of her fighting chance and a second argument is needed to show that it is philosophically tenable to subject ethical ideals to the resultant empirical constraint (i.e. to water them down that far). The trouble is that the easier one makes it to complete one of these arguments, the harder it will be to complete the other.

For example, suppose we say that the average person has a fighting chance to acquire a virtue only if it is easy for her to acquire it. It will then be simple to read the situationist data as showing that the resultant empirical constraint is not satisfied. However, it will be very difficult to vindicate the corresponding philosophical proposition that "an ideal of virtuous character has normative purchase only if it is *easy for the average human being* to acquire the relevant character trait."

Let us now consider a second alternative. On this interpretation, the only claim that a theory of virtue makes about anyone's actually having the (full measure of the) "virtuous cross-situationally consistent character trait of honesty" is a claim about "some" people, namely, the few exemplars or models of honesty. Accordingly, as long as a small number of people have the virtue of honesty, then enough people have it to satisfy the empirical commitments of the theory. Notice that although the scope of a theory of virtue will be (in one way) narrower here, as compared to the previous alternative, its empirical exposure will be greater, since the theory will now claim that some people actually have the virtue of honesty.

Still, this claim is entirely consistent with Hartshorne and May's data.[6] While the average correlation of 0.23 between any pair of their behavioral measures of honesty plainly excludes there being many subjects whose own *individual* average correlation (over any pair of the honesty measures) was much higher than 0.23, it is consistent with there being some subjects whose individual average correlation was much higher than 0.23. It is consistent, in other words, with there being a small number of individuals who were cross-situationally consistently honest. Hence, from Hartshorne and May's overall average cross-situational consistency correlation of 0.23, it does not follow that "no one has the virtue of honesty" or even that "next to no one does." But then, on this second interpretation, neither does it follow that "not enough people have the virtue of honesty."

It would be natural to object – as, in effect, Doris (1998, pp. 511–13) does object – that a theory of virtue whose scope is restricted to a few exemplars is not of much interest, either practically or theoretically. To command our attention, a theory of virtue must be shown to have some clear relevance to most people (better yet, to everyone). This much is certainly difficult to deny.

Fortunately, there is also no need to deny it, as help on this point is available in a surprising corner. Recall that some contemporary theories eschew the traditional definition of virtue as a species of character trait. They define virtue instead as a kind of occurrent state – in the simplest case, as a kind of occurrent act. Hurka (2006) argues that occurrent act theories of virtue are immune to the situationist critique. To see why they are immune, consider an occurrent requirement to act honestly – for example, the requirement not to cheat on this occasion.[7] The normative purchase of this requirement does not depend on any possibility of the agent's having or acquiring any disposition to perform acts of the relevant kind (however this kind is construed). Empirically, it depends only on the possibility of the agent's performing the occurrent act, i.e. of his not cheating then and there. Since none of its data casts any doubt on this possibility, occurrent act theories of virtue are unscathed by situationism.

It is common to treat occurrent act theories of virtue and traditional theories as diametrically opposed to each other; and for some purposes, they are.[8] However, there is also a core component of occurrent act theories to which traditional theories can, and should, help themselves. I have in mind the conception of (individual) virtues as sources of occurrent act requirements on individuals. On this conception, the very existence of a normative requirement not to cheat on this occasion (say) constitutes part of the normative relevance of the virtue of honesty, since "honesty" is itself the source of the requirement (and of kindred others).[9] This highlights a significant aspect of the normative relevance of the virtues, an aspect that not only applies to everyone, but is also immune to the philosophical situationist's critique.

A traditional theory of virtue should incorporate this conception of individual virtues. It should do so, first and foremost, because that conception is anyhow correct. But incorporating that conception would also spell out one obvious way in which the virtues remain normatively relevant to everyone, even if only a few exemplary individuals are expected fully to acquire the corresponding virtuous character traits.

Now it may be further objected that this reply does nothing to rescue the traditional definition of virtue, since it merely conjoins to the traditional theory some free-floating truths (albeit, about virtue) that have nothing to do with its hallmark definition. But that would be a mistake, for the truths in question can readily be made to have something to do with the traditional definition of virtue as a species of character trait. The truths about the specific occurrent act requirements issued by a given virtue will have a firm footing in that hallmark definition, rather than floating free from it, as long as a traditional theory reserves some privileged role for the exemplars of that virtue in identifying those same requirements.[10] A well-known, albeit extreme example of such a privileged role is given by Hursthouse's (1999) claim that *all* right action (and, a fortiori, the occurrent requirements issued by any particular virtue) is *defined* in terms of how a virtuous agent would characteristically act in the situation. But less extreme privileged roles for exemplars are also possible, not to mention much more plausible.

Further to articulate the second alternative, then, a theory of virtue so interpreted will make different claims with different scopes. On the one hand, it will (only) claim that "some" people actually have the virtuous cross-situationally consistent character trait of honesty. On the other hand, it will also claim that "everyone" is required to act honestly, occasion by occasion, whether he or she has the character trait or not. Both claims are consistent with situationism. They are bridged by the distinctive additional claim that the exemplars of honesty have a privileged role in identifying the nature of the acts occurrently required by honesty (i.e. in identifying what it takes to act honestly on some occasion or another), thereby relating everyone *indirectly* to the virtuous character trait of honesty.[11] It is this distinctive bridging claim that qualifies the resultant theory as a "traditional" theory of virtue.

WHICH "CHARACTER TRAITS" ARE THE RIGHT ONES?

Let us now set the issue of scope aside and turn to philosophical situationism's other objectionable inference. We can isolate it by taking the fact that most of Hartshorne and May's subjects were not cross-situationally consistent across Hartshorne and May's behavioral measures of honesty, and asking whether it really follows that most of their subjects lacked the virtue of honesty. To draw that conclusion, one has to assume that Hartshorne and May's behavioral measures properly operationalize the virtuous character trait of honesty. Yet that assumption is objectionable.

To operationalize a cross-situationally consistent character trait, experimenters have to specify a variety of concrete situation–response pairs. In the case of honesty, the situations have to be "honesty eliciting," that is, situations likely to provoke a response that can be readily evaluated as "honest" or "not honest." Hartshorne and May's honesty-eliciting situations include the stealing, lying, and cheating situations described earlier. For each honesty-eliciting situation, the experimenters also have to specify the particular response that counts as the "honest" response. In the cheating situation, for example, Hartshorne and May specify "not copying" as the honest response.

We can distinguish three separate respects in which Hartshorne and May's concrete situation–response pairs fail to operationalize honesty properly. Philosophically, the most important of these is that their behavioral measures do not take account of the normative sensitivity of a virtuous character trait's responsiveness to situations. Unlike with some kinds of character trait, the responses characteristic of a virtuous trait do not simply respond to the situation as such. Rather, they respond to some reason for action present in the situation; alternatively, they respond to the normative requirements imposed by some value at stake in the situation (e.g. the value of honesty).

Reasons for action, however, can be neutralized – defeated, cancelled, preempted – by (other) features of a concrete situation, even if those features do not change the identity of that situation under some abstract or mechanical description. Hence, two concrete situation–response pairs may appear equivalent – from a certain point of view, anyhow – despite the fact that the relevant reason for action is operative in only one of them. But the adequacy of a given concrete pairing as a behavioral measure of honesty depends on the reason to act honestly remaining operative there. Otherwise, the concrete situation does not call for any particular response by the agent after all, at least not as far as honesty is concerned.

Hartshorne and May's lying situation illustrates the difficulty well. Ordinarily, making a false report counts both as "lying" and as "trait-contrary" behavior for honesty. A situation presenting an opportunity to make a false report is therefore plausibly regarded as an honesty-eliciting situation and "reports falsely" is plausibly counted as the "not honest" response. Still, like any ordinary moral reason, the reason not to make a false report can be defeated; and arguably, in Hartshorne and May's lying situation, it *is* defeated. For recall that, in their scenario, the false report serves to prevent another child from getting into trouble, i.e. to accomplish some (sufficient) good. In that case, reporting falsely is *not* trait-contrary behavior for honesty – it does not contraindicate possession of the virtuous trait – because the *reason* for action to which the virtuous trait responds is not operative in the situation. So the lying situation is not an adequate behavioral measure of honesty.

A second respect in which Hartshorne and May's behavioral measures are inadequate is perfectly generic, in the sense that it does not stem from anything particular to the virtues as a subset of character traits. In fact, the objection is best explained by reference to one of the fundamental tenets of social psychology, which situationists themselves emphasize greatly. Ross and Nisbett call it the "principle of construal":

302   GOPAL SREENIVASAN

The impact of any "objective" stimulus situation depends upon the personal and subjective meaning that the actor attaches to that situation. To predict the behavior of a given person successfully, we must be able to appreciate the actor's construal of the situation. (1991, p. 11)

Since the attribution of a character trait is meant to enable (or at least, to facilitate) predictions of how the bearer of the trait will behave, it seems that the concrete situation–response pairs that operationalize the trait ought to be pairings whose significance is agreed on between the experimenter and the subject (i.e. between predictor and predictee). For example, it seems that the evaluation of specific responses as either "honest" or "not honest" ought to be so agreed on. However, Hartshorne and May used "objective" behavioral measures, meaning that the specification of the particular situations and responses were fixed by the experimenters alone.

To illustrate the resultant difficulty, consider their stealing situation. Some change has been left on a table in an empty classroom and there is an opportunity to take it. Hartshorne and May count taking the change as "stealing," i.e. as the "not honest" response. But someone who believed in "finders keepers" – call her Sally – would disagree. Sally would find nothing wrong with taking the change and, more significantly, nothing inconsistent in both "not copying from the answer key" and "taking the change." Say that is indeed how she responds in the cheating and stealing situations. In scoring Sally as "cross-situationally *in*consistent," Hartshorne and May are really (only) registering their disagreement with her over the correctness of finders keepers, rather than discovering any true behavioral inconsistency on Sally's part. Furthermore, since they disregard her belief in finders keepers, it should come as no surprise that Hartshorne and May would have had trouble predicting Sally's behavior in the stealing situation.

Of course, *morally*, it may well be that Hartshorne and May are correct and that finders keepers is not a valid principle. Let us stipulate that it is invalid. In that case, Sally will turn out to be behaviorally consistent, but also not (fully) honest. Recall that behavioral reliability – and, a fortiori, cross-situational consistency – is only a necessary condition of virtue and not also a sufficient condition. To the other candidate necessary conditions mentioned earlier, we can now add a further one: possession of the correct moral beliefs (e.g. beliefs about the validity of finders keepers).[12] Since Sally has false moral beliefs about honesty, she cannot be a fully honest person, no matter how consistently she behaves. Likewise, whether Hartshorne and May sincerely agree with Sally about finders keepers or not has no bearing whatever on the validity of the principle itself. The two necessary conditions (along with their subcomponents) operate independently.

Hartshorne and May's behavioral measures of honesty therefore fail to satisfy a condition of adequacy on behavioral measures of any character trait, namely, that experimenter and subject agree on the significance of the relevant concrete situation–response pairs.[13] This condition is imposed by the need to license predictions of the subject's behavior and has no consequences for the correctness of any moral belief about the particulars of what honesty calls for.

A final respect in which Hartshorne and May's behavioral measures of honesty are inadequate arises from the fact that relevance – specifically, the relevance of a given honesty-eliciting situation to the normative requirements imposed by the value of honesty – is a matter of degree. We can plausibly distinguish between marginal and paradigmatic cases – or, to borrow from psychological idiom, between highly and not highly prototypical cases – of either "honest" behavior or "not honest" behavior. In this vein, copying from an answer key does seem like a paradigmatic case of cheating. By contrast, pocketing stray change is only a marginal case of stealing, even if one rejects the "finders keepers" principle. Much better examples of stealing would be shoplifting (children) or purse snatching (adults). Morally and psychologically, the expectation of cross-situational consistency is much stronger across situations that elicit paradigmatic cases of honest behavior. Insofar as adequate behavioral measures of honesty should accordingly be confined to paradigmatic cases, Hartshorne and May's stealing situation is not an adequate measure.

ONE-TIME PERFORMANCE EXPERIMENTS

A low ceiling on cross-situational consistency correlations, then, does not entail that traditional theories of virtue are "empirically inadequate." As we have seen, there are at least two gaps on the path from "most people lack character traits" to "not enough people have any virtuous character traits." To begin with, "most people" in the premise does not include enough people to warrant the "not enough people" in the conclusion. In addition, the "character traits" operationalized in the premise are not the right kind to contradict the "virtuous character traits" in the conclusion. Sometimes (normative sensitivity) that is because they do not specifically qualify as "virtuous." Other times (construal, paradigmatic relevance) it is simply because their operationalization is generically defective.

However, as even casual acquaintance with the writings of philosophical situationists makes clear, what I have called the heart of their empirical case – the 0.30 correlational ceiling – is only one thread among many in the tangle of evidence they adduce.[14] At least as much attention is devoted to studies of a rather different sort from Hartshorne and May's, of which Milgram's obedience to authority experiments, Darley and Batson's Good Samaritan experiment, Isen and Levin's dime in the phone booth experiment, and Latané and Darley's bystander experiments are prominent examples. In these other experiments – of which there are "hundreds, if not thousands," as Doris is often at pains to emphasize – a majority of subjects (sometimes more) are not only led to perform trait-contrary behavior, but are apparently so led by a trivial feature of the situation in which the subjects have been placed. What is to be made of this part of the philosophical situationist's case?

As the first order of business, we should distinguish various conclusions that might be drawn from this other evidence. For present purposes, I shall limit myself to two possibilities. On the one hand, there is the proposition that *most subjects lack some cross-situationally consistent character trait*, which I shall call the "official interim conclusion." On the other hand, there is the proposition that *situational variables have a powerful effect on behavior*, which I shall call the "situationist minimum." Let us start with the former.

The official interim conclusion is only an *interim* conclusion because, as we know, even in the best-case scenario, some distance remains between it and the philosophical situationist's bottom-line conclusion, "not enough people have any virtues." But let us now ignore that distance and the previously observed impediments to traversing it. What is more useful to notice here is that the official interim conclusion does clearly follow from Hartshorne and

May's study. In their case, the cross-situationally consistent character trait that most of their subjects lacked was "honesty$_{HM}$," where the subscript indicates Hartshorne and May's particular operationalization of honesty. Functionally, in other words, the official interim conclusion captures precisely the contribution to the philosophical situationist's bottom line made by Hartshorne and May's study. In examining whether the rest of the philosophical situationist's case also licenses her official interim conclusion, we are therefore considering whether this other evidence is on a par with Hartshorne and May's.

To make efficient progress on this question, let me introduce a fundamental structural distinction between experiments like Hartshorne and May's and experiments like Milgram's or Darley and Batson's. The distinction holds between experiments structured as an "iterated trial" and those structured as a "one-time performance." In an iterated trial experiment, each subject is placed in a plurality of eliciting situations, whereas in a one-time performance experiment each subject is placed in a single eliciting situation only. We can actually further distinguish two different species of iterated trial design, depending on whether the "plurality" of situations is constituted by simple iterations of the original situation or by a diversity of specific situations designed to elicit manifestations of the same trait. The second species of iterated trial design thus corresponds to what I earlier called an "explicit investigation" of cross-situational consistency.

Hartshorne and May's study is an iterated trial experiment (indeed, it instantiates both species of this design at once). What characterizes the other experiments we are examining is that they are all one-time performance experiments.[15] In Milgram's famous experiment, for example, each subject is presented with a single incremental sequence of opportunities to "punish" a learner under the instruction of an authority figure (the experimenter); and the aim is to discover at what point (if any) the subject will disobey.

The question before us, then, is whether any one-time performance experiment can license the (philosophical situationist's official interim) conclusion that most subjects lack some cross-situationally consistent character trait. Consider Milgram's experiment. No matter where in the sequence one plausibly draws the line past which the virtue of compassion required his subjects *not* to proceed, most of them crossed the line. So from the standpoint of compassion, the behavior of most of Milgram's subjects was plainly trait contrary. Does it follow that they lacked the cross-situationally consistent trait of compassion?[16]

It all depends on how high we set the degree of reliability required of a trait.[17] If we define a cross-situationally consistent trait as an exceptionless behavioral disposition (i.e. as 100-percent reliable), then it certainly follows that Milgram's subjects lacked the trait of compassion. However, when applied to virtue, that would yield an implausibly strict definition. It would identify virtue with nothing less than utter perfection, "one strike and you are out." In any case, Doris explicitly declines to define his notion of a "trait" as an exceptionless disposition (2002, p. 19). So we can set that definition aside.

Unfortunately, on any other setting, it no longer follows that Milgram's subjects lacked the trait of compassion. In other words, when any lower (and hence, more plausible) degree of reliability is used to define the trait, our license to draw the official interim conclusion disappears. The basic difficulty is that an ordinarily reliable behavioral disposition, even if it is very reliable, is thoroughly consistent with a single episode of "contrary" behavior. To exclude possession of a(n imperfectly) reliable behavioral disposition, we therefore require *repeated* failures.[18] Yet since Milgram's obedience experiment is a one-time performance experiment, his subjects never get the chance to fail repeatedly. By definition, all one-time performance experiments share this fatal defect.

Now it may be tempting, in reply, to suppose that a subject's one-time violation of the requirements of compassion is still best explained by her *lacking* the cross-situationally consistent trait of compassion, even though her violation is logically consistent with her possession of that trait.[19] But however tempting, and however convenient for the philosophical situationist, this would be a mistake. In fact, it would be very close to the same mistake situationists themselves diagnose under the label of the "fundamental attribution error" (Ross and Nisbett 1991, chap. 5). The common element in both mistakes is the tendency to decide the possession of a behavioral trait (either for or against) on an insufficient evidence base – typically, on the basis of a single observation, which is all that a one-time performance experiment can ever yield. Both mistakes are forms of jumping the evidential gun.

By contrast, a true warrant for the attribution or exclusion of a reliable behavioral trait requires a *plurality* of observations of the subject's behavior in trait-relevant eliciting conditions. In the particular case of a cross-situationally consistent trait, as distinct from a temporally stable trait, the plurality of observations has furthermore to be *distributed* over a variety of trait-relevant eliciting conditions. We thereby return to the point that genuine evidence for the (non-)existence of cross-situationally consistent character traits is properly to be sought from the kind of experiment exemplified by Hartshorne and May's study – that is, from at least the second species of iterated trial experiment.[20]

SALVAGE OPTIONS

So one-time performance experiments cannot license the official interim conclusion that most subjects lack some cross-situationally consistent character trait. For present purposes, that leaves us with the situationist minimum as an alternative, i.e. with the conclusion that situational variables have a powerful effect on behavior. Let us simply accept that this conclusion is well supported by the great number of one-time performance experiments on record, as the pertinent questions here do not concern this basic inference. They are, rather, "Just *how* powerful is this effect?" and, more so, "By what argumentative route(s) can the situationist minimum be connected to the philosophical situationist's bottom-line conclusion that not enough people have any virtues?"

I do not know the answer to the first question. But I shall sketch two specific routes one might pursue in answering the second. Since neither will prove compelling, it is also worth saying that it is really the philosophical situationists who owe us an answer to the second question. On the whole, they have been remarkably casual on this point (see Doris 2002, p. 38), especially considering that it is not at all obvious how exactly one is supposed to get from the situationist minimum to their bottom line.

To preserve a measure of tidiness along the first route, let us restrict our attention to one-time performance experiments in which the experimental situation is compassion eliciting. Now suppose we assume that, for any given one-time performance experiment, most people outside the actual subject population *would have* behaved as the *average* subject did in fact behave, had these people somehow found themselves in the relevant experimental situation (either in an experiment or in real life). In addition, suppose we further assume that our first assumption *continues to hold*, even as we go on counterfactually "inserting" a given population into *each and every* one-time performance experiment in our restricted universe. Finally, let us take ourselves to be entitled, on this basis, to conclude that most people have a significant number of compassion-contrary performances on their "composite moral record," that is, on the moral record composed of their actual and counterfactual behavior.

Let me call this the *counterfactual addition* route. Since it is manifestly a loose construction, I shall not pause to examine its various component steps. What I wish to emphasize instead is how far we nevertheless remain from the philosophical situationist's bottom line. If most people have a significant number of compassion-contrary performances on their composite moral record, then we may well be able to subtract a significant margin from the maximum degree of "overall reliability" that most people are able to achieve in relation to compassion. (This notion of "overall reliability" is a generic amalgam of temporal stability and cross-situational consistency, and hence distinct from either.[21] We are forced to resort to it because the counterfactual addition route tells us nothing about the distribution of a person's trait-contrary performances over suitably individuated kinds of eliciting situation.[22])

Nothing follows from this, however, about most people's maximum degree of cross-situational consistency in relation to compassion. Nothing follows precisely because overall reliability is distinct from cross-situational consistency. As a result, the counterfactual additional route fails to deliver the philosophical situationist's official interim conclusion (which is about cross-situational consistency).[23] But while this may be worth noticing, it need not be fatal. For one thing, it might be argued that some minimum degree of "overall reliability" in behavior is also a necessary condition of virtue.

By contrast, a further limitation is crippling: the counterfactual addition route is subject to the same scope objection that afflicts the official interim conclusion itself. The fact that "most people's" maximum overall reliability in relation to compassion is capped in some significant way tells us nothing about the overall reliability that can still be achieved by a "few" exemplars of virtue: neither what the most reliable compassionate person's maximum is nor how many people have achieved that maximum of overall reliability in compassion. Hence, the counterfactual addition route cannot yield the conclusion that not enough people have the virtue of compassion.

A second route to the philosophical situationists' bottom line attempts both to deflect the scope objection and to bypass their official interim conclusion. It begins by taking seriously the bewildering number and open-ended variety of adverse situational influences on moral behavior (compare Sabini and Silver 2005, p. 545). In any given situation calling for a virtuous performance, everyone is exposed to this corrosive array of adverse influences. Moreover, *anyone* (including an exemplar of virtue) can succumb to one of them, and thereby fail to do the virtuous thing. No one with this kind of vulnerability, the argument continues, can really be "relied" upon to behave virtuously, not in the sense that the traditional conception of virtue demands anyhow. Since everyone has that vulnerability, no one has any virtues. Let me call this the *extreme moral randomness* route.

Suppose we swallow this argument (hook, line, and sinker). It might well be resisted, but let us not. For all that, an important difficulty remains. To wit, the extreme moral randomness route proves too much and also proves too little. It proves too much insofar as it fails to distinguish virtue ethics from its relevant rivals. In terms of rivals in moral theory, the threat in question – namely, that of a moral agent's being overwhelmed on a given occasion by a situational influence – applies not only to an agent trying to be virtuous, but to any agent trying to follow *any* ordinary moral rule (compare Sabini and Silver 2005, p. 536 n. 5). Accordingly, if this threat is a problem for virtue ethics, then it is equally a problem for any non-debunking conception of morality (and, a fortiori, for deontology, consequentialism, or what have you).

In terms of rivals in trait psychology, the same threat operates just as well against an agent with a temporally stable trait as it does against an agent with a cross-situationally consistent trait. After all, the adverse influences are precisely situational. They operate within the confines of a given situation and their effectiveness is presumably independent of whether the agent's behavior on that occasion is being compared with her behavior on narrowly similar occasions or with her behavior on trait-relevantly similar occasions.[24] Thus, while Doris (2002, pp. 23, 64) affirms the existence of temporally stable traits, the extreme moral randomness route is actually inconsistent with them.

Granted a modest clarification, the extreme moral randomness route also proves too little. As initially presented, the argument is (deliberately) vague about just how "powerful" it claims the array of adverse situational influences to be.[25] The modest clarification specifies that these situational influences are *not so* powerful as to undermine the agent's ordinary moral responsibility for his behavior, which entails that it is still *possible* for him to do the right or virtuous thing on the occasion. As we saw above, however, the possibility of an agent's performing the act that virtue requires of him is enough to secure the normative purchase of the occurrent requirement he faces in the situation. In turn, the fact that the occurrent act requirements issued by a given virtue have normative purchase is enough to establish the normative relevance of that particular virtue. Although none of this was news for an occurrent act theory of virtue (see Hurka 2006), we learned that a traditional theory of virtue can help itself to this path to normative relevance, too. Yet, insofar as the extreme moral randomness route is consistent with the normative relevance of a traditionally defined virtue, it proves too little.

Of course, the philosophical situationist can always reject this clarification, modest or not. But that would make it all the more clear that the extreme moral randomness route proves too much, since its argument would then lead to a form of moral nihilism. Indeed, we can now refashion our difficulty as a dilemma. Either the extreme moral randomness route accepts the modest clarification or it does not. If it does, it is consistent with the normative relevance of the virtues, even as traditionally defined, and so proves too little. If it does not, it leads to moral nihilism, which undermines all nondebunking moral theories, and so proves too much.

CONCLUSION

Since the situationist critique of virtue ethics is an empirical critique, its fate – like that of any empirical question or set of questions – can ultimately only be decided by empirical evidence. This means that there is only so much we can conclude about it on the basis of analysis alone. It also means it may yet turn out that virtue ethics is empirically inadequate. None of the objections to the situationist critique we have canvassed can inoculate virtue ethics against that possibility (nor were they intended to).

As things stand, we either lack the evidence or we lack the argument(s) to vindicate the philosophical situationist's bottom-line conclusion that not enough people have any virtues. On the evidence side, what would be most directly relevant would be evidence from iterated trial experiments (see note 19) that told us roughly how many people (in the population at large) have behavioral traits belonging to a privileged subset of cross-situationally consistent character traits. Leaving aside the issue of which traits map on to which specific virtues, the precise boundaries of the privileged subset depend on the structure of one's favored traditional theory of virtue (as well as on various moral truths). But even to get in the right general neighborhood, the cross-situationally consistent traits have to be normatively sensitive and their operationalization has to incorporate certain basic points of agreement between the subject and the experimenter. These are necessary conditions of membership in the privileged subset, whatever the details of one's favored theory. Moreover, they are conditions not satisfied by Hartshorne and May's landmark honesty study, which is the best existing evidence available to the philosophical situationist.

On the argument's side, there may be other ways to reach the conclusion that "not enough people have any virtues" from the point that situational variables have a powerful effect on behavior, beyond the few considered here. Despite what I have suggested, then, it may be possible to rest the philosophical situationist's critique on the basis of evidence from one-time performance experiments after all. Finally, of course, it is also possible that some of the arguments I have advanced in defense of virtue are simply mistaken – perhaps, for example, there is some compelling objection to (both versions of) the scope objection, the force of which philosophical situationists can help us to appreciate.

NOTES

1 The example also assumes that copying from an answer key is "cheating" and that pocketing stray change is "stealing."

2 For simplicity, let us understand "traditional theorists of virtue" to include contemporary theorists who adopt the traditional definition of virtue. This will free us from always having to acknowledge that some contemporary theorists of virtue (e.g. Hurka 2001) do not define a virtue as a species of character trait. We shall return to the significance of that theoretical option below.

3 But some explicitly omit this condition (e.g. Driver 2001). Driver also rejects the other two conditions to follow in the text.

4 As Ross and Nisbett (1991, p. 95) explain, this means that "there is almost no gain in accuracy of prediction about situation 2 by virtue of knowing how someone has behaved in situation 1." More specifically, given the 0.13 correlation in the text, knowing that Smith behaved more honestly than Jones in the stealing situation does not even raise the likelihood that Smith will be more honest than Jones in the lying situation to 55 percent, as compared to the baseline (i.e. random) likelihood of 50 percent.

5 One reason to question this, of course, is that Hartshorne and May's subjects were all children (see e.g. Kamtekar 2004, p. 466 n.). But I shall put this point to the side, in order to concentrate on the more general issues at stake.

6 The most we can say here concerns what is *consistent with* their data, since their data do not track the behavior of individuals across situations. Rather, they are reported at the level of a population aggregate. Statements about individuals – e.g. that some of them had high average cross-situational consistency correlations – therefore have to be inferred from aggregate comparisons.

7 For convenience, I shall speak in terms of requirements to act virtuously. But this can be read compatibly with various views about the moral weight or precise deontological status of what virtue calls for in a given situation.

8 Centrally, there is an important question about the priority of acts versus dispositions about which the two kinds of theory essentially disagree. For some discussion, see Thomson (1997).

9 When referring to honesty as the source of occurrent act requirements, it would be better to distinguish the "value" of honesty from the "virtue" of honesty, where the value informs the corresponding virtue. This makes it clear that no metaphysical priority need be claimed for the virtuous exemplar, who can remain metaphysically independent of the source of the requirements to which she responds.

10 Following the distinction registered in note 8, this privileged role can be understood as epistemically privileged (and, in my view, should be so understood).

11 The availability of this indirect reading of the normative relevance of virtuous character traits already casts severe doubt on the claim that an ideal of virtuous character has normative purchase *only if* the average human being has a fighting chance of acquiring the relevant character trait.

12 Interpreted without restriction, this condition will compel acceptance of the unity of the virtues. I reject that conclusion but do not have the space to discuss the issue here. See Sreenivasan (2009).

13 In my 2002 (pp. 65–66), I discuss some preliminary evidence suggesting that adherence to this condition would lead to higher cross-situational consistency correlations than Hartshorne and May found. For a much fuller argument to this effect, see now Snow 2010.

14 Merritt *et al.* (2010) do not even mention it.

15 The distinction is not exhaustive, so there are some situationist experiments that are neither iterated trials nor one-time performances (e.g. the Zimbardo prison experiment). My remarks here are confined to one-time performance experiments.

16 Since consistency is necessary but not sufficient for virtue, the question in the text is simpler than asking whether Milgram's subjects lacked the *virtue* of compassion. For discussion of some of the complications I am leaving out here, see Sreenivasan (2008).

17 Degrees of trait reliability are different from dimensions of trait reliability. Temporal stability and cross-situational consistency are the "dimensions" of reliability we distinguished at the outset, while degrees of reliability range from 0 to 100.

18 The lower the degree of reliability required of a trait, the greater the number of failures needed to exclude the trait.

19 But, even if you have these temptations, why suppose that *this* is a better explanation than, say, the explanation that the subject lacks the temporally stable trait of compassionate-under-the-instruction-of-experimental-authorities?

20 Since *virtues* have to be both cross-situationally consistent and temporally stable, we really want evidence from iterated trial experiments that instantiate both species at once, just like Hartshorne and May's. See note 15.

21 It counts the second trait-contrary performance in a given eliciting situation as diminishing the person's trait reliability to the same extent as a trait-contrary performance in any *other* trait-relevant eliciting situation.

22 Of course, we could always add a suitable assumption to this effect. But then we could also save a lot of bother and simply assume the conclusion outright.

23 There is no requirement that the argumentative route to the philo-
    sophical situationists' bottom line proceed via their official interim
    conclusion, although that is how they appear to argue their case. A per-
    fectly good alternative strategy is exhibited by Miller (2009, 2010), for
    example. In an illuminating discussion of one-time performance experi-
    ments about helping behavior, he argues that the experimental record is
    actually consistent with many people's having *some* cross-situationally
    consistent helping trait. Yet, at the same time, he argues that, of the
    people with some such trait, few actually have the *virtue* of compassion
    because, in many cases, the cross-situationally consistent helping trait
    fails a different necessary condition for virtue. (Many of these people
    characteristically help for the wrong reason, for instance, though there
    is an interesting variety in their wrong reasons). I do not discuss Miller's
    argument in the text because he explicitly concedes the scope objection.
24 With *neither* kind of similarity, it may help to spell out, is the operation
    of the situational influence itself any part of what makes numerically
    distinct situations similar.
25 Here again, any such argument has to strike a balance between making
    its claim weak enough to be plausibly grounded in the data and yet
    strong enough to contradict some actual tenet of virtue ethics.

14 The definition of virtue ethics

Ever since virtue ethics in modern guise came onto the moral theoretic landscape there have been calls for definition or at least clarification about what it is. However, offering a definition of a type of moral or ethical theory such as virtue ethics or consequentialism is not remotely like defining 'bachelor' as "unmarried man." Attempts to distill the essence of virtue ethics in a simple clear formula raise more questions than they answer. For example if we take a common route by claiming that 'virtue ethics' means "a moral theory where character is primary," serious theoretical questions immediately arise. What is meant by 'moral' and should the notion be dispensed with in virtue ethics (see Chappell, this volume)? What is meant by 'primary'? Why should character be primary, as opposed to central? Why should character be primary or central, as opposed to virtue concepts applied to rules or actions for example? It turns out that the task of offering a definition is difficult, complex, and highly controversial. Undertaking this task reaches to the very heart of an extremely rich and varied family of moral or ethical theories. Some but not all of these complexities are exposed in this chapter.

To avoid the sense that definitions of "terms of art" are stipulative, straitjacketing, or of not much consequence, we first need to ask: what functions are served by definitions of virtue ethics? These functions determine their adequacy. First, definitions of virtue ethics should illuminate the structure and basic nature of such theories

I wish to thank the audience of the Philosophy Department seminar at the University of Auckland for helpful discussion of an early draft, and particularly Daniel C. Russell for his patient and useful editorial help.

thereby displaying interesting and deep features which mark them off from major rivals. In the modern development of virtue ethics, these rivals are standardly conceived as consequentialist and deontological (Baron *et al.* 1997; Hursthouse 1999, pp. 2, 7). To satisfy this important demand of a definition of virtue ethics, virtue *ethics* has been distinguished from virtue *theory* (Driver 2001). Virtue theory provides accounts of the nature of virtues of character without necessarily being a type of virtue ethics.

Second, definitions of types of moral theories are a way of identifying and characterizing key features of important traditions in moral thought. For example, definitions of virtue ethics have tended to identify different ancient Greek eudaimonistic theories as being all varieties of virtue ethics. However, definitions which identify virtue ethics with just *one* tradition will in so doing obscure the possibility that other traditions also have a strong claim to be understood in virtue ethical terms. Narrow definitions of this type may on those grounds be inadequate. For example, they may exclude Humean traditions, even though in recent Hume scholarship there has been a move to incorporate Hume into the virtue ethical fold (Cohon 2008a; J. Taylor 2006, p. 276; Swanton 2007a; Darwall 2003). This is important, for it allows us to see moral theoretic features in Hume which have been rendered insignificant, even invisible, in previously prevalent utilitarian readings of his substantive ethics. Increasingly, Confucian and neo-Confucian ethics are also being treated in a virtue ethical manner (Van Norden 2007; Ivanhoe 2000; Angle 2009; Slingerland 2011).

Definitions which identify virtue ethics with just one tradition have a further weakness: problems associated with virtue ethics in one tradition are seen as problems for virtue ethics in general. An example is the well-known "self-centeredness objection" to virtue ethics (see below, pp. 335–6).

Third, a definition of virtue ethics in particular enables us to conceptualize and make salient a type of theory which has been neglected, and is now revived. That revival has carried with it calls for greater clarity about just what virtue ethics is (Baron 2011), a reasonable demand in the light of the first function of a definition of virtue ethics. In this way theorists can understand just what is claimed to have been revived, and just what is claimed to make a novel, and indeed progressive, contribution to moral theorizing.

Fourth, an adequate definition should allow us to recognize subtleties and nuances in virtue ethical conceptions of ethics which are not closed off by oversimplified, even caricatured, conceptions. As a result of the first function of a definition of virtue ethics identified above (interpreted as a pressing need to clearly and sharply distinguish virtue ethics from its main rivals), oversimplified conceptions of virtue ethics of the kinds criticized by Stohr (2006) and Hursthouse (1999) were proposed. Such oversimplified conceptions may have the implications that virtue ethics cannot account for justice as a personal virtue or for rules, requirements, or obligations. (Note that virtue ethics as such is not characteristically intended to offer a theory of justice as an institutional virtue or indeed of other institutional virtues.) Though I believe that an adequate virtue ethics can account for all these features in a theoretically satisfying way, these interesting issues cannot be addressed here. Nonetheless an illustration may afford a sense of some of the subtleties inherent in virtue language. Consider the notion of a generous act. In different circumstances a generous act may be variously required (because not to be generous in the circumstances would be indecent), permitted but not required (for example, a CEO's business donation to a cause to which he has the permission of his Board to donate), prohibited (a CEO may not have the authority to make a *generous* donation), admirable but not required (for example an act of great charity), permitted but not highly desirable (such as a generous donation to a slightly dubious cause, or to a cause that is much less worthwhile than others to which one could have contributed), and so on. The boundaries between these aspects of generosity may be fuzzy, and a substantive virtue ethical theory may elucidate the nature and grounds of this fuzziness.

Fifth, a definition of virtue ethics should reflect the breadth of virtue ethical concerns from Aristotle to the present day. Maybe modern ethics is overly concerned with right action (Chappell, this volume), but even though this issue is of considerable interest to many contemporary virtue ethicists, other issues are also central in their book-length works. Zagzebski (1996) is for example also concerned with the nature of virtue and skill (as is Annas 2011); Hursthouse (1999) with emotion, moral dilemmas, and virtue ethical naturalism; Slote (2001) with the relation between virtue, empathy, and justice; Swanton (2003) with objectivity, the demanding nature of ethics (see also Swanton 2009), virtue and universal love – to list but a few important theoretical issues discussed by these theorists. These discussions can be seen as *applying* what Chappell (this volume) describes as a "revolutionary" turn in the history of contemporary virtue ethics, and as such are quite distinctive approaches to central issues (see below, pp. 318–19). What is revolutionary in the 1950s papers of notably Anscombe and Foot (see Chappell, this volume) was opening up a new framework for moral theorizing. The hard job of developing and deploying that framework in new approaches to issues, ranging from the partiality and impartiality of ethics to the demandingness of ethics, was yet to be done. The task is ongoing. Thus it is a mistake to define virtue ethics narrowly in terms of its conception of right action. My definition will reflect this breadth of concern.

An otherwise plausible candidate for a definition of virtue ethics, offered by Daniel Russell (2009, p. 66) fails to satisfy this fifth desideratum of an adequate definition:

virtue ethics (a) makes the notion of a virtue prior to right action, in the sense that a virtue can be understood apart from a formula of right action and (b) holds that right action cannot be fully understood apart from an account of the virtues.

For instance, there is a case for including Nietzsche within the class of virtue ethicists but as May (1999) argues, Nietzsche would reject the very idea of single actions as "the right unit of ethical evaluation" (p. 113). It is not simply that there is no formula for determining whether single actions are right; rather, ethical evaluation should be "broadly gauged over a longer period of 'lived life'" (p. 113).

Finally, the function of a definition of virtue ethics is to reveal a space for a type of theory which makes a *distinctive* contribution to the solution of problems in theoretical and applied ethics. Perhaps this is the most important function of a definition of virtue ethics. Indeed David Solomon (2003, pp. 68–9) lists no less than ten distinctive and important contributions of genuine "radical" virtue ethics. The claim of distinctiveness should not be interpreted as a claim that there is a distinct, unique set of virtue ethical theses about major problems in moral theory (Hursthouse 1999, p. 7). Rather the proof of the pudding of distinctiveness is in the eating, as different virtue ethicists propose various views centering on virtue notions and the virtues. In the area of applied ethics much distinctive work has already been done, particularly by Hursthouse (1991, 2006c, 2007a). Slote (2001) has applied "sentimentalist" virtue ethics to the issues of care, benevolence, and justice. (See also for a virtue ethical approach to the demandingness of ethics Swanton 2009; for a virtue ethical approach to objectivity Swanton 2003, and 2012; and on objectivity in Aristotle's ethics, Chappell 2005.)

CONCEPTS AND CONCEPTIONS OF VIRTUE ETHICS

Despite the need for a definition of virtue ethics which can be widely endorsed, what constitutes virtue ethics is contested. One approach to intractable disputes about definitions of important concepts and types of theory has been to make a distinction between a core concept and rival conceptions of the phenomenon identified by that core concept. John Rawls, the inspirational figure for this approach, applies the distinction to justice. He claims that the "common element" in rival "conceptions" of justice, which are interpretations of the concept of justice, is the role played by the various conceptions in determining rules for assigning basic rights and duties, and the proper nonarbitrary balancing of competing claims to the advantages of social life (1971, p. 5). The question arises: assuming that there are for example Humean, Confucian, Aristotelian, and Nietzschean conceptions of virtue ethics, can we say that they are all virtue ethical theories insofar as they conform to a single core *concept* of virtue ethics? Unfortunately, complicating the task of providing a definition of virtue ethics is the fact that there are rival putative core concepts of virtue ethics. All is not lost for the enterprise of defining that genre of moral theory, however. One could argue that one concept is superior to the others, and that is the strategy I adopt in this chapter.

Perhaps there is a single *exemplar* which provides an agreed core concept of virtue ethics. Aristotle is widely thought to provide that exemplar. However, for Humeans interpreting Hume as a virtue ethicist Hume may provide the exemplar of virtue ethicist, while for Nietzscheans interpreting Nietzsche as a virtue ethicist Nietzsche may be the exemplar. Aristotle does nonetheless provide an exemplar in a weaker sense: any definition of virtue ethics having the implication of excluding Aristotle altogether from the genre of virtue ethics is fatally flawed.[1]

In this chapter I discuss three core concepts of virtue ethics. The first core concept defines virtue ethics in terms of a tradition, the second in terms of the centrality of the agent, and the third in terms of the centrality of a type of concept. All are construed as offering definitions of virtue ethics as opposed to virtue theory. I conclude that the third is the concept that should provide a definition of virtue ethics. That concept is the broadest, including as forms of virtue ethics all theories conforming to the other two concepts.

Concept (1): eudaimonistic virtue ethics

The first core concept of virtue ethics defines it in terms of a tradition, eudaimonism – from Greek *eudaimonia*, "happiness," "well-being," "flourishing." Eudaimonistic virtue ethics is what I have called (Swanton 2003) a genus of virtue ethics with several subgenera, ancient and modern. But should it be seen as the sole genus, by definition? In very recent times explicit definitions of virtue ethics in terms of eudaimonistic virtue ethics (Oakley 1996) may have been in decline, but it remains the dominant paradigm. Furthermore there remains a very prevalent assumption that a neo-Aristotelian conception of right action is *the* virtue ethical account of right action and is even defining of virtue ethics.[2]

There are three aspects to Concept (1) of virtue ethics as typically conceived.

(a)   A necessary condition of a trait being a virtue is that it at least partially contribute to, or constitute, the flourishing (*eudaimonia*) of the possessor of the virtue.[3]

(b)   Practical wisdom is necessary for excellence of character.

(c)   The basic "thin" concept in virtue ethics is excellence.

I consider each of these claims in turn, arguing that even if true, none should be seen as definitional or partially definitional of virtue ethics. Note that though (b) and (c) are typically held by eudaimonists I am not suggesting that noneudaimonists would necessarily reject those features.

ASPECTS OF EUDAIMONISM (A): THE EUDAIMONIST CONCEPTION OF VIRTUE. Eudaimonism is characterized by its attempt to yoke together the ideas that virtues both make you good *as* a human being and are characteristically good *for* you: indeed if a supposed virtue is not characteristically good for you it is not a genuine virtue (Hursthouse 1999).

At the core of eudaimonistic virtue ethics as standardly conceived is the following claim:

(a1) A virtue is an excellent character trait of humans.

Even (a1) is not truistic, however, and should not be thought an essential tenet of virtue ethics. As we shall see, some prefer admirability rather than excellence as the basic thin concept of virtue ethics. Setting this issue aside, we note problems when considering how excellence is to be understood. In standard Aristotelian virtue ethics (a1) is amplified as follows:

(a2) Virtues (among other things) make a human being good as a human being (good qua human).

Although (a2) is often thought central to virtue ethics it should not be thought of as an essential feature, for there are other possible amplifications of (a1). It may be the case that a virtue understood as an excellence *of* humans may be a role virtue such as goodness qua lawyer, but being good as a lawyer, it may be thought, may undermine one's goodness *as* a human being. In that case (a2) would be problematic. Indeed it may be thought that Nietzsche is opposed to (a2). For him, it may be the case that the best life for a particular human being is a life as a passionate artist, and such a life may be thought not to be a life that is good qua *human* (though it may be good qua artist).

Despite this possibility, (a2) might still be true on the following assumption:

(a3) Virtues making one good as a human being may be "differentiated" according to e.g. role and other factors, and these virtues are compatible with goodness qua human.

Given (a3), the way a virtue such as generosity (for example) is manifested will vary according to whether we are speaking of generosity in a friend, generosity in a business executive acting in his role as business executive, and so on. Virtues specified in what might be called basic form (generosity as such), are described at too high a level of abstraction to provide a full understanding of how they should feature in various kinds of lives. Virtues may be "differentiated" according to, for example, one's cultural location, one's role, one's phase of life, and for Nietzsche one's "type" as e.g. a "herd" type or a "higher" type. If differentiated virtue is constrained by the basic form of the virtue, so that for example zealous advocacy in a defense lawyer cannot take the form of what has been called "hyperzeal" (excessive forms which would breach the demands of loyalty and other basic virtues [Dare 2004]), then (a2) may be true.

For the purposes of discussing eudaimonism as a core concept of virtue ethics, let us not tarry over these issues but assume the truth of (a2). Now eudaimonists subscribe, not only to (a2), but to an even more controversial thesis:

(a4) Virtues are necessarily good *for* their possessors (at least characteristically, i.e. in the absence of bad luck).

Though eudaimonists appear to affirm both (a2) and (a4) as amplifications of (a1), the affirmation of (a4) (as opposed to (a2) alone) is a distinct and further move and should not be regarded as an essential feature of virtue ethics. In both Hume and Nietzsche, feature (a4) is prominent in many virtues but is hardly essential in all. Although for Nietzsche, as I interpret him, affirming one's own life is some kind of imperative, being characteristically good for the agent is not necessarily the point of, or even a necessary condition of, many or most virtues. Rather, redeeming culture from mediocrity by fostering a climate which allows "higher men" to be developed or flourish is a major end for Nietzsche, even if that end should be indirectly sought. For Hume things are even clearer: important virtues may be virtues because they are useful or agreeable to oneself, but what makes other traits important virtues is their usefulness or agreeability to others (P. Russell, this volume).

Forging a connection between (a1) and (a4) via such concepts as *eudaimonia* and natural goodness (Foot 2001; Hursthouse 1999; Annas 2005) is an ongoing and fascinating problem in eudaimonistic virtue ethics. There may even be a conception of happiness – beatitude in medieval virtue theory (Wetzel 1992; Porter, this volume), and eudaimonia in Stoic thought – where that connection may be thought conceptual. Here beatitude/eudaimonia is regarded as being by definition invulnerable to the contingencies of misfortune and the absence of external goods, and virtue and only virtue is seen to possess that quality of invulnerability. At any rate, however the connection between (a1) and (a4) is to be forged, the framework within which that task is prosecuted should not be seen as defining of virtue ethics.

ASPECTS OF EUDAIMONISM (B): "HARD" AND "SOFT" VIRTUE ETHICS. Consider now the second feature of the eudaimonistic tradition to be discussed: the claim that practical wisdom is necessary for virtue. Should endorsement of this view be seen as partially definitional of virtue ethics? First let us discuss the claim. According to Russell (D. Russell 2009) there is an important distinction between what he calls "Hard" and "Soft" Virtue Ethics. In Hard Virtue Ethics, phronesis (practical wisdom) is an essential part of every virtue. Soft virtue ethics denies this. A stronger position, maybe we can call it Super Soft Virtue Ethics, claims that practical wisdom is not an essential part of *any* virtue. Slote's (2001) "agent-based" virtue ethics (see below, p. 328, and van Zyl, this volume) is of this type; admirable or good motives but not practical wisdom is essential for virtue.

To understand Hard Virtue Ethics as defining of virtue ethics would be to make a substantive tradition in virtue ethics, with its favored account of virtue itself, defining of virtue ethics as such. Such definitional moves are becoming less frequent I believe; nonetheless it is important to clarify the distinction between Hard and Soft Virtue Ethics for the belief that practical wisdom is central to virtue and ethics generally is commonly seen as a distinctive feature of virtue ethics. And the nature of wisdom as part of different virtues is indeed a fascinating issue. The possibility is open that different virtues make different demands on just how much practical wisdom, and of what type, is proper to a given virtue in different types of context. Justice, especially as a virtue in judges acting in that role, requires a very high degree of wisdom and of a certain type: a wisdom that arguably does not partake in excessive discretion and imposition of moral views. By contrast, virtuous creativity in the talented, as Nietzsche claims, is marked by experimentation and living "unwisely" and "imprudently": the "genuine philosopher lives unphilosophically and unwisely, above all *imprudently*, and bears the burden and duty of a hundred attempts and temptations of life – he risks *himself* constantly" (Nietzsche 1973, §205, p. 132). Nietzsche clearly does not mean here that creative virtue is compatible with stupidity and self-indulgent wanton recklessness. "Unwise" is contrasted with "wise" in the sense of cautiously prudent, not with "wise" in some deeper sense, of for example, "being true to oneself." A certain imprudence, not desirable in someone with heavy responsibilities, is deemed to be a hallmark of the highly creative individual. Recognition of this fact does not make one a Soft Virtue Ethicist, though some may be "harder" than others.

ASPECTS OF EUDAIMONISM (C): EXCELLENCE OR ADMIRABILITY? The third aspect of the eudaimonist tradition that may be thought defining of virtue ethics is the view that excellence is the fundamental thin concept of virtue ethics. Nor is this view confined to eudaimonism: it is presupposed in Robert Solomon's (2003) virtue ethical interpretation of Nietzsche.

Let us see how excellence and admirability, both candidates for the basic thin normative concept of virtue ethics, may come into tension. In Aristotelian orthodoxy, as we have seen, it is a necessary condition of a trait being a virtue in an individual that she possesses practical wisdom, at least to a sufficient extent. According to a model suggested by Mencius and Slote (Slote 2007) – a version of Soft Virtue Ethics – a virtue is a disposition of fully developed emotion and motivation, for example having a *fully developed* compassionate *heart*. Such a disposition may be in tension with a fully developed practical wisdom which may require in the agent (especially if he is a general in Ancient Rome for example, or even a doctor in modern times working long hours as a registrar) a certain detachment, even coldness or ruthlessness.

Such a view would show a tension between admirability and excellence on the following assumptions.

(1) It is compassion rather than practical wisdom that marks out what is truly admirable.

(2) Even if a fully developed compassionate heart is admirable it may fail to be an *excellent* disposition since its possessor may lack practical wisdom and knowledge of rituals, conventions, or practices (Hourdequin 2010).

(3) It is a sufficient condition of a trait being a virtue that it be admirable.

There is another source of tension between admirability and excellence. For some, such as myself, it is a sufficient condition of a trait being a virtue that it be excellent, even if not admirable, because for example too "minor" or too easy to achieve. For others, however, it is a necessary condition of a trait being a virtue that it be admirable, and this rules out the "small virtues." Hunt (1997, p. 19) claims for example that "cheerfulness and gracefulness make one an attractive person but not, of themselves, an admirable one." Since, according to Hunt, the notion of a trait of character is conceptually connected to factors relevant to whether one is an admirable person, cheerfulness and gracefulness are ruled out as character traits, let alone virtues. Given differences in the thin concepts of admirability and excellence when applied to virtue, it would be a form of definitional fiat masking substantive issues to define virtue ethics in terms of excellence rather than admirability (or vice versa).

Concept (2): virtue ethics as agent-centered

According to the second concept of virtue ethics the agent (as opposed to virtue notions in general) is in one way or another central to moral theorizing. This section concentrates on explicating the ways in which virtue ethics is often understood as agent-centered (by definition). It is in the last section that I show that a broader concept of virtue ethics – where virtue ethics is seen as centered on virtue notions – is superior for definitional purposes.

It is often thought that virtue ethics is concerned with who we are as opposed to what we do (Rachels 2003). Yet Anscombe's view, a view that is widely credited with ushering in the revival of virtue ethics, concerns the application of virtue terms to *actions* rather than character or motive – "it would be a great improvement," she writes, "if instead of 'morally wrong,' one always named a genus such as 'untruthful,' 'unchaste,' 'unjust'" (1958, p. 10). Furthermore, many (e.g. Hursthouse 1999; D. Solomon 1997) have criticized the view that virtue ethics is not well equipped to offer action guidance (Louden 1984, p. 229) or to account for moral requirement (though they will reject certain metaphysical conceptions of that idea [Anscombe 1958]). Despite this, the basic idea that virtue ethics is agent centered in one or other sense is often thought defining of virtue ethics (Annas 1993).

The understanding of "agent centered" has two main dimensions of variation.

(a) Virtue ethics may be thought to be either character-centered, where a character trait is seen as a complex disposition, or as centered on inner states of the agent which may not always be dispositions but which help constitute or build character, notably motives, emotions, or intentions.

Some believe that virtue ethics by definition is character centered, as suggested by what Watson ([1997] 1990) calls "the primacy of character" thesis. For Watson, "an ethics of virtue is...the...general claim that action appraisal is derivative from the appraisal of character" (p. 58). However, though they have agent-centered views, both Garcia (1990) and Slote (2001) reject the primacy of character thesis. Garcia (1990) claims that "I doubt that character assessment can be conceptually basic in moral thought because I doubt it can be more basic than assessment of actions as virtuous or vicious" (p. 82). Yet Garcia's view is agent centered, since what is basic is the assessment of actions as e.g. benevolent, and "an action is benevolent only if it is done from certain intentions" (p. 82).

Zagzebski's "exemplarist" virtue ethics (2004, p. 39) is also a theory where a basic component of virtue (motivation), rather than character itself, is "fundamental." Since she gives a naturalistic account of a good motive in terms of good emotion (p. 39), it turns out that emotion is fundamental on her view.

There is a second main dimension of variation in agent-centered virtue ethics.

(b) Whether or not agent-centered virtue ethics is character centered or motive/intention/emotion centered, the idea of agent-centeredness can be interpreted in a strong or weak way.

(b1) *Strong agent-centeredness.* The evaluation of action as e.g. right or required is wholly derivable from the evaluation of character, motive, or intention, where those features in turn are evaluated as excellent or admirable

without appeal to further features (such as value or
flourishing) not wholly reducible to virtue.

(b2) *Weak agent-centeredness.* The evaluation of action as
e.g. right or required is wholly derivable from the evaluation of character, motive, or intention, where those
features in turn are evaluated as excellent or admirable
by appealing to further features (such as value or flourishing) not wholly reducible to virtue, but not wholly
independent of virtue.

It is important to distinguish weak agent-centered virtue ethics
from types of virtue theory which are not species of virtue ethics. If
a theory of the nature of virtue holds that a trait is a virtue if it is a
disposition of appropriate responsiveness to value, where the nature
of value is itself understood as wholly independent of virtue, the
resulting virtue theory would not be a virtue ethics but a species of
axiology (value-centered theory) (as in Hurka 2001). What is rejected
by virtue ethics in general are "list theories of the good" which list
so-called values or goods such as pleasure understood as values or
goods entirely independent of virtue.

We may illustrate the difference between the claim that being
valuable or a good is *derivable* from virtue concepts, and the weaker
claim that being valuable or good is not wholly independent of virtue
concepts, in the following way. Consider the difference between
the status of pleasure and failure as goods or bads. For Aristotle,
pleasure, unlike failure, is in some sense a *good*: that is, unlike
failure, it is something that is properly sought by human beings.
However, pleasure as such is not good *"without qualification"* since
vicious pleasures are *not* properly sought by human beings (Aristotle,
Nicomachean Ethics x.5–6). Though the status of pleasure as good
without qualification is not wholly *derivable* from virtue concepts,
that status is not wholly independent of virtue concepts. By the
same token, failure can be seen as in some sense a "bad" since it is
not properly sought by human beings; it is something to be avoided.
However, it is not bad *without qualification*, since failure may occur
without laziness, fecklessness, or other vice, and may be borne with
dignity, uncomplainingly, and nobly by a virtuous agent.[4] Failure
untinged with vice and borne nobly has some aretaic (virtue-related)
value. It cannot be true then that there are only two options, either

the value of pleasure is wholly derivable from virtue, or the value of pleasure is entirely independent of virtue. If these were the only two options we could not distinguish between the aretaic value of temperate pleasure and failure borne nobly.

The same point applies to forms of virtue ethics according to which the status of a trait as a virtue or vice is determined by its connection to human or agent flourishing as opposed to value in general. For eudaimonists, flourishing is not understood entirely independently of virtue (Broadie 2007), even though on modern conceptions the impossibility of flourishing without (sufficient) virtue may be difficult to fathom (Hooker 1996).

Both strong agent-centered and weak agent-centered virtue ethics are well represented in the literature. A version of strong agent-centeredness is Slote's "agent-based" virtue ethics (Slote 1996, 1997, 2001) (see van Zyl, this volume). For example Slote understands rightness (or wrongness) in terms of the motives of the agents performing the acts evaluated:

> (V1) A wrong action is one that reflects, exhibits or expresses an absence of "fully developed empathic concern for (or caring about) others on the part of the agent" (Slote 2007, p. 31).

A weak agent-centered virtue ethics is that of Hursthouse. For example on her account:

> (V2) "An action is right iff it is what a virtuous agent would characteristically (i.e. acting in character) do in the circumstances" (1999, p. 28).

What makes someone a virtuous agent is that she "has and exercises... the virtues," and the virtues are what an agent needs for flourishing (p. 29). For her, what makes an agent flourish is not wholly derivable from virtue.

Concept (3): virtue ethics as centered on virtue notions

On the third concept of virtue ethics, virtue ethics is not necessarily agent centered in either the strong or the weak sense, but is rather centered on virtue notions in general. These may apply to features other than dispositions of character, motives, or intentions of the agent. Virtue notions include the "thick" virtue concepts as applied to acts (e.g. "generous" or "just") and to what Hursthouse (1999) calls the "V-rules" (such as "Be kind," "Be just," "Don't be callous"). Concept (3) of virtue ethics is more inclusive than Concept (2) since it includes both agent-centered and non-agent-centered species of virtue ethics.

Virtue notions also include the targets or aims of virtue, such as the target of the virtue of justice or kindness. The targets of virtues determine the practical success of an agent when acting. On Concept (3) of virtue ethics, criteria of success need not be reducible to the quality of an agent's character, motives, or intentions; nor are they reducible to consequences of actions. For example, successfully meeting the targets of virtues of respect (proper decorum, respect for protocol, and so forth) is not (or not wholly) determined by quality of intention or motive, or by consequences. Again, virtues of love or amity will have as an important target the appropriate *expression* of affection, love, support. Well-motivated loving behavior may miss its target in its infelicity of expression. The virtues of connoisseurship will have as their targets proper appreciation. Targets of individual virtues will thus vary according to the point and function of those virtues.

Virtue notion–centered conceptions of virtue ethics allow for several non-agent-centered conceptions of right action. These include the following.

(V3) An action is right if and only if it conforms to a rule of virtue (such as "Be kind"), where conformity to a rule of virtue is not understood in terms of the choices of virtuous agents.

On this account, the thick virtue concepts are properly applicable to actions, in part, by virtue of a naturally "shapeless" (Little 2000, p. 279) descriptive "resultance" base. These are features *in virtue of which* an act is properly describable as e.g. kind (Dancy 1993). What sorts of acts can properly count as kind is ascertained by reflection on the evaluative point of kindness (Williams 1995a, p. 206). The descriptive resultance base of virtue concepts as applied to acts precludes the application of certain virtue terms to certain acts, regardless of the choices of virtuous agents: it would be impossible for an act to be called kind when it is the act of a school principal deliberately reducing a seriously ill-disciplined pupil to tears, even though the act is benevolently motivated (for the student's own good);[5] impossible for an act (even one chosen by a virtuous agent) to be called just while violating legitimate rules of justice; impossible for an act to be called honest though a lie, even where the lie may be called for.

Another option for a virtue notion–centered conception of right action that is not agent-centered is what might be called a target-centered account of right action (Swanton 2003; see van Zyl, this volume). Here the rightness of acts is not determined by what virtuous, well-motivated, or well-intentioned agents would do or choose, but by their success in hitting the targets of relevant virtues. This understanding of right action is suggested by what I regard as a plausible reading of Aristotle.

According to Aristotle (*Nicomachean Ethics* VI.2, 1139a16–1139b2; see Aristotle 1976) the aim of practical intellect is to arrive at "practical truth":

> To arrive at the truth is indeed the function of intellect in any aspect, but the function of practical intellect is to arrive at the truth that corresponds to right appetition.

The proper operation of practical intellect requires virtue, and as Aristotle claims "virtue aims to hit the mean" (II.6, 1106b16–24). Hitting the mean is the (highly abstractly specified, but multidimensional) target of the virtues, which virtuous agents aim to hit. On this reading, truth in practical matters (hitting the mean – the targets of the virtues) is the general *aim* of practical wisdom. Virtuous persons do not determine practical truth "in the sense of actually constituting (or 'constructing') the truth about particular ethical questions" (Broadie 2007, p. 120).[6]

It is true that Aristotle claims that a "virtue is a purposive disposition, lying in a mean . . . and determined by that which a prudent man would use to determine it" (II.6, 1107a1–2). For Aristotle, what is *used* to determine the mean is indeed, in characteristic cases, the wisdom or reasoning of the (or a) virtuous person, given the absence of universal principles governing most situations, and given the considerable complexity of hitting the mean (for as Aristotle claims there are many ways of missing it: acting at the wrong time, in the wrong way, for the wrong reasons, to excess or deficiency, with respect to the wrong people, deploying the wrong means or instruments, and so on; e.g. II.6, 1106b20–3). The virtuous person is for Aristotle the authoritative figure, for it characteristically takes practical wisdom (rather than rules) to *work out or judge* what is right. Finally it is consistent with the target-centered account that excellence in action (as opposed to mere rightness) requires that an act be done *in the way* a virtuous agent would perform it (Aristotle 1976, II.4).

This kind of position suggests the following virtue notion–centered criterion of right action, where "right" may refer to acts that are commended, required, or permissible, depending on context.

> (V4) Right acts are those that hit the targets of relevant virtues, or at least are those that are sufficiently successful, relative to sufficiently many contextually relevant aspects of the mean (e.g. right reason, right extent, right manner), which together constitute the targets of the relevant virtues.

There is a distinction between strong and weak forms of virtue notion–centered virtue ethics, analogous to that drawn above. (V4) will be a form of strong virtue notion–centeredness if the targets of the virtues are evaluated (as genuine targets of genuine virtues) without appealing to further features that are not wholly reducible to virtue notions. On the weak virtue notion–centered version of (V4), what makes something a target of a virtue (e.g. that the emotions proper to the virtue are fitting or appropriate to the world) is assessed by appealing to further features not wholly reducible to virtue notions, but not wholly independent of them.[7]

Because more than one type of virtue notion may be central in virtue notion–centered ethics (for example virtue notions applied to acts, character, or the targets of virtues) there is complexity and variation in the way these notions could relate to each other. One might distinguish types of virtue notion–centered theory in terms of Kagan's (2000) notion of a "primary evaluative focal point." A primary evaluative focal point is a feature such as an action or a rule, which is evaluated directly in terms of that property which is the ultimate source of justification of the theory (such as consequences or character) and relative to which other (secondary) features are evaluated. The notion of a primary evaluative focal point is illustrated by Kagan with rule consequentialism. Here, rules are the primary evaluative focal point insofar as they are evaluated directly in terms of the property which is the ultimate source of justification of the theory, namely the goodness or badness of consequences. Acts are evaluated indirectly in terms of the rules, and so are not primary evaluative focal points.

Virtue ethics is conventionally thought to have a single primary evaluative focal point (namely an agent-centered feature, such as the character of the agent). It is also conventionally thought that this focal point is evaluated directly by appeal to the property of being needed by the agent for flourishing, with acts evaluated indirectly in terms of the primary evaluative focal point (as in (V2)). In (V1) by contrast, acts are evaluated directly in terms of the ultimate source of justification of the theory (admirability of motive). On conceptions of virtue ethics where virtue notions in general are central, it is possible for acts to be the primary evaluative focal point or for there to be no primary focal point at all, as I illustrate below (pp. 332–3). Further complexity arises if we reject the assumption that there are properties which are ultimate sources of justification as opposed to central sources of justification. Nonfoundational virtue ethical theories which are weakly agent or virtue notion–centered would reject the very idea of ultimate justification.

Do all forms of virtue ethics necessarily have a primary evaluative focal point? Concept (3) of virtue ethics allows for the possibility of virtue theories which are everywhere direct (Kagan 2000), having no primary evaluative focal points. Such a theory may have the following features:

(a) Traits are directly evaluated according to their point or function as virtues of character in the life of a good human being. That point or function is determined by their targets or aims. Some virtues are dispositions targeted at the well-being of the agent, but by no means all. Others are targeted at environmental good, the social fabric, the good of others, the raising of children, the preservation and appreciation of valued aesthetic and cultural objects, productivity, and so on. What makes a trait a virtue is determined directly by its target(s), and it is not a necessary condition of a trait being a virtue that it at least partially constitute or contribute to the flourishing (*eudaimonia*) of the agent. Such a theory then may not conform to Concept (1).

(b) Acts are directly evaluated (as right) in terms of their hitting the targets of virtues.

(c) Conformity of acts to virtue rules for action such as "Be kind" is directly ascertained in terms of correct application of virtue concepts to acts (see above, pp. 329–30, under (V3)).

(d) The sphere (domain of concern) of a virtue is directly evaluated as being the *proper* sphere of a virtue of character by reference to the point or function of that virtue in the life of a good human being. For example, on Hume's view, the point of the *virtue* of justice is respect for the rules of justice (essentially those that pertain to property), as opposed to general utility or personal good, even though the rules themselves are evaluable in terms of long-term consequences for human good. But that does not imply that the sphere of the personal virtue of justice is consequences for the good of humans, either collectively or individually.

THE FAVORED CONCEPT OF VIRTUE ETHICS

I offered above several functions to be served by definitions of virtue ethics, and these determine the adequacy and superiority of definitions. I focus here on three salient functions, which yield the following three criteria for determining the superiority of a concept of virtue ethics. I argue that these suggest the superiority of Concept (3).

(a) Assuming that a definition of virtue ethics has plausibility as a definition of virtue ethics, the more inclusive is that definition the better it is, other things being equal.

The point of this criterion is that exclusion of conceptions will be seen as arbitrary unless there is good reason to exclude them, relative to the function of including moral theoretic traditions which have good claim to be regarded as virtue ethical. Since Concept (3) would include as forms of virtue ethics all theories conforming to Concepts (1) and (2), and more besides, it fares best on this criterion.

Indeed, with interpretations of such figures as Hume, Nietzsche, and the Confucians as virtue ethicists, and the development of varieties of virtue ethics inspired by them, the task of developing a definition of virtue ethics that is more inclusive than traditional eudaimonistic definitions has become more urgent. Humean and Nietzschean virtue ethical interpretations for example have enriched the landscape of substantive ethics, and the interpretation of important philosophers. Here is one example. According to May (1999, p. 25) Nietzsche's "ultimate standard of evaluation" is the "supreme standard" of "life-enhancement" and this may be thought not to involve virtue notions at all, but rather raw notions of power as such, for example. For many, such an interpretation makes his views immoralist or at least unattractively egoistic. If this is a correct interpretation of Nietzsche he should not be understood as a virtue ethicist. However, on my view, his notion of life-enhancement inextricably involves virtue notions largely understood negatively through the idea of distortions of the will to power, and captured in Nietzsche's extremely rich account of the psychology of the "mature individual" throughout his works. This idea in turn has to be understood through an array of virtue and vice notions (Swanton 2005, 2011b). My own inclination is to read both Hume and Nietzsche as having a virtue ethics not conforming to Concept (1) and probably not conforming to Concept (2) (but see Slote 1998a). Yet virtue (and vice) notions are central in their theories.

> (b) A second criterion of superiority of a definition of virtue ethics is its ability to exclude conceptions which are plausibly not virtue ethical relative to the core rationale(s) for such exclusion: in relatively recent times, the demarcation of virtue ethics from consequentialism and deontology.

A major point of that demarcation is the claim of proponents of virtue ethics that theories of that type can make progress on intractable issues not satisfactorily resolved by rival theories.

The application of this criterion raises the issue of the fuzziness of the idea of centrality in my favored Concept (3) of virtue ethics. I agree with Watson (1990, p. 451) that virtue ethics as a type of moral theory should be seen as "a set of theses about how certain concepts are best fitted together for the purposes of understanding morality," and I have understood this idea of fit in terms of the centrality of virtue notions. However, it seems reasonable to say that a theory is virtue ethical if virtue notions are *sufficiently* central in that theory. There may be debate and even vagueness about what counts as sufficient. For example, does a moral theory grounding virtue in responsiveness to valuable properties satisfy the criterion of weak centrality only if there are *no* items whose value is wholly independent of virtue?

An affirmative answer to this question would raise problems for environmental virtue ethics. According to Holmes Rolston III (2005, p. 70) an environmental virtue ethics is committed to the view that "excellence of character is what we are after when we preserve those endangered species," making it appear that for virtue ethics natural objects such as trees and rivers cannot have value independent of excellence of character. But is environmental virtue ethics committed to the implausible view that *all* valuable things such as human beings, rock formations, ancient kauri trees, have value only if for example they are handled virtuously, are created virtuously, are themselves virtuous, promote human virtue, and so on? The solution is not to claim that there cannot be a plausible environmental virtue ethics, but that the thesis of the weak centrality of virtue notions should not be understood as committed to this strong view. It is enough that for weak virtue notion–centered virtue ethics, standard values or goods such as pleasure, achievement, play, creativity, and knowledge are not understood as values or goods entirely independently of virtue.

Even understood in this way, theories subscribing to the weak centrality of virtue notions are distinguishable from, for example, virtue consequentialism, on the assumption that value in general on that theory is understood as wholly independent of virtue. Again, deploying my basic definition of virtue ethics in terms of centrality of virtue or virtue notions in my *Virtue Ethics* (2003), Baron (2011) argues plausibly and in some detail, that for Kant such notions are not sufficiently central for him to qualify as a virtue ethicist. (For other examples of debate about whether or not Kant's virtue theory can be understood as a type of virtue ethics, see Hill 2008; Johnson 2008). Fuzziness is not an inherent vice: what counts as "sufficiently central" can be a matter of interesting debate.

> (c) Thirdly, a core concept of virtue ethics is superior *ceteris paribus* if it makes room for the inclusion of theories which are plausibly virtue ethical, and yet does not inherit the problems arguably besetting other more traditional conceptions of virtue ethics.

Overly narrow concepts of virtue ethics may fail on this criterion. Here I mention (but cannot here discuss) a problem allegedly afflicting Aristotelian and more generally weak agent-centered forms of virtue ethics. This is the problem of the alleged self-centeredness of virtue ethics: basically the objection that the "moral agent [should] keep his or her own character at the centre of his or her practical attention" (D. Solomon 1997 p. 169). This and other forms of the objection have been well addressed by virtue ethicists but "deeper level" versions are still thought problematic and should be taken seriously (Toner 2006). Concept (3) of virtue ethics, which allows for non-agent-centered direct forms of virtue ethics, is not inherently vulnerable to this objection.

Although Concept (3) performs best on criterion (a) and I believe does well on criterion (c), a lingering problem remains. Although Concept (3) excludes some virtue theories as virtue ethical (see criterion (b)), is Concept (3) too inclusive? There are two tests for this. The first is whether deployment of that concept enables us to exclude on good grounds conceptions which are plausibly not virtue-ethical relative to the core rationale(s) for such exclusion: the demarcation of virtue ethics from rival types of theory. I think this test is sufficiently well satisfied (after all virtue consequentialism is excluded; see above, p. 335). Furthermore, we should heed Baron's warning to avoid a "silly protectionist exercise" (2011, p. 34) in demanding strict demarcations between types of theory. The second test is whether virtue ethical theories conforming to Concept (3) (e.g. those inspired by neo-Confucianism, Hume, and Nietzsche) can offer a broader range of solutions or approaches to a range of moral problems relative to their rivals than those supplied by narrower concepts of virtue ethics. These must be at the same time sufficiently distinctive, important, and innovative. What would count as "sufficiently distinctive" will be itself contested, and will be judged by the qualities of the individual work rather than by conformity to some definition of what counts as distinctive.

Finally it should be noted that even in theories where character is not a primary evaluative focal point, for a variety of good reasons character will generally occupy a very important place in such theories.

CONCLUSION

It is encouraging to see that work in virtue ethics is moving away from the negative exercise of claiming superiority over rival types of theory to the much more interesting task of applying virtue ethics to traditional thorny problems in moral philosophy. The official topic of this paper should not disguise what is really at stake in an adequate definition of virtue ethics as a family of theories: the capacity of virtue ethics to offer a distinctive genre of moral theorizing, providing new approaches to old problems, such as the distinction between the moral and the nonmoral, partialism versus impartialism in ethics, the demandingness of ethics, and objectivity. Its reach is also now extending to virtue notion–centered discussions of epistemology and the nature of rationality. It should be made clear that no virtue ethical contribution should be seen as partially defining of virtue ethics: there is plenty of scope for disagreement among virtue ethicists about the best way to resolve important issues. What they have in common is that they are centered on virtue notions.

The definition of virtue ethics is an important issue in the refinement of our understanding about approaches to the resolution of substantive issues in moral philosophy. Rather than closing off possibilities for creative approaches, a good definition should open up space for new solutions to perennial problems. Accordingly I believe virtue ethics should be seen as a family of moral theories with several genera and species. Genera may include Humean and Aristotelian; species, actual Hume and actual Aristotle. And of course species of contemporary virtue ethics may take inspiration from a wide variety of figures, resisting incorporation within a single genus.

NOTES

1 See further McAleer (2007).

2 For example, in his 2010 Svensson claims that virtue ethics is "often associated with, in essence," such an account (p. 255), though he acknowledges that eudaimonism is not essential to virtue ethics (p. 259, n. 4). As late as 2012 Russ Shafer-Landau was asserting in the textbook *The Fundamentals of Ethics* that "virtue ethics insists that we understand right action by reference to what a virtuous person, acting in character, would do" (p. 253).

3 This thesis must be distinguished from the one that (all, most, the most important, certain specified) virtues are necessary for flourishing (D. Russell, Chapter 1 of this volume).

4 See the example in my 2003 of Prada's dignified loss to Team New Zealand in the America Cup defense at Auckland.

5 I thank Charles Pigden for this example.

6   She continues: Aristotle "does not explain ethical truth as what the *phronimos* reliably apprehends: he explains the *phronimos* as reliably apprehending ethical truth" (p. 121). Indeed Slote (1997, p. 178) describes Aristotle as an "act-based" theorist in the sense that being virtuous in relation to action "involves being keyed into facts independent of one's virtuousness about what acts are admirable or called for." On the target-centered view, however, the facts constituting practical truth are not describable independent of virtue notions, specifically virtue notions as applied to acts. Hence the target-centered view is virtue notion–centered. The proper application of virtue notions to acts is a matter of dispute: my own preference is to understand this in line with (V3) above, but developing this view is beyond the scope of this chapter.

7   If a view is not at least weakly virtue notion–centered it cannot be described as virtue ethical. For example, R. Solomon describes my view as understanding virtues as dispositions to be in various kinds of ways responsive to "an independently justified set of values" (R. Solomon 2003, p. 140). If that were my view it would not be virtue ethical on this account, for it would not be even weakly virtue notion–centered. However, that is not my view in my 2003.

BIBLIOGRAPHY

Ackrill, J. 1999 "Aristotle on Eudaimonia," in N. Sherman (ed.), *Aristotle's Ethics: Critical Essays* (Rowman & Littlefield)

Adams, R. 2006 *A Theory of Virtue: Excellence in Being for the Good* (Oxford University Press)

Adkins, A. 1960 *Merit and Responsibility* (Oxford University Press)

Allen, M. 1984 *The Platonism of Marsilio Ficino* (University of California Press)

Alzola, M. Forthcoming "Character and Environment: The Status of Virtues in Organizations"

Forthcoming "Role Virtues," *Journal of Business Ethics*

Angle, S. C. 2009 *Sagehood: The Contemporary Significance of Neo-Confucian Philosophy* (Oxford University Press)

Annas, J. 1988 "Naturalism in Greek Ethics: Aristotle and After," *Proceedings of the Boston Area Colloquium in Ancient Philosophy* 4: 149–71

1993 *The Morality of Happiness* (Oxford University Press)

2004 "Being Virtuous and Doing the Right Thing," *Proceedings and Addresses of the American Philosophical Association* 78: 61–75.

2005 "Virtue Ethics: What Kind of Naturalism," in S. M. Gardiner (ed.), *Virtue Ethics, Old and New* (Cornell University Press)

2006 "Virtue Ethics," in D. Copp (ed.), *The Oxford Companion to Ethical Theory* (Oxford University Press)

2007 "Ethics in Stoic Philosophy," *Phronesis* 22: 58–87

2011 *Intelligent Virtue* (Oxford University Press)

Anscombe, G. E. M. 1957 *Intention* (Blackwell)

1958 "Modern Moral Philosophy," *Philosophy* 33: 1–19

1981 *The Collected Philosophical Papers of G. E. M. Anscombe*, vol. 3: *Ethics, Religion and Politics* (Blackwell)

Aquinas, T. 1973 *De regno*, ed. R. Spiazzi (Marietti)

Árdal, P. S. 1966 *Passion and Value in Hume's* Treatise (Edinburgh University Press)

1976 "Some Implications of the Virtue of Reasonableness in Hume's *Treatise*," in D. W. Livingston and J. T. King (eds.), *Hume: A Reevaluation* (Fordham University Press)

Aristotle 1894 *Ethica Nicomachea*, ed. I. Bywater (Oxford University Press)

1962 *Politics*, trans. T. A. Sinclair (Penguin)

1976 *Nicomachean Ethics*, trans. J. A. K. Thomson, revised by H. Tredennick (Penguin)

1980 *The Nicomachean Ethics*, trans. with intro. by D. W. Ross, revised by J. L. Ackrill and J. O. Urmson (Oxford University Press)

1985 *Nicomachean Ethics*, trans. T. H. Irwin (Hackett Publishing)

Armstrong, A. E. 2007 *Nursing Ethics: A Virtue-Based Approach* (Palgrave Macmillan)

Audi, R. 1997 *Moral Knowledge and Ethical Character* (Oxford University Press)

Baier, A. 1991 *A Progress of Sentiments: Reflections of Hume's Treatise* (Harvard University Press)

1994 "Hume, the Women's Moral Theorist?" (Repr. in *Moral Prejudices*, Harvard University Press)

2008 *Death and Character: Further Reflections on Hume* (Harvard University Press)

Baillie, J. 2000 *Hume on Morality* (Routledge)

Banks, S. and Gallagher, A. 2009 *Ethics in Professional Life: Virtues for Health and Social Care* (Palgrave Macmillan)

Barnes, J. (ed.) 1984 *The Complete Works of Aristotle*, 2 vols. (Princeton University Press)

Baron, M. 2011 "Virtue Ethics in Relation to Kantian Ethics: An Opinionated Overview and Commentary," in L. Jost and J. Wuerth (eds.), *Perfecting Virtue: New Essays on Kantian Ethics and Virtue Ethics* (Cambridge University Press)

Baron, M., Pettit, P., and Slote, M. 1997 *Three Methods of Ethics: A Debate* (Blackwell)

Batson, C. D. 1987 "Prosocial Motivation: Is It Ever Truly Altruistic?" in L. Berkowitz (ed.), *Advances in Experimental Social Psychology* (Academic Press)

Battaly, H. (ed.) 2010 *Virtue and Vice: Moral and Epistemic* (Wiley-Blackwell)

Beaman, A., Barnes, P., Klentz, B., and McQuirk, B. 1978 "Increasing Helping Rates through Information Dissemination: Teaching Pays," *Personality and Social Psychology Bulletin* 4: 406–11

Beauchamp, T. L. and Childress, J. F. 2009 *Principles of Biomedical Ethics*, 6th edn. (Oxford University Press)

Beecher, H. 1966 "Ethics and Clinical Research," *New England Journal of Medicine* 274: 365–72

Björkman, B. 2006 "Why We Are Not Allowed to Sell That Which We Are Encouraged to Donate," *Cambridge Quarterly of Healthcare Ethics* 5: 60–70

Blomme, R. 1958 *La doctrine du péché dans les écoles théologiques de la première moitié du xiie siècle* (Publications Universitaires de Louvain)

Blum, L. A. 1990 "Vocation, Friendship, and Community: Limitations of the Personal–Impersonal Framework," in O. Flanagan and A.O. Rorty (eds.), *Identity, Character, and Morality: Essays in Moral Psychology* (MIT Press)

Bolsin, S., Faunce, T., and Oakley, J. 2005 "Practical Virtue Ethics: Healthcare Whistleblowing and Portable Digital Technology," *Journal of Medical Ethics* 31: 612–18

Booin-Vail, D. 1996 "Don't Stop Thinking about Tomorrow: Two Paradoxes About Duties to Future Generations," *Philosophy and Public Affairs* 25: 267–307

Brady, M. 2004 "Against Agent-Based Virtue Ethics," *Philosophical Papers* 33: 1–10

Broadie, S. 1991 *Ethics with Aristotle* (Oxford University Press)
      2007 "Aristotle and Contemporary Ethics," in *Aristotle and Beyond: Essays on Metaphysics and Ethics* (Cambridge University Press)

Brody, J. K. 1988 "Virtue Ethics, Caring and Nursing," *Scholarly Inquiry for Nursing Practice* 2: 87–96

Brucker, J. 1743 *Historia critica philosophiae* (Breitkopf)

Buchanan, A. E. 2009 "Human Nature and Enhancement," *Bioethics* 23: 141–50
      2011 *Beyond Humanity? The Ethics of Biomedical Enhancement* (Oxford University Press)

Budé, G. 1535 *De transitu Hellenismi ad Christianismum libri tres* (Estienne)
      1775 *Opera Omnia* I (Basel) (Repr. Gregg Press, 1966)

Burke, J. 1985 Speech to the Advertising Council, in W. M. Hoffman and J. M. Moore (eds.), *Management of Values: The Ethical Difference in Corporate Policy and Performance* (McGraw-Hill Book Company)

Burnyeat, M. F. 1980 "Aristotle on Learning to be Good," in A. O. Rorty (ed.), *Essays on Aristotle's Ethics* (University of California Press)

Cafaro, P. 2004 *Thoreau's Living Ethics: Walden and the Pursuit of Virtue* (University of Georgia Press)

Cannold, L. 1998 *The Abortion Myth* (Allen & Unwin)

Carroll, A. 1981 *Business and Society: Managing Corporate Social Performance* (Little, Brown)

Chaiken, S., Giner-Sorolla, R., and Chen, S. 1996 "Beyond Accuracy: Defense and Impression Motives in Heuristic and Systematic Information Processing," in in P. M. Gollwitzer and J. A. Bargh (eds.), *The*

Psychology of Action: Linking Cognition and Motivation to Behavior (Guilford Press)

Chan, W.-T. 1963 *Instructions for Practical Living and Other Neo-Confucian Writings by Wang Yang-ming* (Columbia University Press)

Chappell, T. 1993 "The Virtues of Thrasymachus," *Phronesis* 38: 1–23

2005 "'The Good Man Is the Measure of All Things': Objectivity without World-Centredness in Aristotle's Moral Epistemology," in C. Gill (ed.), *Virtue, Norms, and Objectivity: Issues in Ancient and Modern Ethics* (Oxford University Press)

2011 "Glory as an Ethical Idea," *Philosophical Investigations* 34: 105–34

Chen, A. Y. S., Sawyers, R. B., and Williams, P. F. 1997 "Reinforcing Ethical Decision Making through Corporate Culture," *Journal of Business Ethics* 16: 855–65.

Ching, J. 1976 *To Acquire Wisdom: The Way of Wang Yang-ming* (Columbia University Press)

Churchill, L. R. 1989 "Reviving a Distinctive Medical Ethic," *Hastings Center Report* 19: 28–34.

Cialdini, R. B., Brown, S. L., Lewis, B. P., Luce, C., and Neuberg, S. L. 1997 "Reinterpreting the Empathy–Altruism Relationship: When One into One Equals Oneness," *Journal of Personality and Social Psychology* 73: 481–94

Clark, S. R. L. 1977 *The Moral Status of Animals* (Oxford University Press)

Coase, R. H. 1937 "The Nature of the Firm," *Economica* 4: 386–405

Cohon, R. 2006 *Hume's Morality: Feeling and Fabrication* (Oxford University Press)

Cohon, R. 2008a *Hume's Morality: Feeling and Fabrication* (Oxford University Press)

2008b "Hume's Artificial and Natural Virtues," in S. Traiger (ed.), *The Blackwell Companion to Hume's Treatise* (Blackwell)

Colish, M. L. 1990 *The Stoic Tradition from Antiquity to the Early Middle Ages*, vol. I: *Stoicism in Classical Latin Literature* (Brill)

Collins, J. and Porras, J. 2002 *Built to Last: Successful Habits of Visionary Companies* (HarperCollins)

Coons, C. (Forthcoming) "The Best Expression of Welfarism," in M. Timmins (ed.) *Oxford Studies in Normative Ethics*, vol. 2 (Oxford University Press)

Coope, C. 2007 "Modern Virtue Ethics," in T. Chappell (ed.), *Values and Virtues* (Oxford University Press)

Cooper, J. M. and Hutchinson, D. (eds.) 1997 *Plato: Complete Works* (Hackett Publishing)

Copp, D. and Sobel, D. 2004 "Morality and Virtue: An Assessment of Some Recent Work in Virtue Ethics," *Ethics* 114: 514–54

Crisp, R. (ed.) 1996 *How Should One Live? Essays on the Virtues* (Oxford University Press)

    2005 "Hume on Virtue, Utility and Morality," in S. M. Gardiner (ed.), *Virtue Ethics Old and New* (Cornell University Press)

    2010 "Virtue Ethics and Virtue Epistemology," *Metaphilosophy* 41: 22–40

Crisp, R. and Slote, M. (eds.) 1997 *Virtue Ethics* (Oxford University Press)

Dancy, J. 1993 *Moral Reasons* (Blackwell)

Dare, T. 2004 "Mere-Zeal, Hyper-Zeal and the Ethical Obligations of Lawyers," *Legal Ethics* 7: 24–38

Darwall, S. 2002 *Welfare and Rational Care* (Princeton University Press)

    (ed.) 2003 *Virtue Ethics* (Blackwell)

    2006 *The Second-Person Standpoint* (Harvard University Press)

Das, R. 2003 "Virtue Ethics and Right Action," *Australasian Journal of Philosophy* 81: 324–39

Davie, W. 1999 "Hume and the Monkish Virtues," *Hume Studies* 32: 139–53

de Waele, A. 1620 *Compendium ethicae Aristotelis ad normam veritatis Christianae revocatum* (Elzevir)

Dees, R. H. 1997 "Hume on the Characters of Virtue," *Journal of the History of Philosophy* 35: 45–64

Diels, H. (ed.) 1882–1909 *Commentaria in Aristotelem Graeca*, 23 vols. (Reimers)

Dodds, E. R. 1951 *The Greeks and the Irrational* (Cambridge University Press)

Doris, J. 1998 "Persons, Situations, and Virtue Ethics," *Nôus* 32: 504–30

    2002 *Lack of Character: Personality and Moral Behavior* (Cambridge University Press)

Doris, J. and Stich, S. 2005 "As a Matter of Fact: Empirical Perspectives on Ethics," in F. Jackson and M. Smith (eds.), *The Oxford Handbook of Contemporary Analytic Philosophy* (Oxford University Press)

Doviak, D. 2011 "A New Form of Agent-Based Virtue Ethics," *Ethical Theory and Moral Practice*

Drane, J. F. 1988 *Becoming a Good Doctor: The Place of Virtue and Character in Medical Ethics* (Sheed & Ward)

Driver, J. 1989 "The Virtues of Ignorance," *Journal of Philosophy* 86: 373–84

    2001 *Uneasy Virtue* (Cambridge University Press)

Edmundson, W. 1998 *Three Anarchical Fallacies* (Cambridge University Press)

Emery, K. 1983 "Reading the World Rightly and Squarely: Bonaventure's Doctrine of the Cardinal Virtues," *Traditio* 39: 183–218

Engstrom, S. and Whiting, J. (eds.) 1996 *Rethinking Duty and Happiness: Aristotle, Kant, and the Stoics* (Cambridge University Press)

Epley, N. and Dunning, D. 2000 "Feeling 'Holier than Thou': Are Self-Serving Assessments Produced by Errors in Self or Social Prediction?" *Journal of Personality and Social Psychology* 79: 861–75

Farrelly, C. 2007 "Virtue Ethics and Prenatal Genetic Enhancement," *Studies in Ethics, Law, and Technology* 1: 1–13

Feinberg, J. 1972 "The Nature and Value of Rights," *Journal of Value Inquiry* 4: 243–57

Feinberg, J. 1986 "Wrongful Life and the Counterfactual Element in Harming," *Social Philosophy and Policy* 4: 145–78

Festinger, L. 1957 *A Theory of Cognitive Dissonance* (Stanford University Press)

Ficino, M. 2001–6 *Platonic Theology*, ed. and trans. M. Allen and J. Hankins, 6 vols. (Harvard University Press)

Foot, P. 1977 "Euthanasia," *Philosophy and Public Affairs* 6: 85–112
    1978a "Moral Arguments," in *Virtues and Vices* (University of California Press)
    1978b "Moral Beliefs," in *Virtues and Vices* (University of California Press)
    2001 *Natural Goodness* (Oxford University Press)

Frank, R. 1988 *Passions within Reason: The Strategic Role of the Emotions* (W. W. Norton)
    2004 *What Price the Moral High Ground? Ethical Dilemmas in Competitive Environments* (Princeton University Press)

Frankfurt, H. G. 1981 "Freedom of the Will and the Concept of a Person," in G. Watson (ed.), *Free Will* (Oxford University Press)

Freeman, R. E. 1994 "The Politics of Stakeholder Theory: Some Future Directions," *Business Ethics Quarterly* 4: 409–21

Freeman, R. E., Harrison, J., and Wicks, A. 2007 *Managing for Stakeholders: Survival, Reputation, and Success* (Yale University Press)

Friedman, M. 1970 "The Social Responsibility of Business Is to Increase Its Profits," *New York Times Magazine*, September 13

Fröding, B. 2011 "Cognitive Enhancement, Virtue Ethics and the Good Life," *Neuroethics* 4: 223–34

Gaita, R. 1991 *Good and Evil: An Absolute Conception* (Routledge)

Garcia, J. L. A. 1990 "The Primacy of the Virtuous," *Philosophia* 20: 69–91

Gardiner, P. 2003 "A Virtue Ethics Approach to Moral Dilemmas in Medicine," *Journal of Medical Ethics* 29: 297–302

Gaus, G. 1996 *Justificatory Liberalism* (Oxford University Press)

Gaus, G. 2010 "Coercion, Ownership, and the Redistributive State: Justificatory Liberalism's Classical Tilt," *Social Philosophy and Policy* 27: 233–75

Geach, P. 1977 *The Virtues* (Cambridge University Press)

Gelfand, S. 2000 "Hypothetical Agent-Based Virtue Ethics," *Southwest Philosophy Review* 17: 85–94

Ghoshal, S. 2005 "Bad Management Theories Are Destroying Good Management Practices," *Academy of Management Learning and Education* 4: 75–91

Gigerenzer, G. 2000 *Adaptive Thinking: Rationality in the Real World* (Oxford University Press)

Gilbert, D. 2005 *Stumbling upon Happiness* (Alfred Knopf)

1982 *In a Different Voice* (Harvard University Press)

Girod, J. and Beckman, A. W. 2005 "Just Allocation and Team Loyalty: A New Virtue Ethic for Emergency Medicine," *Journal of Medical Ethics* 31: 567–70

Goldberg, D. 2008 "Pragmatism and Virtue Ethics in Clinical Research," *American Journal of Bioethics* 8: 43–5

Gollwitzer and J. A. Bargh (eds.), *The Psychology of Action: Linking Cognition and Motivation to Behavior* (Guilford Press)

Gottlieb, P. 2009 *The Virtue of Aristotle's Ethics* (Cambridge University Press)

Graham, A. C. 1989 *Disputers of the Tao: Philosophical Argument in Ancient China* (Open Court)

H. S. Richardson (eds.), *Liberalism and the Good* (Routledge)

Hacker-Wright, J. 2007 "Moral Status in Virtue Ethics," *Philosophy* 82: 449–73

2010 "Virtue Ethics without Right Action: Anscombe, Foot, and Contemporary Virtue Ethics," *Journal of Value Inquiry* 44: 209–24

Haidt, J. 2001 "The Emotional Dog and Its Rational Tail: A Social Intuitionist Approach to Moral Judgment," *Psychological Review* 108: 814–34

2006 *The Happiness Hypothesis* (Basic Books)

Hampton, J. 1993 "Selflessness and Loss of Self," *Social Philosophy and Policy* 10: 135–65

Hare, R. M. 1994 "Methods of Bioethics: Some Defective Proposals," *Monash Bioethics Review* 13: 34–47 (Repr. in L. W. Sumner and Joseph Boyle, eds., *Philosophical Perspectives on Bioethics*, University of Toronto Press, 1996)

Harman, G. 1998 "Moral Philosophy Meets Social Psychology: Virtue Ethics and the Fundamental Attribution Error," *Proceedings of the Aristotelian Society* 99: 315–31

1999 "Moral Psychology Meets Social Psychology: Virtue Ethics and the Fundamental Attribution Error," *Proceedings of the Aristotelian Society* 99: 315–31

2000 "The Nonexistence of Character Traits," *Proceedings of the Aristotelian Society* 100: 223–6

2001 "Virtue Ethics without Character Traits," in A. Byrne, R. Stalnaker, and R. Wedgwood (eds.), *Fact and Value: Essays on Ethics and Metaphysics for Judith Jarvis Thomson* (MIT Press)

Harris, C. E., Pritchard, M. S., and Rabins, M. S. 2008 *Engineering Ethics: Concepts and Cases* (Wadsworth)

Hartman, E. 2006 "Can We Teach Character? An Aristotelian Answer," *Academy of Management Learning and Education* 5: 68–81.

2008 "Socratic Questions and Aristotelian Answers: A Virtue-Based Approach to Business Ethics," *Journal of Business Ethics* 78: 313–28

Hartshorne, H. and May, M. 1928 *Studies in the Nature of Character*, vol. I, *Studies in Deceit* (Macmillan)

Haybron, D. M. 2008 *The Pursuit of Unhappiness* (Oxford University Press)

Hayek, F. 1978 "Why I Am Not a Conservative," in *The Constitution of Liberty* (University of Chicago Press)

Held, V. 2006 "The Ethics of Care," in D. Copp (ed.), *The Oxford Handbook of Ethical Theory* (Oxford University Press)

Higgs, R. 2007 "Truth-Telling, Lying, and the Doctor–Patient Relationship," in R. Ashcroft, A. Dawson, H. Draper, and J. McMillan (eds.), *Principles of Health Care Ethics*, 2nd edn. (John Wiley)

Hill Jr., T. E. 2005 "Ideals of Human Excellence and Preserving Natural Environments," in R. Sandler and P. Cafaro (eds.), *Environmental Virtue Ethics* (Rowman & Littlefield)

2008 "Kantian Virtue and 'Virtue Ethics,'" in M. Betzler (ed.), *Kant's Ethics of Virtue* (Walter de Gruyter)

Hirschman, A. 1982 "Rival Interpretations of Market Society: Civilizing, Destructive, or Feeble?" *Journal of Economic Literature* 20: 1463–84

Hoffman, M. L. 2007 *Empathy and Moral Development: Implications for Caring and Justice* (Cambridge University Press)

Holland, S. 2010 "Scepticism about the Virtue Ethics Approach to Nursing Ethics," *Nursing Philosophy* 11: 151–8

2011 "The Virtue Ethics Approach to Bioethics," *Bioethics* 25: 192–201

Homer, J. S. 2000 "For Debate: The Virtuous Public Health Physician," *Journal of Public Health Medicine* 22: 48–53

Hooker, B. 1996 "Does Moral Virtue Constitute a Benefit to the Agent?" in R. Crisp (ed.), *How Should One Live? Essays on the Virtues* (Oxford University Press)

Hourdequin, M. 2010 "The Limits of Empathy," paper read at the American Philosophical Association, Pacific Division, conference, March 31–April 3.

Huemer, M. 2008 "In Defence of Repugnance," *Mind* 117: 899–933

Hume, D. [1739–40] 2000 *A Treatise of Human Nature*, ed. D. F. Norton and M. J. Norton (Oxford University Press)

[1740] 2000 *An Abstract of A Treatise of Human Nature*, in *A Treatise of Human Nature*, ed. D. F. Norton and M. J. Norton (Oxford University Press)

[1748] 2000 *An Enquiry concerning Human Understanding*, ed. T. L. Beauchamp (Oxford University Press)

[1751] 1998 *Enquiry concerning the Principles of Morals*, ed. T. L. Beauchamp (Oxford University Press)

[1757] 1993 *Natural History of Religion*, in *A Dissertation on the Passions, The Natural History of Religion*, ed. T. L. Beauchamp (Oxford University Press)

[1757] 2007 *A Dissertation on the Passions*, in *A Dissertation on the Passions, The Natural History of Religion*, ed. T. L. Beauchamp (Oxford University Press)

[1777] 1985 *Essays: Moral, Political, and Literary*, rev. edn., ed. E. F. Miller (Liberty Classics)

[1778] 1983 *The History of England*, 6 vols., foreward by W. B. Todd (Liberty Classics)

[1779] 1993 *Dialogues concerning Natural Religion*, in *Dialogues and Natural History of Religion*, ed. J. A. C. Gaskin (Oxford University Press)

1932 *The Letters of David Hume*, 2 vols., ed. J. Y. T. Greig (Oxford University Press)

1975 *Enquiries Concerning Human Understanding and Concerning the Principles of Morals*, 3rd edn, ed. P. H. Nidditch (Oxford: University Press)

1978 *A Treatise of Human Nature*, ed. L. A. Selby-Bigge (Oxford University Press)

Hunt, L. H. 1997 *Character and Culture* (Rowman & Littlefield)

Hurka, T. 2001 *Virtue, Vice and Value* (Oxford University Press)

2006 "Virtuous Act, Virtuous Dispositions," *Analysis* 66: 69–76

Hursthouse, R. 1980–81 "A False Doctrine of the Mean," *Proceedings of the Aristotelian Society* 81: 52–72

1987 *Beginning Lives* (Blackwell)

1990–91 "After Hume's Justice," *Proceedings of the Aristotelian Society* 91: 229–45

1991 "Virtue Theory and Abortion," *Philosophy and Public Affairs* 20: 223–46

1993 "Slote on Self-Sufficiency," *Journal of Social Philosophy* 24: 57–67.

1995a "The Virtuous Agent's Reasons: A Reply to Bernard Williams," in R. Heinaman (ed.), *Aristotle on Moral Realism* (Westview Press)

1995b "Applying Virtue Ethics," in R. Hursthouse, G. Lawrence, and W. Quinn (eds.), *Virtues and Reasons: Philippa Foot and Moral Theory: Essays in Honour of Philippa Foot* (Oxford University Press)

1996 "Normative Virtue Ethics," in R. Crisp (ed.), *How Should one Live? Essays on the Virtues* (Oxford University Press)

1999 *On Virtue Ethics* (Oxford University Press)

2006a "Practical Wisdom: A Mundane Account," *Proceedings of the Aristotelian Society* 106: 283–307

2006b "Are Virtues the Proper Starting Point for Morality?" in J. Dreier (ed.), *Contemporary Debates in Moral Theory* (Blackwell)

2006c "Applying Virtue Ethics to our Treatment of the Other Animals," in J. Welchman (ed.), *The Practice of Virtue: Classic and Contemporary Readings in Virtue Ethics* (Hackett Publishing)

2007a "Environmental Virtue Ethics," in R. L. Walker and P. J. Ivanhoe (eds.), *Working Virtue: Virtue Ethics and Contemporary Moral Problems* (Oxford University Press)

2007b (revised) "Virtue Ethics," *Stanford Encyclopedia of Philosophy* (online)

2008 "The Good and Bad Family," in L. Thomas (ed.), *Contemporary Debates in Social Philosophy* (Blackwell)

Hutcheson, F. [1726] 2004 *An Inquiry into the Original of our Ideas of Beauty and Virtue*, 2nd edn., ed. W. Leidhold (Liberty Fund)

Hutton, E. L. 2002a "Moral Reasoning in Aristotle and Xunzi," *Journal of Chinese Philosophy* 29: 355–84

2002b "Moral Connoisseurship in Mengzi," in Liu Xiusheng and P. J. Ivanhoe (eds.), *Essays on the Moral Philosophy of Mengzi* (Hackett Publishing)

Imber, J. B. 2008 *Trusting Doctors: The Decline of Moral Authority in American Medicine* (Princeton University Press)

Inwood, B. and Gerson, L. (trans., eds.) 1988 *Hellenistic Philosophy* (Hackett Publishing)

(trans., eds.) 1994 *The Epicurus Reader* (Hackett Publishing)

Irwin, T. 1989 *Classical Thought* (Oxford University Press)

2000 "Ethics as an Inexact Science," in B. Hooker and M. O. Little (eds.), *Moral Particularism* (Oxford University Press)

2007 *The Development of Ethics*, vol. i: *From Socrates to the Reformation* (Oxford University Press)

2008 *The Development of Ethics*, vol. ii: *From Suarez to Rousseau* (Oxford University Press)

Ivanhoe, P. J. 2000 *Confucian Moral Self Cultivation*, 2nd edn. (Hackett Publishing)

2002 *Ethics in the Confucian Tradition: The Thought of Mengzi and Wang Yangming*, 2nd edn. (Hackett Publishing)

2007a "Literature and Ethics in the Chinese Confucian Tradition," in B. Wilburn (ed.), *Moral Cultivation* (Rowan & Littlefield)

2007b "Filial Piety as a Virtue," in R. Walker and P. J. Ivanhoe (eds.) *Working Virtue: Virtue Ethics and Contemporary Moral Problems* (Oxford University Press)

2009a *Readings from the Lu-Wang School of Neo-Confucianism* (Hackett Publishing)

2009b "Pluralism, Toleration, and Ethical Promiscuity," *Journal of Religious Ethics* 37: 311–29

2011 "Moral Perception in McDowell, Wang, and Mengzi," *Dao: A Journal of Comparative Philosophy* 10: 273–90

Forthcoming "Kongzi and Aristotle as Virtue Ethicists," in Li Chenyang (ed.), *Character and Moral Cultivation: East and West*

Jacobson, D. 2002 "An Unsolved Problem for Slote," *Philosophical Studies* 111: 53–67

Jansen, L. A. 2000 "The Virtues in Their Place: Virtue Ethics in Medicine," *Theoretical Medicine* 21: 261–76

Jensen, M. and Mechling, W. 1976 "Theory of the Firm: Managerial Behaviour, Agency Costs, and Ownership Structure," *Journal of Financial Economics* 3: 305–60

Johnson & Johnson 1940 *Credo* (Johnson & Johnson)

Johnson, R. 2003 "Virtue and Right," *Ethics* 113: 810–34

2008 "Was Kant a Virtue Ethicist?," in M. Betzler (ed.), *Kant's Ethics of Virtue* (Walter de Gruyter)

Jost, L. and Wuerth, J. (eds.) 2011 *Perfecting Virtue: New Essays on Kantian Ethics and Virtue Ethics* (Cambridge University Press)

Kagan, S. 2000 "Evaluative Focal Points," in B. Hooker, E. Mason, and D. E. Miller (eds.), *Morality, Rules, and Consequences: A Critical Reader* (Edinburgh University Press)

Kamtekar, R. 1998 "Imperfect Virtue," *Ancient Philosophy* 18: 315–39

2004 "Situationism and Virtue Ethics on the Content of our Character," *Ethics* 114: 458–91

Kant, I. 1785 *Grundlegung zur Metaphysik der Sitten* (Hartknoch)

1797 *Die Metaphysik der Sitten* (Nicolovius)

1996 *Metaphysics of Morals*, ed. and trans. M. Gregor (Cambridge University Press)

Kass, L. 1989 "Neither for Love nor Money: Why Doctors Must Not Kill," *Public Interest* 94: 25–46

Kawall, J. 2002 "Virtue Theory and Ideal Observers," *Philosophical Studies* 109: 197–222

2003 "Reverence for Life as a Viable Environmental Virtue," *Environmental Ethics* 25: 339–58

2009 "In Defense of the Primacy of the Virtues," *Journal of Ethics and Social Philosophy* 3: 1–21

Kent, B. 1995 *Virtues of the Will: The Transformation of Ethics in the Late Thirteenth Century* (Catholic University of America Press)

  2003 "Rethinking Moral Dispositions: Scotus on the Virtues," in T. Williams (ed.), *The Cambridge Companion to Duns Scotus* (Cambridge University Press)

Kornegay, R. J. 2011 "Hursthouse's Virtue Ethics and Abortion: Abortion Ethics without Metaphysics?" *Ethical Theory and Moral Practice* 14: 51–71

Korsgaard, C. 1986 "Aristotle on Function and Virtue," *History of Philosophy Quarterly* 3: 259–79

  1993 "The Reasons We Can Share: An Attack on the Distinction between Agent-Relative and Agent-Neutral Values," *Social Philosophy and Policy* 10: 24–51

Kraut, R. 1979 "Two Conceptions of Happiness," *Philosophical Review* 88: 167–97

  1999 "Politics, Neutrality, and the Good," *Social Philosophy and Policy* 16: 315–32

Kraye, J. 1991 "Moral Philosophy," in C. Schmidt *et al.* (eds.), *The Cambridge History of Renaissance Philosophy* (Cambridge University Press)

  1996 "Philologists and Philosophers," in J. Kraye (ed.), *The Cambridge Companion to Renaissance Humanism* (Cambridge University Press)

Kupperman, J. 1999 *Learning from Asian Philosophy* (Oxford University Press)

Kurlander, J. E. and Danis, M. 2007 "Organisational Ethics in Health Care," in R. Ashcroft, A. Dawson, H. Draper, and J. McMillan (eds.), *Principles of Health Care Ethics*, 2nd edn. (John Wiley)

Lebacqz, K. 1985 "The Virtuous Patient," in E. Shelp (ed.), *Virtue and Medicine* (Reidel)

LeBar, M. 2004 "Good for You," *Pacific Philosophical Quarterly* 85: 195–217

  2009 "Virtue Ethics and Deontic Constraints," *Ethics* 119: 642–71

Lenman, J. 2005 "The Saucer of Mud, the Kudzu Vine and the Uxorious Cheetah: Against Neo-Aristotelianism in Metaethics," *European Journal of Applied Philosophy* 1: 37–50

Leopold, A. 1966 *A Sand County Almanac* (Oxford University Press)

Li Chenyang 2000 "The Confucian Concept of *Jen* and the Feminist Ethics of Care: A Comparative Study," in Li Chenyang (ed.), *The Sage and the Second Sex: Confucianism, Ethics, and Gender* (Open Court Publishing Company)

Lieberman, M. 2000 "Intuition: A Social Cognitive Neuroscience Approach," *Psychological Bulletin* 126: 109–37

Lines, D. 2002 *Aristotle's Ethics in the Italian Renaissance (ca. 1300–1650): The Universities and the Problem of Education* (Brill)

Little, M. O. 2000 "Moral Generalities Revisited," in B. Hooker and M. Little (eds.), *Moral Particularism* (Oxford University Press)

Litton, P. and Miller, F. 2005 "A Normative Justification for Distinguishing the Ethics of Clinical Research from the Ethics of Medical Care," *Journal of Law, Medicine and Ethics* 33: 566–74

Liu Xiusheng 2002 "Mencius, Hume, and Sensibility Theory," *Philosophy East and West* 52: 75–97

    2003 *Mencius, Hume, and the Foundations of Ethics: Humanity in Ethics* (Ashgate)

Long, A. A. 1988 "Socrates in Hellenistic Philosophy," *Classical Quarterly* 38: 150–71 (Repr. in *Stoic Studies*, Cambridge University Press, 1996)

Lottin, O. 1942–50 *Psychologie et morale aux xii et xiii siècles*, 6 vols. (Abbaye Du Mont Cesar)

Louden, R. 1984 "On Some Vices of Virtue Ethics," *American Philosophical Quarterly* 21: 227–36

Luban, D. 2003 "Integrity: Its Causes and Cures," *Fordham Law Review* 72: 279–310

Luker, K. 1984 *Abortion and the Politics of Motherhood* (University of California Press)

Luther, M. 1523 *Von weltlicher Obrigkeit* (Wittenberg) (Repr. Hänssler 1996)
    1883 *D. Martin Luthers Werke* (Hermann Böhlau), vols. 1 and 11

MacIntyre, A. 1981 *After Virtue*, 1st edn. (University of Notre Dame Press)

MacIntyre, A. 1984 *After Virtue*, 2nd edn. (University of Notre Dame Press)
    1988 *Whose Justice? Which Rationality?* (Duckworth)
    1991 *Three Rival Versions of Moral Inquiry* (Duckworth)

Mackie, J. L. 1977 *Ethics: Inventing Right and Wrong* (Pelican)

Makeham, J. 2010 *Neo-Confucian Philosophy* (Springer)

Marenbon, J. 1997 *The Philosophy of Peter Abelard* (Cambridge University Press)

Markus, H. R. and Kitayama, S. 1991 "Culture and the Self: Implications for Cognition, Emotion, and Motivation," *Psychological Review* 98: 225–53

Martin, M. 2006 *From Morality to Mental Health: Virtue and Vice in a Therapeutic Culture* (Oxford University Press)

Mathews, F. 2001 "the World Grow Old: An Ethos of Countermodernity," in D. Schmidtz and E. Willott (eds.), *Environmental Ethics: What Really Matters, What Really Works* (Oxford University Press)

May, S. 1999 *Nietzsche's Ethics and his War on Morality* (Oxford University Press)

May, W. F. 1994 "The Virtues in a Professional Setting," in K. W. M. Fulford, G. Gillett, and J. M. Soskice (eds.), *Medicine and Moral Reasoning* (Cambridge University Press)

McAleer S. 2007 "An Aristotelian Account of Virtue Ethics: An Essay in Moral Taxonomy," *Pacific Philosophical Quarterly* 88: 208–225

McCloskey, D. 1996 *The Bourgeois Virtues: Ethics for an Age of Commerce* (University of Chicago Press)

McDougall, R. 2005 "Acting Parentally: An Argument against Sex Selection," *Journal of Medical Ethics* 31: 601–5

   2007 "Parental Virtue: A New Way of Thinking about the Morality of Reproductive Actions," *Bioethics* 21: 181–90

   2009 "Impairment, Flourishing and the Moral Nature of Parenthood," in K. Brownlee and A. Cureton (eds.), *Disability and Disadvantage* (Oxford University Press)

McDowell, J. 1979 "Virtue and Reason," *Monist* 42: 331–50

   1980 "The Role of *Eudaimonia* in Aristotle's Ethics," in A. O. Rorty (ed.), *Essays on Aristotle's Ethics* (University of California)

   1995a "Two Sorts of Naturalism," in R. Hursthouse, G. Lawrence, and W. Quinn (eds.), *Virtues and Reasons: Philippa Foot and Moral Theory* (Oxford University Press)

   1995b "Eudaimonism and Realism in Aristotle's Ethics," in R. Heinaman (ed.), *Aristotle and Moral Realism* (University College London)

   1996 *Mind and World* (Harvard University Press)

Melanchthon, P. 1843 *De Aristotele*. In *Opera quae supersunt omnia*, ed. C.G. Bretschneider and H. E. Bindseil (Schwetschke), vol. 11

   1850 *Enarrationes aliquot librorum Ethicorum Aristotelis*. In *Opera quae supersunt omnia*, ed. C. G. Bretschneider and H. E. Bindseil (Schwetschke), vol. 16

Menn, S. 1997 "Physics as a Virtue," *Proceedings of the Boston Area Colloquium in Ancient Philosophy* 11: 1–34

Merritt, M. 2000 "Virtue Ethics and Situationist Personality Psychology," *Ethical Theory and Moral Practice* 3: 365–83

Merritt, M., Doris, J. and Harman, G. 2010 "Character," in J. Doris *et al.* (eds.), *The Oxford Handbook of Moral Psychology* (Oxford University Press)

Milgram, S. 1974 *Obedience to Authority: An Experimental View* (Harper & Row)

Miller, C. 2003 "Social Psychology and Virtue Ethics," *Journal of Ethics* 7: 365–92

   2009 "Social Psychology, Mood, and Helping: Mixed Results for Virtue Ethics," *Journal of Ethics* 13: 145–73

2010 "Character Traits, Social Psychology, and Impediments to Helping Behavior," *Journal of Ethics and Social Philosophy* 5, www.jesp.org

Moore, G. 2002 "On the Implications of the Practice–Institution Distinction: MacIntyre and the Application of Modern Virtue Ethics to Business," *Business Ethics Quarterly* 12: 19–32

2005a "Corporate Character: Modern Virtue Ethics and the Virtuous Corporation," *Business Ethics Quarterly* 15: 659–85

2005b "Humanizing Business: A Modern Virtue Ethics Approach," *Business Ethics Quarterly* 15: 237–55

2008 "Re-imagining the Morality of Management: A Modern Virtue Ethics Approach," *Business Ethics Quarterly* 18: 483–511

2009 "Virtue Ethics and Business Organizations," in J. D. Smith (ed.), *Normative Theory and Business Ethics* (Rowman & Littlefield)

2012 "The Virtue of Governance, the Governance of Virtue," *Business Ethics Quarterly* 22: 293–318

Moore, G. E. 1903 *Principia Ethica* (Cambridge University Press)

Murdoch, I. 1970 *The Sovereignty of Good* (Routledge & Kegan Paul)

Narveson, J. 1967 "Utilitarianism and New Generations," *Mind* 76: 62–72

Nederman, C. J. 1991 "Aristotelianism and the Origins of 'Political Science' in the Twelfth Century," *Journal of the History of Ideas* 52: 179–94

Nietzsche, F. 1973 *Beyond Good and Evil*, trans. R. J. Hollingdale (Penguin)

1996 *On the Genealogy of Morals*, trans. D. Smith (Oxford University Press)

Noddings, N. 1986 *Caring: A Feminist Approach to Ethics and Moral Education* (University of California Press)

Nussbaum, M. 1986 *The Fragility of Goodness* (Cambridge University Press)

1988 "Nature, Function, and Capability: Aristotle on Political Distribution," *Oxford Studies in Ancient Philosophy*, supp. 1: 145–84

1990a "Aristotelian Social Democracy," in R. B. Douglass, G. M. Mara, and H. S. Richardson (eds.), *Liberalism and the Good* (Routledge)

1990b *Love's Knowledge* (Oxford University Press)

1992 "Human Functioning and Social Justice: In Defense of Aristotelian Essentialism," *Political Theory* 20: 202–46

1993 "Non-Relative Virtues: An Aristotelian Approach," in M. Nussbaum and A. Sen (eds.), *The Quality of Life* (Oxford University Press)

1995 "Aristotle on Human Nature and the Foundations of Ethics," in J. E. J. Altham and R. Harrison (eds.), *World, Mind, and Ethics: Essays on the Ethical Philosophy of Bernard Williams* (Cambridge University Press)

2006 *Frontiers of Justice: Disability, Nationality, Species Membership* (Harvard University Press)

2011 "Perfectionist Liberalism and Political Liberalism," *Philosophy and Public Affairs* 39: 3–45

Oakley, J. 1994 "Sketch of a Virtue Ethics Approach to Health Care Resource Allocation," *Monash Bioethics Review* 13: 27–33

1996 "Varieties of Virtue Ethics," *Ratio* 9: 128–52

2009 "A Virtue Ethics Approach," in H. Kuhse and P. Singer (eds.), *A Companion to Bioethics*, 2nd edn. (Blackwell)

Oakley, J. and Cocking, D. 2001 *Virtue Ethics and Professional Roles* (Cambridge University Press)

Parfit, D. 1984 *Reasons and Persons* (Oxford University Press)

Park, K. 1988 "The Organic Soul," in C. B. Schmitt *et al.* (eds.), *The Cambridge History of Renaissance Philosophy* (Cambridge University Press)

Pasnau, R. 2002 *Thomas Aquinas on Human Nature: A Philosophical Study of Summa Theologiae Ia 75–89* (Cambridge University Press)

Pellegrino, E. D. 1995 "Toward a Virtue-Based Normative Ethics for the Health Professions," *Kennedy Institute of Ethics Journal* 5: 253–77

2007 "Professing Medicine, Virtue Based Ethics, and the Retrieval of Professionalism," in R. L. Walker and P. J. Ivanhoe (eds), *Working Virtue: Virtue Ethics and Contemporary Moral Problems* (Oxford University Press)

Pellegrino, E. D. and Thomasma, D. C. 1981 *A Philosophical Basis of Medical Practice* (Oxford University Press)

1988 *For the Patient's Good: The Restoration of Beneficence in Health Care* (Oxford University Press)

1993 *The Virtues in Medical Practice* (Oxford University Press)

Pence, G. 1980 *Ethical Options in Medicine* (Medical Economics Company)

Percival, T. 1803 *Medical Ethics, or a Code of Institutions and Precepts Adapted to the Professional Conduct of Physicians and Surgeons* (Classics of Medicine Library, 1985)

Petersen, P. 1921 *Die Geschichte der aristotelischen Philosophie im protestantischen Deutschland* (Felix Meiner)

Pico della Mirandola, G. 1942 *De hominis dignitate*, ed. E. Garin (Valechi)

Pitson, A. E. 2002 *Hume's Philosophy of the Self* (Routledge)

Porter, J. 2005 *Nature as Reason: A Thomistic Theory of the Natural Law* (Eerdmans Press)

Posner, R. 1983 *The Economics of Justice*, 2nd edn. (Harvard University Press)

Post, S. G. 2003 *Encyclopedia of Bioethics*, 3rd edn. (Macmillan)

Pronin, E., Lin, D. Y., and Ross, L. 2002 "The Bias Blind Spot: Perceptions of Bias in Self versus Others," *Personality and Social Psychology Bulletin* 28: 369–81

Putnam, H. 2002 *The Collapse of the Fact/Value Dichotomy and Other Essays* (Harvard University Press)

Rachels, J. 1975 "Active and Passive Euthanasia," *New England Journal of Medicine* 292: 78–80

2003 *The Elements of Moral Philosophy*, 4th edn. (McGraw-Hill)

Radden, J. and Sadler, J. Z. 2010 *The Virtuous Psychiatrist: Character Ethics in Psychiatric Practice* (Oxford University Press)

Railton, P. 1984 "Alienation, Consequentialism, and the Demands of Morality," *Philosophy and Public Affairs* 13: 137–71

Rasmussen, D. and Den Uyl, D. 1991 *Liberty and Nature* (Open Court)

2005 *Norms of Liberty* (Penn State Press)

Rawls, J. 1971 *A Theory of Justice* (Harvard University Press)

1993 *Political Liberalism* (Columbia University Press)

Reid, T. (1969) *Essays on the Active Powers of the Human Mind*, with an introduction by B. Brody (MIT Press)

Reisch, G. 1512 *Margarita philosophica nova* (Grüninger)

Richards, N. 1984 "Double Effect and Moral Character," *Mind* 93: 381–97

Rist, J. 1994 *Augustine: Ancient Thought Baptized* (Cambridge University Press)

Rogers, W. A. 2004 "Virtue Ethics and Public Health: A Practice-Based Analysis," *Monash Bioethics Review* 23: 10–21

Rolston III, H. 2005 "Environmental Virtue Ethics: Half the Truth but Dangerous as a Whole," in R. Sandler and P. Cafaro (eds.), *Environmental Virtue Ethics* (Rowman & Littlefield)

Rosenzweig, P. 2007 *The Halo Effect: . . . and the Eight Other Business Delusions that Deceive Managers* (Free Press)

Ross, L. and Nisbett, R. E. 1991 *The Person and the Situation* (Temple University Press)

Ross, W. D. 1930 *The Right and the Good* (Oxford University Press)

Russell, D. 2005 *Plato on Pleasure and the Good Life* (Oxford University Press)

2008 "That 'Ought' Does Not Imply 'Right': Why it Matters for Virtue Ethics," *Southern Journal of Philosophy* 46: 299–315

2009 *Practical Intelligence and the Virtues* (Oxford University Press)

2010 "Virtue and Happiness in the Lyceum and Beyond," *Oxford Studies in Ancient Philosophy* 38: 143–85

2012 *Happiness for Humans* (Oxford University Press)

Russell, P. 1995 *Freedom and Moral Sentiment: Hume's Way of Naturalizing Responsibility* (Oxford University Press)

2006 "Moral Sense and Virtue in Hume's Ethics," in T. Chappell, ed., *Values and Virtues: Aristotelianism in Contemporary Ethics* (Oxford University Press)

2008 *The Riddle of Hume's Treatise: Skepticism, Naturalism and Irreligion* (Oxford University Press)

Sabini, J. and Silver, M. 2005 "Lack of Character? Situationism Critiqued," *Ethics* 115: 535–62

Saenz, C. 2010 "Virtue Ethics and the Selection of Children with Impairments: A Reply to Rosalind McDougall," *Bioethics* 24: 499–506

Sandler, R. 2007 *Character and Environment: A Virtue-Oriented Approach to Environmental Ethics* (Columbia University Press)

Scanlon, T. 1998 *What We Owe to Each Other* (Harvard University Press)

Schauber, N. 2009 "Complexities of Character: Hume on Love and Responsibility," *Hume Studies* 33: 29–55

Scheffler, S. 1988 "Agent-Centred Restrictions, Rationality, and the Virtues," in S. Scheffler (ed.), *Consequentialism and Its Critics* (Oxford University Press)

Scheffler, S. 1992 *Human Morality* (Oxford University Press)

Schmidt, C. *et al.* (eds.) 1991 *The Cambridge History of Renaissance Philosophy* (Cambridge University Press)

Schmidtz, D. 1992 "Rationality Within Reason," *Journal of Philosophy* 89: 445–66.

 1994 "Choosing Ends," *Ethics* 104: 226–51

 2001a "The Language of Ethics," in C. Davis (ed.), *Ethical Dilemmas in the Water Industry* (American Water Works Association)

 2001b "Are All Species Equal?" in D. Schmidtz and E. Willott (eds.), *Environmental Ethics: What Really Matters, What Really Works* (Oxford University Press)

 2006 *Elements of Justice* (Cambridge University Press)

Schmidtz, D. and Willott, E. (eds.) 2001 *Environmental Ethics: What Really Matters, What Really Works* (Oxford University Press)

Schneewind, J. 1990 "The Misfortunes of Virtue," *Ethics* 101: 42–63

 1997 *The Invention of Autonomy: A History of Modern Moral Philosophy* (Cambridge University Press)

Schofield, M. 2006 "Aristotle's Political Ethics," in R. Kraut (ed.), *The Blackwell Guide to Aristotle's Nicomachean Ethics* (Blackwell)

Sellman, D. 2011 *What Makes A Good Nurse: Why the Virtues are Important for Nursing* (Jessica Kingsley)

Sen, A. 1987 *On Ethics and Economics* (Blackwell)

 2009 *The Idea of Justice* (Harvard University Press)

Sennett, R. 1998 *The Corrosion of Character: The Transformation of Work in Modern Capitalism* (W. W. Norton & Company)

Shafer-Landau, R. 2012 *The Fundamentals of Ethics*, 2nd edn. (Oxford University Press)

Shaftesbury, Earl of [Anthony Ashley Cooper] [1711] 1964 *Characteristics of Men, Manners, Opinions and Times*, ed. J. M. Robertson (Bobbs-Merrill)

Shelp, E. (ed.) 1985 *Virtue and Medicine* (Reidel)

Sherman, N. 1994 "The Role of Emotions in Aristotelian Virtue," *Proceedings of the Boston Area Colloquium in Ancient Philosophy* 9: 1–33

    1997 *Making a Necessity of Virtue: Aristotle and Kant on Virtue* (Cambridge University Press)

Shun, K. 1997 *Mencius and Early Chinese Thought* (Stanford University Press)

Sideri, K. 2008 "Health, Global Justice, and Virtue Bioethics," *Law and Bioethics* 23: 79–101

Sidgwick, H. 1907 *The Methods of Ethics* (Oxford University Press)

Slingerland, E. 2011 "The Situationist Critique and Early Confucian Virtue Ethics," *Ethics* 121: 390–419

Slote, M. 1992 *From Morality to Virtue* (Oxford University Press)

    1993 "Virtue Ethics and Democratic Values," *Journal of Social Philosophy* 24: 5–37

    1996 "Agent Based Virtue Ethics," in P. A. French, T. E. Uehling, Jr., and H. K. Wettstein (eds.), *Midwest Studies in Philosophy* xx, *Moral Concepts* (University of Notre Dame Press), 83–101

    1997 "Virtue Ethics," in M. W. Baron, P. Pettit, and M. Slote (eds.), *Three Methods of Ethics: A Debate* (Blackwell)

    1998a "Nietzsche and Virtue Ethics," *International Studies in Philosophy* 30: 23–7

    1998b "Justice as Caring," *Social Philosophy and Policy* 15: 171–95

    2001 *Morals from Motives* (Oxford University Press)

    2007 *The Ethics of Care and Empathy* (Routledge)

    2010 *Moral Sentimentalism* (Oxford University Press)

Smith, A. [1790] 1976 *The Theory of Moral Sentiments*, 6th edn., ed. D. D. Raphael and A. L. Macfie (Oxford University Press)

Smith, K. (1947) Introductory to D. Hume, *Hume's Dialogues Concerning Natural Religion*, ed. K. Smith (Bobbs-Merrill)

Snow, N. 2010 *Virtue as Social Intelligence: An Empirically Grounded Theory* (Routledge)

Solomon, D. 1997 "Internal Objections to Virtue Ethics," in D. Statman (ed.), *Virtue Ethics: A Critical Reader* (Edinburgh University Press)

    2003 "Virtue Ethics: Radical or Routine," in M. de Paul and L. Zagzebski (eds.), *Intellectual Virtue: Perspectives from Ethics and Epistemology* (Oxford University Press)

Solomon, R. 1992 *Ethics and Excellence: Cooperation and Integrity in Business* (Oxford University Press)

2003 *Living with Nietzsche: What the Great "Immoralist" Has to Teach Us* (Oxford University Press)

Sparrow, R. 2011 "A Not-So-New Eugenics: Harris and Savulescu on Human Enhancement," *Hastings Center Report* 41: 32–42

Sreenivasan, G. 2002 "Errors about Errors: Virtue Theory and Trait Attribution," *Mind* 111: 47–68

    2008 "Character and Consistency: Still More Errors," *Mind* 117: 603–12

    2009 "Disunity of Virtue," *Journal of Ethics* 13: 195–212

Stalnaker, A. 2007 *Overcoming Our Evil: Human Nature and Spiritual Exercises in Xunzi and Augustine* (Georgetown University Press)

Stark, A. 1993 "What's the Matter with Business Ethics?" *Harvard Business Review* 71: 38–48

Stohr, K. 2006 "Contemporary Virtue Ethics," *Philosophy Compass* 1: 22–7

Stohr, K. and Wellman, C. H. 2002 "Recent Work on Virtue Ethics," *American Philosophical Quarterly* 39: 49–72

Sumner, L. W. 1996 *Welfare, Happiness, and Ethics* (Oxford University Press)

Svensson, F. 2010 "Virtue Ethics and the Search for an Account of Right Action," *Ethical Theory and Moral Practice* 13: 255–71

    2011 "Eudaimonist Virtue Ethics and Right Action: A Reassessment," *Journal of Ethics* 15: 321–39

Swanton, C. 1993 "Commentary on Michael Slote's 'Virtue Ethics and Democratic Values,'" *Journal of Social Philosophy* 24: 38–49

    2001 "A Virtue Ethical Account of Right Action," *Ethics* 112: 32–52

    2003 *Virtue Ethics, A Pluralistic View* (Oxford University Press)

    2005 "Nietzschean Virtue Ethics," in S. M. Gardiner (ed.), *Virtue Ethics, Old and New* (Cornell University Press)

    2007a "Can Hume Be Read as a Virtue Ethicist?" *Hume Studies* 33: 91–113

    2007b "Virtue Ethics, Role Ethics, and Business Ethics," in R. L. Walker and P. J. Ivanhoe (eds.), *Working Virtue: Virtue Ethics and Contemporary Moral Problems* (Oxford University Press)

    2009 "Virtue Ethics and the Problem of Demandingness," in T. Chappell (ed.), *The Problem of Moral Demandingness: New Philosophical Essays* (Palgrave Macmillan)

    2011a "Virtue Ethics," in C. Miller (ed.), *The Continuum Companion to Ethics* (Continuum)

    2011b "Nietzsche and the Virtues of Mature Egoism," in S. May (ed.), *Cambridge Critical Guide to Nietzsche's On the Genealogy of Morality* (Cambridge University Press)

    2012 "Robert Solomon's Aristotelian Nietzsche," in K. Higgins, D. Sherman, and M. Clancy (eds.), *Passion, Death, and Spirituality: The Philosophy of Robert C. Solomon* (Springer)

Taylor, C. 1989 *Sources of the Self* (Harvard University Press)

Taylor, G. 1985 *Pride, Shame, and Guilt* (Oxford University Press)

    2006 *Deadly Vices* (Oxford University Press)

Taylor, J. 2002 "Hume on the Standard of Virtue," *Journal of Ethics* 6: 43–62

    2006 "Virtue and the Evaluation of Character," in S. Traiger (ed.), *The Blackwell Companion to Hume's Treatise* (Blackwell)

Taylor, R. 2002 *Virtue Ethics: An Introduction* (Prometheus Books)

Thomasma, D. C. 2004 "Virtue Theory in Philosophy of Medicine," in G. Khushf (ed.), *Handbook of Bioethics: Taking Stock of the Field from a Philosophical Perspective* (Kluwer)

Thompson, M. 1995 "The Representation of Life," in R. Hursthouse, G. Lawrence, and W. Quinn (eds.), *Virtues and Reasons* (Oxford University Press)

Thomson, J. 1997 "The Right and the Good," *Journal of Philosophy* 94: 273–98

Tiberius, V. 2006 "How to Think about Virtue and Right," *Philosophical Papers* 35: 247–65

Tien, D. W. 2004 "Warranted Neo-Confucian Belief: Knowledge and the Affections in the Religious Epistemologies of Wang Yangming (1472–1529) and Alvin Plantinga," *International Journal for Philosophy of Religion* 55: 31–55

    2010 "Metaphysics and the Basis of Morality in the Philosophy of Wang Yangming" in J. Makeham (ed.), *Neo-Confucian Philosophy* (Springer)

    2012 "Oneness and Self-Centeredness in the Moral Psychology of Wang Yangming," *Journal of Religious Ethics* 40: 52–71

Tiwald, J. 2011 "Self-Love, Sympathy, and Virtue: Dai Zhen's Defense of Self-Interest," *Journal of Chinese Philosophy* 38: 29–45

Toner, C. 2006 "The Self-Centredness Objection to Virtue Ethics" *Philosophy* 81: 595–617

Tonkens, R. 2011 "Parental Wisdom, Empirical Blindness, and Normative Evaluation of Prenatal Genetic Enhancement," *Journal of Medicine and Philosophy* 36: 274–95

Tu Wei-ming 1976 *Neo-Confucian Thought in Action: Wang Yang-ming's Youth (1472–1509)* (University of California Press)

Valla, L. 1972 *De vero falsoque bono*, ed. M. Lorsch (Adriatica Editore)

    1982 *Dialecticae disputationes*, ed. G. Zippel (Antenore)

van Hooft, S. 1999 "Acting from the Virtue of Caring in Nursing," *Nursing Philosophy* 6: 189–201

    2006 *Understanding Virtue Ethics* (Acumen)

Van Norden, B. W. 2007 *Virtue Ethics and Consequentialism in Early Chinese Philosophy* (Cambridge University Press)

2008 *Mengzi: With Selections from Traditional Commentaries* (Hackett Publishing)

van Zyl, L. 2000 *Death and Compassion: A Virtue-Based Approach to Euthanasia* (Ashgate)

2007 "Can Virtuous People Emerge from Tragic Dilemmas Having Acted Well?" *Journal of Applied Philosophy* 24: 50–61

2009 "Agent-Based Virtue Ethics and the Problem of Action Guidance," *Journal of Moral Philosophy* 6: 50–69

2011a "Right Action and the Non-virtuous Agent," *Journal of Applied Philosophy* 28: 80–92

2011b "Rightness and Goodness in Agent-Based Virtue Ethics," *Journal of Philosophical Research* 36: 103–14

Veatch, R. 1988 "The Danger of Virtue," *Journal of Medicine and Philosophy* 13: 445–6

Vitz, R. 2009 "Doxastic Virtues in Hume's Epistemology," *Hume Studies* 35: 211–29

Vives, J. 1785 *De causis corruptarum artium,* in *Opera Omnia* vi, ed. G. Mayáns (Università de València) (Repr. Gregg Press, 1964)

Vlastos, G. 1995 *Studies in Greek Philosophy II: Socrates, Plato, and their Tradition,* D. W. Graham (ed.) (Princeton University Press)

Walker, R. L. 2007 "The Good Life for Non-human Animals: What Virtue Requires of Humans," in R. L. Walker P. J. and Ivanhoe (eds.), *Working Virtue: Virtue Ethics and Contemporary Moral Problems* (Oxford University Press)

Walker, R. L. and Ivanhoe, P. J. (eds.) 2007 *Working Virtue: Virtue Ethics and Contemporary Moral Problems* (Oxford University Press)

Watson, G. 1971 "The Natural Law and Stoicism," in A. A. Long (ed.), *Problems in Stoicism* (Athlone)

1984 "Virtues in Excess," *Philosophical Studies* 46: 57–74

1990 "On the Primacy of Character," in O. Flanagan and A. O. Rorty (eds.), *Identity, Character, and Morality* (MIT Press)

Weber, M. 1994 "The Profession and Vocation of Politics," in P. Lassman and R. Speirs (eds.), *Political Writings* (Cambridge University Press)

Weed, D. L. and McKeown, R. E. 1998 "Epidemiology and Virtue Ethics," *International Journal of Epidemiology* 27: 343–9

Weil, S. 2006 *Cahiers* VI, 2, in *Œuvres complètes,* ed. F. de Lussy (Gallimard)

Welchman, J. 2003 "Xenografting, Species Loyalty, and Human Solidarity," *Journal of Social Philosophy* 34: 244–55

Wenzel, S. 1984 Introduction to *Summa Virtutum de remediis anime* (University of Georgia Press)

1986 "The Seven Deadly Sins: Some Problems of Research," *Speculum* 43: 1–22

Werhane, P. 1991 *Adam Smith and His Legacy for Modern Capitalism* (Oxford University Press)

1999 *Moral Imagination and Management Decision-Making* (Oxford University Press)

Wetzel, J. 1992 *Augustine and the Limits of Virtue* (Cambridge University Press)

White, N. 2006 *A Brief History of Happiness* (Blackwell)

White, S. 1992 *Sovereign Virtue* (Stanford University Press)

2002 "Happiness in the Hellenistic Lyceum," *Apeiron* 35 (supp.): 69–93

Wiggins, D. 1980 "Deliberation and Practical Reason," in A. O. Rorty (ed.), *Essays on Aristotle's Ethics* (University of California Press)

Wilkinson, S. 2010 *Choosing Tomorrow's Children: The Ethics of Selective Reproduction* (Oxford University Press)

Williams, B. 1980 "Justice as a Virtue," in A. O. Rorty (ed.), *Essays on Aristotle's Ethics* (University of California Press)

1985 *Ethics and the Limits of Philosophy* (Harvard University Press)

1993 *Shame and Necessity* (University of California Press)

1995a "Replies," in J. E. J. Altham and R. Harrison (eds.), *World, Mind, and Ethics: Essays on the Ethical Philosophy of Bernard Williams* (Cambridge University Press)

1995b *Making Sense of Humanity and Other Philosophical Papers 1982–1993* (Cambridge University Press)

Williams, B. and Smart, J. J. C. 1973 *Utilitarianism: For and Against* (Cambridge University Press)

Williamson, O. 1975 *Markets and Hierarchies: Analysis and Anti-Trust Implications* (Free Press)

Wollgast, S. 1988 *Philosophie in Deutschland zwischen Reformation und Aufklärung, 1550–1650* (Akademie Verlag)

Wolter, A. B. 1997 *Duns Scotus on the Will and Morality*, 2nd edn. (Catholic University of America Press)

Wong, D. B. 1988 "On Flourishing and Finding One's Identity in Community," *Midwest Studies in Philosophy* 13: 324–41

Yearley, L. H. 1990 *Mencius and Aquinas: Theories of Virtue and Conceptions of Courage* (State University of New York Press)

Zagzebski, L. 1996 *Virtues of the Mind: An Inquiry into the Nature of Virtue and the Ethical Foundations of Knowledge* (Cambridge University Press)

2004 *Divine Motivation Theory* (Cambridge University Press)

2006 "The Admirable Life and the Desirable Life," in T. Chappell (ed.), *Values and Virtues: Aristotelianism in Contemporary Ethics* (Oxford University Press)

2007 "The Admirable Life and the Desirable Life," in T. Chappell (ed.), *Values and Virtues* (Oxford University Press)

Zwolinski, M. and Schmidtz, D. 2005 "Virtue Ethics and Repugnant Conclusions," in P. Cafaro and R. Sandler (eds.), *Environmental Virtue Ethics* (Rowman & Littlefield)

INDEX

Abelard, P., 77–8, 80
abortion, 198, 202, 208–11
action assessment, 173, 176–8, 186, 193
action guidance, 18, 159, 173–7, 179,
     185–7, 193, 198, 228, 325
Adkins, A., 29
Annas, J., 8, 30, 72
Anscombe, G. E. M., 8, 14, 150–62, 167,
     169, 197, 318, 325
Anselm, 88
Aquinas, T., 57, 71, 80–6, 89, 130, 132,
     135, 136, 139, 169
aretē, 16, 29, 126, 151
Aristotle, 8–18, 21, 31, 34–40, 49–51,
     72–4, 89, 101, 105, 112, 124–45,
     149–52, 169, 187, 188, 205, 216,
     221, 245–8, 252–6, 260–2, 292, 319,
     327, 330–1
  ancient Aristotelians, 81
  contemporary Aristotelians, 30,
     163–7, 197–217, 240–1, 270–4,
     282–5, 320
  medieval Aristotelians, 77, 81, 86–9,
     162
  on politics, 268–82
Augustine, 75, 79, 89, 132

Bentham, J., 125, 152
Bonaventure, 79–80
Brady, M., 185
Buddhism, 56–7, 60

Cassian, J., 76
Christianity, 70–90, 113–15, 125,
     129–36, 140, 141, 156
Chrysippus, 42–7

Cicero, 29, 35, 45, 74, 79, 132, 135,
     151
Confucianism, 49–66, 316, 336
consequentialism, 37, 39, 153, 172–3,
     181–8, 195, 221, 225, 238, 309,
     315–16, 331, 334–6
Crisp, R., 172

Daoism, 57
de Waele, A., 135
deontology, 39, 143, 149, 172–5, 208,
     221, 224–5, 228–30, 309, 316, 334
dilemmas, 23, 175–92, 317
Doris, J., 253, 261, 290, 296–8, 304, 306,
     310

emotions, 16, 35–6, 43, 73–88, 92–7,
     104, 106, 108, 151, 245, 317, 324–6
Epictetus, 46, 216
Epicurus/Epicureans, 13, 30, 40–2, 48,
     115, 128, 132
eudaimonia, 7–26, 29, 128, 130, 152,
     167–8, 205, 246–7, 259, 320–3, 332
eudaimonism, 7–26, 164, 316, 320–3,
     333
euthanasia, 199–202

Ficino, M., 131
flourishing. See happiness
Foot, P., 8, 150, 154–5, 158–62, 165–7,
     198, 199–202, 318

Garcia, J., 326
Gaus, G., 279
Gregory the Great, 76
Grotius, 137–40

happiness, 7–26, 29–30, 32–48, 50–1, 55,
    75, 83, 93, 98–9, 103–4, 110, 115,
    124–31, 132, 134, 137, 141–5, 166,
    200, 230, 232, 240, 246–8, 260, 262,
    268, 271–6, 320–3
Hare, R., 154–8
Hartshorne, H. and May, M. A., 293–311
Hayek, F., 285
healthcare, 202–8
Hill, T., 224–5, 230–2, 235–6, 335
Hobbes, T., 136–7
Homer, 29–30, 124, 167
Hume, D., 49, 51–2, 55, 92–115, 125,
    138–41, 153, 163, 166, 181, 240,
    245, 270, 316–36
Hursthouse, R., 8, 13, 36, 174–81, 190,
    191, 192, 198, 202, 205, 208–11, 217,
    270–4, 277–84, 299, 317–21, 328–9
Hutcheson, F., 51, 181

Jacobson, D., 185
Johnson, R., 178

Kagan, S., 331
Kant, I., 25–6, 125, 140–1, 151–2, 156,
    163, 167, 221, 236, 335

Lenman, J., 161, 165–6, 171
Locke, J., 163, 278–84
Lombard, P., 77–8, 80
Luther, M., 89, 133–4

MacIntyre, A., 124–6, 136–9, 162–4, 203,
    240–1, 244, 254–60
Macrobius, 74, 78–9
McDougall, R., 211–14
McDowell, J., 8, 14, 25, 160, 165,
    167
Melanchthon, P., 131–5
Mencius. See Mengzi
Mengzi, 49, 52–6, 59–63, 324
Milgram, S., 253, 261, 304–6
Mill, J. S., 125, 152, 221
Moore, G. E., 153–4
morality, 18, 25–6, 125, 150–62, 266,
    337
Murdoch, I., 189

nature, 8, 13–16, 40–8, 49–63, 82, 84, 93,
    104, 113, 125–33, 162–8, 283

Nietzsche, F., 156, 161, 318–24, 333–4,
    336
Nussbaum, M., 8, 13, 166, 167, 216,
    270–82

Oakley, J. and Cocking, D., 205–7
Ockham, 130

pain, 41–2, 93–9, 105–12
Parfit, D., 225–8
passion. See emotions
Pellegrino, E. and Thomasma, D., 203
Plato/Platonists, 29–34, 37–9, 72–5,
    128–9, 131, 151–2, 166–7, 268–9
pleasure, 13, 32, 36, 41–2, 93–5,
    105–10
Plotinus, 79
prebirth testing, 211–14
Pufendorf, 138–40

Radden, J., 208
Rassmussen, D. and Den Uyl, D.,
    274–85
Rawls, J., 160, 279, 319
right action, 150–2, 172–94, 205, 208,
    221–5, 299, 317–20, 329–31
roles, 124, 202–17, 249, 321–3
Ross, L. and Nisbett, R., 295,
    301
Ross, W. D., 126, 175, 188
Rousseau, J.-J., 138, 163
Routley, R., 231
Russell, D., 30, 191, 275, 318,
    323

Sadler, J., 208
Saenz, C., 213
Scanlon, T. M., 283–4
Schneewind, J., 139–43
Scholasticism, 74–89, 137
Scotus, D., 87–90, 130
Seneca, 47, 74, 132
sentimentalism, 181, 270, 319
sentiments, 51–2, 92–112
Shaftesbury, 51, 138
Sidgwick, H., 152–5
Slote, M., 51, 181–7, 190, 193, 269–70,
    276–80, 317–28
Smith, A., 51, 138, 140, 163, 240, 245–6,
    258, 270

Solomon, D., 318
Solomon, R., 240, 244, 324, 336
Stoicism, 30, 42–8, 73–6, 129, 132, 135, 269, 322
Swanton, C., 50, 187–94, 277–9, 317, 319, 320

Taylor, C., 162

utilitarianism, 125, 141–3, 149–52, 174, 198–209, 215, 217, 224–35, 241–4, 251, 260, 316

van Zyl, L., 202
virtue ethics, distinguished from virtue theory, 316
virtues
  as excellences, 16–18, 73
  benevolence, 98, 100, 181–3, 188–93, 270
  charity, 100, 140

courage, 29, 31, 43, 82, 85, 100, 189, 205, 256
justice, 29, 30, 42, 43, 82, 85–6, 97–9, 250, 268, 333
kindness, 329
piety, 62
temperance, 43, 82, 84, 85
theological, 70, 75–86, 129
wisdom, 16, 17–18, 29–48, 73, 74, 82, 86, 126, 236, 245, 254, 271–80, 323–4, 330–1
virtus, 126, 151
Vives, J., 134

Wang Yangming, 49, 56–61, 63–6
Watson, G., 326, 334
William of Auxerre, 78–9
Williams, B., 160, 161, 163–6, 167, 169, 175

Zagzebski, L., 317, 326

OTHER VOLUMES IN THE SERIES OF CAMBRIDGE COMPANIONS

FREGE   *Edited by* THOMAS RICKETTS *and* MICHAEL POTTER
FREUD   *Edited by* JEROME NEU
GADAMER   *Edited by* ROBERT J. DOSTAL
GALEN   *Edited by* R. J. HANKINSON
GALILEO   *Edited by* PETER MACHAMER
GERMAN IDEALISM   *Edited by* KARL AMERIKS
GREEK AND ROMAN PHILOSOPHY   *Edited by*
    DAVID SEDLEY
HABERMAS   *Edited by* STEPHEN K. WHITE
HAYEK   *Edited by* EDWARD FESER
HEGEL   *Edited by* FREDERICK C. BEISER
HEGEL AND NINETEENTH-CENTURY
    PHILOSOPHY   *Edited by* FREDERICK C. BEISER
HEIDEGGER 2nd Edition   *Edited by* CHARLES GUIGNON
HOBBES   *Edited by* TOM SORELL
HOBBES'S 'LEVIATHAN'   *Edited by* PATRICIA
    SPRINGBORG
HUME 2nd edition   *Edited by* DAVID FATE NORTON *and*
    JACQUELINE TAYLOR
HUSSERL   *Edited by* BARRY SMITH *and*
    DAVID WOODRUFF SMITH
WILLIAM JAMES   *Edited by* RUTH ANNA PUTNAM
KANT   *Edited by* PAUL GUYER
KANT AND MODERN PHILOSOPHY   *Edited by*
    PAUL GUYER
KANT'S 'CRITIQUE OF PURE REASON'   *Edited by*
    PAUL GUYER
KEYNES   *Edited by* ROGER E. BACKHOUSE *and*
    BRADLEY W. BATEMAN
KIERKEGAARD   *Edited by* ALASTAIR HANNAY *and*
    GORDON D. MARINO
LEIBNIZ   *Edited by* NICHOLAS JOLLEY
LEVINAS   *Edited by* SIMON CRITCHLEY *and*
    ROBERT BERNASCONI
LOCKE   *Edited by* VERE CHAPPELL
LOCKE'S 'ESSAY CONCERNING HUMAN
    UNDERSTANDING'   *Edited by* LEX NEWMAN

LOGICAL EMPIRICISM   *Edited by* ALAN RICHARDSON
   and THOMAS UEBEL
MAIMONIDES   *Edited by* KENNETH SEESKIN
MALEBRANCHE   *Edited by* STEVEN NADLER
MARX   *Edited by* TERRELL CARVER
MEDIEVAL JEWISH PHILOSOPHY   *Edited by*
   DANIEL H. FRANK *and* OLIVER LEAMAN
MEDIEVAL PHILOSOPHY   *Edited by* A. S. MCGRADE
MERLEAU-PONTY   *Edited by* TAYLOR CARMAN *and*
   MARK B. N. HANSEN
MILL   *Edited by* JOHN SKORUPSKI
MONTAIGNE   *Edited by* ULLRICH LANGER
NEWTON   *Edited by* I. BERNARD COHEN *and*
   GEORGE E. SMITH
NIETZSCHE   *Edited by* BERND MAGNUS *and*
   KATHLEEN HIGGINS
NOZICK'S 'ANARCHY, STATE, AND UTOPIA'   *Edited*
   by RALF BADER *and* JOHN MEADOWCROFT
OAKESHOTT   *Edited by* EFRAIM PODOKSIK
OCKHAM   *Edited by* PAUL VINCENT SPADE
THE 'ORIGIN OF SPECIES'   *Edited by* MICHAEL RUSE
   and ROBERT J. RICHARDS
PASCAL   *Edited by* NICHOLAS HAMMOND
PEIRCE   *Edited by* CHERYL MISAK
PHILO   *Edited by* ADAM KAMESAR
THE PHILOSOPHY OF BIOLOGY   *Edited by*
   DAVID L. HULL *and* MICHAEL RUSE
PIAGET   *Edited by* ULRICH MÜLLER,
   JEREMY I. M. CARPENDALE *and* LESLIE SMITH
PLATO   *Edited by* RICHARD KRAUT
PLATO'S 'REPUBLIC'   *Edited by* G. R. F. FERRARI
PLOTINUS   *Edited by* LLOYD P. GERSON
QUINE   *Edited by* ROGER F. GIBSON JR.
RAWLS   *Edited by* SAMUEL FREEMAN
THOMAS REID   *Edited by* TERENCE CUNEO *and*
   RENÉ VAN WOUDENBERG
RENAISSANCE PHILOSOPHY   *Edited by* JAMES HANKINS
ROUSSEAU   *Edited by* PATRICK RILEY
BERTRAND RUSSELL   *Edited by* NICHOLAS GRIFFIN

SARTRE *Edited by* CHRISTINA HOWELLS
SCHOPENHAUER *Edited by* CHRISTOPHER JANAWAY
THE SCOTTISH ENLIGHTENMENT *Edited by*
   ALEXANDER BROADIE
ADAM SMITH *Edited by* KNUD HAAKONSSEN
SOCRATES *Edited by* DONALD MORRISON
SPINOZA *Edited by* DON GARRETT
SPINOZA'S 'ETHICS' *Edited by* OLLI KOISTINEN
THE STOICS *Edited by* BRAD INWOOD
LEO STRAUSS *Edited by* STEVEN B. SMITH
TOCQUEVILLE *Edited by* CHERYL B. WELCH
VIRTUE ETHICS *Edited by* DANIEL C. RUSSELL
WITTGENSTEIN *Edited by* HANS SLUGA *and*
   DAVID STERN

For EU product safety concerns, contact us at Calle de José Abascal, 56–1°,
28003 Madrid, Spain or eugpsr@cambridge.org.

www.ingramcontent.com/pod-product-compliance
Ingram Content Group UK Ltd.
Pitfield, Milton Keynes, MK11 3LW, UK
UKHW042142130625
459647UK00011B/1149